WHICKER'S WORLD DOWN UNDER

'Classic old-style reporting, and it delivers the goods.' *Observer*

'He has singular gifts. His trick, his genius perhaps, is to ask short questions and to offer his subjects generous lengths of rope in case they want to flog, or better still, hang themselves...' *Sunday Telegraph*

'Whicker's genius – like Professor Higgins's – is to treat all interviewees in exactly the same way, gently pushing them along into saying something interesting, sometimes despite themselves. Perhaps his greatest skill is his ability to tackle the serious themes in a slightly bantering way and yet bring out the arguments as effectively as more self-important journalists, without mounting a soap box.' *Daily Mail*

'Whicker relates to it all in his relaxed, quizzical, slightly amused style.' *The Times*

'Just as thorough a warts-and-all study of Australia as was his excellent American tour.' *Standard*

'A real treasure trove.' *Sunday People*

'Good on yer, Alan.' *Star*

'I was delighted.' Terry Wogan, *BBC-1*

'Very good reading.' Ned Sherrin, *Radio 4*

'Hard to put down.' *Weekend*

'Stands out like a glass of claret on a tray of tinnies.' *Evening Post*, Bristol

D0320427

WHICKER'S WORLD DOWN UNDER

Alan Whicker, the renowned television inter-
viewer, has travelled the globe endlessly to meet
some of the world's most famous and most extraordinary people. He has worked in television for
over thirty years and during this time has
received almost every award the industry has to
offer. These have included the Screen Writer's
Guild Award for the Best Television Documentary Script, the Royal Television Society's Silver
Medal for Outstanding Artistic Achievement,
the University of California Dumont Award for
Excellence in Television Journalism, and the
British Academy of Film and Television Arts
Richard Dimbleby Award for the year's most
important contribution to factual television.

WHICKER'S WORLD
DOWN UNDER

Australia Through the Eyes and Lives of Resident Poms

ALAN WHICKER

Photographs by Valerie Kleeman

Fontana/Collins

First published in Great Britain by
William Collins Sons & Co. Ltd 1988
First issued in Fontana Paperbacks 1989

Copyright © Alan Whicker 1988

Printed and bound in Great Britain by
William Collins Sons & Co. Ltd, Glasgow
·

CONTENTS

Contents

Contents

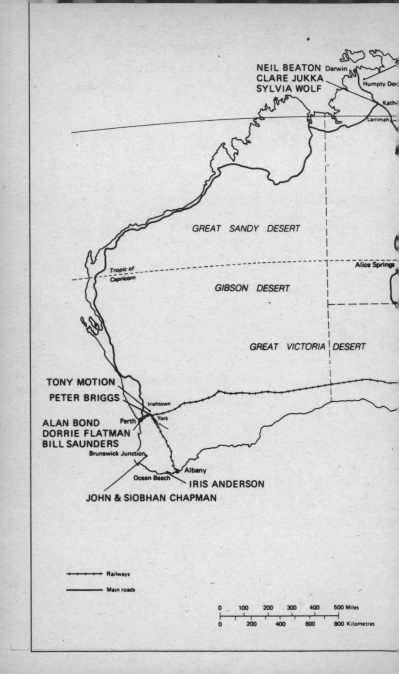

NEIL BEATON
CLARE JUKKA
SYLVIA WOLF

Darwin
Humpty Do
Kath
Larrimah

GREAT SANDY DESERT

Tropic of
Capricorn

Alice Springs

GIBSON DESERT

GREAT VICTORIA DESERT

TONY MOTION

PETER BRIGGS
Irishtown

ALAN BOND   Perth   York
DORRIE FLATMAN
BILL SAUNDERS
Brunswick Junction

Albany
Ocean Beach   IRIS ANDERSON

JOHN & SIOBHAN CHAPMAN

┼─┼─┼─┼─┼ Railways
───────── Main roads

0   100   200   300   400   500 Miles
0   200   400   600   800 Kilometres

NOEL ALLEN
TOM LAW

SID SMITH

TONY SHAFFER
DIANE CILENTO — 15° S
Miallo •
Port Douglas • DIANA BOWDEN
Cairns BILL MOULL
Tully • MIKE POPLE
Townsville
SALLY HURLEY
Charters Towers • Ravenswood
EDDIE FARRELL
GEOFF & EDIE TAYLOR

GREAT

SIMPSON
DESERT

DIVIDING

Warburton Creek

Coopers Creek

STURT DESERT
PAT ROBERTSON
Brisbane
Southport — PATRICK KILVINGTON
North Star
Moree • JANE MAKIM
DAVID HILL
RANGE
'SLIP' DE COURCEY
MITCHELL
Hunter
Valley LEN EVANS

Darling

Lachlan
Sydney

Adelaide
Murray
Canberra •
JOHN AKISTER
JOE BUGNER
GEORGE CAMPBELL
EDMUND CAPON
JANE DEKNATEL
DENNIS GOWING Melbourne PHILLIP EMANUEL
WILTON MORLEY JOHN & ELEANOR DIANA FISHER
ANNETTE WILDE ALLISTON TONY GREIG
JEFF HARDY
Three Hummock Island • MALCOLM HATTON-WARD
JIM JAGGS
DEREK LLEWELLYN-JONES
Launceston ROGER SMITH CHARLES NOBLE LOWNDES
SUE BECKER NIGEL MILAN
PETER BARNARD Hobart •

For the pertinently named
Dorothy Fremantle
(as was – before she collected hyphens)
with love

SEARCHING FOR
THE WIZARD OF AUS

For two hundred years, precisely, Britons have been crossing the world to live in Australia – a land on the way to nowhere. At first, 160,000 of them went reluctantly, in chains; but as their prison camp softened into a Promised Land, others left home eagerly, searching for a better life ...

We're about to meet some of the Poms, the Welsh and Scots and Irish who're 'Living with Waltzing Matilda', and through their eyes and lives take an inside look at their new nation in its celebratory Bicentennial Year ... You may have seen some of them, briefly, in *Whicker's World* on BBC1 when, as Australia heads into her third century, I took to wondering: *does* the rainbow end, Down Under?

The first settlers had been cast ashore on a strange and forbidding island full of exotic vegetation and unknown animals – reluctant founding fathers bound together by terrible isolation. As they pushed the frontiers back and the numbers within the stockade increased, it was natural for them to share a campfire. That tradition remains. Most migrant men settle into Australia without hesitation – though women may dream and hanker after home.

Many of us have considered leaving Britain, at some time or other. In one mighty bound across the world we could escape our weather, unemployment, crime, crowds, taxes, traffic, vandalism, strikes and all frightful things to come ... and head, unencumbered, into our dreams, into a land moulded and *created* by migrants – where you spend your lunch break sunbathing on the beach and never need an overcoat.

But migration, like marriage, should only be undertaken with the assumption – at least – that it will last forever!

Those who do leave, defeated perhaps by conditions at home, hope to be better off elsewhere, to find a fuller life. Some wish to make their fortune, some to keep it. *All* go to trouble, expense and occasionally heartbreak uprooting themselves and starting anew in an untried environment where they must strive harder than the natives, merely to keep afloat. Not everyone Exits Laughing ... as they set off down the yellow brick road in search of the Wizard of Aus.

Many Poms find him, somehow; only a few get lost. So what drives them to pull up their roots and head for an unknown land at the bottom of the world? Desperation over work, and those first coloured neighbours – or romantic dreams and wanderlust? Most of them believed their hopes could be achieved more easily, that ambition would flourish – down *there*.

In any new homeland migrants soon find adaptability is imperative; they need a quick acceptance of new behaviour, new climate, new neighbours, new vocabularies, new values. Not all of them – and especially not the wives, who do not have their husbands' structured lives – not all are resilient enough to absorb this break with family ties and familiar social patterns. It takes a while for the roots to go down, and sometimes they *never* do. Expatriate Stress has become a recognized mental condition, and some immigrants feel like visitors until the end of their days.

Up until the Sixties Australian governments selected immigrants, paid their fares, eased their departures and arrivals – which may explain why migrants to Australia were often less enterprising than those to America, who were on their own from the start in a striving society that had no time for losers and provided no safety nets. Australia remains a much *younger*, less ferociously worldly country than the United States.

Emigration once meant relinquishing everything; you would never see your loved ones again. The First Fleeters took eight wretched months to reach Botany Bay, and did not expect the chance of a return journey. Those who followed took six months and, much later, six weeks. Now you land in Godzone, slightly woozy, within a day – at the cost of a few weeks' income.

To discover how reality compares with images and hopes, I've just travelled all the states, eavesdropping upon the attitudes of a cross-section of migrants and learning what it's like to be on the inside, looking out.

Most of them had quickly taken aboard the fact that the British are no longer Australia's chosen people. Poms now have no inalienable right to the spoils, even though the nation was created by the toil of our ancestors, its culture and customs are British as can be, they obey traffic lights, drive on the left, build roundabouts, pay their taxes, serve Devonshire teas – and beat us at all the right sports.

Before the European Community, Britain was Australia's chief trading partner, providing 30 per cent of the imports, absorbing 20 per cent of their exports. Now, despite fish and chips, uniformed schoolchildren and a suburban society speaking the same language – roughly – the continent has floated away towards its Pacific neighbours and the United States.

Australia is as big as Europe but most of it is unsuitable for cultivation or an agreeable life, because across two-thirds of the land evaporation exceeds rainfall. This oldest continent is mostly dry and empty; too much geography, they say, and not enough history.

It still has only 16 million people, more than three-quarters of them living along a ribbon of coastline at the bottom right-hand corner. They're city dwellers, and as familiar with kangaroos and koalas as Britons are with lions.

Over the years I must have made a small contribution towards their growing population, which should reach 19 million by the turn of the century. The first *Whicker's World Down Under* programmes went out on BBC in 1959, and thousands of viewers' letters showed the national fascination – or was it yearning? – for a distant sunlit land of wide golden beaches that had no beggars or conspicuous consumers. Six o'clock swill and mandatory tomato ketchup were disregarded.

When I later reported from my beloved Norfolk Island – an idyllic speck in the ocean between Australia and New Zealand – scores of families sold up and travelled across the world on the strength of those programmes to create new homes upon that little piece of Switzerland floating in the South Pacific. I returned after ten years, to check, and found them all suitably content.

In the Seventies *Whicker's Walkabout* on ITV had the biggest audience of any documentary series ever, much to our surprise, pushing the then unassailable *Coronation Street* from the top of the ratings. We could only assume this was because it was shown during a bitter winter while Britain suffered austerity, strikes, shortages, and national gloom. Millions watched to see if Australia did indeed offer the promise of easy living – wondering whether, perhaps, one day . . .

I constantly meet people who, like the chambermaid at Darwin's Diamond Beach Hotel, declare, 'You're the reason we came out!' Like many others, Alan Woodroof, a Sydney property man and amateur opal-cutter, explained his last quarter century down under: 'I saw *Whicker's World* and decided, *that's* the place for me!' I have yet to walk into an accusatory complaint – so for once television did something right.

After its rude and abrupt birth, the history of Australia is blessedly uninteresting. Little has happened: no wars, drama or turmoil. The deep, deep peace has only once been disturbed: a few wartime Japanese bombs on Darwin caused a passing panic.

Today, despite its material abundance, the Promised Land is winding down, economically. The manufacturing sector is half the size it was ten years ago and the standard of living has been propped up by money from overseas: net external debt has climbed from $7 billion in 1980 to $80.7 billion in September 1986, and every family with three children now owes $30,000 to some foreign bank. So Australia slips down the OECD income-per-head table from top to sixteenth, and if the debt path is to be stabilized some economists expect the Australian dollar to depreciate by one-third before 1991.

Though the world no longer needs Australian raw materials, the unions still require high wages for *un*skilled labour – while Asian competitors flourish, and work longer for less. The lucky land is running out of credit, as well as luck.

The instinctive Australian reaction has always been: 'No worries, mate – she'll be right!' and she always has been. Uranium, gold, iron ore, nickel, aluminium were discovered on cue, easily available and in enormous quantities. Wars demanded her food and commodities. OPEC forced up the prices of oil, gas and coal.

So Australians have never found it necessary to become

aggressive money makers; something always turned up to save the Down Under Micawber. Until today. This is 'Realism Time', if Australia is not to become a kiwi-fruit republic.

The shock-wave from such looming austerity has been felt in British homes, long sustained by the comforting thought that even if the United Kingdom did go to the dogs, there was *always* Australia ...

Well, there still is – though in 1988 they're only letting in 110,000 migrants, and 125,000 in '89. Today they just advertise for businessmen – 2500 of them – who can each bring £200,000 or so into the country, and create employment. Australia can no longer afford more unskilled in her dole queues – yet determined immigrants still manage to infiltrate, legally or illegally.

Unemployment has kept official arrivals below the levels of the prosperous Sixties, when up to 160,000 landed each year – the same number as those original convicts, though *they* were spread over eighty years. Some Australians still remember the last surviving English convict: Samuel Speed, of Perth, who did not die until 1938.

Migration was always from northern Europe. Half a century ago 98 per cent of the people in the biggest city, Sydney, were of British descent. Then in 1972 the Government abandoned the white Australia policy and 180 years of Anglo-Celtic identity; immigration-office windows slammed shut in London and Edinburgh, while those in Yugoslavia, Turkey and Vietnam stayed open – putting some strain upon the Australians' tolerance and changing forever the look and flavour of the land. Since the end of White Australia, 100,000 Indo-Chinese refugees have been admitted. Most of these migrants work hard and do well; as an old-Australian told me, ruefully: 'Greek men don't play golf ...'

Yet even today the largest *single* source of migrants remains the United Kingdom: 12,040 of us went out in 1985–86 – though that's less than 16 per cent of the total. More than 24 per cent arrived from the East – from Vietnam and the Philippines, China and Taiwan, Hong Kong and Malaysia.

These new migrants have softened and illuminated the land, spurring it on from semi-emancipated colonialism towards Pacific cosmopolitanism. Millions still wait in Asiatic queues, knowing

Australia's migration programme is humanitarian, as well as economic.

So in a nation where everyone is either a migrant or descended from one, where one person in every four is a *post-war* migrant, it might seem the old WASP Diggers and Graziers are fading away – but they remain in control, where it matters. Anglo-Saxons hold the reins, the old guard sets the anthropological tone and can even show a certain palpable xenophobia. More than three-quarters of Australians are of British or Irish origin.

There's still a queue of Britons anxious to reinforce their ranks, to experience the ease of Australian life – those long weekends surrounded by the warmth and honesty of a people used to welcoming strangers. Poms, however, face a prickly love–hate, a distinctive blend of derisive affection, contemptuous envy. After two hundred years the ambivalent attitude remains. It takes new-Australians some years to realize that Pommy-Bastard is two words ...

Bodyline bowling, the European Community, the aliens' queue at airports, Maralinga, wheat subsidies, nuclear warships, Test Matches, visas – there's always something to keep the pot simmering. Scots, Welsh and Irish escape the hostility – which is a joke, of course. But then again ... it isn't.

In the Australian television series *Anzacs*, for example, the thick, malevolent characters in ill-fitting uniforms are Poms, naturally – they're the real enemies, not the Boche. We did the same sort of thing to ourselves, in *Gandhi*. The lame *60 Minutes* programme shows an interview with a discontented migrant couple twice, then follows them back to England to record their relief at returning home – chasing the whingeing Pom stereotype around the world.

There must of course be some Poms who are unhappy, if Australia's large proportion of Anglo-Saxons is being topped-up each year by another 12,000; but I have to report that in six months' research and filming, seeking them out in every state and at every level of society across Australia, I never found a *real* whinger – the kind they tell stories about in pubs.

As a television man making programmes, I'm not sure whether I was pleased or displeased, lucky or unlucky – but that's the way it was. Most Poms I met had thoughtful and interesting things to say, casting new light upon an unusual land and, though not everyone was totally content, a true-blue whinge was hard to find.

As you will read – or have seen – some were nostalgic, while others had not bothered to holiday in Britain even though they could well afford return fares starting at around £650. Everyone in my cross-section, from megamillionaires to dustmen, from surgeons to prawn fishermen, was totally unwhingeing.

During filming Peter Hearsum drove me round Sydney in his white Mercedes hire car. He had been working in an Elephant and Castle tailoring shop before taking a £10 assisted passage: 'In '69 I found people a bit abrasive – and I was *bashed* on Epping Station within the first week! I didn't think that was too receptive. I was going out Saturday night and this chap came up and thumped me to the ground. I said, "Why'd you do that?" He said, "Because you're effeminate." The only thing I can put it down to is I had my best suit on at the time ... That was *my* welcome.'

Peter had walked innocently into a true Australian mood: the pointless punch-up. What the blues are to American blacks, satori to Zen Buddhists and sorrow to romantic poets ... the punch-up is to Australians. It has an inescapable aimless quality, strikes swiftly from nowhere, solves nothing – and leaves everyone disgruntled.

Hearsum hoped he had never whinged: 'But in those days the reception was not too comfortable. Some of the hostels were absolutely dreadful: whole families in one room, living out of each other's pockets. There must have been times when I compared Australia with England, although it was pointless doing so because you can't expect to come 14,000 miles and find the same country with the same attitudes – plus you're Public Enemy No. 1, being a Pom.

'You see, no good news *ever* comes out of England, it never has. You never read anything good about England in the Australian Press. It seems incredible, but after twenty years you'd think I would have read *something* positive about England. Unfortunately, I haven't ...'

Tricia Lovell, from Coventry and the currency exchange bureau at Brisbane Airport, summed it up after ten years in Australia: 'It's like being torn between two lovers. When I'm here I wish I were there – and when I'm there I want to come back.' That was my nearest whinge. Australian papers, please copy.

Everyone seems fascinated by royalty, at least. Anything about Princess Diana or Fergie is seized upon – though a Pom may be suspected of patronizing the colonials should he appear to know *too* much about them.

Even on such sure ground, there are exceptions; when the Duke of Kent visited the Pilbara in the scorched Western Australian desert, he met the State Secretary of the Transport Workers' Union, John O'Connor, at a poolside reception. Mr O'Connor finally put his beer down to take the proffered hand and observed gracefully: 'You've got a weak chin, just like the rest of the Royal Family.'

Standing among migrants and attempting royal conversation, chin out, the Duke asked how long it took an Englishman to become Australian. 'Three days, for Poms,' Mr O'Connor volunteered. 'Three days after they're dead.'

Irish unionists apart, Australia's brightest and best will deride and scorn Britain – but make a dash for London at the first opportunity. Success abroad is still intensely important, as Barry Humphries explained: 'Living too long in Australia is like dancing with your mother all night at a party.'

Despite an indifference to anything British that is not royal or athletic, Australians are upset by reciprocal disinterest in their country and complain that the world sees them through a cruel kaleidoscope of kangaroos, barbies and technicolour yawns – the image they propagate in their advertising, both national and beer. Sir Les Patterson and Paul Hogan may be lovably lecherous and golden-hearted, but socially neither is totally ept.

Sadly, you rarely meet a Crocodile Dundee – though Dame Edna is everywhere, trilling, 'Excuse I!' Also everywhere, and thankfully, are lovely girls looking the way Californian women *think* they look: lithe, tanned, blue-eyed, golden-maned. Such goddesses are 'treated with ignore' by local men who regard them as par for the course and nothing to make a fuss about. Australians like women who 'scrub up all right' and form an attractive background, but don't expect to see them in control.

Sonia Smirnow directs public relations for Sydney's best hotel, the towering Regent. She came from the other side of the tracks, she says, and one night returning home on the bus met a former neighbour who asked where she was working. When she said, 'In an hotel,' he instantly assumed she was a barmaid and congratulated her upon achieving a good job.

The point is, she could *not* bring herself to disabuse him! She couldn't say: 'No, I'm an executive with a lot of people working for me.' A Tall Poppy's bad enough – but a Tall Poppaea ... !

When I first visited Sydney in the late Fifties the taxi drivers were nut-brown Diggers in shorts, wiry and laconic. Today most are New Australians who can't speak English and are uncertain how to reach the Opera House. I was once relieved to get one of the older fellers who knew his way to the airport – a dinky-di Aussie. It transpired he was a German, born and raised on the Shanghai waterfront with a Chinese wife and a psychologist son in California. He hoped to retire to Penang, and had little time for foreigners.

In the Melbourne phone book, a non-British name has made it into the top fifty for the first time: the 1280 Nguyens outnumber the Cooks and the Coopers. However the Top Ten remain resolutely Anglo-Saxon: Smith, Williams, Jones, Brown, Taylor, Anderson, White, Johnson, Thomas, Martin.

Australians can take anything, except criticism. They will request it, beg for comment, seek input from the world outside ... but it is wiser to stick to lavish praise. A quick compliment could save slow traction – and there's much to be complimentary about.

Admittedly they choose strange heroes for their rare and grudging approval: 'He's a *great* little battler,' someone said, with admiration; 'Lazy bugger's never done a day's work in his life!'

What gladiators were to the Romans, kamikaze pilots to the Japanese and astronauts to the Americans ... little Aussie battlers are to the Australians. These legendary heroes always fight valiantly against all the odds – and *lose*! Ned Kelly had to fail as a criminal to become the antipodean white knight. Gallant defeats are also celebrated. Anzac Day.

Corruption is a recurrent topic, and Australians disapprove – mildly. In New South Wales, where each year 15,000 'crims' pass through twenty-three jails, there is a very high tolerance level for corruption, which throughout Australia reaches up through parliaments into judiciaries. Only one or two publications are brave enough to tackle this national malady, for it needs to be proved in court that not only what was said or written was true, but that such publication was for the good of the community. This is not easy. So the status remains quo, and well-known crims go to charity balls.

The annual turnover of organized crime has been estimated at £380 for every Australian. Commissions set up to investigate crime have been hurriedly called off – when the trail led straight back to the politicians! The Costigan Commission was formed to examine the role of one trade union notorious as underworld enforcers, and enquiries revealed Labour Party misconduct. After four years' investigation Labour regained power – and the Commission was closed down. Few of its recommendations were carried out.

At the time of the 1984 election a government minister was awaiting trial for selling early releases from prison; a High Court judge, Mr Justice Murphy, was under examination for urging junior magistrates to favour underworld characters and asking them to put in a word for 'my little mate'; two New South Wales police commissioners had been forced out of office by scandal; seventy detectives were under investigation; Post Office staff were using the mails to import heroin – and immigration officials were accused of selling visas to Asian prostitutes. Enquiries, as they say, continue.

When I suggested it was more Central American than Anglo-Saxon, the Minister for Corrective Services for New South Wales, the Hon. John Akister – an orphan from a Cumbrian workhouse – suggested such easygoing morality might have something to do with the climate!

Australians are not too concerned when others get away with it, and are little interested in what goes on in the next town – let alone the next continent. Only the BBC World Service or ABC's excellent Radio Australia, beamed overseas, help visitors retain a nail-hold on life as we know it in the world outside.

As we refuelled at Bombay, my Qantas jumbo was parked next to a PanAm clipper; we took off for Sydney and PanAm flew on to Karachi – where it was murderously hijacked. This drama appeared briefly in the Sydney newscasts, but was quickly replaced as lead story by a missing child from Vaucluse. It could well have been a road accident in Parramatta or a gas leak in Woolloomooloo.

As in Britain, much breakfast television is designed for eight-year-olds and not *half* as mature or thoughtful as the programme which follows on one channel: *Sesame Street*.

It is difficult for Europeans to comprehend the vast emptiness of Australia, where you travel hundreds of miles without a change of scenery. The black-top road that surrounds the continent was only completed while I was there, in 1986.

Leaving Darwin on the Stuart Highway and heading south through the heartland the first roadsign says: Tennant Creek 969, Alice Springs 1479. Admittedly that's kilometres, but braced behind a hire-car steeringwheel, teeth gritted, the Alice doesn't sound *much* closer at 924 miles! There's no speed limit, so you can put your foot down and go flat-out for days, watching only for animals and giant road-trains.

At Katherine – first stop, a mere two hundred miles south – Dr Clare Jukka told me she had to think hard before referring a patient to a specialist in a southern city: 'It's like sending them from London to Egypt – would you do *that* every day?'

Between Albany and Perth in Western Australia another wonderful highway drives straight across an empty red landscape. Through burnt grass and gum trees, it undulates towards the horizon like a rollercoaster, mile after mile. Only the flavour of the tarmac changes: from vanilla to strawberry, from blue to grey ... Every hour or so, another car.

Australia is one of the few lands where it is still possible to get away from people. In the outback – where the highest recorded temperature was over 53°C (128°F) – you sink into wonderful silence without one unnatural sound; no evidence of man's existence in the red dust, the terracotta cliffs. Only the wind, and the flies ...

Where you have a magnificent outdoors, indoors may seem unimportant; Australians live extremely well but, in the main, not very comfortably. Through endless suburbs, 'bungs' march towards every horizon. With all that space they have no need to huddle, yet roofs reach out to touch reassuringly. Some houses with long thin backgardens are still built directly on the road – as though their occupants feared being out of sight and sound of other people.

In the cities all is new, gleaming and plentiful; services run smoothly – when not on strike – and standards are high. There are few pressures: streets are clean and mostly safe, there's a sense of order and fair play instead of menace, and no hint of riot or revolution.

In the bush little has changed; communications improve, but life remains harsh – a three-year drought can wipe out generations of toil.

Despite the expensive tyranny of distance – a long day's flight from anywhere, which means travellers start and end their holidays exhausted – Australia will be a target for international tourism when fully discovered, a safe and friendly destination in an increasingly hostile world. An influx of Americans followed the Libyan and Chernobyl upheavals; Europeans arrive by the jumboload to visit relatives; Queensland attempts to cope with a growing flood of Japanese descending upon the Great Barrier Reef and finding the Gold and Marlin Coasts better and cheaper than Hawaii, and what's more – *there* be koalas! Australia's superb long-distance airline, Qantas, encourages the coming millions towards one of the last unexplored places on earth which also has the infrastructure for comfort: wilderness, with bathrooms.

A weird two-airline monopoly of duplicate flights is traditional, Ansett and Australian Airlines taking off for everywhere in tandem. Qantas is forbidden to fly passengers domestically – not even those it has brought from overseas – so its luxurious long-haul aircraft often fly almost empty 2500 miles across the continent, wings and profits clipped by their owner, the government.

Most visitors do not stay long enough to become aware that the local work ethic is weak: unskilled workers are highly paid, so there is little incentive to acquire skills. Where sun shines and beaches invite, it does not seem imperative to invest in the future; few Aussies have ambitious goals. Back in the Twenties, D. H. Lawrence arrived in New South Wales with Frieda and stayed in a seaside bungalow at a place called Wyewurk. Lawrence was captivated; he thought it was an aboriginal word ...

Today constant labour troubles recall the silly-strikes in the United Kingdom during the Fifties and Sixties when there was full employment and unionists could afford to be petulant – and would you believe, the poor old British get the blame! Most trade union officials defending their picket-lines on television have northern accents and are known as Pommy stirrers.

The labour force is so powerful that unionists around the world see Australia as a workers' paradise. There are some 330 craft unions, most led by the hard Left, and sometimes corrupt. Once they worked to improve the lot of their members, but many have degenerated into power-centres peddling political ideologies. They are disliked or feared by those outside their stockade, but provide the ruling Labour Party with four-fifths of its income.

While I was there a factory went on strike when the canteen menu offered only two desserts; another suffered a walk-out because only one flavour of ice cream was available. A worker was fired after taking thirty-five 'sickies' in two months; his colleagues came out instantly. The Firemen's Union put a ban on after-hours fire-fighting.

A strike in the New South Wales Government printing office delayed publication of the Budget – because the first-aid room was not staffed twenty-four hours a day. The opening of the new Perth Airport terminal was delayed because electricians refused to install lights unless a qualified nurse stood at the bottom of each ladder.

A stage-hand at the wonderful Sydney Opera House was convicted of stealing, and fired. His eleven colleagues walked out, leaving 4500 concert-goers standing in the cold two hours before the performance, and cancelling a later programme for 15,000 school-children. The dispute went routinely to arbitration next day.

Mineworkers' unions insist that water trucks sprinkle dusty roads – even when it rains; their mine machinery works about five hours in each eight-hour shift. Crews of diesel locomotives have to be replaced every two or three hours – because shovelling coal was once so tiring. Grain is loaded on to ships by conveyer belts worked by inflated gangs of once-upon-a-time sack-carriers; the belts are switched off for tea-breaks ...

At Melbourne a railway union struck because members of another union were using their engine whistles too frequently. A union radio programme reported indignantly that crane drivers sometimes had to work in the *rain*; they didn't say anything about the overseers' whips.

Bricklayers are forbidden to lay more than three hundred bricks a day; one extra brick would cause, as the Pommy shop steward announced severely, 'A state of disputation.'

Not surprisingly, Australian labour is the most highly priced in the world: eight times more expensive than Taiwan, six times more than Singapore – higher priced, even, than the United States. In Korea – a Pacific competitor – electronics factories work a twelve-and-a-half-hour day, with two days off each month. Australians get fifteen paid holidays a year, plus a month's annual leave – when they get $17\frac{1}{2}$ per cent more than their wages to make up for missing overtime. Out of fifty-two weeks they work about forty – and have an automatic allocation of sick-days, without the tiresome necessity of being ill.

Needless to say, the unions are not alone in damaging the economy. Australia possesses a rich store of natural resources – but a poor store of the know-how and ability to process them. Workers have their lavish quotas of 'sickies', but executives take 'stress leave'. In sleepy tropical Cairns – which Conrad would recognize – businessmen retreat to cottages up in the Tablelands, to escape the pressure.

A Swiss survey recorded that Australian industrial management skills were lower than those of India, Turkey and Mexico . . .

The land is one vast paradox: huge mass with tiny population; high-wage economy with low productivity; Third-World balance of payments with First-World financial sophistication. Industries heavily protected by tariffs and barriers, worked by rigidly unionized labour, have left the country in a poor position to adjust to its declining financial fortunes. Yet there is little poverty. Citizens may grumble about the effects of taxation and recession, but by world standards they live magnificently.

The nation is fiercely democratic and for its electorate of ten million, voting is compulsory. The world's first parliamentary elections by secret ballot were held in Victoria in 1856; female suffrage was introduced in South Australia in 1894. The politicians rarely live up to this proud record, for even in that universally devious vocation they appear unusually insincere and self-serving.

Most migrants arrive at Sydney's poor old airport – little changed since I first landed there thirty years ago – to discover, once they escape the queues and delays, that this South Seas place at the bottom of the world is bigger than Birmingham, Manchester, Leeds and Glasgow – *combined!*

The city is curiously expressionless; there is pallor in its style, and little joy – as though no one there has quite recovered from the surprise of actually *being* in such a grand metropolis on the edge of the never-never. The almost unimaginable emptiness of Australia lurking beyond those hills seems to reach down into its teeming streets, draining any exuberance.

Architecturally it is drab. Sydney Cove, where it all began, has been crudely degraded by the construction of an elevated express-way right across it. Some of the highrise blocks on the new Man-hattan skyline are sleek and elegant, but there are no striking civic set pieces – only the usual clumps of nineteenth-century florid. The engaging iron-lace terraces of Paddington lead to posh waterside suburbs of uninspired confusion: nature lavish, man mindless.

I went to a pleasant Sunday barbecue at one large villa, the kind of characterless white blob created for comfortably-off retirees in Torquay in the Thirties – but it had a waterfront, so nature wiped out any disaster of design. It had just been sold for $7 million.

Yet despite man-made mistakes and stodgy air, Sydney remains one of the most beautiful places in the world: pale pure light from the Antarctic goes dancing across that verdant harbour, its winding waterways flecked by yachts and scurrying ferries. The Opera House flutters white and feminine, arching her wings submissively before the massive old Harbour Bridge, which looms macho and brutal above ... Beauty and the Beast, in a fresh and jubilant setting. What a city!

The cultural cringe has now been swept away and Australia brims with confidence. There is no visible class system, as in Britain; no underclass trapped in poverty, as in America. People drive new cars fast and well, heading for the beach with takeaway tubs of fresh oysters. Restaurants have no tables available and, on Sunday, queues. Shops are busy. Citizens show the same derisive contempt for authority and politicians as for the deadly funnel-web spiders lurking in their gardens and, like all Australians, maintain an enviable rapport with their environment.

They are not given to conspicuous expenditure; most are relaxed to the point of falling apart, in clothes designed not to indicate social status but to disguise it. This wards off envy and the fatal 'tall poppy' label – deflecting the devastating Australian levelling instinct.

Their European civilization on the edge of the world is today a blend of old-style Britain, brash America, eager Asia – and boxing kangaroo. Despite its new nationalism, it has not yet decided what it wants to be: a land of untold promise – or easygoing mediocrity? Certainly it remains wholesome and conventional – 80 per cent of the shirts sold are white – but at last some healthy uncertainty is being imposed upon the self-satisfaction. Hard realism has begun to replace 'no worries mate' Micawberism.

Like those first settlers who came ashore to hard labour two hundred years ago, they are in for a testing time during the next five years – but there's always a cheerful readiness to 'Give it a go!' as they face another boring day in paradise.

Once interesting things always seemed to happen somewhere else, but today Australians have a stronger sense of themselves. They may be less than 0.3 per cent of the world's population, but that's *not* the way they come across; among every one thousand of us, they seem to have more impact than the other 997!

So from across this wonderful land, meet some new-Australians, in full cry . . .

THE CROCODILE MAN: MIKE POPLE

Crocodiles have rather bad breath, at times...

Every now and then in some Australian lagoon, creek, swamp or billabong, crocodiles in an almost absent-minded way eat a passing person – or at least take a significant chunk out of someone ... These ancient predators show few good points. They are neither furry nor cute, they do not respond to kindness – they're not even nice to each other, let alone to swimmers or fishermen. On occasion a hefty female will kill her mate, and a male will eat his own young. What's more, they have rather insincere smiles ... In fact, only the estuarine or saltwater crocodile actually attacks humans, while the freshwater crocodile – unique to Australia – is not considered dangerous, though if interfered with may bite. The 'salties', the ones with broader snouts, can grow to at least eighteen feet. One harpooned in Queensland's Norman River measured twenty-eight feet four inches. The 'freshies' only reach nine feet or so. As saltwater crocs also live in fresh water, few approached pugnaciously by nine feet of crocodile would pause to reflect upon the width of its snout; there's always the chance he may not have read the instructions!

In the past two years, nine people have been taken

by crocodiles, and every time someone is snatched the campaign for the removal of their protected status is renewed – 'Exterminate the brutes!' – for during the fifteen years since hunting was curbed it is estimated their numbers have grown from 7000 to 50,000. Unfortunately for the smile on the face of the crocodile, these living dinosaurs have few defenders; perhaps the nearest to that increasingly rare species – a human who actually *likes* crocodiles – is an electrician from Bristol . . .

Mike Pople left ICI in 1969 to travel to Tasmania. Since 1974 he has been a Ranger of the Queensland National Parks and Wildlife Service. A small and chirpy version of Crocodile Dundee with a West Country accent, he spends much of his life protecting crocodiles from themselves, and from others; a most un-ordinary job.

I went with him one breathless night, drifting through some mangrove swamp between Cardwell and Tully as its opaque water lapped and silver fish leapt high into the light around our boat. We whispered and peered through the darkness for the eye-shine of a crocodile. Afterwards, he set a net trap for one of his 'problem' crocs, due to be relocated further from humans. These days, it seems, most crocodiles have *some* sort of problem . . .

That croc's just feeding and sleeping – he's about three years old. You can grab him, if you want! You get them in a crèche when they first get hatched, and they're very communal; they hang around the nest site for quite a long period.

Most problem animals are about the eight- to ten-foot range, being pushed out of the territorial area because they're getting to the size when they can breed. They'll be tolerated by the big males until they get bigger, then they'll get pushed.

They feed at night-time on small fish and turtles, or they'll just be lying there. They sleep in water; it's warmer than the outside air, so they can maintain the body heat far more efficiently.

This is the kind of river in which those two women were swimming when the crocodiles took them? I must say I've no desire at all to go swimming in this!

No, I wouldn't either, because you don't swim where you can't see the bottom, not in mangrove areas.

We have the freshwater or Johnson crocodile, but all these are saltwater or estuarine crocodiles. The freshwater's not a threat in any circumstances. They're quite numerous and only found in Australia. You wouldn't get one much bigger than eight foot – in some areas they may be ten foot, but it's unlikely.

How are you ever going to convince me that an eight-foot crocodile is harmless?

We've done a lot of research on freshwater crocodiles. There's one research study up in the Great Dividing Range a couple of hours' drive from here where they're actually *in* the water with them. You're walking on top of them and you can feel them against your legs!

About a year ago we had a rescue operation up in the Gulf country, at Ascot Station, just north of Mount Isa. With the drought coming on, their water hole was drying up and they wanted us to do something about the crocodiles, to catch them and to relocate them into a large river system. The water hole would have been twice as big as an average room – and there was eighty-plus crocs in there, up to about seven and a half foot! We were amazed.

So we went out and did that. They were all freshwater crocs, and we were in with them and there was no chance of getting bitten at all. The only time you get bitten is when you go to pick one up: it rolls, so you pick it up the right way.

Did the locals at Ascot Station also believe they were harmless?

It took a while! Only the two of us went up, and we needed a lot more help to do it. Eventually we jumped in, and they were quite happy once they saw *us* get in...

There's no record of freshwater crocodiles ever grabbing a leg?

19

In a wild state, no. I wouldn't say that in captivity. They're a very vicious animal in captivity, they go crazy.

The estuarine crocodiles can be found anywhere in any river systems up to the Great Dividing Range – and that's in completely fresh water! That's why people get confused ... A freshwater crocodile has got a very pronounced pointed snout, and it's a lot longer than the other one. Also the scoops on the back of the neck are different.

People are finding it hard to be crocodile-aware ... History shows that all these fatalities are down to stupidity or carelessness, and these recent deaths aren't exceptions: these were European fishermen licensed here in Queensland to fish barramundi. They always fish in the same places, and in this particular spot they ran up to set the nets, and their boat broke down. They don't carry oars or anchors or anything like that, so they decided to walk back across country, back to their bigger boat. The boat would be only thirty feet away, in very fast-flowing water. Anyway, this bloke swam across, and got in the mid-section of the boat. His companion decided she'd walk across because she didn't want to get her cigarettes wet, or something. The water was only up to her waist. Part way across a crocodile grabbed her around the top part of her torso, and carried her along on the top of the water. I think the bloke in the boat got a kick at it as it went past. It was only interested in feeding – nothing else. It just swam off, and went down.

It surfaced a few hundred metres away and he shot at it and missed, and then it went under – and that was the last they saw of it until the next day. They found the body adjacent to one of the nets, with the crocodile guarding it. He'd consumed some of it ...

After these deaths here in northern Queensland there was an outcry of 'Exterminate the brutes'?

It's because people are ignorant of crocodiles, and a lot of the time unfortunately they get a biased side of the story: the media want to put across the sensational bits.

We regard the crocodile as the ultimate villain – it's not a very lovable animal, I must confess.

No, not many people actually bend over backwards to crocodiles, unfortunately. They don't seem to be affectionate to mankind at all, but they have a role to play in the natural cycle of things.

What crocodiles need is a good public relations officer – and you're the nearest they've got!

We still have an uphill battle, I'm afraid, because people believe they've got more right to swim and fish in these river systems than crocodiles have, and it's pretty hard to say what benefits crocodiles bring to mankind. They're the oldest animal we have on earth at this present time...

They're not nice to man or to each other – they're not even nice to their young...

You do get the odd male that gets a bit strange and eats its own offspring, but the females are very protective. They take the eggs and crack them open and assist the young hatchlings out, and even take them to water. They have very maternal instincts.

When I was in Australia in the Fifties and Sixties it was open season for crocs – anyone could shoot them at will.

That's right, but they were fully protected from '72 in the Territory, and '74 here.

But they're on a knife edge now – all they need to do is to take another woman or a child – and there'll be an uproar...

There could be. We'd certainly have to increase our operations, shoot more than we're now actually removing live. People don't realise that by unintentionally feeding crocodiles at boat ramps, where they chuck off crab bait and remains of fish and rubbish, it attracts crocodiles to where people are.

Yet crocodiles do seem to eat human beings in a rather absent-minded way...

It's just a situation that someone being stupid may get themselves into. They may actually find a crocodile that's maybe a bit hungry. It would have to be a big animal – if you get back on the historic records of fatalities you'll find they're all large animals. You don't have problems much below thirteen or fourteen foot, because the crocodiles are too small for a human to fit into their prey size.

But they can still bite off an arm or a leg?

They wouldn't be interested – it's too big to eat. In the Territory the crocodile took that girl but chucked her out – just *too* big. He had a go because she was low in the water and he obviously thought she was a lot smaller than she was; had a go, and basically rejected her.

Tonight they can sense us coming by the vibrations in the water, even though we're on an electric motor. They sense us, they see the lights. If we were trying to *catch* crocodiles we wouldn't be making a sound, we'd be absolutely quiet; you'd just get the motor humming. In some situations we even have hessian bags over the front of the boat to try and stop the water slapping, so there wouldn't be a sound at all.

As far as crocodiles are concerned, we're the only predator?

That's for sure. They've been around so long because they're secretive in their habits: they go right into the back of the creeks, the river systems, the lagoons where man has never gone for literally hundreds of years.

Having a croc on your property must be like living on a busy road; as long as you know it's there and you take sensible precautions, you're reasonably safe?

You have to accept that crocodiles have a place, and their place is a river system such as this. People should be crocodile-aware and not do stupid things like swim and fish, stand in the water, camp adjacent to the banks and chuck rubbish and the remains of food into the water.

Our main worry is problem crocodiles. We don't class a croc less than two metres to be a problem, unless it's round a school or a very popular swimming hole. If there's any kids in there, we may move all the crocs out. Anything over six feet is a *potential* problem.

What about these crocs that attack boats – you wouldn't feel so benevolent if one came off that bank, swam across and took a chunk out of our boat...?

I imagine it *would* be a bit of an upsetting time. That's normally associated with nesting, because the boat is an intruder to that crocodile. The boat could be another crocodile to it, another animal come into its territory. We went through a bad stretch in the Northern Territory: there was one particular river system that's renowned for people getting attacked, boats getting attacked. It's during their mating time, during the wet season, that they get aggressive, very territorial. The females are very protective towards their nest areas. There were quite a few boats attacked, and we had to remove some crocs out of one particular area. But it doesn't happen very often.

It doesn't have to happen very often ... So when a croc's taken a human being, you can shoot him?

Our main priority is to get that animal, yes.

Then you're going to open it up and see if it's got anybody's arms or legs in its stomach?

Our main priority is to confirm that someone has been attacked or taken by a crocodile. When we get a problem, we survey the river and check for signs of where the crocodile is – slides etc. A lot of times you don't actually *see* the animal, just signs of where it's been. You see where the footmarks are. That gives us an idea of where it's sunning itself, because a crocodile being cold-blooded has to get its body temperature increased by the sun. That's when most people see them during the day, and that's how we figure a location and set a trap up.

This is the crocodile trap we developed to make it easy for us to catch crocodiles. It's a big net system: the bait's stashed at the other end and it's connected to this mechanism on the gate. That falls down as the crocodile goes in to grab the bait. It'll automatically try to go out to the water, try to pull the bait – and the door will drop and the crocodile will hopefully be there when we come and find it.

The bait will probably be pig; sometimes it's fish. You have to vary your bait depending on the crocodile's taste.

So you've got your monster crocodile in the net, he's got the pig, he realizes something is wrong – and gets a bit cross? Can't he then fight his way out?

A crocodile can escape out of anything if it's given enough time, so these traps have to be checked every day. A lot have radio alarms, so when the trap goes off it sends a special signal to our base and we get two blokes down here straight away. Once the animal's secured – in other words we tie the head down – it's all right.

You leave a person there, and once someone's *with* a crocodile it's sort of shut down. They've got the ability to shut their metabolism down, and just by having someone wandering around here talking to themselves, that crocodile will be pretty quiet until we can get more people in to shift it.

He likes to have a croc-sitter?

If you went away and left him by himself, he'd go crazy and try and get out of there. They've got so much power – a fifteen-foot animal would smash its way out, in time.

I would have thought once you've caught the crocodile your problems are just beginning?

No, we've found they're pretty easy then. We've got a system to get them out: we tie the jaws up, we get ropes underneath. The first two operators secure the mouth of the trap, and then you put a bag over the croc's head so it can't see. Then it's disorientated and slows itself down, and you get in there.

It's easy to say, 'Put a bag over the croc's head', but how do you do it?

It's not as hard as people think, because they do shut down. They're dangerous, you've got to be careful, and we don't just jump straight on top of it – that would be ridiculous. If it's a small croc we *would*, but a ten- or twelve-foot croc we don't jump on, it's just too dangerous.

I believe you, I believe you.

But you see, the mesh of the net is so small that the crocodile can't really get a bite at you. It could give you a knock with its head and send you flying into the mangroves, no problem. Normally they give a thrash every so often, but if you're careful round them – and everyone *is* careful – you're all right. We've got set procedures we operate.

I should hate to be pushed by a crocodile.

The main problem is people: this is part of a National Park and people come in here swimming, fishing. If they can't see a crocodile they say there's not one around, and they'll still go swimming – and a small child is obviously food size for a twelve- to fourteen-foot crocodile.

A mouthful! Wouldn't it be easier to shoot a dart into a crocodile – to tranquillize, rather than to trap?

You could do that quite easily, but when you shoot a crocodile in the water it'll go straight to the bottom and you just can't find it again. We harpoon crocodiles, with a line attached. With wild-caught animals, they're very stressed, and if we use drugs on a stressed animal there's a good chance that we could kill it. It's what we call post-catcher myopathy, a stress-related problem.

A crocodile will go straight to the bottom and switch itself off, slow its metabolism down for up to two hours, so we work them like a fish, manoeuvre the boats until you get the crocodile to the top and bring it in the boat.

If you harpoon a crocodile, isn't that just liable to make him cross?

It's a special harpoon, it just penetrates the skin like an injection with a hypodermic syringe. It's not a traumatic experience at all.

But when you start hauling him in, won't he know something's happening?

That's something new to him and he would be quite upset about it, naturally. We'd expect that. They're strange creatures, they're very easy to kill in that situation – you can drown a crocodile very easily! People have shot crocodiles many times, wounded them, and they can survive traumatic wounds – yet you can kill them by just leaving them in the water too long. We have to be careful when we bring them to the surface to make sure they take a breath.

It's not easy to give a crocodile the kiss of life . . .

I don't think anyone's prepared to do that – they've got rather bad breath at times!

The skin is valuable, especially from an estuarine crocodile; poachers could sell it for a lot of money?

It's the best skin in the world. If we go on hearsay and information received, poaching is still going on, especially in the Gulf. There is a bit of movement in the stuffer trade, which is little hatchlings one or two years old, because people like them on their mantelpieces.

People also like them as handbags and wallets?

That's right, women do like that sort of thing. Over in Europe, France is the main place where the big tanneries treat the skins. The estuarine crocodile we're looking for here is the most valuable skin; the last price was $20 American per linear inch, and you've got a good width on the belly, so a big crocodile could be quite a few hundred dollars.

Most Poms come out here looking for a new and exciting life, but switching from an electrician in Bristol to a crocodile-catcher in Queensland is a more dramatic change than most. What are your main worries here?

Illegal trafficking of fauna, birds and reptiles.

People who drug parrots and post them to America?

There's a lot of that going on. You can get $2000 for a galah in America, for which you'll pay $10, $15 at the most. Little budgerigars go for about $5 or $6 here, and in some places in America it's $500. Some of the parrots here are very big commercially and probably worth about $500 a pair; overseas they're anything up to $30,000–$40,000.

The big upsurge now is reptiles, because they don't have to drug them, they don't have to feed them. They tape their limbs down so they can't move and put them in the post, simple as that! There's a big business in that. We've had quite a few shipments of snakes.

That might give a curious customs officer a nasty shock!

They *have* done! We've had a few come up in Cairns. They could be venomous snakes, but a lot of the time it's pythons. They're wound up tight, and sealed up. In one instance in Cairns the crate said 'photographic equipment', and it was full of snakes. They weren't packed properly, and it *moved*! That sort of thing's going on all the time.

But some of these government restrictions must puzzle people? Northern Queensland's full of glorious parrots that are classified as vermin, which farmers are allowed to shoot – but not allowed to export!

It's a situation that's not easy to explain. It's a government decision at federal level that they do not want to export our pest species. It's difficult for us to justify, being Field Officers. People say, 'A farmer up the road is shooting galahs, can I go and trap them alive?' and we've got to say, 'No'. They sell for something like $2000 to $5000 in the States.

Some species of pythons are collectors' items in Europe and the States, they go for quite a few hundred dollars. The rarer species, the western taipan that's found in southwestern Queensland, can fetch a *lot* of money, in the thousands. They're the most venomous snakes in the world.

We had a case recently where someone sent reptiles in an Easter egg. For birds and mammals they use suitcases and packing cases. They have to use drugs, and the animals have to be taped down. You get a massive death rate – probably up to eighty or ninety per cent. With reptiles the death rate is a lot lower, maybe only five per cent – I suppose that's why reptile smuggling has increased in the last few years.

But you can't do much about this and you can't stop poaching – there's only a handful of you.

That's the biggest problem. We rely on people assisting us. There's only a couple of us in this district – we haven't got a lot of rangers to do this sort of work. If we're playing around with crocodiles, we're not out looking for bird trappers. Two blokes can't possibly do everything – we're looking at the top end of a volcano.

Even pets can be a problem. One woman kept a kangaroo in her back-yard, in a fenced area. She was menstruating at the time and the animal got sexually frustrated and attacked her – semi-rape, I suppose. It cut her right open with its back legs, slit her open. She had all these stitches. They're big animals that can stand a lot higher than a man, and a lot stronger. You don't play around with them, unless you know what you're doing.

We went and talked to her and recommended we took the animal away and relocated it. She cried and cried – it was amazing – she wouldn't have any of it. She went to the political scene and said she didn't want it to go. She had a very positive attitude, she knew she was in the wrong but she thought we were going to destroy the animal.

They think their animal can't survive in the wild state because there's too many nasties out there, and Mother's not around to look after it. We try and explain the situation and convince them the best thing for that animal is to be put back into the wild state, into a National Park or a reserve.

Can you ever see yourself back in Bristol?

No, I don't think I could. I went back a few years ago and found I didn't know many people, and the whole place has changed and seemed small. You've got a lot of open space here, and we might drive a thousand kilometres in a day to do a job, yet in Bristol it's a major job to go twenty-five kilometres. And there's no crocodiles in Bristol . . .

THE DOWN UNDER 'DUCHESS': JANE MAKIM

I'm the Duchess of North Star, since we got back ...

Jane Makim, born in Welbeck Street, W.1, now lives in a dilapidated fifty-year-old wooden farmhouse amid the endless flatlands near the northern border of New South Wales, outside North Star (population: 100) where crippling drought has shrivelled the soil into dust and farmers' livelihoods into the red. She has no help in the house, and supplies are delivered on the mail-run three times a week. In this harsh, un-giving landscape she looks after Seamus, five, Ayesha, eight months – and nine horses.

Then suddenly, there she was, out of her jeans and into a tamarillo and green silk dress, sitting in Buckingham Palace and Westminster Abbey and watching her sister, Sarah Ferguson, marry Prince Andrew: a transformation scene in true Cinderella tradition, but with Jane as one of the *pretty* sisters.

The Makim property is not easy to find. From Sydney you fly north for a couple of hours to Moree, a small town in sheep country which, in my considered opinion, has more flies to the square inch than anywhere in the world. Another few hours north, then turn right into a confusion of dirt roads, and there through the dust (if you're lucky) is the small homestead built by Alex Makim's father in

1936 and little changed since then – indeed Jane says he protests if they attempt any improvement.

As a basic shelter the elderly house offers a sense of weary impermanence: lino on creaking floors, tired old furniture, an outback bathroom. The front door lets on to a small rudimentary kitchen, where Jane is preparing a chocolate cake; she's tall and slim, with a quick brilliant smile. She loves the life she has chosen – and doesn't even *notice* the flies.

She met Alex in 1972 when he arrived at her home in Dummer, Hampshire, to help with the Ferguson ponies. They were married in July 1976 when she was eighteen and Sarah, her bridesmaid, sixteen. The groom, tall and slim with a certain swagger, is the quintessential rangy outback Aussie. He works three properties of 8500 acres owned with his father and two brothers, but his enthusiasm is polo – so Jane is secretary of the North Star Polo Club. She also rides, with considerable panache.

She was wearing one of Sarah's cast-off sweaters: 'I'm not fussy when it comes to clothes; if I need a pair of jeans I go to Goondiwindi, no problem.' She helped Alex muster some cattle for the market and, as he drove them away, we set off to collect Seamus from the lonely crossroads where the school bus drops him at four o'clock every afternoon, along with a neighbour's daughter.

Sarah's sailor-suited pageboy, internationally known for elegance and enormous yawns during the ceremony, is cocky and enchanting. He has a video of that great day which he'll show anyone, along with some silver cufflinks and his midshipman's fourpence pay for the day – an 1854 silver groat.

It was indeed a great day for a five-year-old – and come to that, quite a change of style for his mother, too ...

From the soft green countryside of Dummer you came here as an eighteen-year-old into the scorched outback – how was it?

An adventure – but I'd been to Africa and other countries, so I was quite used to new experiences. Some days it's a real challenge, especially when you're on your own: the other day Alex got bogged in the dam with the bulldozer and I had to pull him out with the tractor – which is 180 horsepower and quite a responsibility to drive.

He runs the farm with the help of his brother and father, and I have to help quite often – when we sell a lot of cattle like we're doing today; they bring a lot of money. We do our horses together – the polo ponies – we train the young ones together, and that's really rewarding when they go well on the polo field; and we sell them.

You missed all that eighteen-year-old's fun at home, where I suppose you'd have been a Sloane . . .

No I would *not*! I left school when I was fifteen and went straight to a London college. I suppose living in London for two years you grow up rather quickly; also as a child I was lucky to travel to other countries, which also makes you grow up.

Today you're living in quite a basic way; how can I put it . . . you're living simply?

Yeah, but I love it. I have my horses.

You've certainly got your horses, no doubt about that – but you have little comfort and no luxury . . .

Well, I've got a car to get me places, I've got a television, I've got – what else have I got? I haven't got a swimming pool, if that's what you're saying.

Bringing up a couple of young children here must pose a few problems?

Snakes and spiders! I *still* haven't got used to snakes. Spiders don't worry me because we have spiders in England. I don't seem to worry about funnel-webs and redbacks – which I probably should do – but we do have them, yes. I can show you one, if you like?

Thanks – but these flies of yours are tiresome enough. I've always believed there are more flies concentrated around Moree than anywhere in the world!

They're a bit sticky! When I go riding for four hours, I take a can of Airguard with me. We also have kangaroos, wild pigs and emu; brown, black and tiger snakes – we had a tiger snake in our sitting room! You can get carpet snakes which don't actually hurt you, but they come up to twelve feet long! They're like pythons – they have beautiful colouring on their skins, just like a carpet.

How do you handle a poisonous snake in your sitting-room, apart from carefully?

We were a bit dumbfounded. It was Boxing Day, forty degrees, extremely hot. We were watching a documentary on wildlife in Africa – probably one of *your* documentaries – and we sort of thought that the snake was on the television! Alex nudged me, which meant: Get a gun – the four-ten shotgun. I couldn't move very fast because I was eight and a half months pregnant with Ayesha. I was squealing at this stage ... Without exaggerating it was about five feet long! We probably started off saying it was seven, but ...

Five feet is quite long enough to be going on with ...

It *is*, going across the carpet! Then Alex said, 'My goodness, it's a tiger snake, get hold of Seamus.' He was playing in his room – so he was away from it, anyway. Then it slid into the office, realized it couldn't go anywhere so turned round to come back – and Alex blasted it. He obviously only scared it. It went up a crack in the wall, and *stayed* there. We didn't know where it had gone.

Seamus had a torch he'd been given for Christmas and he went around looking for it, shining his torch up cracks in the wall – and he actually *found* it! The scales of the snake stood out – it was stuck half way up this crack. Alex rang his father and said, 'How the hell have you built this house?' He said, 'For Christ's sake don't go blowing holes in my wall!' All *he* was worried about was his house!

Alex said, 'I'm not sleeping in this house another day until I get rid of the snake.' He decided to blast through the wall. He took a punt and hoped he'd hit the middle of the snake. He said, 'You watch it, Jane, I'll go and get the axe.' Then it started to come out of the crack! I started to squeal – I mean, it was still alive! Anyway, he finally finished it off – I've got photographs I'll show you. I'll show you the hole in the wall.

Don't they usually go in pairs, these snakes?

This is the problem: where there's one there's usually about thirty!

So leaving here and going straight to Buckingham Palace must have made you feel you'd gone to another planet?

It was great fun, very hectic, very tiring – I mean there wasn't a day when we weren't talking to some newspaper or doing something, but it was good to get back in my jeans and get dirty with the cattle.

You didn't feel you'd like to stay?

No, no – it was great, but this is my home. Dummer's also my home, I mean I still adore England and my family and everything but *this* is my main home, and Dummer's my second home. I'm very lucky.

When you go back do you feel an Aussie – or still an English girl?

Oh I'm *definitely* an English girl. I'm not an Australian, definitely.

Though your husband is very Australian indeed.

Yes, he's very Australian, but he loves England, loves going there. I grew up at Dummer and your fondest memories are of your childhood, aren't they?

Sarah and I are very close. I'm actually writing a letter to her at the moment, and we do ring up. We probably ring up more than we write, much to – well, it *was* Dad's horror, now it's someone else's horror – my father-in-law's horror! She came here in '78, with Dad; they mustered the cows like we've been doing. Dad loves coming and relaxing and working hard – amongst the snakes and the flies!

I think my biggest memory of the wedding is seeing Sarah and Dad walking down the aisle together and just remembering – though it was slightly different when I got married! – that Dad said funny things to me, walking up the aisle. I'm sure he would have done the same to Sarah, to make her relax. Then when they came up closer to us I think it was a really proud moment, seeing them both looking so happy.

I must say your Mother also looked stunning – she was quite the best-dressed guest.

She looked great. Her life in Argentina is very similar to mine.

But you're closer to your father than to your mother – perhaps because you look more like her?

Yes, everyone says that.

Did you worry much about what you wore?

To start with I did, at Easter-time in Australia when the engagement was announced.

You instantly thought, 'I haven't got a thing to wear'?

No, I merely thought, 'I suppose I'll have to look smart' – but I didn't worry. I obviously wanted to look nice for Sarah, but once we got to England it was easy to get all the smart clothes out again.

You must have been nervous for Seamus, though, as a pageboy in the spotlight?

I was very worried until the first rehearsal, then I realized Sarah and Prince Andrew had had so much to do with all the children they knew them very well and the children respected them – so they behaved *beautifully*. I think that was why – because they got to know them well.

How did Seamus take to Westminster Abbey life?

It came rather quick and went rather quick, but he enjoyed it; he talks about it a lot. Mostly he remembers going in a carriage, kissing Sarah when they arrived at Buckingham Palace, the noise of the band – that was a bit overawing, I think. He said, 'The music was so loud, Mummy!' He and Prince William were reading their programmes upside down and Seamus kept yawning, so Rosanna Roxburghe started to laugh – quite loud actually – and Seamus turned round and said, 'If you don't stop laughing at me I'll cut your finger off with my knife!'

They weren't allowed much to eat in case they wanted to go to the loo, and they weren't allowed *anything* to drink ...

They were very little people, and they all did marvellously. Everybody enjoyed his occasional yawn.

Because they got up early, at six o'clock; but they did well.

The thing is, you like nice clothes – and here you don't normally have much opportunity to dress up?

There's *plenty* of occasions round here to get dressed up. I mean people get dressed up for the country races, for dances ...

Anyhow, after all that excitement would you like to change places with your sister?

Very hard question to answer ... but no – I love my life here. I'm suited for this life.

Evidently; so, back in your jeans, how do you spend your day?

At the moment, because I haven't got any help in the house, Ayesha takes up most of the day. Usually when I've got help, if Alex is working with the tractor I help him with the cattle, sheep, horses ...

Housekeeping? There's only one shop within ten miles, and that's quite a little store.

North Star is quite big, foodwise; it has a mail-run Mondays, Wednesdays and Fridays, so if I'm wanting an emergency, like milk or whatever, that comes out on the mail.

But if, say, you want to go and get your hair done?

What *for?* I can do my hair! I think I've got my hair done once in Moree, for the races; otherwise if I have an occasion that I *have* to get it done, it'll be in Sydney.

If you stayed here for a week you'd be *so* sick of the parties, you'd go very quickly. We have an awful lot of parties. We have a very big sporting complex at North Star – there's golf, tennis, pony club, everything.

So you can dress up and feel like a Duchess?

I've been called the Duchess of North Star since we got back!

Alex, you'd also rather be living here than in Hampshire?

Alex: Absolutely – I'm not a Hampshire man or an Englishman at *all*.

And you've converted Jane into an Aussie wife?

Well she didn't marry me for my castle, that's sure!

It can be a pretty harsh life, this – you can have a drought and lose your livelihood through no fault of your own ...

Absolutely. It's the same as if you're a peasant in Africa; we're probably a bit more sophisticated, that's all.

A friend of mine has sold his three properties and gone back to Sydney because the drought, he said, was the worst experience of his life. He wasn't brought up to it as you were, but for three years he used to look up at the sky and long for rain; he said the experience destroyed him ... You've been through the same thing?

When the rain comes it's better than any tonic, any medicine. It's a funny thing, even the bank manager leaves you alone for a while, as soon as it rains. You can be down the drain, but you just tighten the belt and start again – it's one of those things. Australia was built of battlers and triers, we're built on deluge and drought.

Today, wheat's not worth growing. The only thing that's very good at the moment in Australia is beef, there's a shortfall all over the world. Cotton took a terrific tumble for a couple of years, but now it's just flying through the roof again. It's great to see – gives us heart; even though we don't grow cotton, a lot of our friends do.

What Australia needs is 30 million people – and we need them *yesterday*. We want the right sort of people, the ones that are going to work, we don't want a surplus population of people who just want to be taken care of ...

We have the stability to keep our costs low, we're very efficient farmers selling our product overseas, which is *so* far away: Australia's way down here and the markets are way over *there*. The transport costs are just so vast, and we're nowhere near aggressive enough.

Certainly you're dependent upon transport, upon the wharfies – there's a lot of people between you and your market?

And they all want a cut out of what we're producing! We're still the biggest export earner, the rural sector, and yet we're at everyone's mercy. But we're not done yet, don't worry. We're very resilient. It really makes me angry when you *see* the subsidies they get in England, and the farm lobby's very strong in America too, so I'm told. But right here we have a lot of cheap labour – we have Jane ...

Jane: Cheap?

Alex: We've been exploited by the British for years over the colonies – now we're getting our own back!

Jane: Huh – I'll remember that next time you get bogged in the dam ...

THE MADAM: DORRIE FLATMAN

I'm the only Madam that mixes on the social scene ...

Mrs Dorrie Flatman, a hairdresser from Lyelake Road, Kirkby, Liverpool, sailed to Australia in 1963, taking three daughters and £45. She has lived in Perth for the last twenty years and is certainly a Pom who's made good – if that's the word ...

Running three flourishing businesses, she is now almost a pillar of the Establishment in Western Australia: well known around town, dressed expensively at Louis Féraud, married to Kim, an accountant 21 years younger than she is – younger indeed than her three daughters. They are quite prominent upon the Perth social scene, attending fashion shows, appearing in the gossip columns, giving to charity – for Mrs Flatman is very wealthy indeed.

As you may have gathered, Dorrie Flatman is a proper little Madam ... She runs three of Perth's sixteen brothels which, under Western Australia's unusual Containment policy, are tolerated by the police. Her girls can earn $2000 a week, which in each case means another $2000 for Dorrie – who gets half the take.

Her main establishment in Perth is a neat and carefully anonymous building with thirteen bedrooms on a main road just outside the city centre, its front door always half open. Behind it, a cash desk displays all the credit card signs. The client, if seen to be acceptable, passes through a remote-controlled door into a suburban sitting-room more Maples than bordello, where the television set is always on.

A bell summons the girls on duty for consideration. They dash chattering down the hallway in their lingerie and leotards, and encourage the waiting men with smiles and polite but restrained conversation. Those not chosen and taken up them stairs return to the kitchen, pick up their knitting, remove their suppers from the microwave – and chat about children; their cosy domestic scene has only briefly been interrupted.

Presiding over this anthology of pros – Dorrie, a Madam for the last twenty-four years. A sensible Liverpool lady, her matter-of-fact tenacity would have brought success in almost any business. She is brisk, no-nonsense, ready to answer directly any question you can think of about her esoteric life, since you're interested.

She takes great care with her appearance, dressing at an exclusive boutique in Perth, dieting carefully, putting aside three mornings a week for the hairdresser and one for aromatherapy and a facial. She recently submitted to operations upon both her eyes to restore her sight, and has been able to discard her heavy glasses.

For relaxation she visits the Perth Casino – on Saturday afternoons taking her mother so the perky eighty-three-year-old Liverpudlian may wrestle with the pokies for a few hours.

Her husband Kim was a boyish bank clerk contemplating life as a missionary fourteen years ago when he married into her three-brothel family – and lived happily every after. He now looks after Dorrie's double-entry book-keeping, and also does most of the cooking in their new $400,000 home on one of Perth's better estates. Every day he collects her from her place of work in a flash red sports car, and drives home to prepare the supper.

Dorrie's is very much a family business: Bridie McFarrell is one of her 'sitters' – the women who manage brothels. Once upon a time, back in Liverpool she'd been a *baby*sitter for Dorrie. Now, after a chance meeting in Australia, this soft-spoken abandoned wife runs her branch-brothel in Fremantle, where they have not yet painted-over the sign indicating the establishment's previous use: the Fremantle Fitness Centre. 'Wrong exercises!' said Bridie.

She and the other sitters control a happy hoard of harlots, a fanfare of strumpets whose numbers fluctuate: sometimes forty-five, sometimes only twenty-five girls in Dorrie's three houses. All operate two shifts.

Generally they are bright and cheerful. Bridie told me that to kill time they sometimes play charades. Their looks are commonplace – at best – but most are articulate and sympathetic. They pity men, rather than hate or scorn them; I frequently found it quite hard to avoid asking, 'What's a nice girl like you . . .?'

Many of these 'working girls' – as they call themselves – have been prostitutes most of their adult lives. They leave occasionally to rejoin the straight world, but usually drift back again. They see their daily chores as just another job and, once the heavy make-up is off and the street clothes on, slip back easily into everyday anonymity.

Their drug is money. Once used to that daily wad of dollars from the House reception desk as they go off shift – tax already deducted – it becomes almost impossible to contemplate eight hours in an office or shop for a tenth of the reward.

So they do their time in Dorrie's parlours, dreaming of an uncomplicated future with a family in some suburban home – which is always just a year or two ahead. Meanwhile in their suburban fantasy world they wait patiently and cheerfully for real life to begin . . .

After their wild sexual binge in the Seventies, Australians are now picking wearily through the post-party debris, considering old discarded values, and sampling new ones. AIDS arrived in 1981, so celibacy is one of today's hot topics – though not thought likely to catch on. Some two hundred girls work in Perth's sixteen Contained brothels, with another one hundred and twenty operating outside the system. These are tolerated provided they follow certain simple rules: no underage girls, no drugs, no men involved in their operation . . . Police have found Containment the ideal way of keeping the lid on prostitution among the city population of about a million, so the Madams of approved brothels operate securely within a closed-shop, protected by the police – if not by the law.

This policy of semi-legal prostitution has not been imitated elsewhere in Australia where, in numbers at least, the problem is far greater: Victoria's 4000 prostitutes are believed to entertain 45,000 clients a week. A Parliamentary select committee estimated that in New South Wales 2000 prostitutes conducted 49,000 sexual transactions each week, and earned $263 million a year.

Commissioner Brian Bull, Chief of the West Australian Police, believes the state operates an ideal system – and certainly he faces little public criticism. Containment frees prostitutes from the parasitical pimp and prevents organized crime getting its hands upon the flourishing brothels of Perth and Kalgoorlie, thus contributing considerably to the prosperity of at least one contented Liverpudlian . . .

I was a hairdresser in Liverpool, Great Elm Street. In 1963 things were getting from bad to worse, so I decided it was time to emigrate. I had a problem: my first husband was the problem – drinkwise. I thought at that time making a change and coming to Australia would get rid of all those problems, but it didn't change the situation at all. I got the forms and just said: 'Sign here.' He signed the papers, and because I had daughters we were accepted in a very short time; at that stage they were looking for people with families to come here.

I arrived, believe it or not, with three children, £45 and my husband. He was a dock labourer, but when he came here I think he worked *once*; he was an alcoholic, and I ended up divorcing him.

When we got to Australia the conditions were completely different for hairdressers to what they were in England, which meant that I had to go back to school. I didn't want to do that because I thought I was *well* past going to school after all that time in hairdressing so I applied for a job with door-to-door selling, which I enjoyed very much. Anyway, I was always watching the paper ads for something better – I always felt there *was* something better. With the fashions, you were on commission only, so if you didn't work you got nothing. It was good, but I worked seven days. Then I saw an ad in the paper asking for a masseuse. Well, I'd done scalp massages so I thought, 'There can't be anything much different in this . . .'

I went after the job – and when I got there I nearly died! It was all young girls, and I didn't have a clue: I thought a masseuse, you know, was just a masseuse. Anyway, they told me the position was filled. As I was walking away the man that owned the place, a German, came after me and asked if I'd ever done any management work. I said I'd had staff working for me – so he asked would I be manageress, and he would train me. Which he did.

There were three girls at the time, and I didn't know what was going on! This was near the post office in George Street. It wasn't a house, it was a set of offices with a shower, a massage studio. After a few weeks he said I was capable of looking after the place while he went on holiday. Then he rang up from Acapulco and said he wasn't coming back, would I like to buy the place? I didn't have the money, but he said I could put so much in the bank until the amount he wanted was there, and then the place was mine. I think it was £5000 but in that type of business you'd make it back, and there was no tax in those days. I often had to pay tax, but the girls didn't.

Massage parlour was just a euphemism for brothel – you must have known what you were running?

No. I didn't. I didn't know at that stage.

But Dorrie, you're a very sharp lady – are you really telling me you didn't know what was going on?

No, because nobody had ever said anything, and I was just sitting there. The only way I found out was, one of the girls was off, we were short-staffed and somebody come in for a massage – so I went in to do the massage. When I told him to have a shower he said 'What about the *rest*?'

I went straight out and got one of the girls and said, '*What's* the rest?' And she told me! So I said, 'Oh – will you look after him?' When she came out I said, 'Why didn't you tell me?' She said, 'I thought you'd freak, I thought you'd sack the lot of us.'

I said, 'I've been chasing people away when they were asking funny things on the telephone – I've been turning business away.' So then I knew how to answer the phone, and what to say.

You came to terms quite quickly with the fact you were running a sort of brothel?

Oh yes, it didn't worry me. I finished up buying the place. A few more girls came looking for work and there was only the couple of rooms there – so I opened another one. And after a few weeks, another one. I finished up with seven in Sydney.

Then the law changed: they brought out a new law where a policeman could go into the place on his own and could actually talk to the girls, get undressed – and you could get pinched. So I left them running the place and said, I'm going up north to see what it's like there.

Had you been pinched by then?

No, never in Sydney. I didn't *wait* to get pinched. Anyway, I was going to Darwin but I got as far as Perth and changed my mind: I looked around, and liked it. I found out there was only two houses operating. I found premises, went back to Sydney and folded everything up. I didn't sell anything, I just closed them and told the family I was coming over, if they wanted to come with me. My oldest daughter, Dorrie, was married and had a couple of children; she was married to a sailor from Liverpool, and had her hands full. Irene worked for me in the business as a receptionist, answered the telephone and took appointments; she was married to an Australian sailor.

You're a very maritime family ...

Anyway, they all came over to Perth. It was all massage parlours there, which was good.

But by now what you were opening was a brothel?

It was a brothel, and I'd never run a brothel before, a straight-out brothel, which was a bit new to me.

What did you have to learn?

It was run completely different. A massage parlour, a client would come in those days and pay £2.10s for a massage. The girl was on a weekly wage. What she made in that room was her own – that's why I never knew what was really happening. I never saw any money, you see. In a brothel the clients pay the Madam or the 'sitter' and it's split down the middle.

You couldn't advertise in those days, you couldn't put anything in the paper, you couldn't have business cards – you had to depend on word of mouth. So you get taxis everywhere and you tell the drivers; you'd go to nightclubs and tell the doorman where you were. And slowly, very slowly, it built up. It wasn't called anything, because we didn't have to register a business name. It was just *there*.

And what was the competition like?

There *was* no competition. See, there were two old ladies, they were quite happy to plod along. I wanted something bigger and better, so when the clients found out that it was a nice place, they started coming. This was '67.

The police were lenient as long as you didn't do anything out of the ordinary ... There were rules and regulations where they didn't allow you to open up after ten o'clock because that's when the trouble would start, with the men coming out of the pubs. We didn't open on a Sunday, and you weren't allowed to have more than two girls working on the premises at the same time.

My husband was here with me, but things were getting a bit worse with him 'til in the end I said, You've got to go. At that stage, although it wasn't Contained like it is now, a blind eye was turned: it was tolerated, but women had to run the places on their own. You couldn't have boyfriends, you couldn't have husbands – so I suggested he went back to Sydney to live with his sister, because I wanted a divorce.

What was this Containment regime?

Well, years ago anybody could come and open up. You'd get visits from the police if the place wasn't being run properly and clean, or if there was any complaints from neighbours, and you'd be closed down.

In 1976 when the Royal Commission into prostitution came in, it was accepted fact. They said, 'We know the places exist, we might as well just tolerate them, but we won't allow any more to open.' The places that were operating at the time were going to be left Contained, within the police policy. So now nobody can open up another brothel. If they want to come they have to buy into an existing one.

How many Contained brothels are there?

I'd say about fourteen.

And you've got three of them?

Yes.

It's a good business to start with – but even better because the competition has been limited by the police?

That's right.

You'd brought your girls with you – how did you go about finding others?

They find you. Once they found out there was another house and it was somebody a lot younger running the place and it was nicer, they'd come to you looking for work.

And how about these girls – are they all golden-hearted whores putting their little daughters through school?

I'd say they're very soft-hearted; I think ninety-five per cent of prostitutes are very soft-hearted.

They're not lazy, avaricious, venal girls who don't want to do any real work?

Some are. Some come to this business 'cos they can't be bothered doing a normal job, but others come with a purpose: they've got families to keep, a lot are single mothers, deserted housewives, people saving up to buy a home, girls that can't get a job anywhere else. Jobs are very hard to get at the moment.

What sort of girls do you prefer?

I like the single mothers because they've got a purpose to work and they're reliable.

What are you looking for?

Personality. Looks don't really matter as long as the personality is there.

Looks don't matter – I'd have thought your clients would have gone for the pretty girls every time?

No, I find you can have a really stunning-looking girl and a homely girl – and the homely girl will be the better earner.

Because she's non-threatening – is that it?

I think the men that come in here think a homely girl will do more for them than the beautiful girl, because the beautiful girl could possibly be just in love with herself.

Is a good figure important, or doesn't that matter either?

No, you've got Greeks and Italians, they like really fat girls.

But most of your girls seem tall and skinny.

Yes, but one girl that's been working for me a couple of years has just left, she was buxom – we call them buxom, not fat. You get guys ringing up for a lady that's got big boobs, you've got the Japanese or the Asians who like slim ladies, preferably blonde, you've got all your different tastes.

You get a businessman in a hotel, he'll ring up for an escort, for the most stunning lady we've got. We'll only send to the top hotels. He gives his name and room number, we then ring the hotel and ask them to put us through to that room and if he answers, we know it's all right. If he hasn't given us the name he's registered in, we just don't send the girl.

Do you tell them what to wear when they're working?

I tell them, 'No jeans, no slacks' – to wear what brings out the best in them. If they still don't look right, I'll suggest something or I'll go and get something for them.

These girls dashing backwards and forwards seem to be in some sort of leotard?

Lingerie – lingerie or bathers.

With your experience as a Madam for twenty-four years, what makes a good prostitute, a girl you're pleased to employ?

It doesn't matter if she's big, it doesn't matter if she's skinny – as long as she's got *personality*. Every guy that comes in, she lets him think he's the one she's been waiting for. Honest, clean, willing to work – and she's got an aim. If she comes and says 'I want to buy a house', you know she's going to be a good worker.

So what makes a good Madam – you were never on the game yourself?

No. You've got to understand the girls, you've got to be mother to them. They come to you with their problems and you've got to be able to listen to them and not be hard on them; you've got to understand what kind of work they're doing and what they go through. It's not an easy job.

It must be the most distasteful job in the world . . .

Yeah, you get a lot of people turn round and say, 'It's easy money.' It's *far* from easy money.

Some of these girls are well-educated?

We had one girl who was an art teacher; she was with us for a few years. She was a deserted housewife and had four children; there was no way she could keep them the way she wanted to on a pension, plus she had to put herself through school as well.

A lot of girls come to work in Western Australia for the weather; they also come because they can't really work where their families are – they're frightened to be sprung. We get a few girls from Sydney – not as much as we used to because now it's legalized there. If things get too tough for them, they come over here for a while.

You get Germans, Italians; at the moment there's Asians, Taiwanese coming here. A few English ... I've had four girls come to me this week and couldn't take them because they weren't twenty-one.

How many girls are working for you?

At the moment, in William Street, I have fourteen – that's day shift and night shift. There's about twenty-five between the three places. Day shift is ten o'clock to six, the evening shift six to 1.00 a.m. Friday and Saturday they work 'til 3.00 a.m., maybe 3.30 – depends if it's busy. The majority of them work five days a week. If they want to, they'll work double shifts. They don't *have* to.

If money is the driving force, when they've earned a pile do they quit?

Some do. Some of them don't do anything with their money, others are quite thrifty: they buy property or a business, and then quit. There was one girl working for me for about twelve years and I think she finished up with *exactly* what she started with – nothing to show for it.

However, I calculate you must be one of the wealthiest women in Australia ...

I don't think so!

But if your girls can earn $2000 a week – which means that's another

$2000 for you – and you've got anything from twenty-five to forty-five girls working for you – you must be picking up about $3½ million a year?

(*Laughs*) That $2000 a week, that might only be one girl out of the twenty-five who would earn that kind of money, and the girls don't work seven days a week. Some work three days a week, some two – the most they'll work is six. It's a rewarding business, but the taxman gets quite a big chunk of that.

That's why the girls can buy homes, they can buy cars. Before they were paying 20 per cent tax they couldn't – because they couldn't say where they got the money *from*.

It was black money and they had to put it in the mattress? I suppose they don't get social security if you fire them?

Oh no, they can't do that.

So the police are friendly, the girls are legit – you're really part of the Establishment now? You're a Madam who's on the social scene?

Yes, I go to all the functions. I'm the only Madam in Perth that mixes on the social scene – I don't think any of the others ever do. Everything that's going on we get invitations to: for instance, the Louis Féraud parade is all charity, you go and buy; Ann Vincent of I Capricci, she runs the charity side. Then we were invited to Princess Jah's place a few months ago. No animosity. But people only know what they read in the papers – they have visions of the Mafia and that kind of stuff. If people are talking to me it's a bit tricky when they say, 'And what do you do for a living?'

So what do you say?

Well, to put it the nice way, I just say I run an escort agency. If they don't like it, they change the subject quite quickly, but nine times out of ten, their *curiosity*! Oh they've read about that, what's it like? There was one woman one night, she was giving everybody a headache. I don't think she was anybody, really, she was just putting on airs and graces. She come up and she said, 'And what do *you* do for a living, dear?' And I said, 'I'm a brothel Madam.' She just walked away! Everybody standing around burst out laughing and said, 'Good on ya, she was a pain.' And that was the end of it.

You're going out for your own pleasure – you're not drumming up business?

No, no, no – the people that go to the functions where I go wouldn't be clients, anyway.

So who are your clients?

Well, the naval people when they come in, because they've been at sea for such a long time. At the moment the Japanese boats are in. They used to be very good clients – now they're straight to the casino! They're the biggest gamblers, you see, so we've lost them. The average lonely migrants. One or two French people, but it's mostly Greeks, Italians, Yugoslavians, Norwegians. Since the Vietnamese have come in, we get a lot of them – they're the ones that came over on the boat, the refugees. A lot of people over on business trips. We have quite a few English people, but when the English ships came in they hadn't got any money. The Australian Navy haven't got any money. The American sailors, when they come in. With the Italian and Greek communities you've got a lot of single people amongst them, though a lot of the married men come because their women are different – after they had their family they're there just to cook and clean, and they chase the men out for their entertainment.

Generally, I'd say, people that can't get a girl. Lonely people. You would get quite a lot of young ones coming in who're going out with a girlfriend, so rather than get frustrated – because they know they'll get knocked-back by the girl – they come in here first.

Of all the nationalities you cater for, who do you find are your most troublesome clients?

In the past we've found the Macedonians have been the worst, because they tend to treat their women a bit rough.

I don't even know who the Macedonians are ...

I think they're Greeks, they're on the border somewhere, but they're *very* aggressive people. If they pay for something, they think they own it, that kind of thing. They don't wait to see what a girl is like, they go in there: 'Do what I want, I've bought you ...' They're very, very rough in the room. It's just their personality.

If a girl finds somebody's rough like that, she's got a panic button near the bed. She'll press it and the whole lot of us will be up the stairs two at a time! If the door's locked we've got one master key that'll open every door. There's safety in numbers: this is why girls tend to come to a brothel to work instead of on their own.

You get all walks of life, you get pensioners, you get men in wheelchairs, you get doctors, lawyers – they don't actually tell you what they do, but you know when they come in that they're prominent. The *really* prominent ones won't come into a brothel, the very well-known ones – they ring in and have a girl sent out.

But if you're taking credit cards, you know who they are?

Very well-known people never pay by credit card: they pay cash. We do accept all the major cards: bankcard, Visa, Master Card, Diners, American Express ... We're registered as Mammasan Bistro – it looks a bit more discreet on the receipts.

You've got a number of regulars?

Yes, the girls build their own clientele up: you get a client come in, ask for a particular girl; she could be busy in a room for an hour, so he'll sit and wait for her. He won't see anybody else.

If some of these girls can take home $100,000 a year, it's easy to understand why they don't want to be secretaries!

That's right – but then you get girls that only last two days; they can't handle it. It's nerve-wracking, because you've got these men just supposing you've got ten men in one day ... trying to please them. Lonely people that's depressed and whatever. You've got to be mother, lover, wife, you've got to be *everything* to them.

It could be very distasteful, too.

It can be. It can be.

As you say, it's not everybody's job.

The situation with this house is if somebody comes to the door and they're too drunk, they just don't get past the door. Other houses haven't got the same security, so they're in before you can get rid of them and it's very hard to get them out. This is where the police come in.

You can be pinched for taking anybody under the age of eighteen: they class it as carnal knowledge. If you look at some of them that come in, you've got to ask for ID because they just don't look anything like eighteen.

One day a mother rang up and said it was going to be her boy's eighteenth birthday; he'd told her he'd never been with a girl before and she thought it would be better if he came here to start him off, rather than go and pick somebody up on the street. She asked if that would be possible, and I said yes.

Anyway, she sent him in and he was looked after. She rang up afterwards and thanked us. We've had a man come in with a son, the same thing: a birthday present! I think it's the right thing to do, actually.

There again, a man in a wheelchair would find it very, very hard to get a girlfriend, and even though they're crippled they've still got the same functions and the same feelings; so rather than be frustrated, they come in here.

This is the main office; if anybody wants me, this is where they'll find me. My daughter runs the place on the day shift and Kim, an English girl, runs the place at night-time. My other daughter helps on a Friday, Saturday and Sunday night. One of my daughters used to run the place over the road, now we've got these other ladies: they're good. And a lady that used to mind my children in England, in Liverpool, runs the place in Fremantle.

I enjoy coming in; if I was home, I'd stagnate. What would you do with yourself! I tell the girls, I'll be in three o'clock 'til six. Half the time I'm in at half twelve, one o'clock. I get fed up outside, so I go in to work.

Last Saturday I was married fourteen years to Kim! He's twenty-one years younger than me.

How did his parents react to your marriage?

Not very good. First, because of the age difference. They didn't know who I was at that stage – they thought I was a hairdresser! I kept saying no every time he asked, because of the age difference and because I had two daughters older than him.

Their son was marrying a woman twenty-one years older than he was who owned three whorehouses – how could they object to that?

Well, Kim was a bit on the religious side at that stage and his mother was more or less horrified. They didn't come to the wedding. I said, 'Eh, I just want to go out quietly if we're going to get married' – so Irene, my daughter and her husband, stood for us.

We got married in a registry office and didn't tell anybody else until we came back. He only told his mother a few days beforehand.

Are they reconciled to you now?

I got on brilliantly with them afterwards. Kim's father died the same year as my dad; we were the best of mates.

Kim had friends who were missionaries in Borneo and it was his one ambition to go there. It's something he's always wanted to do. And now and again he gets that little twinge that he'd like to go, but you know after all these years he's more accustomed to it here. He likes it. I don't think he'd want to be a missionary now.

Would you consider going off with him to Papua–New Guinea?

No way – where would I get my hair done?

So when you got married again, Dorrie, were you not tempted to give up the business?

No, I couldn't give the business up because of my livelihood.

But you've been making a fortune every week since 1965 – you must have a few quid tucked away by now . . .

It doesn't last forever, does it? Unless you've still got money coming in, it's not going to go very far. I wasn't the kind of a businesswoman that could invest . . .

You married an accountant, for goodness sake!

Kim wasn't an accountant when I married him: he was working in a bank at that stage and going to night school for accountancy. My books – when I used to do them – were a mess. I'm hopeless at figures.

You're a very level-headed capable lady and no flies settle within several hundred yards of you – so I'm sure your affairs were in excellent order! What do you do with it all, Dorrie, now you don't have to stuff it into the mattress?

I'm thinking of the grandchildren, so I'm putting it into property. I used to go overseas quite a lot – I went to Hong Kong in June – and I always took one or two grandchildren with me. I took two of them on a world trip: one was six, one was ten; now they're eighteen and twenty-two. I took them to Disneyworld, took them on a safari in Africa.

You do seem to be supporting your entire family . . .

No, they work for their money. They get paid their wages, same as everybody else. They put their hours in.

You must spend quite a lot on your appearance, on having your hair done, as an old hairdresser.

Yes, I go on Monday, Wednesday and Friday. I like to keep it neat. I love fashion parades – I'd go anywhere to a good fashion parade. We go to most of the charity functions, they put on some good shows.

You've just had an operation on both your eyes to improve your sight; have you also had cosmetic surgery, as your daughter has?

No, I haven't had a facelift at all. I probably will (*laughs*). Now that I've seen hers, I think I will.

Yours has always been a growth industry: if you now pay tax and you're legit, can you see yourself going public?

If it was legalized, I don't see any reason why not. It's a business, the same as any other business – more acceptable now than what it was years ago.

This is a family business: your husband, your daughters, your babysitter . . . are you planning to hand it on to the next generation?

Yes, I would.

When you'll retire to a little cottage outside Liverpool?

No, I like Perth. I'd go back to Liverpool to see the rest of the family, but I don't think I could live there again.

Do you feel any stigma as you walk down the street? Are there people here who disapprove, who don't regard running a brothel as an everyday occupation?

I should imagine there'd be quite a few. I have heard, sometimes when you go out: 'Oh, it's *that* woman.'

Most people would see this as a fairly grubby business . . .

Yes, mostly people that don't know anything about us. The disapproval comes from people who've never met you, who would only have heard about you on the news.

Nobody knew who I was before I gave evidence at the Royal Commission, only the people that mixed in the scene. The functions I go to, everybody knows who I am, and I don't have any problem with it. If I book in advance, I'm given a good table. Holly Wood – he's the social writer for the *Sunday Times* – he's a very good friend. Holly used to work for me when I had Feathers restaurant. Juanita from the *Western Mail*, I get on very well with her. We give to the charities, so we always get the invites.

Kim's the only man around – the entire establishment is run by women. You don't have bouncers, so if you get some stroppy drunk, who handles him?

If you can't talk them out of being stroppy, you'd send for the police – but they've got to be *really* bad before you do that. People get argumentative, but a woman can nearly always talk herself out of anything. Ha! This is what I've found over the years ...

What sort of facilities do you provide your clients?

There's a bubble spa bath, there's blue movies. Almost anything a client wants we can supply: discipline, bondage, fantasies. If a guy wants a girl to dress up as a nurse, we've got the nurses' outfits. School uniforms. Any fantasies. When they come to a House like this they're always looking for something just a little bit *different* to what they'd get at home. It's always the same line: the wife doesn't understand him, doesn't understand his needs. He needs that something extra.

We get pensioners; sometimes you look at them and they're too old to walk up them stairs – so you let them go into one of the rooms down here! Some of them that's been coming for years, you've seen them grow old, you know; it's strange.

Who are the biggest spenders?

I would have to say the Japanese. You can have someone come in – the minimum is $30, $120 for an hour – but if they want a bubble spa bath it's $140 an hour, with the girl. If they want to spend a couple of hours it goes up and up; we've had one man spend

$1500 in one night, where he finished up taking two or three girls in with him for a few hours.

There's no alcohol allowed, but they can have soft drinks if they like, they can have tea, they can have coffee ...

If you're spending $1500, a cup of tea's a bit unexciting, isn't it?

Yes, but he can send out for a bottle of champagne if he wants it; we can always go and get it for him.

In these permissive days, with so many girls around giving it away, you'd think your professionals might find business harder to come by?

They're a different class of girl: the girls that go to hotels and just pick a guy up for the fun of it, they call them 'charities' – that's the nickname, the charity girls. In one way or another, they charge.

They're pleasant solitary women who want some company – they're not charging, surely?

No, but they're looking for something more concrete: they're looking for lasting relationships, and a lot of guys want the trimmings without the relationships.

To be honest, in these days it's surprising to me that men need to come to a whorehouse ...

Some of the guys I've seen here, I can't understand *why* they've got to come in; some really really good-looking guys. It could be that as he's paying for the girl, it's *his* girl and he can do as he likes – and there's no strings attached.

You make them pay in advance when they come to your booking office?

They don't pay me at the booking office. They go to the room with the girl, she gives him the menu – the list of prices – he decides what he wants. Then she takes the money and brings it down. We put the amount on the book and the time she goes in the room and we allow maybe five, ten minutes over her time. Anything longer we get on the intercom and tell her, in case she's having any problem getting out. Sometimes you get a guy carried away and doesn't want to leave the girl, he doesn't want to come out of the room.

Come in number twenty-six, your time is up! Then you charge him extra, I presume?

Yeah, we tell 'im if he wants to stay longer he's got to pay more.

The meter's ticking ...

We don't really *push* it, you know, on the dot – but we give them a fair length of time, and then they've got to go.

You must have a number of dissatisfied customers?

Yeah, you get your dissatisfied ones. You'll get a guy that says the girl was no good – he didn't do anything, he was ripped off with his money. I'll just ask the girl, 'What in fact *did* you do?' If she says, 'He was too drunk, he couldn't do anything,' I'd say, 'Well you've had your time, if you were drunk it's your fault, not the girl's.' If the girl was indifferent to the man and just didn't like him and couldn't be bothered with him, well then I'll give him his money back and tell him to see another girl. I've done that a few times.

You give the girls their money at the end of the shift but you hold back their tax – so apart from being a brothel-keeper you're a tax collector as well?

The taxmen come in maybe once a month, sometimes more, to see if you've got any new girls. They interview the girl and give her a file number – so this is where Kim comes in, he's the accountant. I collect the tax off the girls, the tax goes to him. He then helps the girls to fill in their tax returns. At the end of the financial year the girl gets a group certificate. If the girls have got families, nine times out of ten they'll get rebates.

You'd think in many ways it'd be simpler for a girl to be a freelance and work in a park or an hotel, or pick them up in the streets?

But the kind of girls we've got working here wouldn't do that because they're too frightened.

Of the men or of the police?

The men; it's too dangerous – one girl was murdered here two months ago. This escort agency had sent the girl out to a house, but didn't do any checking at all. The girl gets there, and it was an *empty* house – the people had moved out that day. She was murdered. They still haven't got him.

I never send a girl to a private house unless I know who it is and I've known him personally for a long time. We've got one guy, he used to be a bouncer in a nightclub that we had, he was in a car accident and he's now a paraplegic. He likes to have a girl, but he's in a wheelchair and lives way out, so I'll send somebody out there; but normally I won't send to a house at all.

The girls find a safety in numbers, and there's no way they'll try anything outside, there's too many things happen. One girl that was a single operator, the guy tied her to the bed. He could have killed her, it could've been a couple of days before she was found. Terrified the life out of her – she says there's no way she'd work on her own again.

At what age would a girl feel she's too old for all this excitement?

We've had girls here still working at fifty, fifty-one. They can still look quite good at that age, if they look after themselves. You get guys ringing up asking if we've got fourteen-year-olds; we get calls for mature ladies.

How old is a mature lady?

A mature lady would be anything between forty and fifty. One place in Perth called Happy Haven advertise in the *Sunday Times* for ladies wanting work, twenty-one to fifty-one.

You'd think by the nature of the job they'd not be very reliable?

Some of them aren't, some of them are. You get somebody like Lola, the Indonesian girl, she's like clockwork. She's very popular, very reliable, she's here on the dot, quarter to ten every morning. She doesn't muck around like some of them.

The most unreliable girls are drug addicts: they've got no sense of time, no sense of honour, no nothing, and sometimes when they come for a job you can't pick it up because they're on their best behaviour. Sometimes it'll take a week before it actually starts showing – then you've just got to get rid of them. The unreliable ones last a week, maybe two weeks at the very most. Say they're supposed to start at ten, they come running in at half past ten with the most unreal excuses you've ever heard in your life: 'Oh I've been in an accident and I've got to have two weeks off.'

But you can dismiss a girl within two minutes – she hasn't got any job protection?

I just tell them to go and empty their locker, just go. If they've been very bad they ask if I'm going to blacklist them – in other words, am I going to let the other Madams know, so that they can't get another job.

I'll sack a girl if she swears. I say, 'You may be a prostitute but you can still be a lady, you don't have to use that language.' I find you don't get trouble in a house if you act like a lady: you talk like a lady then the clients will treat you like a lady. This is why we've got a good House.

I've seen your advertisements in the Sunday papers, you even advertise in the Sydney cinemas . . .

That's for inter-state travellers. If all the advertising in the news-papers stopped tomorrow, the taxi drivers would still give us business 'cos they know where we are, we've been here so long, we're known. We advertise, 'Relax in a bubble spa with two or three beautiful young ladies. We have the Best in the West! Come and see Lola for a tantalizing strip' – words to that effect. Lola also has another speciality; I advertise her as being very naughty and needs spanking. We get a lot of clients for that, they like to spank a girl and it's not many girls like to be spanked.

But Lola puts up with it?

She likes it – she doesn't mind it at all.

Whatever Lola wants, Lola gets!

There's a girl off today, it's her birthday so she's having a party tonight with her *straight* friends who don't know she's a worker – the girls don't say prostitute, you just say 'worker', because they're working same as anybody else, that's the way they look at it. Anyway this girlfriend of hers has decided to go to the party – as a hooker!

So she's waiting now to see what her friend's definition of a hooker is: probably very high stilettos, black mesh stockings, very short skirts, very low cut front – an Irma la Douce type. This is what people think the girls look like.

What is your girl going as?

A bunny girl. On Christmas Eve here we're going to have a party in this very room. The girls want to have a fancy-dress, so I asked, 'What's the theme?' The Best Little Whorehouse in Texas! I said OK – as long as I can be Dolly Parton.

Parties for their birthdays, that's something they work out for themselves. Twice a year the girls get a piece of jewellery off me, for birthdays and Christmas. One year they'll get a ring, the next year a pendant, then they'll get a bracelet; it mounts up when they stay for a while.

You've never been asked to pay protection money to the local villains – never had an offer you couldn't refuse?

I did once, years ago. A guy came in and said, 'Who is the owner? I'd like to speak to you quietly.' I took him out and he said, 'It's time you took a partner.' I burst out laughing: 'Meaning you?' 'I've got four guys outside in a car and either I'm your partner or we'll tear the place apart.' I said, 'That's what *you* think.'

Anyway, there was a client coming in who was a regular – a great big six-foot-four black guy; he was walking through the back door as this feller's standing there, and I said, 'See what I mean – I've got all the protection I need.' He was a bouncer in a city nightclub, this black feller. This other guy, the heavy, had come from Sydney. I said, 'If you're not out of this door within two minutes you'll go right through it, head first.' He said, 'I'm just going to talk to my mates. I'll be back.'

I rang the coppers, because they were only down the corner then, in James Street. They were here within two minutes and he was put on the next plane back to Sydney. They said, that's *exactly* what we don't want. So you've got your protection there, with the police.

What relationship do you have with the police, now you're Contained and quasi-legitimate?

If we do something wrong, we get more or less rapped over the knuckles for it. If we've got any problems, we can go to them. All in all, they're all right.

There are no backhanders involved?

No, none at all. The Vice Squad, they get transferred and moved around a lot.

To make sure they don't get backhanders?

It's not to make sure they don't, it's because if they want promotion they have to do so many years in this place, so many years in another place. Because they move around you don't get to know them so well, so that cuts all that out. The man in charge now used to be on the Fraud Squad – he's been on the Vice Squad maybe a couple of years. They treat the girls quite good. Every Monday morning, girls go to be registered; the main reason for that is to make sure there's no girls under twenty-one – a girl can come to me with her sister's birth certificate. If she goes to the police they can check it out and make sure she's over twenty-one.

They like to keep a register of who's in what house. If a girl leaves me she just rings up and says, I've left Aphrodite's and I'm going to work somewhere else, and they just move her file to that address.

I was involved with a gay sauna once; unfortunately I couldn't stay with that. I was more of a silent partner and I don't *like* to be a silent partner, I like to see what's happening and what's going on.

They wouldn't let a woman on the premises?

No – well, I wouldn't even *want* to go on the premises.

If you had your life over again, Dorrie, would you still choose to run brothels?

Yes I would. I was a hairdresser before and I was bored to death with it! I said when I came to Australia I'd never touch another head as long as I lived. But this business, you meet so many people it's never boring, it's never dull. We've had hairy-scary times, you know, running round getting chased by the police, but I wouldn't change it.

Do your neighbours know what you do?

If they recognize the name at all, they never say. I don't broadcast the fact, I don't go and knock on the door and say, 'I'm Dorrie Flatman the brothel Madam', I just don't do that. If somebody asks me I'll tell them.

Your mother's now living with you in Perth – how does she feel about her hairdresser daughter running a brothel?

I first told her in England, before anyone else did. I thought, 'Somebody's going to, so I'm going to tell her myself.' She didn't really quite know what it meant. I explained to her what it was and she said, 'Will you get into trouble for this?' and I said, 'Well you *can*.' Anyway she came over and I brought her into the House and introduced her to everybody. She sat and had a cup of tea and said, 'Aren't the girls beautiful? I wish I was younger.' I said 'Why?' and she said, 'I'd be your cleaner' (*laughs*).

So what would she tell her friends, back in Liverpool?

They all knew who I was. When I went over I used to go to the Pension Club and they used to ask me, 'What's it like, what do thee do, what kinds of people come in?'

Your daughters all married husbands from the straight world outside, and yet they've all blended in; nobody said, 'I wouldn't marry the daughter of a Madam, I wouldn't marry somebody who works in a whorehouse'?

I haven't had anybody say that, no.

Do you think any of them find the business at all distasteful?

No, not at all.

What about your grandchildren? Do you think some of them wish that dear old Gran had another occupation?

I don't think so. My eldest grandson is now twenty-two and he's come to the House on occasions to pick me up and give me a lift home, but anything Grandma does is all right by him. He doesn't say anything. I've got a granddaughter of eighteen and one of her girlfriends said, 'When your grandma dies, will you inherit the business?'

A growing sense of double-entry book-keeping! How old were they when they discovered Gran was running a bordello?

Paul would have been about twelve, because at that time I was in the headlines a lot because of the Royal Commission. Even though his mother never took the newspapers home, his friends used to tell him, 'Your grandma's in the paper again.'

Did he know what a brothel was?

These days the kids do know, yes. When the schools are on holiday we get all kinds of phone calls, and we know they're kids.

Do their schoolmates give your grandchildren a hard time?

No they don't – they think it's great!

So you're living an ordinary suburban life, fetching your grandchildren from ballet school, going to charity functions – yet you're doing a very un-ordinary job that would shock most people.

Going back a few years I think it would, but it's getting more accepted. No one seems to bat an eyelid any more when you mention the word 'brothel'.

It seems to me that the acceptance of the straight world, of the respectable world outside, is quite important to you?

Yes – if they don't accept us then we've got problems because we start getting moved around again.

If somebody wanted to buy the brothel we're in now, what would you ask for it?

We've got thirteen rooms and the building itself is worth about $250,000. Then you've got the goodwill – so I really wouldn't sell it under six or seven hundred thousand dollars because it would be the top place in Perth, the biggest place. One of the old ladies sold out Happy Haven – she had two businesses and she sold the two for a couple of hundred thousand dollars. There's an old property, the Scarlet Garter – I've been told there's only four rooms but it's quite a busy place. She wants something like $600,000, but she has a prime position in the city – Hay Street.

There's a quiet period at the moment but sometimes you're rushed off your feet, as they say?

Yeah, when the American Navy's in. We had two aircraft-carriers in at the same time, which means they've also got the accompanying small ships – and when you get something like twenty thousand men in Perth with not very much for them to do ... we're exceptionally busy. We might only be closed for an hour before the next shift starts. We've had ten girls kept non-stop, and I'd say that they would have taken between twenty and thirty clients each.

That's three hundred clients in one shift! What makes a good bordello, incidentally – what makes this a better brothel than certain other brothels I could mention?

The size, for one. Plenty of room to move around – not poky little cubicles. The sitters, the management – you're fair with the girls and they're fair with you – a happy family atmosphere.

What about illness – are you worried about VD, about AIDS?

AIDS was a big scare when it first started.

Well it certainly hasn't got any better – it's far worse now.

But we know more about it – everybody was ignorant. We thought if anybody just winked at you, you were going to get it. We made it compulsory that the girls had to use condoms. If the clients ring up and say they don't want to wear one, we just don't take them – for their benefit and ours. I mean, you don't want this going round. To ease the girls' minds on what it was all about, the lady from the VD clinic came over with pamphlets and had a talk to the girls. Anything they want to know, they can go down to the clinic and ask any time.

Normally the more AIDS is explained to people, the more worrying it becomes . . .

Only if they don't understand it. You've got to use condoms for safe sex. All right, so you can get the odd one that might break – but it's lessening the chance of catching AIDS.

We've had a very quiet two weeks. There's been so much on in Perth; we have golf tournaments and if it's on television they'll stay home to watch it, they'll stay home to watch cricket, you've got the Cup yacht racing, there's an Expo been on and the Elton John concert . . .

One day it was quiet and in Indonesia, where Lola comes from, the superstitious people always go and put salt on the doorstep to bring visitors – so she went and did that. We laughed about it, but within two minutes there was a client in who paid her $140! He'd only just gone and another one came in.

The Test Matches, the America's Cup, the Pope's visit – how do these occasions affect your business?

If we were on the route the Pope would take, I'd be inclined to close that day.

Because you're a Catholic, or because it wouldn't be a good day for business?

Not because I'm a Catholic, but you've got to show a little bit of respect. If you're on the route where the Queen comes through you show a bit of respect – so it's the same.

This is a most orderly disorderly house, Dorrie; from what quarters do you attract criticism?

People that don't know how the place is run, they only read books or see movies, and it's based on that. Jealousy. You've got the churches that are against you, but then again they're now starting to accept the fact. It's changing.

I certainly wouldn't want a brothel next door to me ...

Nobody does, nobody does – this is why to open a house you look around and try to find a place without any neighbours. This is classed as an industrial area, which is the best place to have one. You really wouldn't go into the suburbs.

You wouldn't want a brothel next to your home.

No, I wouldn't; although I'm a Madam, I wouldn't.

All those slamming car doors! What are the men who come here looking for?

Companionship. Someone to talk to.

Can't they find that in the pub for the price of a beer?

No, not really. One man told me he comes here a lot and he's never had sex. He likes to find a girl he can talk to that will listen to him, maybe ask her to go out to dinner. The girls don't do that unless they go as an escort – then it's going to cost them a bit: $120 an hour, plus taxi. The girl won't go out for less because while she's off the premises she's losing money. Time to a prostitute is money.

You'd think the girls might begin to hate and despise men, having this kind of life and having to cater to all these whims?

They don't. The girls class this as a job. I've said to them, 'It's like working in Coles or Woolworths, you've got your rules and regulations, you have to look after your clients. I advertise you open at a certain time and you close at a certain time, so you've got to be here at that time – you don't walk in and out when you feel like it. It's the same as trying to sell a dress; you've got to look after your clients, or they don't come back.'

I suppose the girls sometimes feel sorry for the clients?

Nine times out of ten they do. I've had them come down and say, 'I felt *awful* taking that man's money, he's a real sweet guy, he's got problems'. But then, it's their living – if they did that with everybody they wouldn't *have* a living.

That's the story of the golden-hearted whore, which can be a bit hard to believe . . .

Yes, because they're not all the same. You get your good ones and your bad ones, but the bad ones don't last long, the good ones are here for a couple of years, maybe longer. The bad ones are really hard as nails.

Could you imagine opening a branch-brothel back in Scotland Road, Liverpool?

No, I don't think there's any money there, I don't think the men would be able to afford us – plus the fact Liverpool men used to always say they never had to pay for it. Whether they did or not, I don't know.

One wonders why Australian men have to pay for it, to be honest.

There was a shortage of women: a lot of men come from overseas – you've got your Greeks and Italians and it's quite common over there for people to frequent these places . . .

Is there anything you wouldn't let clients do, or pay for?

We won't let a client be rough with the girls. If a girl comes down and says, 'I don't want to see him again, he's really bad', he won't get through the door again.

Yet you go in for bondage here, discipline, sado-masochism and all those games?

Yeah, but that's when the guy's paying for it, that's his kick and that's why he's coming to a brothel because he couldn't get it at home. We've only got one discipline mistress.

If he pays for it, he can have anything – that's what you're saying?

Yes, that's right.

But there can't be many girls who'll put up with that sort of thing?

There isn't. It's very hard to get a discipline mistress, a *proper* discipline mistress. You get the girls that will do a slight discipline, a slap or humiliation – as they call it – but they just can't cope with the heavy discipline.

Does it help if they're lesbian and hate men?

It does, because they can put all their aggressiveness there – but then they can go a bit *too* far! We did have one girl I had to let go because she was too aggressive.

Guys were carried out on stretchers?

I wasn't very happy, because you don't know what damage you can do. They just lay into somebody – I'd be frightened.

After all these years observing human nature at close range – and often at its most debased – does anything shock you?

Not any more, no.

Nothing?

Nothing.

That's rather sad.

I don't think there's anything left to shock me; you hear it all when you're in here ...

THE SLEUTH AND THE SWAMI:
TONY SHAFFER AND DIANE CILENTO

Inside my typewriter – a wasps' nest ...

Tony Shaffer (ex-lawyer and advertising man who wrote
the overpowering *Sleuth*) lives with his wife Diane Cilento
(actress, artist and once Mrs Sean Connery) in a moun-
tainside house with wide verandahs and stained glass
windows, rearing up like some Disneyland tropical
cathedral amid two hundred acres of rampant rainforest
near Miallo, north of Mossman.

He left the Law after losing an *undefended* divorce action
for his client – 'thus adding to the history of British
jurisprudence' – and followed his twin brother Peter
(*Amadeus, Equus*) into playwriting.

Diane, his vital and talented wife, has lived in Far North
Queensland for ten years, arriving from her life in Putney
(as Mrs James Bond) and a Gloucestershire commune
at Sherborne (as guru). Here at the edge of Australian
civilization in a place she calls Karnak, Mrs Shaffer once
again guides students seeking to change their lives. She
teaches meditation, tranquillity, non-toxic food preparation, an holistic approach to the twentieth century and
all that good stuff – and they obligingly pay her not
inconsiderable fees, tend her garden, milk her goats and
whitewash her walls. Everybody seems happy with this
arrangement.

Observing all this emerald incongruity from his air-conditioned study on high, the menacing figure of Shaffer: tight white wiry hair and mauve spectacles. He has totally recovered from a brain tumour, and amid such esoteric surroundings rewrites his latest play, *Murderer*: 'Thirty horrible minutes of blood and gore before anybody says a *word* ...'

With controlled intensity he paces the room – as did the mocking Laurence Olivier playwright-figure in *Sleuth*. It is faintly alarming. His conversation is astringent, his plays brutal, his inspiration creeps out from the dark side of human nature.

Beyond the rustling sugar-cane outside, tropical life revolves lethargically around the coming tourist invasion and the price of sugar, while within Karnak Mrs Shaffer instructs her smiling future-people. Somehow it seemed an odd place to plan a murder ...

Diane: Commune is such a funny word – sounds like the battlements in Paris or something. It isn't like that. We have about two hundred acres; we're very lucky because we've got a river.

You're the Bhagwan, the Rajneesh of northern Queensland?

I'm not the Bhagwan or whatever; I just have a future community here, a place where people can come and live for about six months and learn to propagate trees and meditation and time and motion study, have a creative project, do all sorts of wonderful things, make films ...

So Tony, have you come back from Broadway to be part of this propagation – are you an instructor?

Tony: No, I don't believe in teaching anybody anything.

This is a relaxing tropical scene, a place where people lie around – is your muse stimulated here?

69

I think, no. I think it is stimulated from other places, because one works in a medium which doesn't have any *being* here. Very few people are actually writing for the movies or the theatre here; one can't say honestly there's enormous stimulation in that direction, so one goes away quite frequently not to get left behind, so as not to seem *totally* ignorant of what people are doing in London and New York – and indeed Hollywood. That's the real axis of the English-speaking theatre, surely.

If Hollywood heard you were here, they'd give you up for dead?

They probably do anyway, but this contributes to that mori-bundity. I think from time to time it's necessary to walk up and down Hollywood Boulevard or Sunset, just to assure people one is still breathing. It's something one's agent demands. You can see what people have been doing quite quickly, and renew a few con-tacts; usually they're quite nice and one leaves with a piece of work to bring back here. Now they don't altogether *like* you doing that because they like to control you, and controlling you means having you there where they can call you up and – as they say in their own parlance – 'take breakfast meetings'. They like to have you around, otherwise they believe that you are virtually uncontrollable, if not unemployable.

I'm not saying they're wrong, I suspect they're probably right, because what happens is that you tend to ride your horse off in a totally different direction to the one that they think you're going to take. Each piece of work will take three or four months, and after that you can end up with a piece of work so far away from what they think you're going to come up with that automatically you can get into a lot of trouble. It doesn't matter that it is worse or better than what they imagined they were going to get, it is *different*, and originality is probably the dirtiest word in the movie business.

If you compound that by surprising them, you can get into a lot of trouble – so I try from time to time to go and write where the people are who are doing the producing, just to relieve them of that anxiety.

How then did you sneak Sleuth *into production?*

No one knew me then, you see, so I could ...

You could get away with murder!

That's right, get away with murder. Exactly.

But do they expect you to come here and create? As I said, the tropics are for lying around in, not for white-hot typewriters ...

Diane: Strangely enough what's happening now – and I've been here ten years – is that you're all coming to us. They're making films here, it's a bizarre thing – you sit in Port Douglas and meet everyone you know; everybody's arriving. Yes, this sort of weather *is* lethargic in a certain way, but our winter is a very stimulating time.

Yet Tony's writing is particularly urban and sophisticated, is it not?

True – that's why he gets on so well with the Australians! They think he's a wonderful caricature of an Englishman.

Tony: Which shows *exactly* how far from the truth they are – on this subject as indeed on all others.

When you entertain friends here, do you step down from the dinner table stimulated?

Depends what we've been eating! At a local restaurant the other night – which I shall not name – I stepped down envenomed, not to say *poisoned*. It took twenty-four hours to recover.

You've been a lawyer, an advertising man, a dramatist – all professions demanding some wit; do you find the necessary stimulus here?

Um, not a lot. Take the case of one world-famous wit: I suppose Mr Oscar Wilde would come high on the list, and quite recently at a dinner party in this very house I did suggest to a man who wanted to sue someone that if he did that, he might find himself over his head by someone suing *him* – being forced to, because of the inflammatory nature of what he was suggesting. Then, I said, he'd find himself in the same position as Oscar Wilde.

'Who?' he said.

If this begins to indicate the difficulty at these dinner parties of making anything of a world statement or a witty remark that depends on something known further south than Cairns – you'd be right. It's heavy going sometimes.

So this is a pull-up-the-drawbridge place for you?

Very much so. We rely on visiting firemen quite a lot in that way. People *do* come here, and are increasingly coming here – in fact I think we're going to get far too many of them. In view of local developments, it's becoming a very big tourist area – and I don't know that the standard of wit is going to increase enormously because we have eleven thousand Japanese dumped in our laps ...

Sleuth was about sadism and humiliation, was it not? Murderer, your latest, is even more macabre I'm led to understand ... whereas here one feels relaxed and benevolent and the worst thing that can happen is for a coconut to fall on your head – yet you're sitting here in your ivory tower thinking fiendish thoughts!

Fiendish, indeed fiendish. Both those plays were actually written first time round away from here. *Murderer* has been rewritten here, and has become even more fiendish than it was the first time round.

Must be that venomous meal you had the other night!

It's a genuine black comedy now; previously it was just black.

You are fascinated by murder – you even sat in on the Yorkshire Ripper trial of Sutcliffe?

That's true, I wanted to see what that little fellow was about. I don't know how I imagined I was going to do that, because the guy's about five foot two and looks as if butter wouldn't melt in his mouth – or indeed in the mouths of anyone around him – but there was a *lot* more that melted when he was operating. The curious thing is that he was plainly completely schizophrenic; he could do what he did with his nasty little bag of tricks, his hammer and his chisel and his other ghastly implements, and then return to his wife and say, 'Well, where's me cocoa?' and forget totally – and I think he *did* forget totally – what he'd done, because he's not a tremendously good actor, from what I saw of him. That's what I wanted to find out.

There was a policeman who spotted him, who knew it was him all the time – not, unfortunately, the man who was conducting the case, the head of the Yorkshire constabulary who really made a fearful mess of the whole thing. Not wholly his fault, he was sent a tape which turned out to be a hoax, but he should perhaps in his position as a skilled policeman have realized that earlier. But I had to go and see Sutcliffe himself for that reason. Yes, one *is* fascinated. Could *we* do what he did, is it possible? That seems to me the question.

I think anyone can probably kill someone else in a temper, but that's not the same thing at all. It's forming the *decision* to do it, doing it, carrying it out – and this is what he did. Now I think what happens in a case like that, what is interesting is that the guilt grows. He gets – if it's not too silly a word – *bored* with what he's doing: 'Oh God, have I *got* to go out and do all this again' when that mood comes upon him.

My point is that your interest in the macabre can hardly be stimulated in this placid atmosphere?

Diane: Not true, not true.

Hidden depths in these dark primeval forests?

Tony: Oh hidden depths, indeed. Yes, there's a certain Wagnerian ring to that up here.

Diane: It is a very peculiar place here, because we have ladies eaten by crocodiles and things that nobody knows how they happened. The wonderful rumble after that is quite delicious to Tony.

Your brother Peter chooses to live in New York, which suffers a different sort of killing ...

Tony: You can get killed by the water there! I lived in New York for many years in the Seventies. We both lived on opposite sides of 89th Street, he on the river and me on the park. Between us lay the no-man's-land of Amsterdam Avenue and Columbus.

I once tried to get Peter out of New York when he'd lived there then for five years; he got out of the car in the Holland Tunnel and said: 'I've gone as far as I'm going.'

Diane: All the things you're saying about witty stimulating conversations, etc.: one does have to contend in a certain way with the stultifying climate, but at the same time there is an extraordinary sort of reward here.

Yet Sydney, with three million people, one of the biggest cities in the southern hemisphere, has only three theatres.

It is a shock, absolutely, horror; there seems to be something very slack about the way people look at their entertainment, or their information. It's got to be something really extraordinarily sensational to rip them away from the footie or whatever it is, the beach ...

This country's very body-orientated. Everybody is not intellectual, they're body-orientated, just as the English are not body people. They have an extraordinary youth who use up an enormous amount of their body thing but don't get very much shoved into their heads. That's why they become avid sportsmen – I mean followers of sport, they become avid sort of barrackers. Their passions are only really aroused by that sort of adherence, not by theatre and not by whether somebody's going to take over a newspaper empire.

Tony: If there isn't any theatre, they can't be expected to turn on to it. The trouble is, even those three theatres in Sydney are not constantly doing different plays, because invariably every season there is a big smash – a musical – in the old days from America, more recently from England, that'll go into the Theatre Royal and stay there for a year, or maybe eighteen months. That knocks out one of the three. That can happen to one of the others, so what's offered in the course of a season, or even two seasons, is *one* musical! This is scarcely the spectrum of world theatrical literature, is it, in our first city – the style of which is considerable.

Diane: It's not going to be in the entertainment area that Australia develops. Australia has that sort of energy, and they send people like me over to England every year. Even now you don't really make it in Australia until you've gone to England or somewhere else and come back – and then they don't like you because you've been out of the country! They don't like tall poppies anyway.

With all that, there is a sort of strange evolution of films and things here. Because it's such a huge undeveloped country, things are beginning to seep through, even into the hinterland like this, and make it. I'm the director of a theatre here and we play in a radius of about one thousand miles, which for England would be unheard of. We just sort of run up and down the coast and do these shows, and at least we're actually trying to make people think about things in a theatrical sense. I don't say they've entered into the real psyche of anybody yet, but I do think it's going to get there some day, because Australia is a country of the future. It's an unpopulated place that's like nowhere, except maybe Alaska or the South Pole.

And this country has an extraordinary facility for making people – I don't say sparkle, like you said about people that go to America, but making them at home, giving them a place which is regenerative for their own spirit. This country does do that, and I think that's why Tony lives here.

Tony: Sometimes the tropics *follow* you – by which I mean that last year I went to New York, and after being there a month I thought it was about time I did some work. I therefore took the case off my typewriter to discover inside it – a wasps' nest! They had pursued me to New York City. All the keys had been covered with a lot of nasty brown goo.

I took it down Fifth Avenue to a man who was meant to be able to repair typewriters and he said, 'My God, what is *this?*' I said, 'The secretions from a wasps' nest.' He was furious. He said, 'You must be living in some strange place – and you can't be doing all that amount of work if the wasps get in there.' Good thinking.

Diane: Those wasps are the bane of our lives, because every book we had, as you opened it huge streams of old clay came falling out, so we knew we had to have an air-conditioned place – that's why we built the house.

Stevenson and Conrad and Somerset Maugham – even Noel Coward – were all stimulated by the tropics: all those torrid dramas among the tea planters' wives and ships' captains ... But those were in the days when going to Calais was an adventure. Today these tropics are instantly available to many more people ...

Tony: I don't know that Stevenson's two great books have anything to do with the tropics, in terms of stimulation; Jekyll and Hyde?

Surely Treasure Island *could hardly be more tropical?*

Not really – the only scenes that are decent in that book are the opening eighteen chapters, all set in the Admiral Benbow Inn. As soon as he gets to the tropics the novel's a disaster, everyone knows that – in fact Stevenson himself said so.

So Diane, you're alone in the jungle with one of nature's critics.

Diane: Right, that's why we pour cold drinks into him, all very kind, keep his fevered brow away from the tropical sun . . .

THE BILLIONAIRE: ALAN BOND

*We're generating between two and three
billion a year ...*

A thirteen-year-old boy left Perivale School in Ealing to
make his fortune, and the next year became an apprentice
signwriter. After forty years he's still a member of the
Painters' Union – but is also a megamillionaire and all-
Australian hero controlling assets of $3 billion, give or
take. He can be ruthless enough; the name's Bond – *Alan*
Bond.

His family settled in Fremantle, where he set about his
career in the classic way: selling newspapers. He left
school at fourteen and, while signwriting, bought and
sold smallholdings with such success that at twenty-one
he was a millionaire. With shrewd but risky deals and
close shaves, he clambered on to the West Australian
property roller-coaster: from boom to bust, and back
again.

His was a hard-driving, larrikin style. On bare dunes
north of Perth at his Yanchep property he painted the sand-
hills green to make his sales-brochure pictures look better.
He was booked for having bald tyres on his Rolls-Royce –
it was that sort of life – but he was in the fast lane.

Today everyone has a story about Bondy. A viewer
wrote to tell me that Bond was sleeping in his garage at

Melville in 1952; 'He was a young bloke in a mess –
eighteen yesterday, and married. The kid had nowhere
to go, but he was a bighead who said he wouldn't be
painting all his life.' That proved true, yet it still plays a
role: a few decades later Bond had his local nineteenth-
century church repainted and redecorated to match his
daughter Susanne's wedding dress – and returned to
its original colour when the four hundred guests had
departed.

We all remember where we were when President
Kennedy was shot; Australians remember what they were
doing the day Bondy won the America's Cup in September
1983 after four tries, when the whole town came singing
and dancing into the streets of Perth at five in the morning . . .

Strange that a twelve-metre yacht race should take on
such national significance – it is after all a minority
sport for the super-rich; yet Bond became the saviour of
Australia's honour, the nation's only folk hero, and his
symbol – an unlovely yellow boxing kangaroo on a hard
green flag – was the focus of the nation's new-found pride.

The Bond family became soap opera and Australia's
answer to the royals. Eileen Bond, the legendary Big Red,
is known for her whirlwind vivacity and generosity with
champagne, for her raids by private jet upon her favourite
Melbourne shop, which she kept afloat almost single-
handedly during a recession. She's good at parties and
launching ships: 'I've got a *great* swing!' They met at a
Sacred Heart convent dance class, and there are four
grown-up children: the eldest, John, is Executive Director
of the Corporation.

Bond is now the tallest poppy of them all. Even in the
1987 America's Cup defeat he did not break trust, for
Australia IV lost in the heats to another local thruster,

Kevin Parry, who was not much liked in Perth even before his *Kookaburra* went on to be wiped-out, allowing the Cup back to the US. All Bond lost was the $30 million he had spent on the challenge.

I went to talk with him in his ultra-modern home in Dalkeith, on the banks of the Swan River. Like most Australian houses, however lavish, it stood crowded in by other properties: from the road we could see Big Red in her first-floor room, preparing.

The house is a blend of Versailles and Virginia Water. As is traditional with the newly rich, Alan Bond has gone heavily into art. His is an eclectic collection: French Impressionists and colonial Australian paintings share pride of place with a Perspex box displaying a pair of Michael Jackson's white socks . . .

On his dining-room table the centrepiece is a replica of the Cup – which he will never lose; Eileen had made sure of that by ordering Garrard's to create a copy, for £38,000.

I was with Alan just before her forethought paid off: 'As one door slams, you just go out and bash down another.' So to compensate he bought Kerry Packer's communications empire for £422 million, to establish the first broadcasting network across Australia and to add to all that the Bond Corporation already owns – which, looking around Perth, appears to be everything in sight . . .

I'm Chairman of the Bond Corporation; our family has over 50 per cent of the stock in that. We control some 48 per cent of the national beer market across Australia and we're the largest wine and spirits company in Australia; we're doing other brewing activities right throughout South-east Asia. We have media interests, television stations both state and national, radio stations; we're one of the three or four largest property developers in the country. Then we have our mining interests – oil exploration and development, coal mining and gold mining, and we're involved in nickel and cobalt. We're in China and we have a major property investment in Hong Kong. We're the number one airship producer and manufacturer in the world.

Do you control everything yourself, or are you a delegater – do you hand over and go sailing?

Any large business can only be built on the basis of delegation, profit centres, areas of responsibility.

You're not a hands-on boss?

It's too large to be hands-on on a daily basis; we have management systems. I like to play a role in picking all our chief executives – that's terribly important, because you pick people who want to succeed themselves. So we have an ability within the organization for many individuals to become multimillionaires.

You've been on a financial roller-coaster in the past – and it was often a close-run thing! Are you now impregnable – could you ever go bust?

I suppose anybody could, but I don't think we can ... We're generating between two and three billion a year in sales, and one to two million dollars a day in gross profits before taxes and depreciation, so it's a large company today. We export our beer to forty countries, we export coal to members of the ASEAN region, we sell our oil domestically and overseas, we're growing.

You've just borrowed $1.8 billion?

That's right, unsecured for fifteen years.

How do you sleep nights?

Obviously if you're able to borrow, you must have assets, net worth and cash flow to be able to repay those dead instruments. Matter of fact, if you can borrow at fixed rates, our average rate of between 7 per cent and 12 per cent means that we're paying that sum of money back in ten to fifteen years – by when $1.8 billion will probably only be worth $100 million! It's a matter of how you perceive the world in long-term strategic planning. We have a twenty- to fifty-year corporate plan.

The investment in private homes has been very rewarding. My headquarters are here in Perth – the world headquarters of the Bond Corporation. Our international headquarters are in Hong Kong, so I have a house there. We spend a lot of time in London, but I prefer to stay in houses rather than hotels – so when I finish work I can at least have some semblance of relaxation.

You're living in Belgravia, and there was a report you were going to buy Paul Getty's Sutton Place – but it wasn't posh enough!

That's not *quite* right: I had a look at it but didn't like the inside, I like it to be more homely. The one I have in Hertfordshire *is*; whilst it's large, it's quite intimate – you don't feel as if you don't belong in it. The Getty mansion is fantastic on the outside but it lacked internal planning and I didn't feel it would have been a home at all. I was looking for a home, not a castle – and I think it was overpriced, at £10 million. I made them an offer of about £6 million.

I've now got thirteen hundred acres in Essex and a fifteenth- to sixteenth-century house which I've restored internally and externally, and a lovely Cromwellian tithe barn – it's fantastic, a lovely property.

All in all, it's not bad for a signwriter from Hammersmith!

I was only thirteen when I left England, so I didn't learn to paint until I came to Australia!

Do you now feel one hundred per cent Australian – or are you still a Pom at heart?

When I get off the plane every time I go to London, I feel like I'm coming home – so I don't know whether you ever lose the roots of your founding country. Maybe in later years I could return to England; who knows?

Do you think you could have achieved all this in any other country, or has Australia – and Western Australia in particular – some sort of magic formula?

I really believe I would have done it anyway. Even now we're moving into England and America in quite a large way. We've already commenced the development of airships; we're in property and many other investments in England, not least a little bit of farming. We farm here in Australia, so it was logical for us to buy farming property in England – and I've bought a farm in Hertfordshire.

How has such success and achievement affected you personally? We met some fifteen years ago, and I detect you're much more confident now: you're handling the Press, you're on television all the time, and whenever you make an announcement it's treated here with the solemnity of a senior statesman ...

You mature. You get a little older – and perhaps a little wisdom comes with age. When you have a large business and you play a large part in the communities you're involved in, trying to see things happen in a better way, then you become a public figure and your statements *should* be taken seriously, if you're serious about them.

You're now taking on the Unions, making bellicose public pronouncements about them ...

You have to stand up. You can't give in to pressure, and certainly some of the unions in Australia aren't prepared to abide by the laws of the land. That's the reason we then take them to the courts. I don't believe that if you strike, you should be paid; it's *your* choice if you strike, but I don't believe you should be paid by the company and that cost added to the cost of its products.

The plumbers and gas-fitters gave you a going over, and now the Builders' Union has been holding up the completion of your Perth hotel resort?

We've built a hotel there in twenty months – twenty-five floors! I don't think you could build a hotel anywhere in the world in twenty months, so we haven't done a bad job; but at the same time we could do better because we have to be competitive in the world scene, and when you get elements that won't complete something you have to take them on, make your point and stand up for your rights.

I've heard stories of explosions, of arson – so it's getting rough?

We had one quite serious case: forty-nine sticks of gelignite were placed around a crane, and it was blown up! I can't say whether the union were involved in that or not, because we never did find the culprits – but one can suspect it. We made security stronger, and we've now got things in order, and they know that we *will* stand up to them.

I've been a member of the Painters' Union for twenty-five years. I kept my membership when I went into other businesses, so I can talk on the floor level. In West Australia we have the largest breweries and 95 per cent of the market, so obviously we would be a very easy target for industrial problems – and we've only lost four days in four years! So, we do have good industrial relations.

Do you ever feel concerned with your own personal safety – kidnapping?

Like everybody in a high-profile position, you've got to take the necessary precautions. I do that.

I think it's important that if you've made a lot out of an economy and a country has been very good to you – as Australia has to me – that when as businessmen you see things that could be changed and you might well be able to bring about that change, you should stand up and speak out about it. I think that's the proper thing for you to do.

You're sounding as though you could be persuaded to join the New Right party?

(*Laughs*) I think the New Right's too extreme. Quite frankly, I don't approve of them, yet. I believe there is a place for unionism in this country and in most industrialized countries in the world: the working man has to be represented, and that is a system which is not going to be changed – you've got to face the reality of it – in the foreseeable future. So we've got to try and make it better, so we can work within it.

I believe Australia will address the problems she's got. Right now in the ASEAN region there's probably no better place to invest; there are 2.4 billion people, and Australia is the Switzerland of the Pacific rim. This Asian growth market is the *only* growth market left, for the next hundred years.

You're Australia's first billion-dollar borrower: what now drives you on? Are you ever going to be sated, commercially?

One has to balance one's life, for a start; that's very important. I enjoy collecting paintings – I get a lot of fun out of that. I like to play tennis. Things have got to be kept in balance, and I don't think growth for growth's sake is necessarily good. Certainly we're expanding into the United States and Great Britain and I believe we'll continue to expand, because we have a long-term plan for twenty years. The minute I'm not prepared to drive our company on, then I would step down and let somebody else take the chair – and maybe do something else with my life.

I don't bring balance sheets and work home. I start early in the morning and I finish by six or seven at the latest. The climate of course means that you've got another four to five hours to enjoy outside activities, which you can't do in other countries: that's the great quality of life in Australia.

With this quality of life, how does Australia treat one of its tallest poppies?

There is a section of the community that is anti anyone who's successful, whether in business or anything else. A successful politician will attract adverse comments, which is unfortunate. We still have in Australia that knocking – we call it knockerism.

And they go for the jugular, don't they?

Yes, they do. I think it's probably something to do with the competitiveness right throughout the schooling system here. If you win you get *all* the colours; if you don't win then you're considered to have done very badly. The system of the Olympic games – where it was sufficient to compete and not necessarily to win – is not heralded here in Australia. They *expect* you to win ...

Attitudes towards you must have changed totally when you won the America's Cup – you were the national hero?

It was quite fantastic, really. I became, of course, a household name through that. It was the first time I have any recollection of a nation actually joining together to celebrate something. I'm thrilled to bits about it, you know – it was Australia actually beating that great giant out there.

Your Prime Minister took his first drink for years, people were weeping in the streets, you were the hero of a television mini-series – it was an event such as Australia hasn't seen before.

The Crocodile Man: Mike Pople

The Madam: Dorrie Flatman

The Down Under 'Duchess': Jane Makim

The Sleuth and the Swami: Tony Shaffer and Diane Cilento

The Billionaire: Aland Bond

The Financier: Charles Lowndes

The Outback Hostess: Sylvia Wolf

The Psychologist: Bill Saunders

The Impresario: Wilton Morley

The Paradise Islanders: John and Eleanor Alliston

The Bush Publican: Sid Smith

The Kangaroo Lady: Iris Anderson BEM

The Radio Man: Nigel Milan

The Gay: Jeff Hardy

The Sex Expert: Professor Derek Llewellyn-Jones

The Prawner: Bill Moull

The Minister: John Akister

There wasn't a unity like that since the last world war. The people were united. It became a personal thing, because it was small Australia fighting that great might of America ...

It was good for your business, I'm sure – what did it do for you personally?

I got a great sense of satisfaction, quite frankly, being able to bring some credibility to Australia's technology, to its management skills and to the sheer determination of all the crews involved in it for so long. It took us nearly fourteen years to win that Cup.

Does that mean Bondy will always be a goody from now on?

Oh no, if you lose the next race, they soon forget. Like any sport, you're there during the height of your excellence and you're soon forgotten thereafter ...

THE PSYCHOLOGIST: BILL SAUNDERS

This catalogue of carnage
is largely ignored . . .

Bill Saunders, darkly outspoken, is a clinical psychologist in drug and alcohol abuse at Perth's new Addiction Centre. A bachelor of thirty-six from Portsmouth, he had been Director of a Glasgow University Alcohol Studies unit and Senior Lecturer at the Paisley College of Technology.

He felt mildly guilty about deserting the National Health Service in 1986, for his lectures always explained that our most popular and acceptable addiction is also Britain's third largest killer – alcohol kills ten times as many youngsters as heroin and cocaine combined; indeed two-thirds of all drug-related deaths involve alcohol. Heavy drinkers carry twice the average death risk – so jolly old booze does far more than release inhibitions.

Bill Saunders found Australia also needed him: a nation of sixteen million suffers twenty thousand deaths annually from alcohol and tobacco, though less than two hundred from opiates. So his message to the fortunate and convivial burghers of Perth is: alcohol is *far* more dangerous than any hard drug. In their lucky country drink is behind every other murder, every other road death, three-quarters of the assaults, a third of the drownings, almost half the suicides . . .

The Scottish government decided in 1979 that professional workers needed more training on addiction problems – especially alcohol problems. I was at Glasgow University lecturing on psychological medicine – I'm a psychologist, which I think is a more appropriate profession to deal with drug problems; I don't think medicine gives a fair view.

But Perth is a long way from Paisley and Glasgow – it's prosperous, modern, clean, full of fresh air and sunshine. Why did they need someone with your anti-addiction skills?

Responding to alcohol and drug problems is not just about poverty and desperate social-economic circumstances. Drugs are freely and widely available, and because this is a community which has lots of leisure pursuits, lots of drugs are used.

Where life is so much easier and people are more affluent, are their problems not less?

The problems are different. The problems are overwhelmingly those of alcohol and tobacco, as they would be in Britain, but here it's more the regular use of alcohol – alcohol is everywhere, the community is *saturated* in it! The Australians head the league of the English-speaking peoples in terms of their ability to drink. They actually shade the Scots into the distance, and by quite a long way!

So here is a community which has become used to having alcohol distributed into it at a very high rate indeed, from the bottle shops and hotels. Drinking is very much a way of life. To try to do anything about alcohol here is very much akin to trying to control the right to use guns in the States.

Certainly beer seems central to life, part of the fabric – the America's Cup is sponsored by beer, the Melbourne Cup is supported by another brewery; the most attractive buildings on every street corner are the pubs – it's often the only building in town that's been restored . . .

That's certainly true of Fremantle: they've done a magnificent job in restoring that. But one has to strike a balance: alcohol is an interesting drug, a nice drug, a drug which is used well and wisely on most occasions by most people. The problem, especially in Australian society, is that it increased its alcohol consumption by about fifty per cent in the last two decades, so what you have now is a situation where with people moving into their thirties, forties and fifties, you're getting lots of regular-use harm. There's lots of people turning up in the hospitals whose livers, brains, hearts etc. are being quietly eroded by their regular use of alcohol.

So addiction can be a problem no matter how good your life and how good your surroundings?

Indeed, some studies show it's at both ends of the spectrum, it's when life is either very comfortable or very *un*comfortable that the drug alcohol tends to get misused.

You believe drug and alcohol abuse exists because the experience is pleasurable, not because the addict has some psychological tendency?

Let's be careful what we're talking about; I mean anyone who drinks can experience alcohol-related problems, it's not just a prerogative of one or two funny *odd* people. And there's no evidence whatsoever that alcoholics, so-called, are really different from the rest of us. So what we're looking at is intoxication; this is the ordinary person going out on a Saturday night and drinking one or two drinks too much – and that results in a whole range of problems. We have road accidents, we have knifings, family arguments and the rest.

So there's no such thing, you're saying, as an addictive personality? We're all equally susceptible?

Some people just put more energy into it than others, and you *have* to put energy into developing a drug problem. I mean that idea about heroin: you take one hit and you're hooked for life! It's a media myth. The person that gets hooked on heroin has to put a lot of time and energy into doing that.

What we're really talking about is a lifestyle given over to alcohol, a lifestyle given over to tobacco. I mean, tobacco addicts will get up in the early hours of the morning and go and find a slot machine, so they'll have a cigarette first thing. They'll actually organize their day around their supply. What's happening is people saying, 'I *need* this drug in order to function comfortably.'

To over-simplify, you're suggesting that heroin and cocaine are not really too worrisome, but alcohol and nicotine and opiates are very dangerous indeed?

Alcohol and nicotine are the drug problems here. Most Government drug initiatives – especially the ones in Britain – are focused on heroin, when in fact of course they should have focused on alcohol and tobacco. That's not to say that heroin and heroin-abuse problems do not merit concern, but it's a matter of prioritizing things: if you've got limited resources in terms of the anti-drug abuse, then what do you tackle? I'm quite clear about this: we need to tackle alcohol and tobacco, and I'm very pleased to see that what's happening in Australia – it didn't happen in Britain – is that those products are actually on the agenda for debate in the current campaign against drug abuse.

You were telling the nurses at your lecture that Alan Bond was not a local hero, but a villain?

No, I'm telling you – I was telling them – that he's really a *drug baron*! Right, he promotes and pushes his drug with amazing lack of resistance into this community. He's now been able to get the licensing laws extended so that twenty-four hours a day Perth people will be able to drink. That is very curious when you see the Government on the other hand saying they're going to get tougher on cannabis users and the supply of illegal drugs: any movement now of $10,000 in a bank account could be open to police scrutiny, your telephone could be tapped; we're going to have better coastal surveillance – with the idea that we're going to cut off the supply of the illegal drugs and that will cure the problem. Yet with alcohol the problem's supposed to be cured by pumping *more* of it into this community! It's a nonsense.

I was saying he was a pusher, if you like, of the drug that's the greatest problem in this society. The figures from alcohol are really quite daunting – we're talking one in two of the road traffic accident fatalities, one in three of the drownings, one in every five admissions to general medical wards – the people are there for their pancreatitis or their gastritis, alcohol-related to their drinking habits. This is not in any way people who are seen to be alcoholics, this is just the ordinary normal Australian.

Spontaneous abortion is now well known to be related to alcohol consumption. If you want to look at assault – 78 per cent of assaults here are alcohol-related, one in two murders, something like 40 per cent of suicides. If these figures were from heroin there'd be *such* an outcry, yet this catalogue of carnage is largely ignored. Society's become inured to it.

There are said to be between thirty thousand and one hundred thousand heroin addicts in Australia, among sixteen million people . . .

Let's be careful about what we mean by addicts: are we talking about users? No one knows how many heroin users there are in any community because it's an illegal behaviour, it gets hidden. Most figures are dreamt up by the media, and then reported by the media to the media, and they get themselves very anxious about it.

If you want to talk about addiction you've got to talk about the five or six million Australians who use more than twenty cigarettes a day. One in four of them will die from that drug use, and there are probably some four or five million really addicted people. They far outweigh the number of people who may use heroin. And let's be careful: it's nice to say 'heroin addicts', but what you're often talking about is people who use heroin on a recreational basis, who will use it now and again, take it up, put it down.

I'm not recommending it as a good thing to do, because I think the risks of getting problems with heroin are high – but the risks of getting into trouble with tobacco are *very* high indeed. The majority of people who start smoking will develop a tobacco addiction.

If you smoke cigarettes you can go on smoking for forty years, if you take crack, you're an addict tomorrow . . .

You're only a crack addict tomorrow if you listen to the *Panorama* programme and believe what they say about that! There is no such thing as a drug which overwhelms your will instantaneously. What crack is is very pleasant, it's a nice thing to do, right, so what people like is the pleasure. Now there are lots of other human behaviours that are pleasurable; your first kiss, I suspect, led you to carry on kissing – so there we are: the instant addictive behaviour!

We want to be very careful we don't allow that sort of media rhetoric to take away from the evidence. There will be recreational cocaine users, there will be recreational cannabis users, there are recreational heroin users, so let's get this in perspective.

The people who get into trouble with crack are highly likely to be already in trouble in other areas of their lives. They'll be unemployed, they'll have little hope for the future, they'll be desperate in certain areas of their lives — and then crack or whatever drug is a very nice solace. But instantly addictive – no, I'm sorry.

You believe that drug abuse exists because the experience is pleasurable, not because the addict has some psychological dependence?

That's correct. The majority of people will use drugs because they find it pleasant, and people don't do things that are unpleasant, as a general habit. We know people do things that are rewarding, so *all* of us use drugs – it's not as though there's a group who will use drugs, and the rest of us don't. It's part of the human condition. You can't find a society throughout the world that doesn't have *some* form of drug use embedded into its culture, so it does seem to be a natural human behaviour.

I can remember returning from America several years ago and devoting part of my radio programme to AIDS – which few people in Britain had heard of at that time. I discussed it with a young and liberal doctor who said, in effect, 'That's a lot of newspaper rhetoric.' He was suggesting it was being sensationalized, that AIDS wasn't all that serious, that the numbers were infinitesimal – and what about all the people who're knocked down by cars . . . ? Aren't you now doing exactly the same thing with hard drugs?

No we're not, because the whole mechanism of addiction is moderately well understood. We know that what addiction is about is *not* being over-controlled by the drug, that you don't give up your will, you don't give up your ability to think. At the end of the day people choose to take up or put down drugs. OK, so what they're doing, mainly, if they're introduced to a drug, is saying, 'I'm going to experiment with this.' The overwhelming majority of people who use cannabis will try it sometimes and then, depending on their life style, will either take it up or will not. And the same with alcohol and the same with crack, if you like.

The police here in Western Australia say that nine out of ten hold-ups, muggings, are drug-related.

Yes, probably people who're intoxicated with *alcohol*, we know the evidence on that ... I would argue against the suggestion that they do hold-ups in order to fund their heroin habit. That's got nothing to do with heroin, that's got to do with the fact that heroin's *illegal*. Because it's illegal there's a black market, because there's a black market it's expensive. You cannot legitimately go out and buy heroin, so therefore because you're already doing something illegal, doing another illegal behaviour is just part and parcel of that. You do not see it as being greatly different.

Perth is a most conservative city, yet your stance is decidedly liberal — even permissive. How do they take to you?

Moderately well, I hope. One of the reasons I was brought here was to try and raise the quality of the debate about drug use.

Broaden the outlook?

And broaden the outlook, yes. We're running postgraduate and undergraduate courses, so our aim is to gradually develop a group of people who can speak about drugs in a more informed, objective and rational manner. That does seem to be lacking, to some extent.

Don't they see you as somebody coming in and saying: strontium-90 is good for you?

I don't think so because all the time I try to balance it by saying, 'Look, OK, I'm not condoning heroin use, I'm not condoning cannabis – but let's be sensible about this. It's no use making these things into drug-horrors while ignoring the ones that *really* do the damage.' I'm arguing for a consistency across the board ...

You're crying in the wilderness, I suspect, if you're saying, 'Don't drink too much beer' in Perth!

Yes, it may well be, but that's an experience most people in the addiction business would have in Britain too, especially coming from Glasgow. If you want to see a big powerful industry, the brewers and distillers in Britain are very powerful indeed and have resisted strongly any attempts to curtail their activities.

What were your initial impressions of Australia?

It's about ten years behind the times. The media is very poor here, it's atrocious. I've done a couple of radio programmes, and they were quite appalling. A lot of the stimulation I got in Scotland was related to that type of work. I miss Radio Four in the morning, the *Today* programme; I miss good news broadcasts; I miss going to watch Portsmouth play – but that's just a long-term addiction! I miss my Glaswegian friends for that articulation and laughter. The cinemas here are better, superb. Financially it's no different at all: I'm as broke here as I am there.

There was the Libyan thing, there was the Russian nuclear explosion, and I think: 'Thank God I'm in the southern hemisphere.' Since coming here the pace of my job has dropped by seventy per cent. The sheer harassment of working in Glasgow – it was so busy, I'd get there at 7.30 in the morning and still be there at eight o'clock at night. I had to work at the weekends. Now I don't do any of that and I tend not to work in the evenings. I'm totally changed!

I'm going to live longer. I've just read bits of the Royal College of Physicians' report about the state of British health. Looking at the life expectancy rates in Glasgow, I could expect another twenty years, at best. I may well be looking at thirty here.

At your Western Australian Institute of Technology, are your facilities much better than they were in Paisley?

Coming from Paisley College, it's chalk and cheese! I'm working in a beautiful campus, the sun shines, there are twelve thousand bright clean articulate students – it really is *very* different indeed. Sometimes I'm just walking around the campus and I have to sort of shake my head to believe my good fortune.

I come through the city and I watch the blue rivers sparkle in the sunshine and I still sometimes marvel at the fact I'm here! At the moment I don't feel as though I belong to it, because it's all rather too wonderful.

Makes Paisley seem Dickensian?

Poor old Paisley! I certainly have a lot of sympathy for the Scottish situation, but from a personal point of view the quality of my life has changed radically for the better, no doubt.

Do you feel any sense of guilt, because the living's too easy?

In Glasgow you were aware that what you were doing was urgent and important and necessary. Occasionally, being English in Scotland, I used to say I was up there doing missionary work – and there *was* a flavour of that, it really was quite desperate stuff!

Here, that's missing. What you do have sometimes is the feeling, 'well, if these rich comfortable people want to rot their livers with alcohol, why should we be too concerned about it?' There is a bit of that. Maybe that's just a Presbyterian Scottish hangover that will pass.

Now you've got used to the relaxed life, would it be difficult for you ever to return to Scotland, or to Portsmouth?

It would probably be impossible – and that's after only nine months! The reason would largely be to do with climate and style of living. Here you can finish work at 4.30, walk down to the river, hire a little catamaran and have some fairly good sailing for an hour. I don't play the piano, but I *will* learn to play while I'm here, or something like that. It might not be the piano, it might be hang-gliding ...

Scotland is beautiful, Glasgow is vibrant – but it's got every known inner-city problem; what of Glasgow do you miss?

That vibrancy, the sense of sharp-cutting humour, the tensions at the Glasgow–Celtic football matches or England versus Scotland at Hampden Park. The quick wit and the acceptance of the *desperation*, sometimes, of Glasgow. It really was a charming place to live, but the sun didn't shine and it was hard work and the public transport system was ineffective and it's just a lot more hassle to have to work and live in Glasgow than it is here.

This is a very ordered society, it's structured, conservative – and I was a little disappointed! I like the young people, but I didn't think they were quite as vibrant as I'd been used to. I was sitting on a bus and this punk rocker came on and he really was *splendid*: full regalia, green spiky hair, the earring, the lot. The people were all sort of tut-tutting. I thought, '*Great* – how refreshing!' He sat down and the bus quietly filled up and this old lady got on and, lo and behold, my punk rocker stood up, moved nicely out the way – and offered this old lady his seat! I thought, 'Look, you haven't *quite* got the role right – more practice required!' But that's a very charming thing to happen.

In Glasgow the buses wouldn't *stop*, the drivers are so aggressive and disgruntled. People had to be equipped with parachutes to get off. Here not only will they tell you your time to get off, but if you've got a pushchair or pram they'll actually stop the bus to hook it on the back – and off you go! The public service is of a much higher order.

On one occasion I got on the wrong bus; I was at the end of the trip and wasn't quite sure where I was going. We actually drove round the block, and he dropped me off where I could catch another bus – then he went back to his route again! The Glasgow Transport Executive weren't doing *that* sort of thing . . .

But do you find life here lacks a bit of zing?

It's an interesting question, but how much zing does one *need?* It's about balance again. I mean, this week I've been to a piano concert, there's been a rock concert, I've been to a lively seminar, I went out to dinner, I went to the movies, the Test Match is on, there's a yacht race off the coast – even the Pope's here. How much more can you cope with? And you can go to the beach as well. Too much zing can be dangerous to your health . . .

THE IMPRESARIO: WILTON MORLEY

The country's run by rather fierce middle-aged women...

Wilton Morley looks like a thin version of his father Robert Morley. He arrived in Australia in 1973 at the age of twenty-one, and soon went into business as a theatrical producer. He had hard times and good times – the best of which came from the esoteric *Rocky Horror Show*, which made him $4 million.

He brought Lauren Bacall out in *Applause*, which was good financially but rather a strain personally as he had to escort her around the capitals for five months. Miss Bacall, not known for generosity, had a tendency to send back her Sunday morning breakfast because room service was asking $11.59 and she would *not* be ripped off.

While I was in Australia he was planning to bring out Anthony Quinn in *Zorba the Greek*, and presenting *Aren't We All* with Claudette Colbert and Rex Harrison. Australian Equity had tried to ban these venerable stars from parts they had made their own in New York and London, but was overruled by the Federal Immigration Department.

Wilton, who enjoys the Australian pace, told me, 'I've never pushed the idea of being a Pom – that's a dangerous thing to do. The Englishmen that've come here have largely been the trade union members they absolutely hate who make life difficult for everybody, or upper-class English twits. I was once asked to speak at an old public schoolboys' luncheon, and there was nobody under about eighty. Anyway I got $200 – that was the main thing . . .'

As we talked in the Melbourne theatre at the start of his tour, the well-controlled voices of Colbert and Harrison floated across their elderly matinee audience and out into the foyer. I wondered whether the fact that he was Robert's son and Sheridan's brother had driven him out to Australia . . .

A bit. I suppose they did – but it certainly helped when I got here. There was a certain amount of credibility to it, and when you start putting on plays you have to try and find the money *somewhere*. I suppose they thought they weren't about to get ripped off by Robert Morley's son! But yes, it did a bit in England – I felt I wanted to get away if I was going to go into the theatre business. It's been very hard for Sherry, always being compared with Robert; I didn't really want to have to tackle that.

I worked for a while in a theatre company here, and then went into business on my own and lost a lot of money with my first play, called *Same Time Next Year* – which a lot of producers do, I suppose, but I battled on and then I had a success.

A play called *The Elocution of Benjamin Franklin* got me off the ground – a one-man play about a transvestite elocution teacher, which was *not* the sort of thing you'd think they'd go to in Australia – but then when you've lived in Australia for as long as I have, that's exactly what they go to! It was about this strange transvestite who taught little boys and eventually gets seduced by a little boy, rather than the other way round. It was an enormous success for me here.

Why do they go for that in Australia?

There is that sort of image of Australia – that it's a frightfully macho place where people go into the outback. Of course the people who live in the cities never go *near* the outback. Also Sydney has the largest gay population outside San Francisco, so all the myths are in fact not true.

You brought Lauren Bacall out, you've now got Claudette Colbert and Rex Harrison – they're all a long way from your Rocky Horror success...

I buy all the things from London and America, so I go every year and have a look at what's on and decide what I think is going to work here. Largely, if things have been a success in London and America, they do tend to work here as well.

Aren't We All *worked in both places – so how's it doing here?*

It's going *quite* well in Melbourne – about break-even at the moment, but we've only been out two weeks...

They wouldn't rather have a transvestite elocution teacher?

Well, they might, you just never know, but you can't *keep* giving them transvestite teachers and *Rocky Horror Shows* – though every time I run into a little problem I bring back *The Rocky Horror Show* and it *is* in fact what they seem to like best here, because it's only an hour and a half so they can get out of the theatre by 9.30, it doesn't have a big plot to think about, and they can whistle the songs. That's what they *do* seem to like, that's been the biggest success. I don't know if that says something about Australia – perhaps it does...

I would have thought this would have been a winner and the coach trade would pour in to see stars they've watched on their screens for the last fifty years...

We bring very big names out now, but when I first came here the people coming out were Patrick Cargill and Derek Nimmo and television people. I don't think they now want to see – to be unkind – Leslie Phillips and Norman Wisdom any more, which is what they had a diet of all the way through the Fifties and Sixties. Every sitcom telly star from England came out in a vehicle – a not very good vehicle – and usually when their series had washed up. I think Australians got wise that they were being given second-rate English Ray Cooney comedies, and they got sick of that...

After a while they started getting their own film industry and became a bit more sophisticated and decided that having old stars coming out from England was *passé* – even my father I've brought out, and he lost me a lot of money! For a number of years I put on plays like *Steaming* and *The Dresser* without names, and it worked very well.

When I first came here, as soon as you got off the plane they said, 'How do you like Australia?' They were terribly nervous you were going to say, 'I don't like it as much as England'. In *infuriates* them if you compare England to Australia.

Now there's this enormous nationalism here, and they don't care at *all* what anybody thinks. They think this is a better country to live in than America and England. In some ways it is and in some ways it isn't, but there's a fervent nationalism ever since they won that silly boat race in New York... I think the America's Cup probably started it as much as anything else – but it's a very dangerous thing, nationalism, and it's sad there's no kind of in-between: they've gone from being terribly insecure to being enormously overconfident, and that's a shame. I hope it levels out, eventually.

Do you find this a better place to live?

I came when I was twenty-one and it's been very good to me. I've made a nice living and I can get back to England when I want to, but I like the way of life. I'm not a terribly hard worker and I find the idea of going to the beach in the afternoon quite nice. It's a Mediterranean way of life: they have a kind of 'she'll be right' attitude.

In many fields it's easier to succeed here than it is in New York, certainly, in London, probably...

Oh yes it *is*: one can be a big fish in a small pond very quickly and very easily, and that has its attraction in life. There's not a lot of competition, there's not a lot of people producing plays, it's a nice living, I understand it, I've been doing it for ten years. There's something fun about taking a show to Mount Isa or Alice Springs or New Zealand, I love travelling around. It suits me.

We had the most extraordinary experience of taking *The Rocky Horror Show* to Mount Isa, where they'd never had *anything*. The man at the theatre said they'd had Frank Ifield and 'Les Girls' in the past ten years. I said, 'Well this is a cross between the two – you'll *love* it.'

People would get up in the middle of the performance and go out to the bar and have a drink and come back in, as if it was a wartime concert. Then the man who ran the theatre said, 'I hope you won't mind, I'm having a little wedding ceremony. I'm the registrar here and I'm marrying some people between the six o'clock and the nine o'clock shows – do you mind if I use the set?' It was the kind of experience one wouldn't have missed for the world! There's a lot of pioneering here, you know, in a sense.

One misses the proximity of Europe, but then you can go to Hong Kong or Japan or the Far East quite easily, and that's interesting. I think there *is* a certain lack of culture here. Sure you give that up – you give that up for sunshine and money and pretty girls! Sure one gives up things to live here – but then you give up things to live in England, don't you?

Television seems curiously pleased with itself here – is the theatre audience equally undemanding?

I think they're probably less demanding, the theatre audiences, than they are in New York and London. They may be more honest than New York. I mean, you go to the theatre now in New York and they get up and applaud the orchestra, the overture! They have this extraordinary thing of leaping to their feet every five minutes because they've been told this is a wonderful play. This is a much realer audience, they don't give a stuff what the Press say. No reviewer can close you overnight, it works on word of mouth. It's an honest audience – but sure, probably a little less sophisticated.

You can't afford to be too experimental?

No, not at all. There are plays I would like to do which I haven't done because I've thought they're a little too *avant garde*, better done by subsidized companies: Stoppard, for instance. I love Stoppard but they don't like Stoppard much here, it's too English. We did *Noises Off*, which is Michael Frayn's big comedy, but his other plays like *Benefactors* wouldn't work here – I don't think they'd know what they were about. Ayckbourn again is a little English for them.

Is there an advantage in being a personable single Pom here?

I went to an American school for some years, so I don't really have a discernibly English accent and I've never pushed the Pom thing: I don't think that's a sensible thing to do. The upper-class

Englishman is considered a bit of a joke here. I think there's an advantage in being personable wherever you are, but it's a very dangerous thing to be a snob in Australia, a very dangerous thing.

What does your very English father think of it?

He likes Australia for the first ten minutes and then, when he can't get the news or he can't get the story he's been following in England the week before, he gets annoyed that every newspaper has a bathing beauty or a dog being born on the front page. Then he gets irritated. He likes it for about a week, then he gets bored and wants to go off.

This is the interval, now. This is quite an elderly audience you'll see coming out in a moment, because it's a Wednesday matinee. I'd say the average age of the audience will be about seventy today – probably haven't been to a show for quite a long time.

But still a bit younger than your stars . . .

Just! I think it's not sensible that Claudette Colbert tells everyone she's eighty-three because I don't think you want to go and *see* an eighty-three-year-old on the stage. I do rather say, 'Look darling, don't keep mentioning your age' – but she's very proud of it, as you know, and sweet . . . If you told people she was fifty-three they'd believe it, of course, because she looks so young.

Rex is a worldly man who's lived in many countries, what does he make of Australia?

Well, Rex is not young; he's seventy-eight and he spends a lot of time in the hotel, and then he has to come and do the show. He finds the women here *extraordinary*. He thinks the country is run by rather fierce middle-aged women – which it probably is. He thinks the men are all rather timid or rather gay, or both. At the Melbourne Cup, which he was exposed to yesterday, it was very hot and he had a lot of rather large women bossing him around.

The general misconception about Australia is that it's run by men in shorts running along Bondi Beach, and of course it's not: the Australian women are quite fierce and really do run the country.

They both think the audiences here are a bit slow. Rex said to me, 'I can't hear the minds ticking over like I can in New York and London . . .'

THE OUTBACK HOSTESS: SYLVIA WOLF

Mother said, 'You were such a lady when you left...'

Sylvia Wolf left Hayes in 1969 and – looking for the real Australia – hit the Northern Territory with some impact. A warm and jolly lady, she descended upon Katherine, then an unsuspecting outback town with a population of 1400 sweltering on the Stuart Highway two hundred miles south of Darwin.

A considerable life-force, she ran a small club where she established a reputation among the local drinkers as a fun-loving girl with a strong right hook. As the daughter of a reporter on the London *Evening Standard*, she went on to establish a newspaper she wanted to call the *Katherine Bullsheet*, but was persuaded to tone it down to the *Informer*. Then with a government loan she built her own motel even further south into the never-never, and married the Frenchman who put in her spa pool.

Both the motel and the marriage went bust, so she retreated to Katherine – now grown to 6000 people – where she is a JP, manages the best motel, plans to go into federal politics and get married again, though not necessarily in that order.

Having happily abandoned both her English accent and her British passport, she was infuriated at being redirected to Heathrow's alien queue by an intrepid immigration official ...

When I came here in 1969 or thereabouts, nearly twenty years ago, Poms had a worse reputation possibly than they do now for whingeing – and I must admit I agree with it. They were just a pain in the bum. I think they probably expected too much, and maybe the advertising in England was overrated.

I was born in a little place called Hayes, in Middlesex. I don't know if it's still there? I went back when Daddy died and I was horrified, I just didn't recognize it. I went through Southall and gracious me, there were shops with saris in them and everybody seemed to be black!

I didn't actually emigrate – I'm not a 'ten-quid tourist', as they call them. I was going to have a pop around the world and see what was going on, and I was disgruntled in England ...

An unhappy love affair?

Yes, everybody does, don't they? That's all part of growing up.

So it was like joining the Foreign Legion?

If I'd been a man I probably *would* have joined the Foreign Legion. I was doing quite well in England, I was an office manager for a company called Pyrene – fire extinguishers; it was taken over by Chubb Locks. I had about a hundred and twenty staff and I was doing all right.

I was very keen on Enoch Powell; I don't know if he's still going these days, but I was one of his disciples. He was just a bit ahead of himself, and possibly he put it in a manner which people couldn't accept.

So the racial situation drove you out of England – yet you came to the Northern Territory where 20 per cent of the population is black.

Yes, but it's different. The reason I couldn't cope with it was, well, say you had a nice house and an Indian or a Pakistani moved next door, before you knew it you could have twenty or thirty there – and the value of your house would disappear, be nothing. You had to sell it cheaply, and just get out. They didn't really belong there; here I accept that obviously the aborigines do.

Because they're staying in the settlements, not coming to live next door?

Here in Katherine we have what we call fringe dwellers, people that just live under trees. There are others that try and assimilate, are being educated and gradually progressing, but there are still a lot that are a big problem. All governments, whether federal or state, everyone is concerned.

With the Land Rights situation here in the Northern Territory, over 50 per cent of the land is under claim. Most of those claims will go through, so virtually 50 per cent of the land is just given away, and I don't think that's right. I did start the committee called 'One Nation, One Law', because since the Land Rights bill the whites are discriminated against. It's wrong, because it's turned the whites against the blacks, or it *did* do – all right, we're calming down now!

The abos have got Ayers Rock, and they'll have the Katherine Gorge. What worries me here is the fight's gone out of the whites: they're just accepting it now – they've had the guts kicked out of them.

The rot really set in with the Whitlam era. When a government changes they don't necessarily revoke all the laws the other governments passed, so it just went on. And with the aborigines, it's a conscience thing: you see the poor sods lying around on the river bank and you think, 'We've got to do *something*!' I don't know what the answer is – certainly not what they're doing.

So if you get into politics, you'll try to push the pendulum back again?

I'd say at this stage *when* I go into politics because I'm fairly confident that I will be. I'll try and talk some sense into politicians in Canberra, because that's probably where I would be most use. I feel I could probably pick up a seat on the federal scene easier than on the local.

You arrived here and went to work in the Katherine Club serving drinks – in effect you were a barmaid. Now you're a JP, you're running this hotel and you're hoping to be a politician – so you've achieved more than you would if you'd stayed in Southall?

I found England too oppressive. When I got to Australia I was very disappointed with Sydney. Adelaide was OK, but I was looking for the *real* Australia that's advertised overseas, with kangaroos leaping around and these lovely bronze men ... It's a much freer way of life – not so stuffy. There aren't those tiers of class you had in England – and still have, I believe. But I'll just correct you: I wasn't a barmaid, I was the Manager.

Forgive me – but it was a fairly rowdy place?

It was on Saturday afternoons, yes. We used to have what we called the Sporting Peg – that's when the club sponsored different sporting bodies. They'd come back and have a few drinks, and they always used to fight. I mean it was a man's world then, and they used to fight *every* Saturday afternoon.

I'd just *had* it this particular day and I thought, I'm going to really fix them up. So I pulled back the hatch and went out just as one guy swung a punch – and he laid me out! I had a lovely black eye, but when I got up I really knocked the shit out of him, don't worry about that. So yes, it used to get rough. Still happens in some of the clubs.

Sounds as though you were working in a Wild West saloon – they all came through those swing doors!

I guess that's what suited me – I did like it!

Nobody ever said, 'Who's this pushy Pommy sheila ordering us about?'

They probably did – and they'd have got a smack in the mouth for it!

In Katherine today the facilities have improved, the shopping's improved – but I must admit I preferred it as it was. Having been one of the prime movers to get the place changed I suppose I shouldn't complain, but I did prefer it ten, fifteen years ago – although we did get those plagues! Just after I got here we had a bat plague – they're smelly old things – and then a rat plague. It was dreadful! I was terrified, they looked so big. In this old shack I used to live in, we caught about twenty big rats in *one* night – the traps were going off one after the other, it was awful. You'd drive down the street and you'd kill a dozen rats, that's how bad it was at one time. It was just a plague – and then they'd gone. Nobody knows where they came from or where they went to. It just happened.

Some Pied Piper of Katherine! How did the locals take to you?

They loved me, quite honestly. Yes, they really did, because I was prepared to do things. That's how I came to start the newspaper, the business agency and other things I got involved in. Once they got used to me, they really appreciated me. They often used to pick me up – I was a lot smaller in those days, darling, about eight stone nine – so they'd put me on their shoulders and race me around and sing a particular song that perhaps I shouldn't mention now ... It went: 'Hoorah for Sylvie, hoorah at last, hoorah for Sylvie, she's the horse's arse...!'

On top of all this, you're now a Justice of the Peace – what sort of punishments do you dispense?

It's just the Petty Sessions – we have drunks come before us, rowdy behaviour, wives beating up on men and men beating up on wives, things like that – though we did put somebody away for three months...

When we first met some months ago you sounded very Strine; now you're getting a bit more Pommy...

Well, that's because of *you*. When you go I'll have to try and get rid of it again, because hardly anybody would know I was a Pom.

In politics it's not a good idea to be a Pom?

In *most* situations it's not a good idea to be a Pom! The Poms had a bad reputation and to some extent still *have*. Any time that you hear of unrest in the unions, and strikes, it's really noticeable that they seem to be troublemakers. One of our Ministers suggested that as soon as they start causing trouble – send them back! He didn't know I was a Pom when he told me that, mind you...

Do you often go back home to England?

Only once; when my Daddy died I went back, but as soon as I got to Heathrow I felt there was something wrong. I followed everybody else to the place where you show your passports and he looked at me and said, 'Aliens, Madam, over there.' That set me off right from the start! I just felt different, like I didn't belong.

At the gathering of the clan they hadn't seen me for such a long time – thirteen years I think it was – and I was different, totally. In fact my mother said to me, 'What happened? You were such a lady when you left.' I was really peeved.

You didn't tell her you'd been going three rounds every night, back in Katherine?

She wouldn't have understood...

When you first arrived here the ratio of women to men must have been about 1 to 100 – how was your social life?

Unfortunately that's not true; I guess there was about a third women to two-thirds men. But the women – I shouldn't *say* things – they didn't look after themselves... I'd just come out of London, not a bad looking bird – well, the world was my oyster. It was wonderful!

With your inside knowledge of Australian men...

Would you rephrase that?

With your experience, how do you find men in the Territory treat their women?

Mainly dreadfully. I don't mean they knock them around – although some do – but they leave their wives at home. You go to any club now, they're all there on their own. I don't think in the Territory the average male treats his mate properly. They think it's a bit soft to hold the lady's arm as they take her across the road, or open the car door and things like that. Well I guess in England a lot of men aren't doing it any more, either. I didn't see too much of it when I went home – notice how I said 'home'? That's the first time I've said that in *years*. You must *go*!

So as a woman, how do you get along, how do you cope with them?

Oh beaut, because they just treat me like one of the chaps.

You get along with them beaut – yet you married a Frenchman?

Oh God, did you have to bring that up? That was probably the biggest mistake I ever made – and I've made a few – but he used to open the car door and hold my arm going across the road and pull back my chair when I sat down ... That wore off after a while.

Here you are living in the bush about one thousand miles from anywhere –
and you've just had cosmetic surgery?

You don't want to have a look at them do you? Right, yes, well
what happened; when I got here, in the heat – it *must* have been
the heat – my boobs just kept growing. I mean, they were *enormous*,
and any caricature they did of me had these great tits and a big
smile. I thought, I've got to do something about this. I went to
Adelaide and went from a double D to a real smart C...

THE FINANCIER: CHARLES LOWNDES

Your garden turns brown and blows away...

Most young Poms emigrate to Australia looking for a better life for their families. Charles Noble Lowndes was already wealthy and, born in London with a father from New Zealand who had property in Australia but lived in Jersey, entitled to three passports. He enjoyed the rich man's luxury of choice.

Shy, thoughtful, articulate – but not gregarious, not a beer-drinker, not into mateship or sport, he does not instantly appear the ideal migrant. Indeed at one time it seemed he was not: he went to live in a handsome house on one of his three properties in New South Wales, but after a despairing three years was driven off the land by a harsh and relentless drought. 'You have to *live* a drought to understand a drought; it marks the stoicism of the country people of Australia.'

Spirit broken, he retreated to a Sydney harbourside house at Vaucluse with his second wife Susie, from New Zealand, and their three small children. He now runs his property and venture capital consultancy business from Macquarie Street; she runs Hampshire and Lowndes, an up-market dress shop in smart Double Bay, with Anouska Hempel's sister. 'The two rudest women in Sydney,' he says; but their business flourishes.

I had last seen Charles Lowndes, a good friend, twelve years ago, when he thought he preferred Australia to anywhere else but was not quite sure. He has now decided in which world he feels most comfortable . . .

I was born in London, went to Summerfield's at Oxford, then to Canford School in Dorset, and then to Millfield, briefly. My father was a New Zealander, but I was brought up in Britain until I was thirteen or fourteen, when my family moved to Jersey. I'm actually entitled to an Australian, a New Zealand *and* an English passport.

My family bought land in Australia when I was about fifteen. When I left school I came out for six months of every year until I took up permanent residency about six years ago. When one has children, one has to decide where to live. We decided we'd rather bring up our children in Australia as Australians than we would in England or, more specifically, in Jersey.

From a career point of view, I feel more comfortable here than anywhere else, because I know it better. I may not sound like an Australian but I have in fact worked here almost exclusively since 1970. Sydney is going to play a more important role than it does now in the world's most vigorous and expanding financial sector.

Yet even Australia's own Finance Minister said the country's in danger of becoming a banana republic . . .

The problems with the banana republic relate to the varying nature of the economy, where we are not undertaking secondary processing of our raw materials. It's the manufacturing sector which has let the country down. The primary sector continues to produce more and more and better and better agricultural produce and mine produce. It's the unionized secondary industries, the processing industries, that have been unable to compete internationally with the processing of that product.

The service sector and the treasury sector of the economy is actually very advanced – probably the most advanced in the Asia–Pacific region – and *that* is Australia's future. Within this city of Sydney there is a financial capacity to deal with the rest of the world: Sydney is the financial centre of Anglo-Saxons, if you like, in the Asian time zone.

When the markets in London close, the markets here open first in the world – Tokyo's behind us – so the day starts here. It starts in New Zealand, actually, but Sydney is the major overnight trading centre for the world. When New York's closed, London's closed and most dealers are sitting on their phones all night continuing to trade, they're trading on the Sydney market, the Tokyo market, the Hong Kong market. But this is the white man's country for Asia–Pacific, and if you take the Asia–Pacific region as a whole and the link that gives with the US and South America, the whole of this vast ocean – the world's largest – Sydney is its communication centre. We sit towards the bottom left-hand side, and everything radiates up and out from Sydney.

I liked the space, the security of this country – security in terms of personal freedom. I consider that the more dense the population, the more laws are required to restrict personal freedom, so England is far more over-governed than Australia. With the actual physical space, you've more than the usual personal freedom of movement.

I enjoy living in the country, although it's very different here, and *very* difficult – particularly for the wives. So many of the things one takes for granted in Europe are non-existent here: you might have to generate your own electricity, you certainly have to generate your own water. There's no question of a rubbish collection service. If something goes wrong – something as simple as a domestic pump – you've got no water. You've got to fend for yourself, yet this is the land of the five-day week, so you can't get anyone to help – and you can't live without water in a hundred degrees for two days! You've just got to be dependent on your own resources.

All those infrastructure things one takes for granted living in the English countryside are just not available here. You have to be more resilient. It's harsher and it's tougher.

You had four farms, but you lived in the one at Comfort Hill; how far away was that?

Only two hours, very soft country by Australian conditions, not outback. Closely settled, highly desirable southern highlands – the closest bit of country to the south of Sydney.

Susan felt she didn't have enough to do out there?

She had too much to do – all sorts of things she didn't *want* to do! Also domestic matters: to take the children to school was twenty minutes there, twenty minutes back, and again in the afternoon. The shops were fifteen miles away.

It's all those damn things that go wrong, you know, the dishwasher and the washing machine and Charles's bloody pump has broken down and what the hell has he done about fixing it? And it hasn't rained, so we've got no rainwater. Susan's never practised on Australian washing machines. You go ploughing a field and you put your plough through the water pipe to the borehole and bloody water's all over the place.

But I think the thing that really finished us was three *years* of drought. Unless you've lived through drought in Australia – which most Australians have not – it's the most soul-destroying experience. Every morning you wake up and open your curtains and you've got that bright blue sky and that awful bloody sun! It's a creeping paralysis – it must be like sclerosis or something like that, where you know it's going to start in your toes and creep up but you don't know how far it's going to get and when it's going to stop – but you know it *can* come all the way up and kill you.

It's like that with a drought. It goes on for two or three years, every day getting worse. False expectation and false hope all the time. A cloud comes over – nothing happens! You look at the weather every day and you hope and pray and you think, 'Well if that happened and this happened it could develop the right circumstances for rain.' Nothing happens!

All that hard work you've put into the garden outside your window turns brown – and then blows away in front of you! You get a strong wind and you literally see your soil disappear. Those little trees that you protected last winter and nurtured and grew under the most difficult circumstances, you open the curtains one morning and they've actually blown away during the night. They're not there any more in the soil in which you planted them.

You then look beyond your garden fence at your fields, and you see your animals withering and dying. Your income is zero, so you're not just looking at your domestic circumstances, you're looking at your livelihood, gradually and perceptibly dying and disappearing, never to be replaced.

It's very hard to describe it, Alan, but it's a very long slow process of continual disappointment and false hope. A drought can break any day. We had a three-year drought, most appalling, and quite an experience to have lived through.

I think frankly, if I'm honest, it probably broke our spirit for living in the country, because you could spend the next twenty or thirty years of your life putting your heart and soul into your farm and your garden – which you *can* do in your thirties, as we are. You sit there retired at sixty looking at your life's work – and the same damn thing will happen again! It always happens, in Australia. It might be in ten years or it might be fifty years. The drought that we had was the worst ever recorded here, but those records are only there to be broken again.

That's what marks the stoicism of the country people of Australia, who are very different to the city people. If you can survive that, then you have a certain type of person, you have a resilience that people in Europe would not appreciate. You have to live a drought, to understand a drought.

We had forest fires, all those sorts of things: a petrol tanker blew up on the bridge on the highway one day, ran into some nurse who was rather too tired to be driving – and blew up! The bloody flames leapt through our trees.

All sorts of drama: snakes in the kitchen garden; red-bellied blacks and lethal funnel-web spiders ... You can't put your children out in the garden to play – your babies anyway – you've got to be with them all the time. They were all over the place, hundreds and hundreds of them. You try to spray to keep them down, but they're still all over the place.

I was quite happy to live with all the other inconveniences because I really enjoyed the challenge and the space, and it's something I loved doing, but I think even my strength was broken by that drought. I know that Susan's was, and it was entirely justified that it should have been so.

So here we are in Sydney, which is probably where we should always have been, anyway. It's like living in a tourist resort. I can't think of anywhere else I prefer to live. I've looked at some of those

American cities. I love the English countryside, but I don't like living in London. The idea of having to travel an hour and a half in to work, I find shocking. Fifteen minutes from the city I'm in the country here, on the waterfront.

You don't read about violent demonstrations in this country, about Greenham Common, about missiles. We just don't have those sort of tensions. It's the same syndrome as that bus queue in London in the morning: none of those people smile. Here in Sydney on a normal sunny morning there are a few smiles around, because the pressures are just not there. Of course there *are* tensions, as there are within any society; we've got a slightly different mix here to elsewhere, but I believe it *is* less tense – and that's part of the security.

The tensions are between race and race, or union members and non-union members?

There's certainly *that* tension! The unions here are probably more powerful than in the UK because they've not been hit as hard. There's not been that crash which has enabled management finally to talk sense into them. We've got to the brink of that four or five times in the last fifteen years, but that threshold's never been crossed.

The other tensions are the social tensions of immigration, which again are not unique. As always, the newest immigrants work hardest and threaten those who were previously at the bottom of the pile – the new up-and-coming groups of Italians, Chinese, whatever.

When Australians used to make jokes about Poms they would not criticize the British for coming over here and cleaning-up, they would criticize those Poms who came with a haughty attitude – they became the butt of Australian jokes. That was because of Australia's insecurity and inferiority complex.

It's curious that this lucky country, where everything's so good, suffers so much union trouble – I find it absolutely incomprehensible.

That's the nature of the malaise, particularly in the secondary industry sectors. The primary sectors work extremely hard. Farmers, miners work hard, and in the City they work very hard. The manufacturing sectors take it easy to some degree – but can you blame them? They're in a tin shed out there in the western suburbs with the sun beating down, it's bloody hot – and there's the lure of all those beaches.

The Pommy trade union bosses seem to be blamed; is this a stereotype, or is it true?

Some very Leftish-type trades unionists have come from England and run the unions, or held senior positions of influence. We don't have American-style labour contracts, we have English-type unions and all the hullaballoo that goes with them – and a long history of unionism, of course. Britain's first unionists were exported – the Tolpuddle Martyrs came here.

Other than the straightforward criminal situations, the majority of people sent to Botany Bay were guilty of the crime of sedition, which was speaking out against the Establishment. They were frequently the Irish who were, by the nature of the troubles there then *and* now, antidisestablishmentarianists, so there was that natural antipathy.

Over there on The Rocks is where the convicts were put – and there, where the Opera House is, is where the soldiers were put. They stared at each other at rifle point, across this bit of water: these blokes were in irons, and those blokes had muskets, and that has been the structure of this country from its very foundation.

So in fact a division between labour and management has evolved in the same way that the division between management and labour in Japan evolved from the samurai situation. It's evolved from the soldiers *there* and the convicts *there*.

Corruption in New South Wales seems so much worse now – is it just that it's getting more publicity?

Yes, corruption's a major thing in this country. It's practised mainly by the Anglo-Saxons, because they're still the people that run the country. I think only 55 per cent of the population are now of British origin, but 95 per cent of the power still comes from that group.

In the past it's fair to say the majority of the corruption has taken place under a Labour government, to the extent that their officials are perhaps more bribable because they don't have as much money as the Liberals. In New South Wales the story is that the Liberal Askin Government was at the explosion point of corruption.

However, the current Government here – when you talk about corruption in Australia you talk about Sydney, because this is the centre of things – has been in power for ten years, and the corruption has probably got worse. Obviously it's got bigger in volume – everything's got bigger in volume in ten years – but the foundation for this all-permeating corruptive tissue of society was probably the Askin Government.

There's gambling, drugs, prostitution ... but you see, it goes much further than that. People are bound together perhaps by those aspects, but then if you want something else done in society you use those connections, you use the holds that you have over people in one form or another to get things done, whether it be building permits or political favours or justice favours.

There are some very unsavoury characters in Sydney, *very* unsavoury, who are the Mr Fix-its and Mr Do-its. They all like the races and the dogs, and they go along in their Jaguars and open the boot – and it's stuffed full of bloody cash! 'Look at my winnings!' They're going to the races to launder it, you see. They bring along a few mates and say, 'Look what I won today!' They arrived with it in the bloody car!

Corruption started in the military here, with MacArthur. The Rum Rebellion and all that sort of thing in the early 1800s was based on Governor Bligh's attempt to curtail the smuggling and illegal sale, without duty being paid, of the colony's entire rum supply by the officers in the New South Wales Regiment.

You can't ask questions here in NSW, in the Press or on television; you can't ask them because the law of libel is that it must not just be shown to be true, but it must be shown to have been in the *public interest* to have printed it, or to have said it in public.

In terms of the Labour movement, it's a factor that was bred into the foundation of this country. There was a very strong view by the first thousand people who arrived in chains about the five hundred people who were not in chains!

There have been various other factors overlaid on that: there's a very substantial Irish position in this country. I think about 35 per cent of the original settlers, forced or otherwise, were of Irish descent who tended to view the Establishment with as much displeasure as perhaps the Irish do today. That has had the effect of religious–political polarization within the community. They've all tended to drift towards the left-wing, while the descendants of authority tend still to be rather established old-family, old-money, and perhaps represent the right-wing.

You're a businessman – do you think the world is going to have much faith in the Australian dollar for the next five or ten years?

I think it's fallen to the degree where it now presents opportunities. It's important that labour relations are controlled, as they have been in Britain in the last few years – but that's unlikely to occur with the present Labour Government. After all, our Prime Minister is a trade unionist . . .

Australia has failed to deliver for many decades, but it's still a land of potential. That potential will no doubt one day win through. We certainly don't have the street violence that other developed countries have experienced.

Anything that you regret from England, from Jersey?

The age-old story of the inability to get on a plane and go to Paris or Rome for the weekend – those are the regrets. To take my family to Europe for a holiday – it's not worth going for ten days, I've got to go for months to make it worthwhile – costs me $20,000 in air tickets to get them there, with a nanny. Why *go* if you've got to look after three children yourself?

It's a major undertaking, and it's also a major hassle to have three young children on a plane for twenty-four hours. That's also why one has eighteen pieces of luggage – it takes three taxis! It's an organizational nightmare, and *not* my idea of a holiday.

But at least if you stay here in Sydney you haven't got snakes and those deadly funnel-web spiders to cope with, as you had in the country . . .

You *do* have snakes to contend with; you never put your children out to play in the garden without watching, even in an enclosure. Cats are pretty effective, though. There are also funnel-web spiders in the pool – they can live for days under water! They descend, take an air bubble down with them, and disappear for three days . . .

THE PARADISE ISLANDERS:
JOHN AND ELEANOR ALLISTON

*You have a sense of impending disaster
all the time ...*

The story of the Allistons and their Three Hummock Island is out of romantic fiction. Once upon a time a destroyer captain, Commander John Alliston DSO, DSC and Bar, set out from Abbey Cottage, Titchfield, in Hampshire, with his young wife Eleanor. They had married in 1937 and were planning to raise a family far from wartorn Europe – ideally, some place on the 40th Parallel: Chile? New Zealand?

In 1949 they headed for Tasmania, where land was on offer at sixpence an acre, and finally found their sanctuary among the howling winds of the Bass Strait, thirty miles off its northwest corner. The deserted island of thirty-five square miles, without one essential service, has been their has been their home for thirty-six years – so far.

The nearest shop, neighbour or doctor is forty miles away across pounding southern seas – or at the end of a bumpy twenty-five minute flight in a well-worn air taxi. There the Allistons struggled to raise and send out into the world four children and fourteen grandchildren. Both nearing eighty, they still cling to their island like survivalists, alone and staunch and happy.

Three Hummock, a pinprick on the map, has thirty empty beaches, lakes, rivers and those hummocks – one of which they call a mountain. Its prevailing southwesterlies are constant and chill, so they both have that redness of eye once seen only in engine drivers who lived with their heads in the cold onrushing air outside their cabs. There is a small wharf which sometimes sees a visiting boat, and a grass landing strip on a bumpy hilltop upon which mail and food is occasionally dropped by a friendly bush pilot. My chartered aircraft from Smithton landed instead on a long silver beach and taxied towards a lone wooden house, ever so slightly dilapidated. Their homestead is sturdy and adequate, but basic and not very comfortable – the size of its furnishings limited by the space within the tiny aircraft that must transport them.

Eleanor is now seventy-five, a determined dreamer with a practical nature. She rarely bothers to wind a clock or know what day it is, yet musters sheep on foot and copes with any emergency. Each day she moves alone around the island, barefoot but carrying the tape-recorder into which she dictates romantic novels and television scripts written under the *nom de plume* of Minka Jones, in which girls called Tiffany live in passionate conflict with men called Rhett in some sophisticated city of the mind. Despite all her imagination, the lives of Tiffany and Rhett seem *far* less romantic than the true love story of Eleanor and John ...

We didn't particularly pick Australia in the first place; it was going to be either Chile or New Zealand – *anything* on the 40th Parallel.

Has that latitude some special magic?

Yes, it has: we think it's very very good for creating healthy people, for a nice, relaxed happy feeling; it's a good homoclime.

But the weather here can be terrible: wind and rain – it's worse than Hampshire!

It's terrible in a sort of way one learns to cope with perfectly. There's always shelter, you don't have that freezing cold. When we were first married and John was in the Navy, he used to go to St Vincent – which was a redbrick ship – and I think the agony of him trying to get out of bed on an icy morning in Hampshire and go off on his bicycle filled me with a desire to go where he didn't *have* to get out of bed at all, where we managed our own fate and were perfectly free – and we've found this freedom and we've *done* it!

It wasn't that you were such an attractive lady who liked the gentlemen so much that he wanted to get you away from the competition and have you all to himself?

I'd *love* that to be the case! I can shoot a line on that subject, but I'm afraid it wasn't so. It might have been that I felt the same thing about him – but I do think life is so much simpler, just *à deux*.

Had you any idea when you left England what you were getting yourself into?

No idea whatsoever when I walked into this house – with women it's always the house, isn't it? John saw the beautiful land, the trees, the paddocks, the stock – and thought that was absolute bliss. I thought the house was hell, complete hell.

And you've been here thirty-six years and haven't changed a thing!

I *beg* your pardon! There is our pine-encrusted sitting room or whatever you call it, and lovely little kitchen. I must introduce you to an exquisite bathroom – we've done that much! But you see, what we didn't realize was that if we didn't do it ourselves nobody was ever going to come and do it for us. We waited four and a half years for the new kitchen until it was a dangerous venture to walk across the room – we were going through the floor. That was horror, horror.

Have there been moments – apart from your leg going through the kitchen floor – have there been moments when you wanted to give it all away and go back to the city?

Never got as bad as that. No.

Not even when it's cold and wet and windy and the plane can't get in and the larder's empty and you haven't got your mail?

I can honestly say that I'm totally and utterly sold on every aspect of this island. I didn't ever realize or suspect that life could be so satisfying. I used to be fearful, I wanted things exactly the way I wanted them – I *made* them happen. Now it's absolutely too easy, it's like falling off a log, it's just wonderful.

Yet no sooner had you arrived than your baby was taken gravely ill and might have died; that must have foretold what could happen?

You'd think by the law of averages that couldn't happen again. That was the most awful experience. It's a terrifying thing to have a child screaming non-stop at two-minute intervals all through the day, blue in the face – and no way to get it to a doctor, no way to talk to a doctor, 'cos we had no telephone. The radio which we bought from the people who'd left here didn't work, and so there was no way but to light a signal fire – three fires on that rock over there. Finally, just as the boat was going out of sight – they had the wheel tied and they were down below, going back to the mainland – one of the crew went up on deck and said, 'The house is on fire back at Three Hummocks!'

So they answered the signal, came back – and we went off on this ghastly voyage to the mainland, arriving about one in the morning in a dead, asleep village. We finally got him to a doctor and he was operated on.

The boat went back to get John because they thought Warwick was going to die – this little baby boy. I have a picture of these poor characters: John and his little son aged about three, Robert was four, standing at the end of the hospital ward and looking bewildered. They'd had the most dreadful sea voyage to get there. But by that time Warwick, by some miracle, had rounded the corner and was turning somersaults in the bottom of his cot, so all was well.

You have a sense of impending disaster all the time on the island. You don't do silly things, because you know you are alone. And you see, John and I sometimes don't see each other during the day.

He's working on his cabbage patch and you're writing?

121

Or he's writing and I'm out somewhere. He often says, 'I think you should tell me where you're going', and I say, 'It would take all the *joy* out of it if I had to tell anyone where I was going. I'll be back in time to cook dinner and that's that, my lord. That's all you're allowed to know.'

Fortunately, you're both loners; but you don't bother to wind the clocks, you don't know what day it is – do you know when it's Christmas?

No, not necessarily – unless the children ring up and remind us.

Has your curiosity ever led you back to England?

No, never. You see, this is something we haven't had on the island. People say, 'What do you *do* all day? Aren't you lonely?' Look, we're just flat out, we're absolutely desperate all day. I mean, that's true.

I was talking about going around the island: I consider that very important because I take my tape recorder and I do my writing as I go, and I call *that* being busy. I'm walking and exploring and sitting on a rock and thinking, and I may go and have a swim somewhere along the coast there. That's me, being busy!

Housework I'm terribly bad at, and at any rate John adores to come in with his boots filled with mud and walk across the floor – if I'd just washed it, it would be sad; but I haven't, so he's allowed to do that. Then we sweep it up! He has utmost freedom; he loves to be free to do what he likes. Would you say we're free people, or do you find us encompassed by the limitations of the island?

You seem totally free ... Your four children, fourteen grandchildren – do they love the island the way you and John do?

The children do, especially when they're young, but we have two teenage grandchildren and they're showing a distinct liking for discotheques and things like that ...

I live on an island myself – not much bigger but not quite as isolated – and we always say that if friends come all the way to visit it means they really want to see us – they can't just drop in.

That's very true. We have a few old faithfuls who come from England, and that's really nice.

Yet you didn't even bother to have a radio here for the first twenty-odd years.

We *did* have a radio, but it was total bother: it was really badly behaved – something about the atmosphere. I couldn't manage it so we didn't go in for that very much, we just trusted to luck.

What made you finally put in a telephone?

Something absolutely amazing happened; I wrote and enquired how much the telephone would be. It was very expensive – about £4500 in those days – so I wrote back and said, 'I have no further interest in it, thank you very much' – and the next week the pilot brought in a man who was coming to see about the telephone! I hadn't even mentioned it to John, so my face was rather red; but it was just part of a deal with the Telecom people who put a beacon on our mountain – a telephone was needed for their personnel. We've only had it for about fifteen or sixteen years, but then I could ring the children at school – that was *marvellous*.

Did you find bringing them up here made them any different from other children: more solitary, more independent?

At school and university they did very well. They brought their friends home for holidays, and so they were rather popular; they'd take sleeping bags and a tent and sleep all around the island. One lovely morning I remember coming out and looking up to the top of the mountain in the sunrise and with the binoculars I saw them dancing on the skyline! They were dancing to 'Zorba the Greek'; they had a Greek boy teaching them. They camped all over the island and we went in the aircraft and dropped food and messages and things to them. Rather fun.

Yet they all went out into the adult world and took conventional jobs – they were never tempted to come back here and carry on your good work?

By that time there wasn't a living for more than John and me, if there was *that* – if you could call the overdraft that. There was no place for them. John and I had to work the cattle and sheep by ourselves, except in the school holidays. We couldn't give our children payment for what they did. They did an enormous lot for us before they went – they've got a really good stake in the place.

You've made yourselves self-sufficient here – are you totally independent?

No, there's always things like tea and sugar and flour. We don't exactly grow our own wheat, or grind it, but we have a lovely kitchen garden and every single day of the year we've got three varieties of vegetables edible. John orchestrates his garden very cleverly.

He's training me bit by bit to be a good cook. I'm very interested in it, but we only have one meal a day, which is dinner. We don't have elaborate lunches or breakfasts, the usual sideboard array that you would have in England – or did have in England in our time.

Having lived together in this solitary way for thirty-six years, have you not said just about everything there is to say to each other?

No – that's the biggest fallacy in the world! That's a lovely question. I think we're always covering new ground. It's the most amazing experience to know some other person well, *really* well. If we could've talked when we were first married as we can now, what on earth would our marriage have been? A super, super, *super* thing.

It wasn't too bad, even as it stood!

No, we were quite satisfied with it; but I would think it's wonderful in the modern way to be able to say everything to each other. I envy the kids today their wonderful freedom of communication. I don't think we had that: I was very strictly brought up to say only what ought to be said, what must be said. There were things that one didn't say – and that's a great waste of life.

Your eldest son has been divorced, so the content and happiness of your marriage didn't rub off on him?

He didn't have a happy marriage, I don't know why it is. I would think that he's too good-natured and relaxed. Perhaps he shouldn't have been married at all, he's so sweet and unsuspecting and he married at first sight – now that was the wrong thing. He had four little boys, and she's one of those bossy women who say, 'I suspect you're unfaithful to me, so we'll get divorced.' And Robert's simple-minded, I'm afraid, so they were divorced. He then married a second wife exactly the same as the first, to look at and in manner, so he's had two marriages and six children, or five and a half children. She wanted him so badly she got him, and now she's having another one, so that's that! He's fairly successful in business. He should have been a Cavalier with long gold ringlets and purses full of money and getting all the local ladies into trouble in the days of Oliver Cromwell.

Perhaps he should have stayed on the island?

He adores the island. He would have loved to stay, but there wasn't the place for him, and that agitates and infuriates him. He feels that if he could have taken over the whole management he could have made the most wonderful success of it all. I don't know whether that's true or not. John was a first-generation farming gentleman and I certainly was a first-generation farming lady, and between us I think we made a fairly good mess of it!

We adored the life, but if modern techniques and everything were used we could be running a wonderful property here today. It's just that the low prices for our products got us down.

Isolation provides its own problems, doesn't it – you had to get your produce to market?

Business-wise you had everything against you because you took your stock ashore. We did, what, two hundred and thirty trips with stock – with me the mate and John the captain. We loaded them all and took them to market, but people knew we couldn't take them home again; they got into a ring, they ringed around us – they admit it now! They say, 'Hah, we had you on toast.' Oh, it was terrible.

Somebody said to see John's pale face like a lamb to the slaughter while bidding was going on was absolutely pathetic. It was tragic – it was really tragic. He did it so well and he was so energetic and taught himself to shear – and he'd never lifted a finger in his life. He taught himself everything.

We did have a very bad bush fire here three years ago; it swept right across the island in about forty minutes and its flames were all round us. One of the rangers came and told us we had twenty minutes to get out of the house! So we thought, 'What could we take?'

John was so sweet, he said, 'You must take all your manuscripts.'

I thought that was absolutely wonderful! It was worth the whole bush fire just to hear that ...

What would your attitude be if in the middle of a force-ten gale John has a heart attack?

I'd be thankful that he won't have to go and have a heart bypass operation. We've seen a few of these heart bypasses around here and I certainly wouldn't like John to have one – but you've only got to *look* at John to know he won't have a heart attack. I might have an accident and so might he, but I'd be very surprised – he's a wily old bird.

You're not a total recluse – one has the feeling that you enjoy people and you like pretty clothes and dressing up?

Love it, adore it. When we go ashore we stay in the very best hotel we can possibly find, and we simply ring bells and live it up.

What do you enjoy most of all when you're away?

Dancing.

And room service, I take it?

Yes definitely! Ice cream, which we never have here, and everything that we shouldn't eat.

Might it have been easier – certainly more pleasant – if you'd had just a little more money? One feels you were always lurching from one financial crisis to another?

It was true, and people simply couldn't understand it. When I'd go to see the accountant he'd say, 'Now how many calves did you have on the fourteenth of July?' I'd say, 'Our stock in this climate breeds throughout the year, how in heaven's name can I tell you when a bunch of cattle were out in some paddock I haven't yet *discovered*?' He'd say, 'I've got a property in Queensland and it's run by the aborigines and they know to the last calf what was dropped this season.' I'd say, 'You'll probably find there were fifty of them doing what one person is trying to do here. That's not very clever. If you're an aborigine that's the sort of thing you do know – but I know a lot of things they *don't* know.'

I'm sure – how to write romantic novels, for one thing!

They're really lovely things to do.

You escaped to an island, then you escape again into romantic fiction. Who is this other person called Minka Jones who writes about glamorous girls called Tiffany meeting suave chaps called Rhett?

She's just as real – she's the other side of the coin and she has the greatest fun in the world.

She's your alter ego – what you really longed to be?

No. I'm perfectly satisfied with what I've been and am; she's just an extra me thrown in for good measure.

When you're striding up and down this deserted beach dictating your Mills and Boon love stories, does it occur to you that the girls you're writing for are probably dreaming about being whisked off to a paradise island by a good-looking sailor?

Probably, yes – I think there's a lot in that.

I'm still not sure whether it is gloriously romantic here, or just one terrible slog ...

Right, I can put you straight there: it is beautiful, gorgeous, lovely, romantic – no fooling. There's some sort of recipe here that we've got, and it's unbelievably good and it's not phony. It's for real and it's totally satisfying and exciting.

I'm sure many people might dream of living on a paradise island with a beautiful wife or a handsome husband – but almost nobody actually does it.

This is the tenor of the letters I still get in almost every mail, depending on how often it comes. People say, 'I'd simply *adore* to live on an island, it sounds so wonderful, life's so easy – but Mum would be very upset if we went away, so we must stay by her 'til she dies ...'

I'm trying to think what effect this kind of life has had on you: you're certainly self-sufficient, and it's very peaceful; are you a wiser person, do you feel?

I feel I know most of the answers now, quite frankly. I think I do.

Is there anything in life that you still want?

I want an enormous emerald ring. I went into Drummonds when I was in Melbourne last time and John got a bit twitchy, but I knew what I wanted and what it costs and I'm going to earn it, and he's going to help me by earning too.I'm *going* to have it. It'll look absurd, I know.

Can you foresee the day when you'll leave Three Hummock?

Only when I'm dead. But even then I won't leave it, 'cos John absolutely *guarantees* he'll put me on the compost heap so that he can grow some lovely tomatoes out of me.

I thought you were going to say you'd be buried in a lovely little grave under that beautiful tree!

No, because it's too much nuisance for people to look after. I'd rather absolutely vanish into the atmosphere, which is a very quick way. I can't imagine John trying to conduct a funeral for me – he'd be hopeless, he'd get it all wrong, he couldn't do it. I don't want a funeral – I want to get *lost*.

I shall sail into death as easily as anything. I've got no fears. Being dead, I'm sure, is just the same as being alive. I've got no thought of it: if I die, fine. If I don't, fine.

Sometimes when we're in an aircraft and the engine splutters or something like that, I think: 'Isn't it glorious, John and I, here we go, both together, what fun! He won't have to find out how to turn on the toaster.'

I've got a lovely little speech of thank-yous ready when I know the inevitable could be happening. It would be so neat, terribly neat. I'd say: 'You're the most generous and wonderful person I could ever imagine.' That's about all. We'd be holding hands, and it would be simply super ...

A millionaire's existence – without the bank balance . . .

Almost eighty and white-haired, but slim and agile, John ran the island farm; they have just sold their cattle, with great relief, and thus ended a lifetime in debt. He is proud of his tractors and vegetable garden and, perversely, even prouder that their thirty-six years of hard work have had such little impact upon the ungiving and resilient island: almost none of the nine miles of fencing he struggled to erect is still standing. Peacocks and kangaroos swoop about, triumphant.

The Allistons were never able to buy the lease of their rented paradise from the Tasmanian government, so will be unable to leave it to their children. During such a lifetime they have been only *guardians* of their secret sanctuary – Three Hummock Island, population: 2.

John, what made you decide to change your life so dramatically after the War?

You could sum it up by saying that I didn't want to see another gun, another bombed-out thing – I wanted to make something instead of destroying something.

Could you not have done that while staying on in the Navy, or in Hampshire?

I could, but we wanted to go to somewhere where Eleanor and I would have the entire bringing-up of our family. We didn't want any outside influences. In Hampshire we didn't of course visualize

Three Hummock Island, but we did visualize somewhere where we could work as a family.

In the Navy you were within a womb in your warship, surrounded by shipmates, by companionship . . .

The best club in the world.

You left that and came out here to be solitary – not a neighbour within miles.

All I can say about that, Alan, is that there does come a time in your life when you have to take a sharp knife and chop everything away and start again – and that's exactly what we did.

This was a dream – but had you planned how you were going to cope once you'd got here?

No we hadn't, and we got some nasty surprises! For instance I found that in order to live I had to be able to slaughter a sheep and dress it, and somehow keep it and feed the kids with it.

You don't have to do that too often in the Navy . . .

How right you are! But we were sensible enough to go and spend eighteen months jackarooing in the midlands of Tasmania getting paid £2.10s a week, something like that, but we got a free cottage and half a side of sheep a week. It's called a fringe benefit these days, and taxed!

What did you have to give up to come here – what were you surrendering, apart from companionship?

We certainly knew we were taking a risk because we were going to start something which neither of us had any knowledge of – and also we were putting ourselves out on a limb as regards money. All we had when we came here was a retired Commander's pension, which was *very* mean – the Royal Navy has never been known for paying its people.

You'd no experience – you were a Londoner and there aren't any farms in Regent's Park. Could you cope?

Yes, you can; that was a lesson I learned in the War, and I daresay you've seen the same thing too; when the pressure's on, people *learn*. Your ordinary seaman who joins a ship in wartime and only knows how to put on his uniform and do a few knots and splices, he suddenly finds himself a member of a team, and if he doesn't learn fast it's his own skin and the skin of his mates. So he *does* learn, because he's in a tight situation. We were in a tight situation, and we both learned.

You became an instant farmer?

That's right, very good – but as Eleanor says, you really only become a farmer if your family have been farmers for about ten generations. Anything less than that and you're just a Johnny-come-lately.

People putting their lives into land like this would hope to leave it to their children, but you can't do that?

The government were determined never to sell this land; it's always going to be a leasehold, and there's not a living for two families on this island.

Not in thirty-five square miles?

Not as it stands. If you had say $3 million capital to invest here you could possibly earn a bit on that – but you'd do much better moneywise to put it in the bank.

You had to leave the island for three years to work as a mate on a steamer to earn money to put into the place; must have upset you, leaving Eleanor alone?

It didn't work out quite like that because in the Merchant Navy today you only work for six months of the year and get paid for a *full* year – which is certainly not what happens to a farmer! So between voyages I was back here. She was by herself some of the time but Eleanor can cope with that - look, you can't knock Eleanor down with a six-inch shell! She's tremendously resilient.

I like the way she told you that you were going to write a book – and, by George, you wrote a book!

Certainly! If she hadn't given the impetus I would have lazily attended to my cabbages and forgotten the book.

She's a hard lady to argue with ... After so lonely a life, John, after being so solitary, how do you cope when you go back into a city?

The first reaction is to talk the back leg off a donkey. I get rid of all the things I wanted to say that I've been thinking about.

It's strange in this climate that Eleanor hasn't got a refrigerator? You have a washing machine – it must be an affectation ...

Well, perhaps it is.

Don't you like a piece of ice in your pink gin?

No, I'm not a cold-drink man. Another thing is that none of us are mad keen housekeepers, and so refrigerators tend to become like museums. Another point is that our power consists of an engine and you know what a refrigerator is: every five minutes it would be starting up and then five minutes later it would be shutting down – in a week's time I'd have no battery left.

The other thing that surprises me, since we're being rather personal, is that you don't have any pets; I would have thought you'd have had some wonderful dogs?

We realized that the best way to have a dog is when it's a working dog. A dog that merely occupies space in your best armchair quickly becomes a pain in the neck. I don't think farmers, having had the immense pleasure of working dogs, go in for pet dogs. You might have shooting dogs, but then I'm not a shooter and so dogs really aren't *on* on Three Hummock Island.

You've got tiger snakes and copperheads?

We've learnt that the snake is only too delighted to get out of your way, and the only time it's dangerous is if you're silly enough to attack it with a broom inside the kitchen or somewhere like that.

But if you're gardening and you tread on one accidentally?

I retire to a safe distance.

You shoot the possums though?

Yes, simply because I couldn't have a vegetable garden if I didn't. They can go over any fence and they just don't eat something then go away, they pull things up, break branches, create absolute havoc. Reluctantly – because they're beautiful animals – I trap them and then shoot them.

You've also got quite a lot that bites and stings – the flies are awful, and I'm told in the summer they sting too?

Yes, we have quite a lot of stinging flies.

Mosquitoes?

Yes – not bad and not malarial, but mosquitoes.

So paradise has its irritations?

There's no doubt about that, you have to take the rough with the smooth.

You've spent thirty-six years of hard slog on your island – what impact have you had?

Very little – and I'm delighted with that. It really shows that this island is bigger than all us chaps who come along and fiddle around with tractors and spades; it's far stronger.

It's nature reasserting herself ... You put in nine miles of fencing, for example?

A fantastic amount – half of it's fallen down now.

You had up to 1600 head of cattle at one time?

It might have been that – Eleanor probably knows better than I do, because she kept the books. The real figure that counts is that we had better than 300 breeders – and then of course 1500 sheep on top of that.

It was a great relief to sell them all?

Oh terrific, fantastic – first time in our lives we've ever had any money! While we were farming every penny was spent on things like tons of superphosphate, drenches were like liquid gold, all those tools ...

You achieved your dream and it was a terrible slog, but you didn't make a penny out of it – in fact you've been almost bankrupt most of your life?

That's right, too. Well, put it this way: we certainly always owed money, and that was always a bit of a drag on me – so when we finally paid it all off I felt a new man. But let's look at it another way, Alan: we've had three meals a day, we've lived in the place we wanted to live in for thirty-five years, we've raised a family, we've educated them – well, dammit, what more do you want?

But it has been an expensive dream?

I certainly don't think you'd recommend it, unless people were as idealistic as we were. We were certainly idealistic.

Looking back, John, is there anything you'd have done differently?

I'd have been more clever, financially. I wouldn't have thought that you borrowed – and then were able to pay it back simply because your flock would increase at a certain rate and prices would stay the same – which they never do! I might even have done some sort of course in financial things, instead of thinking only of the nuts and bolts.

Do you feel more Australian than British after all these years?

About fifty-fifty.

At the Test Match – who do you root for?

I'm really not interested in Test Matches.

OK – the America's Cup?

A lot of baloney.

I see. So you're completely contented?

I should say, ninety-eight per cent. I'm just trying to think what the other two per cent would be – possibly the fact that we don't see enough of our family.

Are you at all worried that you might have a heart-attack one night when there's a gale and the planes can't land?

I think I'm quite *likely* to have a heart attack, but I'm not worried about it. It would be a very good way to finish it all up – much better than sitting in a bloody bed for a few months with people taking bits out of you and putting them back again.

You're going to be buried here?

We thought the compost heap . . .

Eleanor said the compost heap, but it's not a very romantic thought! Might improve your vegetables, I suppose.

That was the idea.

In fact at the end of the day, an island like this is a rich man's toy – you need money to spend, boats, help, helicopters . . .

That's right, that's right – it's a millionaire's existence, without a millionaire's bank balance . . .

THE BUSH PUBLICAN: SID SMITH

*The Flying Doctor won't come
if you're white ...*

Sid Smith is the man from Larrimah. He's *really* from
Dudley in Worcestershire, where he was manufacturing
haircream.

He became a £10 migrant in 1956 and went to work
for Helena Rubinstein in Sydney, packaging cosmetics.
On his retirement tour of Australia five years ago he
bought – rather to his surprise – the outback pub at
Larrimah, lost in the never-never of the Northern Territory. Ever since then he and his wife Barbara have lived
in searing desert heat and unsplendid isolation.

Larrimah is a good 350 miles south of Darwin or, if
you prefer, 620 miles north of Alice Springs. You are not
fenced-in in the Territory, and there's only one road
that goes anywhere: the Stuart Highway, which drives
straight as an arrow across the red heart of Australia.

There is no speed limit on this excellent road so you
can put your foot down and be carefree – but watch out
for roadtrains! These enormous lorries with two swaying
trailers barrel across the continent, and it's said some
drivers go for thirty-six hours at a stretch, gulping pep
pills to keep almost-awake. At that speed they take some
passing. In my experience they were careful and con-
siderate, but you do hear stories ...

Night driving is not advised, since if you hit a kangaroo or buffalo at 100 m.p.h. the radiator will be in your lap. Not even roo-bars are complete protection. Better start out at dawn.

When you arrive, Sid's desolate pub is just off the road – and serves Devonshire teas! It is almost sixty years old and – don't laugh – is a protected building because of its antiquity. It does have a certain Nissen-hut appeal, a twenty-four-hour licence, and is open 365 days a year; does Christmas dinners too, if you're interested in pudding at one hundred degrees in the shade. Under its tin roof, the pub is mainly two enormous refrigerators, from which the stubbies emerge. This Australian beer bottle usually holds two glasses, but such are the temperatures in the Territory that the Darwin stubby holds two and a half litres! Sid presides on a stool behind the high counter, staring towards the horizon and taking the occasional scotch and dry.

Apart from the pub, Larrimah has a couple of filling stations and a steady population of around sixteen. Sid only has one regular, but in the dry season does reasonably well with coach passengers thankful for a break after hours on the scorching featureless highway.

He greets the parched travellers wearing his pith helmet and carrying a rifle – a solemn Les Dawson figure – and invites them for a swim in Lake Larrimah. They grab towels thankfully and follow him on a deadpan tour around the dusty grounds, with full commentary. This finishes triumphantly at a pink panther fishing in a small brown stagnant puddle of algae in front of the bar. Frustrated tourists carrying swimming trunks have been known to cry . . .

We travelled around Australia for eleven months; never even heard of Larrimah, twenty-four hours before we got here. We came into this place and the chappie behind the counter said, 'Do you want to buy a pub?' We thought he was mad. Three days later we bought the pub.

The whisky was talking?

We weren't drinking in those days. Slight occlusion of the brain.

You thought you were going to drift in and run the place from a deckchair?

We did think we were going to have three days a week off, and work four days; not a bad life really – if you can get three out of seven, you're winning. Instead I think we've had about twelve days off in the last five years.

It's reasonably tidy but it's not inviting – and when you came it must have been even worse?

It was. There were none of the trees around, none of the shelter, none of the shady area. It looked as if it was in the middle of the desert.

Which, in a way, it is.

It is, yes. It's desert weather, quite frankly.

So what's the appeal? You haven't explained how when you saw it you thought, 'This must be mine, all mine.'

No, Alan, and we don't know the answer. I think we just went mad at that particular time. We'd never been in pub business, we'd never done anything like this before – possibly that was the appeal, to try and prove something. It's very hard to explain.

You've made a few quid, presumably, as the coaches keep coming through . . .?

Yes, we're getting over five hundred a year.

But you wouldn't rather be back in Worcestershire living the good life?

Living the good life would be OK, but *can* you live the good life in Worcestershire these days? I don't know. I don't think I could live back there now. It's twenty-two years since we've been there, and it's changed a lot. We listen to Brits who come out here and they're moaning about it all the time. It's a different way of life, I don't think I would fit in.

You're in the middle of nowhere, there are only sixteen local residents, you've got no radio, no TV; tell me the advantages ...

One of the advantages, there's no radio and there's no TV! But I'm getting out now, yes. Five years is enough. We've proved a point, if there *was* one to be proved. We've made a fair job of it – we've planted four hundred and fifty trees, believe it or not.

If you do manage to get rid of this pub, what will you do?

We'll sleep for three months, down the Whitsunday Passage in Queensland: beautiful place. Then we'll probably come back into Darwin; there's still money to be made in the Territory, for how long I don't know.

Did I understand this place is a National Monument under a preservation order?

Yes it is.

Are you serious?

I'm very serious, it's part of the National Trust.

From here it looks like an old cricket pavilion ...

(*Laughs*) Cricket pavilion's not bad at all. It's actually what they call a Sydney Williams hut construction. This was the chappie that built them in the early 1920s to stand the cyclonic weathers – which it does, or it did. We don't have cyclones here, we're too far inland, but up near Darwin where they get them this sort of building could take it. There's three left, and they're all on this National Trust business.

We're also National Trusted because we were part of the Second World War – this was the terminus of the Northern Territory railways and a lot of troops passed through; also the largest airfield in the southern hemisphere was here.

This is an hotel as well, you've got nine rooms which are a mite primitive, perhaps?

139

A mite primitive, yes, rather like glorified concrete boxes – but they're very, very solid.

I don't know if that appeals – does anyone actually stay here?

Oh yes, thank God, yes. It's not a bad place really, our rooms are very cheap: $14 a night – six quid – but they're very solid. You'd need an atom bomb to shift them: concrete, top, bottom and sides. They'll last far longer than the hotels in Darwin.

Of your sixteen locals, how many are regulars?

Er, one regular, a 365-days-of-the-year drinker.

Thank goodness for him.

Yes, he tries very hard, Alan, but he can't keep the pub going. We've got two you could say are regulars, but sometimes they move around the Territory – go out fencing or a bit of droving or whatever. Then they come back.

When you took over you gave them a pubwarming?

We did, and failed miserably! On the inventory was eighty-five pounds of killermeat, beef. I was so much of a Pom, I didn't realize what killermeat was. I thought all meat was killed.

Righto, we'll chop this up into big steaks and put them on the barbecue, everyone will be right. Barbara did marvellous salads and all the business that goes with them, and I'm outside doing this barbecue. I wanted everything to be top hole – but no one could eat the darned stuff because it was like the top of a *table*!

I said, 'What's this killermeat?' Apparently it's meat that's sort of semi-illegal, off the stations. It's any old scrub bull that they can catch, very, very cheap, but you can't *eat* it. Terrible – I failed on that one.

Do you ever get cabin fever out here, do you go troppo?

We get a lot of that. We also call it the mango season: if the mangoes are ripening this is when people normally go slightly skew-whiff, shall I say. But we have a lot of fun amongst ourselves – we *have* to, otherwise we'd go stark raving mad, that's the truth.

If you suddenly get appendicitis what are you going to do?

Hope that God is very close, because you've got a long way to go for any help!

Doesn't the Flying Doctor drop in?

We've only seen him once since we've been here. There we have a bit of a sore point; he *will* if you're a black man, he won't if you're a white man. It may sound as if it's racial prejudice, it *is* – it's against us, though, this time. This actually happens. I've never managed to figure it out. I get very annoyed.

But is that official policy?

Oh Lord, I really don't know about that one, but it does exist. Whether people will admit this to you or not, I don't know, but we have a standard practice here: if you're ill and you're white and you ask for the Flying Doctor, you just say, 'Yes, it's a black person' – and they'll come. This is true.

Is this all over the Territory, or just Larrimah?

It's all over the Territory. There's some funny method they have which I can't figure out. I mean if you're ill, you're *ill*. It shouldn't matter whether you're black, brown, brindle or pink-striped – but that's what exists.

There's no aborigines around here. If they call in we serve them, but they don't stay around. I mean, they own over 52 per cent of the Territory right now and it appears to me that if they ask for more, they just keep *giving* them more. Where it'll end I don't know. The average white person in the Territory's a bit worried about it.

We have a fair system with the bush nurses; they come round all right, and we see a doctor I suppose once every two or three months, something like that – so you can only be ill when they're due to visit. No good being ill when they're not here.

You have snakes?

We've had a few good snakes around: mainly western-browns and death-adders. A young fellow booked in the other day and he'd been here two hours when they struck-up a snake over the road there – so this gentleman went across and picked it up by the tail! The snake promptly bit him in both hands.

It happened to be a western-brown. Now I have it on fair authority that, drop for drop, the venom of the western-brown is as deadly as any snake on the face of the earth, so there's a bit of a panic on. He was *very* sick.

We had two policemen over the road at the time – they were attending a road accident – and they knew about pressure bandages. One of the policemen did one arm and my wife did the other arm. We raced him up to the hospital and got him there in time.

You didn't suck the poison out?

No, you don't do that these days. If he hadn't been extremely fit and young, he wouldn't have survived.

And you can't rely on the Flying Doctor to come in and solve those problems?

No; this was at night-time, for a start, and we've got no landing strip with night-time facilities. If he'd died, it was just bad luck. Terrible place for snakes – terrible snakes in the place, let's put it that way.

Do you ever have any barneys in the bar?

We've only had two since we've been here. One was pretty violent – a knife-throwing – but other than that, nothing extra special. A man just went cuckoo, could be the season, the time of the year. It turned out he was a bank robber from Melbourne and he just decided to throw a knife at me. He was an awful lousy knife-thrower, because I'm a big enough target! We balled him up with a shotgun, and the police came and got him.

How about bikies? Do they come through, riding the range?

We get them through, all the crew from Darwin. We're quite friendly with them now. At first we weren't.

The Darwin chapter of the Hell's Angels?

I don't know what they call themselves – you can never see through the grease. They come in and if you want to have a row with them, you can have a row; if you want to have fun, you can have fun. That's the way it is.

The chap you bought this place from must have been pleased to get rid of it?

Very pleased – he was drunk from morning to night. Very nice bloke, really, just a straight alcoholic.

I suppose it's one way of passing the time ...

Well, it is really – it's a big trappie, as a matter of fact. It's a thing you've got to watch out for, it's too easy – you've only got to turn round and dive right into a bottle. I've been very lucky up to now; I suppose I'm drinking more now than I've ever drunk, but that only runs to about six scotches a day – which is not bad drinking in the Territory. Matter of fact, it's not drinking at *all* in the Territory ...

THE RADIO MAN: NIGEL MILAN

Australians seem to enjoy
seeing themselves ridiculed ...

Australian broadcasting is a curious creation: to the British listener its huckstering is as charmless as American radio. Qualities? Well ... they write good jingles; but with such competition for the marketplace dollar they're concerned about ratings, not quality.

In a land the size and composition of Australia it is easy to see how radio became vital and viable long before television arrived: it welds homesteads together across vast distances and talks to the conveniently concentrated lonely suburbs of the five cities. Sydney's three and a half million support nine commercial stations, and the ABC.

Australian radio discovered long before Britain that call-in audience-participation programmes were cheap, and built loyalty. I heard my first driving back from the country to Sydney in 1970: the Reverend Roger Bush, an early radio cleric, was deftly counselling late-night listeners. It was an obvious and sensible use of parochial radio, and I afterwards put him on *Whicker's World* to explain his role – which seemed to be somewhere between the commercial and the confessional.

Today the ruling voice of Sydney's airwaves is John Laws, reported to have been offered a lifetime contract of

$12 million. By British standards his audience is minuscule: perhaps one or two hundred thousand, yet because he can do his own commercials – 'live reads' – and that advice is often followed, it would seem the money is well paid. Margaret Peacock, wife of a leading Opposition politician, has a much talked about radio programme in Melbourne – and an audience of some forty thousand.

On the small Australian stage, radio personalities have considerable publicity clout: a new contract will be the lead story on the evening front pages, and their romances get the coverage given a US soap opera; in fact they become soap characters themselves, breaking politicians, crying on the air, denouncing, sneering and even – convinced their right to free speech is above the law – going defiantly to jail . . .

A powerful backroom figure on the Australian radio scene today is the son of an East End postman, born in Walthamstow in 1951: Nigel Milan went to the William Fitt Comprehensive, worked in a boutique in Carnaby Street and as a double-glazing salesman; at twenty-six he had become UK Sales Manager for Radio Luxembourg.

He emigrated in 1980 with his Australian wife and went as Sales Director to the failing 2GB station. Made General Manager in 1984, he took it up to number one in the Sydney market, and is now Deputy General Manager of the Macquarie network of nine stations. To encourage loyalty, they gave him a Porsche.

Alert and chirpy and earnest, he remains almost a Cockney – and can hardly believe how quickly he has reached the top of his chosen pile. He said, disarmingly, that going on *Whicker's World* was an accolade that would show his English friends how he had made it, Down Under.

His secret? He had converted the waning 2GB into an all-talk station at the time of the Falklands War – when international news suddenly mattered, even to Australians ...

There are two kinds of Englishmen, basically: those that come here and settle into this community and make a living, but really stay Englishmen; and those that become almost honorary Australians as soon as they get off the plane. I'd be in that latter category, I love this society. I'm now going through that trauma of actually having the registration form at home to *change* my citizenship! I think I'll do it this year because I've got an Australian wife and two Australian children – so I'm kind of outnumbered in my own household.

So what were you selling when you walked in to Australia?

I suppose, a different view. Australia actually is a country that is thirsty for outside input. As a nation, we the Australians recognize our geographical isolation; I think they're always interested in at least giving a Pom or an American or a Frenchman or an Italian, a go – to see if they've learnt disciplines that might be useful.

You think other East Enders would be wise to come here, because there's no class structure?

I went to an Inner London comprehensive, and you're kind of educated to accept the system: it just seems that that's *normal*. When you come here and then you go back, you see it all so much clearer. I was aware there was a class system, but I thought it was breaking down and getting better. Viewing it from Australia, I no longer believe that: I think there's still an entrenched class system in the UK.

You think Michael Caine, Vidal Sassoon and David Bailey would have done better had they come to Australia?

Er, not necessarily the Cockneys. I think they're sort of one out of the pack, really. I actually went to drama school to sort of unlearn my Cockney accent, and I've come here and tried to re-learn it, because Michael Caine and Vidal Sassoon have made Cockneys

146

fashionable. I think they're fashionable in London as well, but if you come from north of the line from St Albans to The Wash, you're probably having it fairly tough.

So today you've become a sort of Sydney yuppie?

Yes. I'm not sure if I like the word or the inference, but I think probably in broad terms, yes, I'm an achiever, and someone who's done relatively well relatively quickly.

You shook a radio station into life, you lifted it from bottom of the ratings to the top; what were you offering Australian radio men that they couldn't find locally?

The advantage of being able to think out of the square, because I hadn't been here. Australian radio, commercial radio, has a sixty-year history – it was established before commercial television. Because I'd come from the outside I wasn't restricted by a level of knowledge of what had happened in the past. I didn't have disciplines set in my mind of how an Australian radio station should operate and sound; and of course I'd been exposed to all-talk in the UK through the BBC and the LBC. I'd had an American trip and seen all-talk radio stations operate in America, so it just struck me as logical that there was a position for an all-talk station in Sydney.

They're fairly laid back here, how did they react to a brand new Pommy pusher coming in?

I think they were pleased that there was someone who was actually going to show them the light! Being a salesman by nature I went and said, 'Let's do this and we'll win; it might take us a time, but we'll win.' We got lucky. The timing to launch a news-talk station was good; the media's becoming more and more sophisticated. We are very physically isolated and that in some ways has set Australian society back. Over the last decade there's been almost a communications explosion within the Australian marketplace.

The other thing that helped us is that we launched in 1980, which was the time of the Falklands War: being a Pom, once the fleet sailed I started flashing constant Falkland crisis updates, much to the disgust of my Australian executives. They thought, 'It won't be war.' There was even some cynicism about the hundred ships setting sail from Portsmouth; they were saying, 'The Poms don't still *have* a hundred ships, do they?'

My view was that once Thatcher had committed the fleet Galtieri was in an untenable political position, so there was going to be war. We had all the advertising positions set up, we actually had a TV commercial already made for when hostilities started!

You could say that Margaret Thatcher and Galtieri increased our audience by thirty-five per cent – and that in a way was the launch of 2GB. We actually considered sending them cases of Dom Perignon, but we thought that might be a little tasteless!

I think 2GB does make a very meaningful contribution to the lifestyle of Sydney. We package news in a very acceptable way for consumers – so in other words, there's a large entertainment quotient on the radio station. There *is* a certain amount of talk-back: listeners ringing in. Talking to the announcers is a very healthy thing because it involves the community with the station.

But it often sounds like a desultory conversation in a bus queue – and about as interesting!

Well the listeners don't think so – it's taken the station to number one! There's a lot of hard news in 2GB; to give you an example of how powerful radio is in this country, John Laws interviewed our Treasurer, Paul Keating, who made that famous statement that if Australia wasn't careful it would become a banana republic. By that night two points had come off the Australian dollar – that's *powerful* communication!

Australian radio's probably the most competitive in the world because in the Americas you've got so many stations competing for the advertising dollar that there isn't enough money to go round. Once you move outside the top two or three stations in any of the cities, the others simply aren't making a bob, so you don't get the quality of programming. Within a city like Sydney, you've only got nine commercial radio stations . . .

Only nine!

How would you like to programme one in Los Angeles, where eighty-four signals go to the market? Here at least five or six stations will be making money, and two or three will be making a *lot* of money.

It's curious how your presenters impose themselves upon the news: I've heard one of them, Mike Carlton, switch off the BBC World Service news – an insert I'd been waiting for, and the bright spot in your schedules – and tell the listeners, 'Look out of your window, you'll see the most wonderful sunrise, it's better than the news.'

Yes, I think that's very sensible of him. You may be the only person here in Australia – being a Pom – who's hanging on for the gems of wisdom from the World Service news!

But I was waiting to hear what's happening in the world, that's what's important, and I don't want my news patronized and trivialized, I want it straight.

I don't think he was trivializing the news, he just stopped it and said he thought it was a spectacular sunrise and rather more relevant to those people living in Sydney. I think that's an eminently sensible decision for him to make. The BBC World Service is not the be-all and end-all, particularly if you happen to be living in Sydney.

On the news here – not just your station, I'm talking about television as well – an accident in the Parramatta Road or a local netball result will take precedence over major disasters elsewhere in the world?

Yes, the more parochial radio can be, the more successful it becomes. Radio's great strength is that it can talk town to town, suburb to suburb, and so we tend to emphasize the parochial nature of the news.

Are you not encouraging Australians to be totally incurious about the rest of the world?

No, quite the opposite. If you gave us a go over a whole week, I think you'd see that 2GB has broadened the news horizon. It's the first pure-news-talk station in Australia. You might argue that in some ways we trivialize the news, but what we do is, we package the news in an entertaining fashion.

Australians are a very unprofound race. I don't think they enjoy sort of pompous profound statements, and that's part of the way 2GB presents itself in the marketplace: it's a very unpretentious radio station. We're communicating to you one to one, whereas I think at its worst the BBC can often talk down to you.

Yet your top men here can be curiously patronizing and often rude to the people who call in – can you explain that phenomenon to me?

I can't explain why it works, but to an extent it's true. We certainly have one or two announcers that take a very aggressive line.

They're horrible! I've heard them jeering at uneducated people who call in, ridiculing foreign accents; and they get terribly cross if articulate callers win the argument – then they cut them off! They need to score off their callers.

Yes but they still ring in, you see. Probably the archetypal proponent of that style of radio is a gentleman called John Pearce who has a thirty or forty year history in this business; John is a very aggressive announcer, tends to trivialize the arguments with people that ring in.

And sneer at them?

But they *know* that before they call, and in a way they ring in to do battle with John, and the audience expects it. John Pearce on a human level is one of the nicest men you could possibly wish to meet, so what you get is really a stage performance, a piece of audio-theatre.

I was listening to one of your presenters this morning abusing some schoolteacher who'd called in with a thoughtful point which contradicted his view. So, why did she do it – and why do other listeners enjoy hearing this intelligent woman ridiculed and cut off in the middle of her argument?

There is that levelling effect here; I think we're growing out of it as a nation.

What does this tell us about the Australians, who are a most amiable people; why do they enjoy a display of public arrogance and bullying and bad manners? Is it that your presenters are saying things the listener would like to say to people?

There might be an element of that. I really don't know the answer, but it's an interesting point because you're quite right – Australians seem to *enjoy* seeing themselves ridiculed. I think that, maybe, is part of the working class, the egalitarian nature, the fear of tall poppies. To some extent there *is* a cruel streak in Australians that likes to see the tall poppies levelled.

I've read this week that for a lifetime contract you're paying one of your top performers $12 million – is that possible?

It's a huge amount of money, isn't it? Yes it is possible, because our top-line announcers attract an enormous amount of advertising revenue.

But he's got an audience of say one or two hundred thousand. A BBC producer would commit hara-kiri if he was only carrying that number of listeners!

Yes, but they all *buy* the products that John Laws tells them to, that's the reality. We can do something in radio here that you can't do in the UK: the announcers can actually endorse products in their own programmes.

Generally speaking the talent gets a much higher proportion of the take here, than in the UK, because all the media operators in the UK have some kind of monopoly – so therefore if you don't work for the commercial station in London, you don't get a gig.

Apart from an ability to bully the audience, what else does a radio man in Australia need to be a success?

When the book of John Laws's life, his biography, was released he was interviewed by Derryn Hinch, who's the morning announcer on our Melbourne radio station; Hinch wondered why he was a success and offered the proposition that his voice gave the female audience the impression that he had large private parts! He said it rather more graphically at the time, I might add – which caused John for the first time in his career to have two or three seconds of mike silence!

There *is* something about sexuality in radio: people create images in their minds of the announcers, what they look like, what sort of people they are. That's one of the reasons radio talent doesn't often transfer well to television. You have to have a warmth, an understanding of the audience you're talking to. You obviously have to have communication skills. Laws, to my ear, would be the best radio performer in the world. He deserves the money.

As the son of an East End postman, do you think you'd have done as well had you stayed in London?

The odds were probably better by coming here. It goes back to the class structure, and the fact that there really is no restriction on your background here. It doesn't matter who you're the son of, what school you went to; everyone's an equal in a meritocracy. You're judged totally and absolutely on performance.

If you're a young unemployed kid in the Gorbals, what are you going to do? You go round and beat up old ladies and break telephone boxes. If you're an unemployed kid here, you pick up your surfboard, go up the north coast and lie on the beach for nine months. That may lose them the work ethic, but it's still not a bad lifestyle. So I think it's a more optimistic society, a happier society.

Australia will probably have another two or three tough years, but we'll get through. It'll still be – if you take the overall quality of life – probably the finest country in the world to live in. There's certain parts of the boondocks which aren't places where you might *choose* to live, but I'd defy anyone to say they couldn't live in Sydney. None of the other state capitals has this international flavour.

I've been back to London twice since we've been out. The last time we were staying with friends in South London, and driving to see my parents in North London I said, 'My God, it's like an Indian city – all these black faces surrounding us!'

I brought my parents out here and my dad was amazed: it was the first time he'd seen a *white* busdriver in twenty-five years ...

THE KANGAROO LADY:
IRIS ANDERSON B.E.M.

There's forty-nine pregnant, down there ...

There are few corners of the world where you cannot find some soft-hearted English lady, caring desperately for animals. At the very bottom left-hand corner of Western Australia, just outside Denmark, 250 miles south of Perth, Iris Anderson dedicates her life to the welfare of orphaned kangaroos.

Her kitchen is strung with old buttoned-up pullovers with knotted arms: from the top of each stares a wistful baby face, looking for its next bottle. In the garden of her modest bungalow are convalescent adolescents.

Iris Anderson was seven when she left Gravesend in Kent after the First World War; her grandfather had performed in Charlie Chaplin's London Mumming Birds troupe, and her mother was an actress. Fifty-one years ago she married Archie, who worked on the roads before he became a policeman. After the last war she started caring for orphaned and injured wild animals: joeys found in their dead mothers' pouches, injured by shooters or hit by cars; also emus, wombats and bandicoots, falcons, cockatoos and kookaburras. She developed an adoption system among local animal lovers who received cured patients for convalescence.

When Archie retired fourteen years ago, two Perth businessmen helped her establish the sanctuary at Ocean Beach, and the state spent $750 fencing her thirty acres; otherwise she receives no support and charges no entrance fee, but has thousands of visitors each year. For children her backyard is the ideal petting park, and her tame animals give much joy to the blind.

Australians have a love–hate relationship with their symbol. Kangaroos leap proudly across the skies on the tails of Qantas and Australian Airlines, a boxing kangaroo fought on their America's Cup flag ... yet they flatten and destroy crops so farmers clamour for mammoth culls of these graceful winsome animals, as vermin. Their skins make the adorably fluffy koala bears every tourist carries home, and hunters shoot them for sport or petfood – while Iris struggles to return her patients to the wild.

Though in her late seventies and besotted by animals, she is certainly no dotty old lady – she is practical and flirtatious, and only leaves her Ark to go to Weight-Watchers. She has never considered returning to Gravesend because their air fares could always be far better spent on her bush babies, and when she buys an electric foodmixer it's for them, not Archie.

'The Kangaroo Lady' has received the British Empire Medal for service in the preservation of fauna; she would *much* rather have had the money ...

Thirty-six years ago my son – he was a little chap – went out shooting, and one of his mates shot a mother roo. Chris was heart-broken because he found a baby in the pouch. Since then, up to '74, when we last counted, we've reared and found homes for 5088 joeys – and there's thirteen years onto that!

Kangaroos have character, but many people here regard them as vermin ...

154

The people who regard them as vermin ought to be shot. Well, they put them on aeroplanes and on coats of arms – and yet they allow all this shooting to go on for pet meat! All these here, their mothers have been killed for pet meat. I get a bit indignant about that.

They're in this fenced enclosure, yet most of them seem to be pregnant; how did that happen?

There's a big old one we call Casanova – he jumps that seven-foot-six fence! The first time he came they were all innocent little does, and they all ended up being pregnant. From then on, every few months, he hops over. Every new doe we get here fascinates him – I'm sure he keeps a watch, out there in the bush! When he sees a new one come in it's not long before they're pregnant. He comes from the bush and jumps that seven-foot-six fence, no problem at all. He rapes all my innocent little does – there's forty-nine pregnant down there.

The does are gentle, but the males can be quite aggressive?

Only if they're cornered, or if people tease them. This big Casanova, I wanted to get him out: I gave him his cake too soon, and went to get the chain and undo it. He pushed his big rump right against me, I couldn't go backwards – and then I made another mistake. I said, 'Move over Casanova', and just touched him light – but to a wild animal I shouldn't have done that. He stood right up on his hind legs, well over six feet tall, and I was worried about his feet – that's where the injury comes from.

They can rip open your stomach . . .

I didn't fancy that, so I went forward – and I slipped on the sand and fell against him! He just put his two hands up and made a terrible noise and frightened the *devil* out of me. Those hands could have done such a lot of damage – so I hit him round the face! Slapped him round the face as hard as I could. I said, '*Don't* you do that to me!' Anyhow, he just looked at me, took off, went round these two paddocks twice and jumped the seven-foot-six fence about a metre above it – and cleared off in the bush. You see – they're *not* savage.

Casanova's not going to hurt you because he knows he's on to a good thing here – you're providing his harem!

Trouble is, if you were here with some cakes or bread he'd take it so gentle, but if I was to walk towards him he moves backwards.

Because you slapped his face: kangaroos don't forget things like that!

They've got a little brain, but they remember kindness and they remember cruelty.

They have kangaroo shoots, don't they?

Yes, which is wrong. You can understand the farmers, it's their living, they get professionals in for that job. They don't waste bullets – they kill outright. It's the people that go out just for fun, go and shoot everything that moves.

What you're doing here is trying to make good other people's actions?

I'm not religious, but I think that if I'm looking after what's been created, well, I'm as good as anyone that goes to church a lot, ain't I?

Of course you are. You're bonkers about animals, Iris, but how do you feel about people?

I like people, but not so much as animals because an animal repays you – everything you do kind, they repay with love. People don't; they forget about it. They do, I find that.

You've never been tempted to go back to Gravesend to see what it's like?

I'd like to, but then I think of all that *money* for the fare. I could build more houses or something for the animals, because when a holiday's over you think, 'God, all that money's gone and I've got nothing for it.'

But you've got your BEM, anyway!

Yes, that was kind, but I'd rather have had powdered milk or something for the babies, because you put a medal in the drawer and forget about it, don't you?

You finance this shelter yourself, nobody gives you any money?

We've got a little donation box – we're not supposed to have, but I leave it there and some people put money in ... Well, the government don't help you. That's what makes me wild, they give grants for a lot of stupid things like, in today's paper, a female wine bar.

A lesbian wine bar!

I never thought of that – no, just a female wine bar. I haven't got a bad mind like you have! (*Laughs*) But what a stupid thing – my kangaroos could do more good. The blind people love to come down and touch and feel the animals. All the schools come here. Think of the goodness these animals do, compared to what a lot of people do ...

THE GAY: JEFF HARDY

Reminding people – but not pushing things down their throats ...

Most British girls I met in Australia confessed that one of the excitements of emigration was the prospect of meeting husky Australian men, bronzed and muscular, striding towards them across the beach, galloping into the homestead, or casually trapping a crocodile. Trouble was, when located, most available hunks tended to wink at their husbands ...

Because of this unmilitant tendency, and because the remaining men seem to marry earlier than Europeans, city women suffer a dearth of escorts and groups of pretty girls sit together in restaurants, being cheerful. Finding a man seems ever more difficult, for in this chase the quarry is rarely in sight.

The theory that Australian men are more interested in sport/booze/mates than in women has been around a long time, reinforcing the nation's macho, chauvinist image. What cannot be denied is that the gay outburst is now highly visible, in Sydney at least. A city where 'poofter' was once one of the dirtier words has become the gay capital of the southern hemisphere; its beauty, splendid climate, and easy-going acceptance of other people's ways has made it sister city to San Francisco.

In contrast, Queensland, under Premier Sir Joh Bjelke-Petersen, is stern with its homosexuals; anti-AIDS measures allow a barman to invoke some 'perverts law' and refuse to serve men he suspects of being gay – which must require nice judgement.

In non-judgemental Sydney I went to observe six thousand homosexuals attending the annual Sleaze Ball in the vast Entertainment Centre – a setting as cosy and intimate as an aircraft hangar. TV cameras were barred – except ours – and in turn the Press ignored the event.

Every permutation gays could devise for themselves passed the turnstiles, each apparition picking up, as part of the festivities, three condoms and some germicidal lubricating jelly – to be going on with. Burly six-foot bruisers with beards would have looked like wharfies – but for their blonde wigs, half-inch eyelashes, fishnet tights and stilettos. Slaves sidled by in chains, imitation nuns had moustaches and high heels, bare-bottomed sailors wore wimples. It was all a long way from Chips Rafferty. I could see they were nudging each other and whispering, 'Who's that freak in the grey suit?'

It is estimated some 50,000 of the 250,000 Sydney homosexuals carry the AIDS virus. At the time of the Ball more than 370 cases had already been diagnosed, and 200 had died; by 1990 they expect 3000 cases. This news did not appear to dampen the Ball's frantic Hieronymus Bosch excitement ...

Its 'visual coordinator' was Jeff Hardy, from Carshalton in Surrey. He'd worked on window display for Fortnum and Mason, and with a theatrical prop company. I wondered what made him decide to come out thirteen years ago at the age of twenty-four – not out of the closet, but out of Britain ...

The feeling that England was slowing down. In '74 I actually left thirteen-foot-high piles of garbage mouldering on the street corners. It seemed that the city was going, and I wanted something new.

You left a country where homosexuality was legal, and came to where it was illegal?

It wasn't a consideration, but it was difficult, or *could* have been difficult, for me because of my lifestyle.

Did you feel any sense of oppression here?

Oh, not oppressed at all. I came here and moved into a very salubrious inner harbour suburb, and it was paradise. I could walk down the garden and swim across to a beautiful cove behind a shark net – very valid if you've come out from England, to be protected from sharks! It was paradise on earth – until I started to look for work.

That was very, very difficult. In England eccentrics are accepted, but Australian eccentrics are mad and therefore quite suspect, so there was an English style which doesn't transcribe to this country. But human nature is human nature the world over, so you run into bigots everywhere and there are a great many, or were a great many, in Australia.

Things seem fairly unbigoted tonight?

It's grown. *This* would never have happened when I arrived in Australia. Parties happened, but this sort of situation is really quite new, and growing. This is the tenth birthday of Mardi Gras, and I've been here for twelve, so I've been part of this extravagance.

Nobody here seems inhibited by AIDS – I would have thought that might have cast some gloom upon the evening?

No, no, because with knowledge there's awareness. It's a fact of life.

I see they're issuing three condoms to everyone at the entrance ...

It's a matter of reminding people – but not *pushing* things down their throats. We live a serious life, I mean it's not all frivolity – this is one of the few occasions when Sydney can really let its hair down, and I think that's very important.

Yet there are said to be 50,000 people in Australia who already have the AIDS virus, and several hundred deaths ...

People are adjusting their lives. They're living a healthier life – maybe not tonight, but generally. It's a very serious matter for the whole world; there's no naivety about it any more, we have the information, we have the back-up teams, we have the support, and it's up to the individual. I think the individuals here are very responsible.

Do Australian gays face any hostility from those who say that AIDS is nature protecting herself, that it's a disease of choice?

Yeah, God's wrath – we've heard every cliché in the book! I can't feel guilty. I don't have it, though. It's the world disease – but what caused the black plague? Rats.

With AIDS, I suppose it's promiscuity?

It was a matter of the extraordinary freedom that stretched the world for gays several years ago. This is actually a very healthy reminder of some semblance of realism and human endeavour, how to use one's freedom. We talk about Australia being a few years behind, but I think with that new freedom – what can one say – they went over the top.

I don't see much restraint or inhibition tonight?

People come here because they want to let their hair down and have a good time, but that doesn't necessarily mean they won't have their conscience – well, conscience is a really odd word. They're aware of AIDS in our society, but it's not something that can subdue a whole nation, or a whole group ...

THE SEX EXPERT: PROFESSOR LLEWELLYN-JONES

Shoot a crocodile in the morning,
lay a couple of ladies in the afternoon . . .

Derek Llewellyn-Jones arrived in Australia in 1965 and is now Associate Professor of Obstetrics and Gynaecology at Sydney University. He is concerned by the lack of body knowledge of his teenage students: using a diagram, he found some unable to locate uterus or vagina. 'The myths are that they're promiscuous, but from what we can tell only 60 per cent of Australian teenagers have had sexual intercourse by the age of nineteen. The media say 40 per cent of the women will have a pregnancy by the time they're twenty. That's nonsense.'

After writing a lot about his subject, Professor Llewellyn-Jones is nationally regarded as a sex expert. He does not much care for the title – though since he's sixty-four and has one son aged thirty-seven and another, with his second wife, aged twenty-two *months*, it seems he may have been reading his own books . . .

If you're a male and write about women, people in Australia think you *must* be writing about sex. It sells books, yes, but I'd rather sell on other things than sex. I mean, *Everywoman* – the first of the books I wrote – had 28 pages about human sexuality out of 340, but that's what got the headlines: 'Gynaecologist says women need sex.' I didn't quite say that – but they *do*, so it was reasonably straightforward.

And in the papers today you're saying that the Victorians were sexier than we are?

As sexy. Comparisons are very difficult to make, but I have a lovely image of a Victorian family in Manchester going to chapel: the man, wearing his black coat and bowler hat, owns a cotton mill. Behind him his wife's rather large, because she's had fourteen children. Then the servants follow. They all go to chapel and then back to that enormous lunch people used to have – used to have in my young days, too, in North Wales – a loaded, groaning table. Then on Monday morning he goes off on't train to London – where there's one brothel to every sixty houses! I'm perfectly sure many of those people were publicly very moral but privately not a *bit*, and I don't think things have changed all that much.

How about morality in Australia today? I went to the Sydney Sleaze Ball the other night and watched six thousand homosexuals prancing around. They'd each been presented upon arrival with three condoms and some lubricating jelly to see them through the evening. Would you regard this as commendable restraint, or encouragement to promiscuity?

I think the gays have been very sensible since the impact of AIDS. They're promoting safe sex and saying, 'Reduce the number of partners.' The condom is to my mind one of the things which should come back – both for heterosexual *and* homosexual relationships. Although women in Western society don't have AIDS, women do get infected with the wart virus, which is a factor in cancer of the cervix – not a very nice disease – and it's certainly a factor in the spread of infections of the pelvis. Condoms prevent both of those, so I'm in favour of condoms. So, roll on condoms!

Gays are aware that condoms are available, and they use them – it's behavioural change people are looking for. I mean, we non-gays can go around saying, 'Isn't it awful, gays are getting AIDS, gays are promiscuous, gays have multiple partners', making the assumption that heterosexuals don't – which is not true.

Most gays, as far as I can tell, live in a quiet relationship with one person, not much talked about. I think heterosexuals putting this view that it's God's curse on homosexuality has been wrong, but it has also let gays look at their own behaviour and decide whether they want to change. To change you need some motive: well, one of the motives is, you don't have to stop sex if you use condoms!

I notice of the Australian AIDS deaths – some 290 up to now – only two were heterosexuals . . .

Yes, I think we followed America, and that's why I see this link between San Francisco and Sydney: the AIDS virus got into America from Africa via Haiti, affected the homosexual community mostly, a few drug addicts – and the homosexuals of San Francisco probably brought it over here. So it spreads and it's a worry and it's not going to go away. So we're back to safe sex – or no sex, if you want – but that's for those who like it that way and the best of luck to them, Australian and British!

Getting back to heterosexual activity, the battle of the sexes is sometimes seen as quite pronounced here in Australia; men and women have their definite places – at opposite ends of the room?

That's gone, thank God, though twenty years ago when I came here I really was horrified to find the men gathered round the keg, and the women at the other end of the room, presumably making lamingtons or pavlovas.

Sure, Australian men like sport, and who wouldn't like beaches – the beaches are there and they're great – but men I believe are sharing a lot of things with women. I've been preaching for years that men and women should do all the same things. I've moved away from that: I think women are better at certain things – mostly the things I don't like doing myself!

Such as?

Such as baby-minding! I've had a fortnight of *that*, and it was a salutary experience.

That'll teach you to write all those books!

That'll teach me ... But there has been a change for many men in Australia; the attitude of swilling beer and going home demanding dinner has gone. Men still go to the pub, but we don't have that awful six o'clock swill where you'd be reaching out for a drink and the bar, *choonk*, went down – you lost three fingers and half a litre of beer.

Everyone rushing to and from the bar carrying those terrible jugs...

Oh that's a sensible way of transporting beer to a table, you get that in the North of England, too.

Yes, but we don't drink out of them.

(*Laughs*) No, you don't.

One does notice that the youngsters here are much less sophisticated, less mature and I suspect rather more wholesome than their American and British counterparts...

They are less mature, age for age, than the Americans – and certainly less articulate. It always amazes me when I go the United States, the great ability of most young Americans to *talk*. In England it's regional: the Welsh talk a lot, the Londoners do. I wonder about the North of England where I worked, where there was the same lack of articulation. It's interesting why Australians aren't articulate, given the Irish background. The Australians say you can't talk much because you've got to keep your mouth closed or the flies get in – but I think that's also a myth.

Each new wave of immigrants must bring its own sexual standards and taboos here, so we're in this mélange; is there such a thing today as Australian morality?

Not in the sense that you could identify the sort of Paul Hogan sexual morality as Australian morality – you know, shoot a crocodile in the morning and lay a couple of ladies in the afternoon. I don't think that exists. There's an Australian morality, but there *is* no normal sexual behaviour because people's sexual behaviours vary from group to group, particularly ethnic groups.

So are you going to be put out of business if there are thousands of Asian ladies arriving who have other attitudes towards gynaecology?

I don't think so for a minute; I think the attitude of the ex-Vietnamese, the ex-South-east Asians, is very similar to the attitudes and behaviour of the Australians – in fact it's quite remarkable. In the second generation there *are* problems: the parents come out and expect their children to accept and adopt their sexual behaviours, but the kids are influenced by other ethnic groups and by Australians – and there conflicts arise, particularly in teenage life.

We did a survey of medical students as an exercise at the beginning of a teaching session, asked them various milestones, simple things like, 'What age were you when you first saw your mother naked?' Going on to: 'At what age did you have sexual intercourse?' Medical students are much later at having first sexual intercourse, and fewer of them have sexual intercourse than people going for arts degrees and particularly people who don't get tertiary education. It's been consistent over a number of years, so there *is* a class difference. A good academic would say they're too busy studying the books, but that's a load of rubbish.

When I came here twenty years ago people talked about, 'going home' – and they meant going back to England. Nowadays people talk about going to England. Gough Whitlam's time as Prime Minister, that period really was the Australian Camelot, if you can say that Kennedy's was the American Camelot. They both ended disastrously, but that brought a big change to people's feelings about Australia.

The older people still feel a great affinity to England, but so do I. Britain was where I was born and brought up, but I now consider myself Australian. What I don't like is this rampant nasty nationalism portrayed in advertisements on Australian television, 'Now we'll beat them!' I think it's dreadful, it's not competitive, it's whipping up the worst side – and yet it sells products. We're going to beat them, of course, whoever they are – but we can do it subtly . . .

THE PRAWNER: BILL MOULL

*Sometimes we dump four tons of fresh fish
over the side...*

As an engineer, Bill Moull worked in Ford's prototype shop at Rainham, Essex. Today he's prawning in the Coral Sea.

The housing situation seemed unpromising for young couples in 1966, so he and his wife Julie became £10 Poms and headed for Melbourne, where he joined International Harvester. After a few years he realized that, despite such an upheaval, he was just doing the same job in a better climate. So they bought a caravan and set off to work their way around Australia; eventually he became a deck hand on a prawn trawler in the Gulf of Carpentaria. After fifteen years trawling he now has his own $150,000 boat, which he skippers one run out of three.

To find him, I set out one night from Port Douglas in a catamaran, heading into the dark sea towards the Great Barrier Reef. After an hour or two, somewhere around Low Island, we spotted the dazzling deck light of Bill's trawler. I scrambled aboard and passed a magical night as shoals of radiant fish were lifted from the sea to tumble in brilliance from the nets and spread in a convulsive iridescent mass across deck trays.

To me this cornucopia looked even more attractive

than those expensive displays in the best fish markets – but to Bill they were mainly trash fish. He was looking for prawns, for the Japanese. What didn't go over the side was instantly sorted, graded and frozen.

Most enchanting of all were our escorting dolphins: half a dozen of them swooping through the waves to collect discarded fish, playing joyfully in the swirling sea. I was amazed to see that, uninstructed, they even walked across the water on their tails – as in the best credit card commercials.

When I left Essex I never dreamed I'd be in fishing. In those days it was an adventure, because we didn't have a home and we had nothing to sell up. We'd just got married, and the housing situation was pretty bad for young couples. Only cost us £10 to come out here, and we thought we could stay for three years – then you're allowed to go back without paying your fare. It was part an adventure, part a holiday and part an exploration. I came out as an engineer and worked for International Harvesters in Melbourne.

So what made you change to fishing, where you can be at sea for twenty days at a time?

I've been away for three *months* at a time! I think in some ways it helps your marriage – a break sometimes does you good.

We left Melbourne looking for we didn't know *what*, just to work for ourselves, something different. We looked at the tourist industry, caravan parks and that sort of thing. I was working as a toolmaker in various places along the way, to build up our capital. We got as far as Karumba on the Gulf of Carpentaria and the only work there was on prawn trawlers, so I said, 'We'll give that a go for a month or so to get a few bob' – and I've been with it ever since.

This is your own trawler, which must have cost you a few quid?

This is $150,000, to value it now. We've got to earn $1000 a night gross to make things work pretty well; that pays the deckhand, the fuel, the upkeep on the boat, and profit on your investment. To earn $500 a night we're virtually going backwards, because we're using about seven gallons of fuel an hour and we're paying $7000 a year insurance, so there's a lot of expenditure. Prawning is a big income on one hand and a big expense on the other, so it sounds good money – but you don't hang on to much.

The fact that you're still doing it suggests you're ahead of the game?

Well, we own the boat – the poor chaps still paying for them are having a struggle. The Australian dollar's been devalued so much we're getting a really good price for export prawns, and that's given us a lift, and fuel is less than two-thirds the cost of what it was last year.

There are Taiwanese and Korean prawning boats around – do you have prawn wars the way there used to be cod wars?

We did years ago, in the Gulf; there were a few shots fired in anger, but now we're all very restricted. None's allowed within the twelve-mile limit. There's a few poachers come in for clams on the reef, but we don't have any trouble with foreign trawlers. The only problem would be outside the Great Barrier Reef where they're fishing for tuna, shark, that sort of thing.

I thought a prawner would be more basic than this, but you've got a lot of sophisticated equipment?

You've got to keep improving every year, or you get left behind. There's getting to be less prawns and more nets flashing around trying to catch them, so if you don't improve your boat you're not in the race. That's a tele-radar; near enough all the electronics on the boat is Japanese: very little English gear, unfortunately. See the fish going through underneath us?

Where they're in shoals, you could see a complete blob of prawns. When I used to work in the Gulf some shoals of banana prawns, the day-time prawns, would get up to 16,000 pounds weight – two or three hours trawling.

Sometimes we dump maybe four ton of fresh fish over the side – that's trash fish, up here in the north. We'll get a lot of trash fish tonight, because the moon is bright. We're very wasteful, we don't save much at all. It just goes back over the side to feed the sharks. Small silver dollar fish, small whiting, what we call banana fish. If you're down in Melbourne a vast quantity could be sold, but there's no market for it up here.

You rarely get anything in the net above about ten inches long, except for sharks. Sometimes you get big turtles, at other times you get ball rays big enough to cover the whole tray and very hard to get off the boat.

If you're out here for three weeks – or indeed three months – are you eating some of the catch?

No, not much fish at all. After you've been knee-deep in it all night, you quite welcome the egg and bacon in the morning! We've got a full-size stove there and we'd eat exactly the same as you'd eat in port: we'd have roast beef or T-bone steaks, we'd have a bit of ice cream, we've got the lot – hot and cold showers. We don't rough it any more.

Quite like the QE2! So the sharks are a worry – any other hazards out here?

In the sorting the catfish are the worst: you're quite likely to get a spike on one of those, and they're *very* painful. You might get one every couple of nights. If you get something called a stone fish, they're deadly and you can die from the spike of that, but they're rare – you might only see one once a trip, and you'd be very unlucky to get a spike.

I lost my finger in the early days when I was working on another boat, got sucked into a turbocharger on a Rolls-Royce diesel. I was off work for a couple of months. I claimed compensation from the insurance company, who said there was a law dating back from the 1800s stating it was only up to £100. So I said, 'That's fair enough – if you're going to revert to those laws, I'll have it in gold sovereigns!' Didn't do me any good.

It *is* a dangerous occupation if you don't watch what you're doing. Those wires, if they snap, could do a lot of bodily harm. Also if we get a tangle-up you've got to go out on the end of the boom and untangle them. In rough weather it's quite bad.

The fish in the nets attract the sharks, which bite holes in them, and we're stuck with a lot of net mending through the day. There is a market for sharks, but you've got to be properly equipped: you've got to cure them and bleed them because they're high in mercury content. They're a damned nuisance to us, anyway. Sometimes you could nearly *walk* on them at the back of the boat, they're that thick when you're pushing the flat fish down and they're fighting each other. You make sure you're holding on pretty well when it's rough weather. I've only ever lost one deck-hand over the side – and he got back on the boat pretty quick...

THE MINISTER: JOHN AKISTER

*One ex-Cabinet Minister is up before the Courts
at the moment...*

John Akister's life had a most unpromising start: an illegitimate child, he was abandoned in a Lake District workhouse, brought up in an orphanage – and did not meet his mother until he was forty-three. In the best Dickensian tradition, he became the Hon. John Akister, a Cabinet Minister in the New South Wales government.

He is responsible for Corrective Services, so we met in Sydney's Long Bay complex of jails, where fifteen hundred hard cases are guarded by nine hundred warders. Under blue skies there was a relaxed, almost holiday atmosphere in the jail yard; convicts lazed around in the sunshine, or played some gentle football. None of the warders was armed, and lone women officials passed among the massed 'crims' – indeed Long Bay has a woman Governor.

'The toughest criminals in the world,' said the Minister in his hesitant Cumbrian accent, as we strolled among them. They did not appear threatening – indeed the only one who paid him any attention was a garrulous old convict, overjoyed at the chance to take his whinge to the very top. The others ignored us and got on with their games.

John Akister is now fifty, with two daughters; he

emigrated to Australia in 1963 and entered State Parliament as a member for the country seat of Monaro in 1976. In 1984 this mild-mannered man was handed the State's political hot potato: running the prisons is regarded as a no-win job – and indeed his predecessor was awaiting trial in jail. As the Minister told me, 'There's a different attitude to crime in Australia...'

Minister, yours is the quintessential rags-to-riches success story: from orphan in a workhouse to Cabinet Minister...

The two things I inherited from my mother were reinforced by the type of life I've had: a capacity for hard work, for long hours, and determination.

You were in the Army, you play rugger, you sing – so you do have the qualifications for a success in Australia!

Yes, but to bring a piece of Old England and try to graft it on to the Australian situation isn't possible, not successfully.

You didn't meet your mother until you were forty-three. Were you not concerned about trying to find her before that?

A lady walked into the Parliament and saw my photograph in the foyer, because mine's the first one, with an 'A'. Her maiden name had been Akister, and because there are few Akisters in this world she thought we might be related; she came from the same district, North Lancashire, the Lake District area. I told her I was an orphan, didn't know my family at all, and she said that she'd make some enquiries among her relatives.

I came home from Parliament one night and the phone rang and a voice said in a very thick Lancashire accent, 'Hello John, do you know who this is?' I said no, thinking it was a constituent who wanted something, and being a bit defensive at that time of the night. Then she said she was my mother! I was quite surprised.

Where the hell have you been for forty years?

No, no, no, I'd never felt that I should lay any blame on my mother. What happened was consequential to the decision she made that she couldn't look after me. She didn't condemn me to that life. I've never, never felt any affection for my mother, never had any feeling that I wanted to know her – but also didn't feel any antagonism.

The story is something out of Dickens, or Boys Own Paper...

It really is Dickensian; when I describe conditions in that orphanage, my colleagues think I'm describing something that happened a hundred years ago.

I left the orphanage at fifteen, did an apprenticeship as an electrical fitter, and at twenty-one went into the Army. I was sent out to Hong Kong with the Lancashire Regiment on a troopship in which we were burnt black by sunshine every day. For twelve months in Hong Kong, even in the typhoon season, the sun shone; then this wonderful trip of eight weeks back to England, again sunbathing all the way. When I got back it was probably the worst winter on record! In Manchester I don't think the sun broke through for six months – and I'd become like a drug addict for sunshine.

The choices were really between South Africa and Australia. Macmillan's speech about the winds of change had gained wide circulation by that time; I thought South Africa didn't have much of a future so I chose Australia because it had a reputation for good sunshine.

I went to have a look at what I'd come to, set off with a pack, slept out every night beside the road, in paddocks, got work with councils, as a shearing-shed hand, a docker, cane cutter, farmhand, anything I could find. I worked my way right around the rim of Australia, up and down the centre, and had a good look at the place.

In the United States every boy's told he can become President one day but, by golly, it takes a lot of money and influence to get him there! You're not exactly President, but I doubt if you'd be a Minister in England now...

I doubt it as well. When I came to Australia I moved up in work experience to a level which if I'd stayed in England I would have been precluded from doing, simply because I didn't have *paper* qualifications. I finished up as the senior draughtsman on the Snowy Mountain Scheme, a huge scheme involving twenty-five years' work, and I was in charge of every electrical drawing on the scheme.

Are you saying that things are easier here, standards are lower – or that there isn't the competition?

I'd say standards are higher. If you can demonstrate you can do the job, that, in many cases, is sufficient for you to *get* the job. The necessity to have been to a certain school, to have reached a certain educational level and so forth, is not so urgent as it would be in Britain.

Today you've got a job politicians see as a hot potato; to take over all the jails in New South Wales means you drew the short straw?

Yes, very much so. It's not a popular job – nobody wants Corrective Services, but it's vital to government because you're influencing hundreds of thousands of people's lives every year. If you get it wrong, then you're imposing on society a huge burden by way of added crime and violence.

The discipline here seems totally different to England: convicts come up and take you by the collar and ask you questions in the exercise yard – I doubt whether that would happen to the Home Secretary in England . . .

It's a quite different culture, here in New South Wales. Because we were founded as a penal colony, a very strong streak of larrikinism runs throughout our society at all levels. That means an anti-Establishment, anti-authoritarian attitude. To try and impose a very strict discipline code on Australians would be counter-productive – you'd have to run this place like a concentration camp and do nothing but force people to salute you and stand to attention and call you 'Sir'. The result would be that you'd never have time for work experience, education experiences, social skills training – in other words there'd be no chance of rehabilitation. The inevitable consequences of a regime *that* tough in jails would be that we'd turn our prisoners into worse criminals than when they came in, and more inclined to violence. We *had* that system here for about 170 years and it didn't work – so we've changed it.

Does that mean this is a soft jail? Certainly these seem the least cowed prisoners I've ever seen in my life.

It's a very tough jail, very strict regime, but personal discipline – as long as it's not abuse to officers, it's not aggression – is a matter for the individual prisoner. We don't insist on heels together, straight shoulders, call everybody 'Sir'. In New South Wales, because we have Sydney, which is the biggest city, we have the toughest criminals and our judges are tougher than any other set of judges in the world. We get longer sentences for the same crimes here in New South Wales than you do anywhere else. It's a tough system here.

Is there any stigma attached to being in jail, is it something you try to hide?

It certainly is with a considerable proportion of the population, but among the majority of Australians you're taken as an individual; if you've done time, that's seen to have been a punishment which you've got behind you, and people will take you at your face value. They don't condemn you forever.

They think fair-do's, do they? Certainly the sight of all these young women wandering around inside the prison yard is quite unexpected.

We've done that quite deliberately. These jails used to be exclusively male, and we found that by introduction of female prison officers and an additional number of nurses, educationalists, welfare officers, they've modified the behaviour, not only of the prisoners, but of the officers as well. Like any army camp, if you put a lot of males together in a confined area you tend to move *down* – your language, your behaviour, your expectations drop down to the lowest common denominator. If you add a leavening of women into the system, then expectations rise. They seek, not favours, but rather to rise in the esteem of people who're of good character, or worthwhile citizens. It has a tremendous modifying effect on the behaviour and the character of the jails, having women introduced into them.

What's more, you have a woman Governor!

Yes, and we've got 1500 people in this complex of jails with about 900 warders to look after them. They're in for every conceivable type of crime: drug peddling, murder, rape, child molestation, arson, fraud, forgery ... Anything you can think of, somebody in here will

176

have *done* it! This is a maximum security jail for very tough prisoners who refuse to go along with the system.

The warders keep a low profile – they're unarmed.

You don't arm warders inside the jail because if they were rushed and the weapon was taken away from them, it would cause a greater problem.

Yet they certainly do in America – they have shotguns at every door!

But they don't go in for rehabilitation. We have a responsibility to the community for what we do in these jails; the old concept of jails inevitably resulted in prisoners being led a draconian life, a strict discipline package, punishments which were often unwarranted and excessive for the infringement that may have occurred, and a level of control by the hardest criminals which operated below the level of control by the officers. The inevitable result was that most prisoners leaving jail were worse criminals than when they came in; they'd learned more skills and were more inclined to violence. The jails were colleges of advanced education in criminality and violence. That's a huge penalty to impose upon the community, as we release 11,000 prisoners a year.

It's still us-and-them in Australia is it?

Yes, it is.

So you've joined them?

Yes, I would have done . . .

Does that help you, politically?

Politics in Australia is quite different to Britain. We're a lot closer to the day-to-day workings of our constituents. Again, they take you at face value. There is a collective view of politicians – which is about twenty places *below* prison officers!

People hate policemen, so I assume they also hate prison warders?

The prisoners do, but the people outside don't hate them – they just think it's not a very attractive job, and not very attractive people would *do* that job.

Your ex-Sergeant-Major from the Black Watch, his sense of discipline would be rather different from your Australian NCO?

Yes, it would be.

So he's not going to be very popular here?

Initially I would imagine he has problems, because the British system is really a system of *discipline*, whereas the Australian system is that you are responsible for your own behaviour and attitudes. In Britain somebody unknown at the top of the pile determines your attitudes and what your behaviour will be, and as long as you comply with *that*, you get by. Here you're expected to show more self-control, more responsibility.

Politics in New South Wales don't seem quite as they should be; one is always hearing about corruption – even in the judiciary here, the Federal judiciary as well . . . That's unthinkable!

I don't think *anything's* unthinkable in any society, but we hear from time to time of the class of giants and demi-gods, as it were, who have been caught with their fingers in the till. In Australia, we *do* have a very heavy criminal scene, internationally as well as nationally.

But among politicians, among judges?

There *is* one ex-Cabinet Minister up before the courts at the moment, and that's not decided yet. Among judges, there's been allegations made and indeed one chief magistrate served time in this jail. It's a real problem, but there's a different attitude to crime in Australia than there would be in Britain. People are not condemned so readily for committing crimes, there's a level of criminal activity which is tolerated: things like SP booking, gambling generally, the traffic laws are not adhered to as readily, a whole strata of activities occur which a community goes along with and does not condemn.

It seems more South American than Anglo-Saxon . . .

Yes, I'm sure it's something to do with the climate – people *change* because of the climate.

The whole legal system is undergoing a bit of an upheaval at the moment?

There are two major facets of our life here in Australia which don't meet the requirements of a democracy, in that people who

178

have responsibility for welfare, the care, the making of good citizens, are unaccountable either individually or as a group. *Our* actions are examinable because they're exposed to public opinion, but the Law is not accountable. It trundles on, on its own merit. Neither the individual judge nor the judges, the legal profession as a whole, is accountable to anybody for what it does, and the most bizarre anomalies, in my view, have emerged in our system: we have a legal system, but it's not a system of justice. With democracy, those who can make and break and destroy people should be accountable.

Corruption seems to be accepted; there's a fair amount among the police, which nobody seems to worry too much about: they think, 'Good on him, he got away with it.' The morality's very different here.

It is – certainly for the successful crim who's never caught. There's a grudging admiration for them. That's because in our earlier days certain characters who were definitely anti-Establishment, definitely anti-authoritarian, people like Ned Kelly – a vicious murderer and a dreadful character really moved into our mythology as defenders of the rights of the ordinary man.

I don't detect corruption in everyday politics, what I do detect is a lack of willingness to set in place the mechanisms which put the frighteners on the crooks, which will catch the big crooks. We catch street crooks in the main and put them into these jails. The very big fellows, the crooked bank managers, lawyers, accountants, stock exchange agents and so forth, we don't catch those.

Politicians ... judges?

Politicians and judges, because it's estimated in Australia, for instance, there's $280 million worth of illegal money floating within our system. To have that sort of money, to finance it, you've got to be a very big businessman, you've got to have access to lawyers, to bankers, to agents, to the Stock Exchange and so forth. We never catch those people – yet they presumably are on the boards of companies, they're Government advisers, they're bankers, and they're representatives of the community. We seem somewhat reluctant to tackle these people ...

THE GRADUATE BUNNY: SALLY HURLEY

Not until I've tried the goods ...

Sally Hurley is the wife of the Director of the new Hotel Casino in Townsville. She would *hate* that description – for this attractive ex-Bunny croupier from the London Playboy Club has stopped regarding herself as 'an executive wife'. She left Ron Hurley and then returned to him – 'on my own terms' – and is now studying psychology at the James Cook University.

She and Ron – then Assistant Casino Manager at the London Playboy – had to marry fast before they came out in 1971 with sixteen other gambling families to open Australia's first casino, in Hobart. Gambling was hard enough for Tasmania to digest – let alone casino managers living in *sin*. Ron went on to establish casinos in Alice Springs, Darwin and Launceston before opening northern Queensland's first five-star hotel and casino in 1986.

Townsville and Sally are both at the crossroads: this rather plain town, where the most interesting building is a television station in a restored terrace, does not have the ramshackle charm of Cairns nor the rainforest of the state's far north, but still waits hopefully for the tourist millions to descend from Japan and America and kiss it into life. The Casino, a brutal but luxurious block on the new and deserted harbour, is seen as a symbol of good times to come.

Sally has moved house so often in the past sixteen years that she never buys a pot plant; now a 'woman in her own right', she works for a degree in psychology and also waits for life to change, somehow ...

Sally, you were a Bunny who ran off and married her pit boss?

I didn't actually run off, I was told to leave when they found out about our relationship! They said I could work permanent nights and he could work permanent days – which is one way of breaking you up. Because of casino security, we weren't supposed to be together: we were working with so much money all the time they thought we could perhaps have a little liaison and I'd slip a few pounds over the table to a friend – and Ron, who would have been watching me, would've shut his eyes. I used to have to do all sorts of strange things, like walk a mile up the road in the middle of the West End at 4 o'clock in the morning – so he could pick me up to drive home. A friend and I actually went down to the Hilton one night and were pushed-off by another couple of ladies who thought we were trying to take their pitch – so *that* wasn't terrific.

Some girls working in that Bunny club made a fortune from the various spin-offs available?

Umm, yes, yes they did – but it's the same in any business: you meet a rich man, whether he's an Arab or a businessman, and you go out with him and there are spin-offs. I mean, they were all beautiful-looking girls. Actually the best piece of advice passed around the place was: don't ever sleep with an Arab, because when you sleep with him he stops giving you all the money and the gifts. So the really smart ones were never actually naughty girls. But it was fun, it was a beautiful time, it was almost like my university. I was fairly naive, very young – but after working there for two years you could *smell* the phoney coming through the door. It just taught you so much about people.

If it was so good, why give it all away and come to Australia?

Ron was offered the position of opening the first casino in Australia, so we got on the immigration trail and came out.

You merely had an understanding then, but Tasmania insisted you were married?

Yes, Tasmania wasn't ready for a casino *and* a casino manager and his lady living in sin, so we were forced to get married along with quite a few other people who came out. It was beautiful – we all went to each other's weddings and there were cries of 'legalized nookie'! We all came out *en masse* – about sixteen families.

Anyhow, it was a very romantic occasion?

There was no romance at all. I didn't really know what was going on, but we were sitting in the movies one day and just before the film started, Ron said, 'We have to get married!' I got all fluttery and excited and sort of melted, and he said, 'Shut up and watch the movie.'

Ron's divorce was very rushed; we had a Tasmanian legal giant come over and push it through. We didn't have a decree nisi, there was no three months wait, he just stood up in court and said, 'Mr Hurley is required desperately by the Australian government,' which in a way was true. 'He has to leave soon and he *has* to be married,' and they said, 'Yes, yes'. We went right out in the sticks somewhere in Surrey and the little judge was quite befuddled by it all and just granted the divorce there and then.

So that was followed by a sort of shotgun marriage?

A big financial shotgun, yes. When we actually arrived in Melbourne it was suicide time. There was a great antagonism between Melbourne and Tasmania: Melbourne was a little jealous because Tasmania got the first casino in Australia and anyone who's jealous denigrates. They told us not to go because they were going to cut the chain and Tasmania would float away into the distance.

I expected the people here, because they're white and they speak English, to be the same as us – and got quite a shock: they think differently. It's something you don't understand. All you knew in England in those days was that they were tall, bronzed athletic people and had long beaches and they canned peaches. I expected walking down the High Street to see horses tied up at posts by the side of the pubs.

You assumed they were basically English at heart, but they're much more open than we are, incredibly friendly, they take you on first meeting as a buddy – which, being English, is quite frightening. To go to someone's home in England you have to be invited at a certain time on a certain day, but over here they'll say, 'Come and have a barbie sometime.' You don't take them up on it, you have to be formal, so we found we were very lonely at first because we were the top of the casino tree and it's difficult to mix with your staff on a social level confidently; causes a few problems. In our loneliness we arrived at someone's doorstep on a Sunday, and we expected them to open the door and say, 'Oh sorry, we're busy' or, 'We have to go somewhere.' There's nothing worse than being socially put-down. The door was opened – and it was like we were life-long buddies! We've been friends with these particular people ever since. The beer and the chops and the sausages came out, and we were just stunned. Very, very different culture.

And how about the tall bronzed surfers?

Don't be silly! When we hit Melbourne I'd never met so many gay people in my life. This isn't a denigration of them, but the sheer numbers just overwhelmed me. Sydney now is a gay paradise – so that goes against our initial idea of what Australia was about.

So how did the people of Tasmania react to escapees from Playboy bringing sin into their serene lives?

They thought it was great. We had a few problems originally in that the big fish in that small pond were a little worried about us taking over, but then they understood and capitalized on the industry and excitement that we brought.

How long before you found your feet, before you felt accepted?

Probably two years. There is a policy in the Immigration Act – I don't know if it's still there – that if you don't stay for the full two years you have to pay your original fare over, and that's a very very good timing figure, we found. We stopped whingeing after two years.

We didn't whinge as much as the others, which really is just saying something is different, but they took it as a criticism because they're a nation – or were a nation – in its adolescence. They've grown since then and become very egocentric: now if something isn't Australian, it's no good. Before it was: 'If it's Australian it *can't* be very good.' They assumed all sorts of things about us that weren't correct – most of all our superiority. Fortunately they've grown up and understood what a terrific country they've got.

It seems to be accepted in this unusually insular society today that you should be incurious, uninteresting and non-foreign – so you lost on all three counts?

Yes, but we were bringing something to them, we were helping them grow, we weren't coming in and *using* them, which they felt a lot of English people did. They viewed English people as escaping, looking for something better – and just denigrating what they found. We were helping them grow, and they liked and appreciated that.

So Sally, although it was a far cry from Park Lane you were happy in Tasmania – yet you eventually left your husband and your marriage broke up?

Yes, it was a difficult time because for twelve or thirteen years I was what's classified as an executive wife: you're working, yet you get no kudos. In fact it's often the other way round: people look at you wining and dining guests who sometimes are *so* boring it's unbelievable – but that's your job: you are the appendage of the manager and there to be gracious and charming and witty. I found I lost my own identity amongst it all. It was a very difficult time for me.

So leaving behind your husband, you moved on to become a woman 'in your own right'?

Yes, which was fantastic.

A real person?

It was great: a voyage of self-discovery which was incredible.

And now you feel realer?

184

Yes.

Yet you've gone back to your husband?

Yes, well ... love calls, doesn't it? I mean we all go through these traumas and if you're going through a trauma of identification you often tend to push away what you thought was the cause. Maybe that was it.

He's now running this casino and hotel, which is a major force in north Queensland, and you've gone back to him under the same sort of arrangement?

No, not under the same arrangement at *all*. On my own terms. In fact the other day one of the executives of the company said, 'Where's your wife?' and he said, 'She's at home studying,' and felt quite proud to say she's *not* an executive wife. I mean, if a man needs a woman to boost him, then he shouldn't be there anyway; if he can survive on his own in those sorts of areas, more credit to him.

You're at the James Cook University, studying?

Psychology and education, at the moment. It's great – I'm discovering things that I knew I knew, but couldn't have put them in words if you'd asked me! It's just fantastic, a voyage of self-discovery. I got a pass on my essay on educational psychological theories.

You have to do a lot of reading?

Yes, but I could go into the library now and stay there for a week and not come out.

In the future, what do you want to be? A solitary psychiatrist?

No, I don't want to be solitary. I'd like to do psychology, if I'm good enough. I might like to bring it into the clinical area and be, as you say, a solitary psychiatrist.

I'm looking now for a degree in psychology, which is going to take me four years. For the first time I'll be able to phone up and say, 'Here I am', and not have to bluff my way into things. If you've got the aptitude but you haven't got the paper qualifications behind you, you always go in bluffing. But it'll be, 'Here I am' on the merits that somebody else has awarded me!

How do you explain bluffing?

Knowing absolutely nothing about it but working very hard. If you've got that assurance you just walk in and everybody thinks you know what you're doing, and you've got no bloody idea. You look confident and get away with it.

So Australia's taken you from Playboy Bunny to would-be psychiatrist?

Not bad, is it! But then to have been a Playboy Bunny croupier was probably well on the way to *being* a good psychiatrist, anyway. It's a people business and if you have an affinity with people you home in on their brains, you feel the vibrations, and if you can understand them you become successful in that field.

At least people are no longer looking at your fluffy tail?

No – I used to drop that down the toilet . . .

After London and then fourteen years in Tasmania, how do you find the Queenslanders – a lot of Australians seem to regard Townsville as a hick town?

I wouldn't use the word! I'd say it's a contented country town, but on the edge of a very large explosion. The Americans and the Japanese are very tired of Europe, they're absolutely terrified of Gaddafi – so the Middle East as a tourist destination is dead. They want vast open spaces – especially the Americans who're always looking for something new, and the Japanese who're always looking for someone to photograph. So Australia as a tourist destination is really going to take off.

Is it a good place to bring up your daughter?

Yes, I feel a little safer in Tasmania. I'd love her to be an Australian woman – but I don't think I want her to marry an Australian man!

You were no stranger to Australian men and Australian manners when you arrived here as a separated woman and first went out on your own?

I don't know if I quite like the way you put that! Yes, I did arrive in Townsville alone as a single female, and found it very very difficult – probably because I'm what they call a Southerner, and considered fair game. I had a few fairly nasty experiences before I understood what was going on.

In the very first nightclub I went to I was introduced to a gentleman by a very dear friend, so I assumed that the gentleman was a gentleman. We were having a chat, and he said he was a pathologist, so I laughed and said, 'I know how much money you make, would you marry me?' He took a few steps backwards, looked at me and said, 'Not until I've tried the goods.' Then he went tweak-tweak on my breasts and said, 'You haven't had a mastectomy, OK, you'll do.'

I was just totally stunned. He was too big for me, and I didn't think my right hook would be enough for him, so I walked away. He came up later and said, 'Have I offended you?' I said, 'Yes, mortally', and he said, 'I don't understand, can we start again?' I said, 'No.'

It was a funny joke and I was supposed to laugh and think he was a terrific guy, but I just couldn't cope with it. If I went up and did a reciprocal action and asked if he'd had his testicles off, I don't know how he'd have felt about that!

But a woman doesn't *do* things like that. You're expected to be feminine and modest, but at the same time you're expected to drop your femininity and your modesty when they start an action like that against you.

So how do women cope here?

With great difficulty! They either go down to the standards that are there – which sounds very unkind but I think it's true; they marry early, or they form very safe little feminine groups which are self-defeating because in the end they become very insular. The men haven't got the courage or confidence to approach these groups. The women depend upon each other, but they don't ultimately find what they're looking for because the men aren't allowed in – or don't *want* to come in. Men won't penetrate that sort of thing; they haven't got confidence in themselves.

Sounds as though your pathologist was fairly confident?

Yes, but he was on his own for the rest of the night!

So the women are in self-protective groups and the men are in the pub?

187

Yes, one big mateship. The drinking mateship originated, if we are to believe the sociologists, from the early days when the very few women here were all married. There were no prostitutes. Standards for women were very high, as they were in limited supply, so to sublimate their sexual desires the men would meet in the pub and have a warm feeling of comradeship. They'd start yahooing – which you still see them doing – and they'd release all that sexual energy. It was in fact not macho to actually *talk* about women or sex.

This is obviously still going: there's no romanticism, nothing between wanting a lady and *getting* her. They're ashamed in that build up of showing feelings towards the lady, and that's very difficult to overcome when you've been used to a comradeship with your men.

We're generalizing, so it's not fair, but I don't find them attractive because they don't care particularly what sort of image they're putting across to you. They don't worry too much about how they dress and how they appear. We have a little instance here at the Townsville races today, where we have a very beautiful lady – I think you've seen her – in the red dress?

That skin-tight red leather! In this temperature she's suffering for her art . . .

She looks superb and she probably took a lot of hours and a lot of money to get dressed up like that. Her gentleman's got a Popeye shirt on – a little cotton shirt with Popeye and Olive Oyl on the back. It's not on.

I notice the men are usually dressed in a relaxed way while the women have made an enormous effort: they're wearing hats and they've bought all sorts of things – some of them through mail order, no doubt – but they have made an effort. The men make no effort at all.

Because the lady's a possession. The men will probably pay for her to look good, but it's patriarchal. He's the dominant one, it doesn't matter what he looks like, he's the prize catch anyway because he's a male. This sounds terrible, but it's so true it's ridiculous.

I love the Australian females – they have a pride in themselves, they're joyful, they're open and I think in ten to twenty years' time you are going to hear a lot more about them, but up until now they've been put in their little boxes, they've been told, 'The only thing you can expect from your lives is to marry this big handsome wonderful brute.' Therefore there's no reason for them to *expect* to be wooed. They do the wooing, most of the time.

How did you find life here, as a suddenly unprotected lady on the prowl, after being married?

Dangerous, actually. There are certain areas where you don't go: you don't go at night along the Strand. Townsville's become a very transient place because you've got the weather and you've got the dole that's easily obtainable. You get a lot of people who'd rather be on the dole in the sunshine than in the cold, which is unfortunate because Townsville people are just fantastic.

I've been used to being treated as a lady and there are situations where I assumed I would be safe. I went out one night, got into the car – and a gentleman flung himself inside and said 'If you scream I'll kill you!' Up until then I hadn't *thought* about screaming at all because the mind was just a blank, but it was a terrific idea. By the time I'd got back into the hotel I was screaming like billy-o!

I sat down and they gave me a cup of coffee, and one of the little doormen came up and said, 'Sally, if I was you I'd be *very* proud of your scream!'

The police came but they weren't particularly interested. An elderly woman was raped two streets away about two weeks afterwards, and no one ever came to ask me if I would verify a description or anything like that – just not interested. You're fair game, and that's the end of it.

It's just, 'If you don't do as I want, then I'll *make* you.' It comes very much from the macho image – 'How dare you turn me down, because I'm the greatest ...'

THE HISTORY MAN: ROGER SMITH

When a migrant goes anywhere,
he burns his boats ...

Roger Smith was born in Crosby and evacuated to Wales, where his father had a paint factory. In 1964 he decided he couldn't stand the approaching urban violence or Harold Wilson, so took his £8 savings, went to Tasmania, borrowed £20,000 and built a motel on the remote south-east coast where the road was not paved.

In 1971, in the middle of the bush at Barton, thirty-eight miles south of Launceston, he discovered some over-grown stone buildings which in 1840 had been a water-mill supplying power for the fledgeling English colony of Van Diemen's Land. It had been built by an earlier emigrant, Andrew Gatenby, a Yorkshireman who in 1822 sailed with his wife, four sons and three daughters to Hobart Town. Their voyage took six months, and they also made good.

Roger, who had once worked on the restoration of Caernarvon Castle for the Ministry of Works, set about moving this crumbling mill back to Launceston, to form part of an entertainment complex. It took ninety days. Painstakingly reconstructed in an old quarry, it now stands alongside a nineteenth-century gunpowder mill, a windmill, a cornmill and a representation of *The Sand-*

piper, an eighteenth-century ten-gun sloop of war, two-thirds its actual size, firing cannon built by the original foundry, while being electrically guided around a man-made lake past a reconstructed foundry with operating blast furnaces ... and so on, and on.

Penny Royal is a sort of Disneyland rebuilt in original stone, not fibreglass, under the sharp eye of Roger Smith, a perfectionist with a fanatical desire for historical accuracy who cannot be the easiest man to work for. His impressive end-product now attracts fifteen hundred visitors a day; there is an appetite for the past in Australia – where a house built in 1964 can be advertised as 'historic' ...

Having achieved all this, Roger is selling up and leaving Tasmania, beaten into defiant retreat by recalcitrant unions. He must be the quintessential example of a poor migrant who works desperately hard in his new home, achieves all he attempts – but is finally forced out by the work practices of the land that provided his opportunities ...

We thought we would go somewhere where it was English-speaking, a high standard of living, reasonable prospects for children and – perhaps I shouldn't say this – no coloured people, because in Liverpool at that time they were burning my factory down and scratching the sides of my car ...

In those days it wasn't safe to walk on the pavement at all. Just days before I left, one Indian – or wherever he came from – jumped from car to car in a traffic jam in Renshawe Street, got hold of my windscreen wiper and threatened to pull it off if I didn't give him some money. I put the money through the window. He snatched it and jumped onto the next car, bent my bumper ...

It was starting then, in 1964, and I was perceptive enough to see the problems that were coming – I read them right! When Harold Wilson announced he was going to socialize Britain I realized there was only room for one of us – and I had to go. This part of the world was as good as anywhere in those days, so I decided to come out here and be enterprising. I came with a Land Rover, £8 in my pocket, a box of tools and a lot of hope and determination.

Australia is quite a way, but Tasmania really is at the end of the line ...

I thought there was a future in tourism and as events have turned out, I'm right; this was an isle basically ripe for development. Also, I liked the historical aspect – this island was before anywhere else with the convicts.

You started in Australia as a labourer – that was considerable demotion after owning your concrete company and being a managing director?

It was the only job I could get. It was the price I was prepared to pay to get on – and everything I've done has been successful so far.

How did the locals take to you?

Not very well, at first. The British in those days – this is twenty-two years ago – were all Poms. But over the years they've got used to my eccentricities and I've become accepted, I think. For twenty-two years I've been flat out. There's been no let up, ever.

This is quite a laid-back island – were they surprised by your get-up-and-go?

You've got to remember that when a migrant goes anywhere, he burns his boats – at least the good ones do. If I was going back, I was going back *successful*. I planned to be successful a lot quicker than I was – but I got there in the end, and I suppose that's what counts.

You borrowed £20,000 from the Tasmanian Government to start a motel out at St Helen's on the east coast – an obscure part of a remote island?

It was so remote that we had no water. It really was the ultimate in pioneering, but with £8 in your pocket what else can you do? Beggars can't be choosers.

I heard that the locals wouldn't let you join their golf club. Why was that?

My golf was atrocious and they were probably worried about their course more than anything! So I thought the only way to really beat people was to get my own course built round the motel.

So you built your own – and wouldn't let them join!

Oh, they could join, but they didn't. Everybody predicted year after year I'd go broke and were amazed that I didn't, and kept going. A few times I sailed close to the wind. I saved my money and Elizabeth was frugal and we worked jolly hard; I cooked all the breakfasts, I did all the waiting-on for lunch, waiting-on for dinner, did all the gardening, did all the accounts. We had thirteen rooms but only one helper, so it was very hard work. We broke even on three rooms, and we often got four and five.

I have to say, you're not the most modest and retiring Pom I've ever met!

I sort of explained to people what I was going to do – and then *did* it. But I did one thing from the start: I got my star organized, and I followed that star. I wouldn't be put off. I wouldn't take no for an answer and I wouldn't see anything fail. So some of the things I produced were not as good as they were meant to be, but with perseverance and determination I made them work, and now they're fine.

You retired at the age of thirty-two, having made your pile; what brought you back to work again?

I discovered the Penny Royal mill in the bush, and I thought, I'll move that to Launceston, stone by stone – and so began the second great era of expansion!

Bringing this place here was like William Randolph Hearst shipping castles across the Atlantic!

It was much more difficult than that. It took me three months to take the mill down, six weeks working day and night, seven days a week, with convoys of trucks through the night, to move the 2500 tons of stone to Launceston, and then another three months to rebuild. I'd spent nearly all my money the day I got the last stone to Launceston – I really didn't have any more to start building it again.

You gave the public instant history; it's like a Disneyland, with real granite instead of fibreglass.

There's real history because the gunpowder mills are precisely as William Drayson had them in 1820, and the cannon foundry again is a real foundry as in those times. And even the ship is a two-thirds scale replica of a ten-gun sloop of war. We did enormous research in London at the National Maritime Museum to get everything exactly right, and it really works – we fire real gunpowder from real cannons. Those cannons were made by a company in Scotland which made the same guns for Nelson.

Is this place your monument?

I suppose it is. My satisfaction is not the money side – that's very nice, of course – but I know that as long as civilization endures, all this will remain, long after I'm under the sod and forgotten.

With all this success, why did your first wife leave you and go back to England?

I think nostalgia, really, coupled with the fact that she once said I was fanatical in my work, which was true, absolutely true. She was very long-suffering, but it was too much for her. Had things been easier for us there would have been less difficulty. Now we're best of friends – so it really goes to show that circumstances cause problems, more than anything else.

She went back to England because she was homesick – but now she's back in Australia again?

When people go back the second time they nearly always realize how good their first decision was!

What would you say your company's worth at the moment?

£10 million, say: five hotels, a village as well, the gunpowder mill, all the tourist attractions.

And how many people work for you?

About two hundred and eighty, in total.

With all this, you're considering selling up and leaving Tasmania?

I suppose everything has a price, and nothing is forever. I'm too young at this stage to stop. With the experience that I have of developing things it would be a tragedy for me to just retire.

You're going to turn your back on your monument and walk away?

Yes, yes, I will indeed. There's no point in doing any more development in Tasmania because the unions here have become so strong, their tactics are so bullying, they're so unreasonable in their approaches, there really is no point in continuing. The government nowadays seems to back them almost to an unreasonable point; the unions force a very unreasonable pay rise and the government will enforce it. As long as they take this attitude of stifling private enterprise, there's no place for my kind of person. I'm needed in other parts of the world, doing other things.

The unions have always been very strong in Australia.

Yes, but they've never been unreasonable before. Now in the last few years they've become *very* unreasonable, they've been pushing for a higher and higher standard of living that the country cannot afford. I'm afraid that a lot of British union people have come out here and caused trouble, and a lot of the Australians – understandably – are very angry about it. I feel so, too. It's certainly a tremendous disincentive to anybody these days to come out. Unless you're very large – and I mean ten times bigger than I am – then you really haven't a chance.

For example, because I wouldn't give in they put a black ban on the cranes, and one of my key workers who'd helped me for many years suffered spinal injury directly through trying to lift something that he shouldn't have lifted, but was loyal enough to do so. He hurt his back, and he's a cripple for life. Now when that happened, that was the end as far as I was concerned – it was just unacceptable. When this sort of thing happens, there's no place here for the likes of me.

You feel resentful against Tasmania? Australia? Or just the unions?

Only the unions. The unions have become too greedy, they're unscrupulous, they're not really looking after the interests of their workers any more. They used to, but not any more. Now it's their own interests, and pushing their own ends. I think countries that allow the unions free range, as Australia has done up 'til now, are going to pay the price and it's going to be a very heavy price because if one hundred people like me leave Australia, if they're forced out because there's no place for them any more, then that is going to have a knock-on effect that will adversely affect the country.

To some extent it happened in Britain – a lot of very enterprising people left twenty-five years ago, going to other parts of the world. I followed them. There has to be room for expansion, there has to be room for the entrepreneur in the world. Even in Russia they need them.

I didn't do all this to make money, I did it because I was inspired. It was a labour of love. I was dedicated to it. Now unions don't like people being dedicated to things.

Have you told them you're leaving?

Yes, and they didn't believe me. They laughed in my face. Now they're wondering why I haven't done any more. They said, 'Oh, you'll change your mind', but I won't.

Where will you go?

Somewhere in Europe – because Europe's the place that has the greatest future. I have various countries in mind that are very happy to have my kind of entrepreneurial skills.

Australia depends on high commodity prices and those unfortunately are brought about by wars. There have been no wars – and hopefully there won't be any for a long time – and therefore the standard of living in Australia *has* to go down. If you look back in history from the First World War and the Second World War, America and Australia have prospered through shortages of strategic materials and food. They prospered out of the suffering of other countries, if you really think about it ...

The Graduate Bunny: Sally Hurley

The History Man: Roger Smith

The Union Boss: George Campbell

The Solitary Pundit: Sue Becker

The Tall Poppy: David Hill

The Koala Man: Pat Robertson

The Champ: Joe Bugner

The Prospector: Eddie Farrell

The Socialite: Diana Fisher

The Garbo: Jim Jaggs

The Disillusioned: John and Siobhan Chapman

The Studio Boss: Jane Deknatel

The Loner: Dennis Gowing

THE UNION BOSS: GEORGE CAMPBELL

When you say you're a Union official,
they look for the horns ...

It's bad enough to be a Pom in Australia – but *far* worse
to be a Pommy stirrer. These are the trade union officials
who go on television and, with strong Yorkshire, Birmingham or Ulster accents, tell viewers there won't be any
buses in the morning, the supermarkets will be picketed,
the petrol stations closed, the airlines grounded or the
opera cancelled ... In a newspaper poll, eight out of ten
long-suffering Australians thought their unions had too
much power.

As the only Third World economy where you can drink
the tap water, Australia has First World living standards,
an industry more backward than Taiwan's – and British-
born trade unions. On their far left and most militant, the
Amalgamated Metalworkers Union: 'When AMW moves,
the rest follow.'

For its 160,000 members there are 168 different job
categories, from Added Shipwright and Agricultural
Fitter, by way of Poker Machine Mechanic and Screwer,
down to Welder Sheet Metal and Worker Electric.

The Union's Assistant National Secretary handling this
industrial nightmare of wage rates would surely be the
prototype Pommy stirrer, had he not come from Belfast.

An apprentice shipwright at Harland and Wolff, George Campbell became a £10 tourist in 1965 at the age of twenty-two. He intended to work his way around the world, but met his wife and his fate in Melbourne, and stayed. He plied his trade and his union enthusiasm along the waterfront, and rose steadily from shop steward to sit within two rungs of the presidency.

I attended a National Day of Protest he had organized in Canberra and caught him in full rant before 2500 demonstrators. When not haranguing everyone in sight, George Campbell is a quiet and attractive man with black eyebrows and penetrating eyes. He lives with his pretty wife Diane and son in a southern suburb of Sydney, five minutes from his local trade union club. He bought their hillside house for $46,000 in 1976 and believes it's now worth about $130,000.

His home is visited twice a day by flights of cockatoos. They gnaw the balcony timber support and also cause considerable havoc in the garden – but as George never has any time for gardening, he's not too worried . . .

There's a perception that unions have too much power. A lot of that's derived from the beat-up in the media about unionism and union power. If you look at some polls they've done in the newspapers on trustworthiness, union leaders run second to car salesmen in terms of public attitude as to whether they're trustworthy or not.

Usually they don't think much of journalists or television people either!

That's right – we're just slightly below those. On aircraft when I'm travelling, someone strikes up a conversation – and I find when you tell them you're a union official they tend to look for the horns. Doesn't worry me; I suppose I'm big enough to be able to look after myself that way.

We've got just over 160,000 members. I think for a number of reasons, we're regarded as the leading union on the Left in the trade union movement in this country – and a lot of unions look to us for a lead. We have members in virtually every industry in the country and they're constantly involved in dispute situations. We're very heavily involved in the political movement through the Labour Party – for example, I'm on the national executive of the party. We have a fair degree of influence there.

Not all that much influence on Mr Hawke, because you've just organized a demonstration in Canberra protesting about him and then you went in and laid the hard word on him?

I did, for an hour and a half. I think that was fairly significant, I really believe they were concerned at that demonstration, particularly because it was their own constituency saying to them, 'We don't believe your economic direction's correct.'

Wall Street and most foreigners seem to blame much of Australia's poor economic condition upon the trade unions ...

Trade union movement, yeah, they do. Again that's a beat-up situation, generally by the media. The media have created a very bad image, I think quite deliberately. I'm not saying there are not situations and circumstances where the trade unions haven't warranted the image that they've received, or that trade unions haven't been guilty in some circumstances, but the Press in this country tend to sensationalize a lot of the industrial relations – for example they very rarely report the result of industrial disputes – they only report the actual impact.

Some of these seem quite ridiculous, seen from the outside. Since I've been here, an airline has been grounded because the stewards didn't like the length of their shirtsleeves, a factory went on strike because there was only one flavour of ice cream in the canteen – such disputes can't be taken seriously?

Those are the more absurd type of industrial disputes, but if you really examine our disputes you'll find at the heart of them is terribly inept management – people who just do not have the slightest idea of how to manage personal relations. They see the fact that they've been elevated into management position as a licence to exercise their absolute power over the lesser mortals below them.

But with all your restrictive practices and that sort of thing, haven't you priced yourselves out of the international market? I mean, 17½ per cent extra pay for going on holiday: when executives come over from America they think they're in Disneyland!

When that came in in the early Seventies the basis of that 17½ per cent was to ensure that when people went on annual leave, they didn't earn less than they were capable of earning when they were working. Even the Japanese get a bonus, so they do, for not working.

On an average your workers are paid eight times more than the Taiwanese, six times more than Singapore – how can you ever drag yourself out of this recession when you face that kind of competition here in the East?

That's a problem we don't believe you can approach from the point of view of us dragging ourselves down. We see that basically as a problem of trying to develop and improve the living standards of workers in *those* countries. Many of them exist under military dictatorships, they're not democracies, they're not free.

It's a very complex issue you raise because, for example, a car worker in the vehicle industry in Australia earns an average of $17,000 a year. His equivalent in the Japanese car industry now earns the equivalent of $44,000, $45,000 a year – but the Japanese can produce cars cheaper than we can.

But George, they don't have a thirty-five-hour week, they don't have all your restrictive practices, they don't have sixteen men doing the job one chap could do . . .

True, I recognize that.

. . . and they have one union per factory. You haven't.

But the union movement in this country recognizes that a lot of change is necessary. We reckon new technologies are essential, we recognize work practices need to be changed – a lot are antiquated – but you can't get the result the Japanese are capable of getting if we rely on the traditional type of management structure we have. The restrictive work practices we have in this country derive out of the nature of the division of labour which management itself introduced, not the work force.

Let me give you an example – since the Labour government came to power real labour costs in the country have dropped by something like 8 per cent below what they were in 1969/70. Profits have increased to the highest levels that they've been for over twenty years – but investment in this country has fallen, in real terms. The flow of investment capital out of Australia's increased from $125 million in 1982/3 to $7000 million in 1985/6. Employers are getting increased profits but they're not reinvested in Australian industry, they're investing it overseas.

Foreign capital, of course, is often reluctant to invest here because of your unions.

But they've got nothing to invest *in*. There's a bit of a myth about strikes. Certainly the working standards of Australian workers are high in comparison to world standards.

If a Taiwanese or Brazilian woke up in Sydney he'd think he was in heaven!

Sure, sure I appreciate that, but think of the standards of workers in the Scandinavian countries, for example. Our concern at the moment is not so much in terms of improving living standards, but in terms of maintaining them, maintaining the lifestyle Australian workers are used to.

As an extreme-Left union do you have a lot of Communist members?

Within the leadership of the union I suppose about a quarter are Communist Party members, or perhaps who've been members of the Communist Party.

So whatever happens, you want to shake the pillars, to bring the system down?

Well, not so much to bring the system down in that sense – I mean people often talk about revolution, but as far as I'm concerned it's also an evolutionary process. As I said at the Left conference which I helped organize here this year, if we want to change the system, we'd better learn how to run it first.

I make no secret of the fact that I want to change the nature of our production process, that I would prefer a socialist society, a society based on socialist ideals, and I make no bones about it. I have fought vigorously for those ideals, I still fight vigorously for them.

So you're a Pommy stirrer, right?

Some people call me that! I'm quite often called a Belfast Pommy.

A Belfast Pommy – so you're consecrated and prepared to devote your life to changing society, while all your Aussie union members want to do is go and lie on the beach! Is that why there are so many Brits running the trade unions?

I think it's a bit of a myth that so many Brits are running the trade unions. There's no doubt that when I came to this country in the Sixties a substantial proportion of unionists – particularly shop stewards – were British migrants, but a substantial proportion of the community were British migrants also.

They say Britain gave Australia its form of government, its culture, its law – and its British shop stewards.

In the Sixties the average worker in this country was concerned only with reading the back page of the newspaper – the racing page – or going to the beach.

Has this changed?

I think they've changed considerably ... I also like to get to the beach when I can, but the point I'm making, Alan, is that there's a much more significant role played in the trade union movement by Australian-born unionists than there was in the Sixties and Seventies.

It seems to an outsider that industrial relations are just the way they were in England twenty or thirty years ago, when there was full employment and people could afford to walk out of a job. Here I find one railway union in Melbourne on strike because another railway union is blowing the engine whistles too much ... It seems you're in that silly-strike period?

I think those sorts of disputes are always going to occur, where individuals are in control of their own environment and they'll take action in it. It's a question not so much of those occurring but of having the structure there to be able to resolve them.

There's a report here in a left-wing paper about work practices in one factory, and this writer ...

He's not quoting me?

No, he's not quoting you, but he writes, 'If a compressor fails on a production unit, an electrician must disconnect the power, a plumber must disconnect the hydraulic line, a fitter must disconnect the bolts, two riggers are required to sling steel cables around the unit, transport workers must lift it, painters must paint it and a lagger must deal with the heat-protected areas.' In doing this it took sixteen workers two days to do a job that one could have done in about two hours.

That type of situation is repeated in a range of industries in this country. It originates out of the sort of management structure which in fact was developed in the nineteenth century, based upon dividing the workforce up and giving them as little knowledge as possible. We don't agree with that – in fact my organization has said we're prepared to cooperate in terms of removing those restrictive types of work practices, but the difficulty is you cannot change these things overnight. They have to be negotiated ...

What's it like, Diane, being married to an old Belfast stirrer?

You get used to it ...

THE SOLITARY PUNDIT: SUE BECKER

Incest is a very dicey subject ...

Driving through the glorious almost empty island of Tasmania I found myself listening each morning to a throaty English voice interviewing local politicians quite firmly, and handling call-ins with no-nonsense perception. As an old radio man I appreciate a job well done, so traced the gravelly Pommy voice back to Sue Becker, a handsome lady of a certain age who is now the significant sound of Tasmania.

I raised the matter of this beery what-ho voice with its owner: 'Don't drink beer.' She settled for 'ginny' – equally unfair, since she takes only wine.

Sue Becker is slim and youthful – as well she should be, for back in the Seventies she was on British television as a pre-aerobic keep-fit goddess. Her series was called, would you believe, *Boomph With Becker*. She was Auntie Mame in leotards.

Her outspoken morning radio programme has run for seven years and is called, more prosaically but with no reflection upon her figure, *Becker's Broadside*.

Greatly daring, I submitted to an interview in the ancient Hobart studios of ABC Radio, a network which can offer Australia's only quality broadcasting – but then break off to lose its entire audience by carrying umpteen hours of parliamentary debate from Canberra. This stupefying blend of banality, boredom and farmyard language can make even Dennis Skinner, Eric Heffer and the notorious Westminster yahoos sound intellectual.

Sue trained as a teacher. Her parents had escaped from wartime Burma to South Africa, and she went to join them. She also lived in New Zealand, Guernsey and New Guinea – where she married a Hungarian and followed him through the wilds. They had a son, but then divorced.

She was working in Sydney when she fell in love with Tasmania: 'It's so English – gentle climate and four seasons – but the Establishment here wonder what I'm going to do next. They're not into controversial programmes – Tasmania's very bland. We prefer to sweep our problems under the carpet! Well, I like to shake them up and give them an airing.'

She lives alone in a pretty 1820 house in a wide tree-lined street upon a hill, surrounded by New Guinea relics and a lovingly tended English country garden. It takes her five minutes to cycle down to the studio and ten minutes back, up the hill. There is still a noticeable amount of boomph in Becker ...

I've had to battle against my accent all the time I've been in Australia. I think it's more acceptable now than it was, say, sixteen years ago, but at the beginning the biggest stumbling block was the voice.

How did the battle show itself?

Well, they send you up. I get a bit hurt sometimes because they don't send up the Irish or the Welsh or the Scottish; it's the southern English accent they send up. I used to get awfully hurt 'cos I didn't find it in South Africa or Canada or New Zealand.

I suppose if you're interviewing the Prime Minister and you sound like a Pom, listeners might think: 'She's not one of us'?

I always wondered why the accent was so important; I thought it should be what you are, what you do, what you say – not so much as *how* you say it. I think it's a hang-up from the old days.

If I go to a cocktail party, I'll know immediately those who disapprove of me – I get that rather frozen look. That slight disapproving air. But against that, a great percentage say, 'Good on you, Sue', for having a go and raising issues that perhaps in the past were not raised. There's a new breed coming up that want things aired, that want things discussed – and funnily enough my greatest supporters are amongst what I call my little old ladies. One tends to think of little old ladies – whose ranks I am rapidly going to join – as very settled in their ways of thinking, but they're not. The older you get, the wiser and more tolerant and open to new ideas you get.

You spend your professional life asking questions – which is an un-Australian activity; Australians are very incurious people.

Very apathetic. It's difficult to stir Australians up. As I've always said, next to the stomach – the great Australian stomach – the national disease is apathy. I think it stems from the time when we really were the lotus-land of milk and honey, and I don't think we've woken up to the fact that we're not.

Australians object to even the mildest criticism – so how do you cope? You're always getting hold of politicians and finding out what they're doing wrong!

Yes – trying to pressure them! They're difficult to get direct answers out of, aren't they? I find it easy, Alan, when I'm on air. That's my job: to question and probe and try to get a direct answer. I find it difficult when I switch off from that to my private life – that's where the pressure's on, and being in a small place you feel the pressure round you.

In Australia when people refer to others as 'outspoken' it's meant to be rather pejorative; they're saying, 'The trouble with him is, he's got too many opinions ... '

That's a label I wear very much round my neck. Well, I sort of barge on regardless. I say, 'Look, love, my home's here, I pay my tax here, I have no money anywhere else' – I don't have any money here either, but never mind – 'so I consider myself a Tasmanian.' But it does come up on dicey subjects, controversial subjects we're discussing on air – such as tourism, when I tell them to wake up and get with it. They'll say, 'If you don't like it, why don't you go back to where you belong?' This is defensiveness which I understand – Tasmania's so small compared with the rest; and of course outside I'm as defensive of Tasmania as any true Tasmanian.

It must be difficult running such a programme in a small community where you're going to bump into the Premier in the afternoon?

Luckily the Premier is one of the few people that's very good: I can have a ding-dong argument with him, and then meet him at a social function and it's 'Hello Sue.' But certainly I get the airwaves telling me of a group who don't approve of me – what I would call the Establishment, the powerful people behind the scenes who really don't want things to change. I get the message quite strongly from them, that frozen disapproving look.

I think some of them love me now because I've been here long enough – I've almost become part of their routine or their furniture, and they respect me. But there are an awful lot who dislike me intensely, and it all started off with the voice – Pommy accent and ginny voice – because it was different. I do irritate thousands of them.

Is there anything you wouldn't talk about, on air?

Incest. I've spoken about homosexuality – naturally, with AIDS, which is a big problem. I've done incest as a topic, but I'm aware it's a very dicey subject to talk about here. The other big problem is that because we're such a small community people are frightened to speak out: their voices are recognized. It's a very sensitive subject – I think there's more incest in an island. It had to be raised because the whole country's become aware of it, after raising child abuse, but in a place like Tasmania incest has been proved to go right across the board: it doesn't know social barriers, so you have your professional as well as your less-educated man committing acts of incest. It was difficult to do because people are not going to come out in a small community because their voices are recognized; they're under enormous pressure, *everybody* will know. People are listening, but they're frightened to ring in.

Tasmania often seems to hide from the world ...

We've still got Acts in force that were made in 1929 and earlier that haven't been updated in any way. We don't have freedom of information, we're resisting what other states are trying to do to cope with the drug problem, we're not going to have condom vending machines, homosexuality's still illegal ... We're very cautious. That's a nice way to put it, isn't it? Very cautious state, we don't believe in rushing into things.

We've got *so* many politicians – we've got fifty-four, for 345,000 people. It's unbelievable, isn't it – and that's just state. We're terribly over-governed and over-ruled, but at the same time they don't seem to be very abreast of the times.

Reading your book *Whicker's New World*, what strikes me about America is that there's not the enviousness that we have.

They love *tall poppies in America.*

They love them. They love individuals, they love their showbiz people that are outrageous and distinct. Australia is getting better, but it's still embarrassed by eccentrics, by individuals, by ambition. There's almost something *wrong* with being ambitious. We're seeing it with Bob Ansett, who's fighting against certain government decisions here. He's an achiever. We *have* to knock our tall poppy. It's a very sad disease Australia's got – I think it stems from a sense of inferiority.

Somebody tells me Tasmania is thirty years behind the mainland?

I thought fifty, actually – but that's its charm, isn't it? As long as we're competitive. I think we fall down in tourism because we're not selling what we're all about – which is the charm of a more leisurely bygone era.

Is it a good place for a lone woman?

Not really – but much better than it was. I think America is the ideal for a lone woman: Americans don't have hang-ups about career women – they rather enjoy women who're independent and go out and do their own thing.

It's still rather a chauvinistic society – I get the feeling the Tasmanian woman's place is in the kitchen ... ?

Yes – or in the bedroom flat on her back, sometimes. Yes, we are. I think Tasmanian men are still basically frightened of career-orientated or independent-thinking women. I'll never forget at one dinner party, it struck home so vividly: I was having a great discussion – they would have called it argument, I called it debate – about something or other and I seemed to be the lone woman battling. When we went into the kitchen to make coffee the hostess said, 'I'm so glad you said that, Sue, we *need* women to speak up for us like that.' But it never occurred to *her* to speak up ...

I always get the impression the men reverse gear when I come along, you know, three steps back. They're a bit frightened of me ...

Because you're the dragon lady – you're going to put them right.

You use the term 'dragon' – was that how somebody described me, or was that one of yours?

One of mine.

But do you see me as a dragon, really?

No, of course not – but I suspect they do.

Yes, they do. This is the interesting part: male men don't see me in that way, neither do Europeans. If there's one at a party in Tasmania, we'll end up somewhere together – Europeans, they're not frightened of me.

Is all this an argument for going back to England?

Look, I've reached the age where my possessions own *me*. The thought of all that in my home there, dragging it back to England! Forget the cost. And I haven't lived in England for so long I don't know how much it's changed. I have my son here, and I must see him. But I do think as you get older, your original roots pull stronger, which is why I chose Tasmania: it's the gentleness of the country, the serenity which to me England's always had – and the four seasons, which I'm passionate about. Tasmania is very pro-British, royalist.

It seems you've just got your life well organized, just as your home is beautifully organized – but are you ever lonely?

Oh yes – any woman who lives on her own is lonely, Alan, if they'd only admit it. I don't really think it's a natural state to be in, not to share your life. I've been married, of course, and have a gorgeous son, but you've got to weigh up the pros and cons. I know I'm very independent, I know that I must work – I simply cannot just Hoover the carpet and wash the dishes, it isn't enough, and I realize men basically don't *want* that in a woman. They want a woman who's the homemaker, who does listen for his final word, who turns to him for advice . . .

I need that in a man too – I mean, I'm not interested in weak men. Strong ones are getting rarer and rarer, and I've never been interested in wishy-washy men. The wishy-washy ones are petrified of me, which is very interesting, but the very quiet, secure male just tells me to shut up and sit down and listen, and of course I *do*!

So I'd have to make my choice. I would have loved to have got married again, but I know that being what I am makes it difficult for a man to choose me as a partner. I think I've accepted that and will live in peace, but with those great periods of loneliness. It's inevitable. And life's a compromise, they say, but I could never do with a half-baked husband – he's got to be totally yummy, or I don't want him. Somebody like *you*, dear . . .

THE TALL POPPY: DAVID HILL

We've reduced our losses
to $1 million a day ...

David Hill is a new brand of Australian bureaucrat, energetic and forceful; no overtones of Sir Les Patterson here – more of Dick Whittington. Born in Eastbourne and deserted by the father he never knew, his family were destitute. He was sent to Dr Barnardo's at Barkingside, in Essex.

At the age of twelve he and his twin brother were sponsored to Australia on the Big Brother scheme as underprivileged children, and sent to a farm school. He left at fifteen and got a job in a Sydney hardware shop, counting nuts and bolts.

When we met he was Chief Executive of the New South Wales Rail Authority and about to take over the musical-chairs post of Managing Director of the Australian Broadcasting Corporation from another Pom, Geoffrey Whitehead. He was already its Chairman. The top position in Australia's BBC carries all the job security of an Italian Prime Minister: in thirteen years five Chairmen have come and gone.

So this Barnardo boy was then leading two of the most demanding public institutions in the land. He had become the most highly paid public servant in New South Wales at the age of thirty-four, as boss of the State Railway and its 40,000 employees. In one month during 1983 he survived thirty-two strikes.

When we met he was on his fifty-fourth tour of inspection, travelling in his magnificent private train like some maharajah: panelled saloons, sleeping cars, restaurants – with a bevy of solemn railway managers jumping to it. David Hill was on tour, and meeting his people.

His rise and rise from nuts and bolts, by way of economic adviser to the former Labour Premier Neville Wran, was relentless. He disclaims any interest in a political career while showing all the necessary push, self-confidence and ambition – yet his is the kind of success that Australians can *almost* tolerate: he plays Rugby League, laughs easily, enjoys good living and descends beaming from his splendid train to greet railway workers with man-to-man joviality that transcends the impatient determination that makes wary executive hearts beat faster.

His train had progressed through Woy Woy, Wyee, Murrurundi and Narrabri when I went aboard in Moree to travel north with this engaging man, heading for Boggabilla on the border. After our conversation in his elegant Commissioner's carriage with its cedar and maple panelling and observation deck ... he ordered the train to stop so I could get off at some wayside halt.

I stood on the deserted platform amid the vast emptiness of the outback as the train obediently moved away and its people settled down to breakfast; it seemed that David Hill from Eastbourne, no longer noticeably under-privileged, was getting ideas above his stations ...

The railways are a very old industry with great social divisions. There's the boss class and there's the working class – this huge historic chasm. It's very English, our railway, and one of the reasons for these visits is to try and close the gap, to let them know we're not another class but just doing a day's work, like them.

We've got twenty-eight unions! Our union structure is exactly the same as you've got in British Rail – we've got an ASLEF and an NUR. They're called different things but they've exactly the same structure, and we're fighting exactly the same fights as British Rail. In the last few years we've probably had as many – if not more – successes than British Rail, but certainly we've got overmanning and outdated work practices and, like the British, we're slowly but surely whittling them away.

You're efficient, you're a 'doer'; how do you cope with Australia's 'she'll be right' attitude?

Australia's fairly industrious. If we have a malaise, I think you can trace most of our industrial attitudes back to the English: the structure of our trade union movement. I remember an old trade union friend saying that one of the difficulties the movement had in Australia was that every time there was a strike and an official was trying to give the union view, it was invariably somebody with a thick English accent from the Midlands – and it's *true*. The structure and culture of our unions – the culture of our industry – has been shaped more by English attitudes than anything else.

Yet you haven't been able to make your railway profitable?

No, but we've succeeded in reducing our losses to $1 million a day. We've effectively halved the real level of operating losses in the last four years, and I regard that as a pretty good result.

Wages account for 51 cents in every dollar of your turnover, whereas with road freight it's 17 cents ...

Yes, but we're now on a railway running up into the north of New South Wales that we have to pay for – while out there our competitor is running on a road he's *not* paying for. We're spending something like $4 million a week maintaining this railroad, that our competitor isn't paying.

And for good political reasons you're still putting railways into the marginal constituencies!

There are marginal constituencies all over New South Wales and we've obviously got to show some sensitivity to them! (*Laughs*)

You bounced into the political arena as the economic adviser to the Prime Minister of New South Wales, but you've turned down a number of safe seats in Parliament?

I've certainly made it clear when approached that I think, as an old English friend in the trade union movement once said, 'Parliamentarians are not a very happy breed.' That's true – I think life in Parliament would be a dog's life; I'm not interested.

Unless you go in at a high level?

Not even interested in that. Look, I've got some wonderful and exciting jobs to do: I run the biggest and most complicated railway in Australia, I'm Chairman of the Australian Broadcasting Corporation – these're absolutely marvellous, exciting and challenging things to do, far more exciting than life in Parliament could be.

One of the disturbing aspects about Australia is the tall poppy syndrome, where people are very sceptical of those in public office. Basically, Australians don't feel *good* about people in public office; there's an assumption that they're ill-motivated, rather than well-motivated.

The media – which reflect community attitudes – and much of the public seem to suspect that your politicians are corrupt?

If not corrupt, certainly they think they're in it for their own good, rather than the public good.

The hand is in the till?

There's some belief of that, which goes back to our old Irish convict heritage. The prevailing view isn't corruption, but that they're in it for their own selfish ends.

When you get into politics – as you inevitably will at some time – which party will you go to?

I'm a member of the Labour Party.

But as we were saying, Australians don't like politicians irrespective of who's in power; they hate them all.

214

Yes, well they hate Pommies too but at the same time they're furtively monarchistic! Australians don't feel uncomfortable about a paradox.

I went back to England last year, back to a little council housing estate outside Eastbourne where I used to live, and I couldn't help but reflect that it's highly unlikely that a kid on that estate will *ever* become the head of British Rail at thirty-three years of age. This says something about the difference between the two countries.

So you're a Pommy achiever, as opposed to a Pommy stirrer?

Some people would say I'm both! (*Laughs, and picks up phone.*) Can you get hold of the conductor? Tell him to hold us here for a while.

It's rather splendid to be able to command the train and the tides – to make the day stop and start like that!

The railways were built before Australia, back before Federation to the colonial days, and the Railway Commissioner was effectively the antipodean monarch – and still to some extent *is*.

You're a maharajah, sitting there?

It's a wonderful culture. The Commission built themselves wonderful carriages like this to go out on inspections; if we've got to travel for three days and three nights on a train, then there's no better way in the world to do it.

When I took the job, I looked at a map on the wall and saw the extent of the railway network: it's about 10,000 kilometres long, and I saw names like Bolivia, Kentucky, North Star ... I said to one of the Secretaries of the railways, 'Is it possible for me to go and have a look at these places that I'm now responsible for?' He not only said 'Yes', but procured this – my *own* train! (*Laughs*) It's been a great adventure. This is our fifty-fourth big tour of inspection in the last few years; we get out about once a month. We can actually run this all around the capital cities of Australia.

The ABC's not going to be able to top this, is it?

No, I worry about that: the ABC can't give me a train to play with ...

You'll be the sixth chairman the ABC's had in thirteen years?

Yes, the ABC is also in trouble, but it's a wonderful institution. It's to Australia what the BBC is to England.

You get the feeling that someone might not be doing you a favour?

The organization's in enormous trouble and it's a very high-risk job because in the end the buck stops with the Chairman. In both commercial and ABC, in addition to our own production we buy the best of English and the best of American – which I'd certainly argue in many cases isn't very high – so certainly we have a range of television you don't have in the UK, and we don't have all the junk they have in America. As for our own production, certainly the ABC has been going through a bad patch; the ABC itself recognizes that and is doing something about it.

But although the ABC does run a few good programmes – most of them from the BBC – it's curiously disliked by viewers, and almost abandoned by them.

There's been a slide in audience away from the ABC to the commercial over a ten-year period, but a lot of that's been due to the advent of colour television and dramatic improvements in commercial television's production of current affairs in particular, documentaries and drama ...

You opted out of life here in Australia for a while, lived in Greece, and afterwards on a happily bohemian houseboat on the Thames. What made you decide to return?

I went back to England after being here for about fifteen years, and in all that time I really still believed I was English. So I went back home – but it wasn't home any more.

A lot of English people do that. They have a bad name here, they call us whingeing Pommies. We come out, we don't settle and we go back to England – and a very high proportion, having gone back, realize England isn't home any more, come back again and make a very satisfactory adjustment. I became Australian two years ago.

Australians have enormous pride in their country, but at the moment it's in a poor way economically.

So is the UK.

But that's no answer to your problems.

The basic problem we've got is that a very high proportion of our wealth comes from exports. We're out at the moment on this train inspecting one of the biggest wheat belts in the world, and the world price of wheat has plummeted. That means the wealth of all these farmers, the wealth of the railways *and* the wealth of Australia is going with it. The largest single source of our declining fortunes has been the collapse of commodity prices world wide. That's a factor regrettably we can't do much about. We're not too pleased, incidentally, that the EEC as well as the United States are subsidizing wheat exports, which is really contaminating world trade and forcing our national income down further.

Many Australians, particularly in the media, feel they have to go to England to make their names. You did it the other way – you're unknown in Europe.

That creative urge you see with so many Australians is understandable – a vast continent and a population of only sixteen million people, there isn't the capacity or the facility for people to develop their creative talents as there is in the United Kingdom and Europe.

So today, what's the view of Sussex from here?

I miss Sussex, you know. One of the things I've never adjusted to is this majestic country – it's just so bold and intimidating. Last year I went right back to Pevensey and we spent a week – we had good weather – walking the South Downs and through Stone Cross Wood and Pevensey Castle, and I must say the English countryside is still in my soul. That's the one thing I don't think I'll ever really get used to in Australia, you know, this vast and craggy intimidating landscape.

You want cosy little English pubs and wrap-around scenery?

I miss the pubs. I don't *mind* standing in a tiled bar with a schooner of cold beer, but I really miss the English country pub, the quaintness of England . . .

I was going to tell you the great paradox about the Australians, and you've probably observed it. They hate the Poms – it's really a love–hate thing – and yet I've gone to Test Matches at the Sydney cricket ground and as it's become increasingly obvious that the English are going to get absolutely thrashed, you'd expect as the contest went out of the game, the enthusiasm for it would diminish and the crowds would die. Not at *all*! The crowds actually increase as the prospect draws nearer of the Poms being beaten by Australia. There's almost a sadistic streak – yet surveys suggest that Australians are more fervently monarchistic than the English.

Are you sure?

Yes, my word! I remember seeing a comparative survey which shows about 77 per cent of English were pro-monarchistic, and something like 81 per cent of Australians! If you want a real indication, we've got the Union Jack in our flag. Now Republicanism has got about – the Republicans are enthusiastic people and their support has doubled from 6 per cent to 12 per cent in the last decade ...

You're expecting a boxing kangaroo on the national flag soon?

That's for the America's Cup. But look: Australians feel comfortable about an excursion into the jingoistic green and gold, but that Union Jack in the corner of the flag has got about a 95 per cent passionate support-rate. It's a great paradox.

I want to see us move in the direction of the Canadians. We have the absurd proposition now where the Queen's representative can dismiss a Government – and did. It's preposterous! Do you know, if Parliament passes laws we still have to have the assent of Her Majesty before the legislation, before the Bill becomes Act? I've become Republican ...

THE KOALA MAN: PAT ROBERTSON

*It had been prearranged
that the Pope would hold a koala ...*

Koalas are impossibly adorable – cuddly toys with fluffy ears, little grasping hands, bright eyes and big black noses. They are loved by all children, and advertising men. Curled up into a woolly ball and snoozing in the fork of a eucalyptus tree, each seems insufferably cute – and should one have a baby in her pouch ... well, it's *too* much. The baby spends the first eight months in there, and afterwards clings to its mother's stomach or back, pushing its head into the pouch for a drink. Only a very seriously grim person indeed would not melt before such a sight.

However, it must be said that, apart from looking captivating, Australia's most appealing animals don't have much character or personality ... In the cute stakes they have some competition from pandas, but *they* can be big and cross and not very sexy – while koalas in a sanctuary may actually be cuddled, for a small fee.

Apart from their looks, which excite universal oohs and aahs and cries of adoration, koalas are fascinating marsupials: they rarely drink and never sweat, they don't make shelters or nests but rely upon thick shoulder fur to protect them from sun and rain. They spend at least nineteen hours asleep, only becoming slightly active at dusk, when they munch leaves for what's left of the day.

Pat Robertson, from Osterley, knows rather too much about koalas to melt easily; he has been running the sixty-year-old Lone Pine Sanctuary at Brisbane since it was bought in 1964 by his father, a Park Royal ice cream manufacturer. His sanctuary has 180,000 visitors each year. It is full of koalas bred in captivity and on parade daily to be photographed with their arms placed around the necks of apprehensive tourists – who've noted how their claws have blooded the scarred arms of their keepers, but are risking a picture anyway.

The long-suffering marsupials – who'd much rather be sleeping or toying with a eucalyptus leaf – are also photographed on the back of Oscar, an equally patient Alsatian.

As though all *that* wasn't enough, Pat Robertson also has a white koala – one of the two albinos known to be alive – which merely compounds adorability; who could resist . . .

At the turn of the century people started shooting koalas for their fur. The shooting reached rather massive proportions. In 1924 there were over two million skins exported, and the koalas really were in danger of extinction, so the various state governments declared them protected fauna and around 1924 banned the shooting. Then in 1926 there was an open season in Queensland for one month – when it's said 60,000 koalas were shot!

In fact from what I've been told by officers in the National Parks there were a lot of people who kept shooting them illegally, and had piled up quite a few skins and couldn't do anything with them. So for political reasons the Government announced a one-month season which made it suddenly legal for these people to dispose of all their koala skins. Since then it's been stopped completely.

Around that time Claude Reid got concerned about the welfare of koalas; he remembered as a boy rowing down the river and seeing koalas in these trees on the banks and decided this must be a suitable place for them. He opened this sanctuary in 1927. At the time people said he was mad: 'Who wants to *pay* to go and see koalas when they've been shot for so long?'

Anyway, he ran the place until 1964, when he wanted to retire. My father decided it was worth buying; he thought, with an eye to the land, that the property would always be worth money. We've got fifty-seven acres on the river, seven miles from town. But also he had a thing about putting something back into Brisbane, so we bought it and my brother and I ran it until three years ago, when my brother retired. He'd had enough. Now I run it.

My father had gone to the States in 1949. He was manufacturing ice cream in England, and had some cafés in north-west London – Park Royal, Ealing area. I was born in Osterley. In 1949 all the ice cream manufacturing equipment was produced in the States, so my father went there for a month's business trip, and then came to Australia. There was no trouble getting money to come to Australia in those days because it was a sterling area, but US dollars were impossible: the day before he and my mother left they got their dollar allowance for one month's stay: £10 sterling, in dollars!

They travelled to the States first-class on the *Queen Mary*, made good relations with some Americans, paid their bar bills on the ship – and they repaid him in dollars. That's how they got enough dollars to survive a month in the States.

He came on to Brisbane and had four weeks of magnificent weather. When he came back to England all he could do was talk about Australia. In 1951 he sold the ice cream factory and said, 'We'll go to Australia for a *holiday*.' And we all knew damn well he wanted to stay.

I was sixteen then, I'd just done my 'O' levels. We came out and stayed with some English friends. My mother wasn't too happy at the time, so in April '53 he said, 'We'll go back to England. If you like it we'll stay, but if you don't we'll sell the business and return to Australia.' My mother said, 'I'll *never* want to come back here.'

We got back to England and after six weeks, in June '53 just after the Coronation, she'd had enough. She couldn't get back here quick enough! Since then I've never really heard her criticize Australia.

When we bought this place my father mortgaged everything – borrowed the entire purchase price at the unheard-of interest rate of 12 per cent. And that was his faith in this place, and the future value of it.

Today there are eight places with permits to display koalas between Nambur and the NSW border, and another eight with applications in – that's in 120 miles! Everyone seems to think if you've got koalas, you've got a pot of gold.

In 1969 we suddenly had five places in Brisbane which bred koalas, we had two drive-through lion parks between here and the Gold Coast, ten miles apart, competing for a very small market. And a few got hurt – we were certainly hurt. People come here on a busy day and say 'My God, there must be good money in this!' But they don't see it on the quiet days.

We're not too badly off because we're low-cost entertainment. If times are tight people have still got *some* money, so we're not affected. We don't enjoy great booms when the economy's flush, but we don't suffer terribly when things go sour.

The biggest problem is the food, and it's made more difficult now by the other places with koalas. We don't have our own eucalyptus plantation, which we should. Up until the last six weeks we were getting all the leaves within about forty or fifty miles, but now we're having to go sixty or seventy miles. We feed the koalas once a day but we normally get our rains in January, February, March – we get about forty inches of rain a year in Brisbane. This year was very dry and in this country you can go from flood to a drought situation. There're still plenty of leaves, but they lose their moisture content, their protein value, and there's a very fine balance between keeping koalas properly fed, and not *quite* properly fed. Getting them to eat 101 per cent of their daily food requirement as opposed to $99\frac{1}{2}$ per cent is very difficult.

Pat, you were the chap who thrust a koala at the unsuspecting Pope on his visit to Australia?

I don't like the term 'thrust'! It had been prearranged that the Pope would hold a koala, but I think when the moment came he got a little bit of a surprise – but he did very well. Fortunately he had his hands together, so it was easy enough for me to hand him the koala ...

It's a natural Papal posture – so you just slapped the koala down into his hands?

Before he really realized what was happening, yes!

Koalas are incredibly cute but, to be brutally frank, they don't have much personality; they're beautiful but dumb. I suppose when you look adorable you don't need a great personality ...

If you could sleep eighteen to twenty hours a day, have all your food brought to you and live in a fair degree of comfort, why, wouldn't you be content?

If you could buy them – and I presume you can't – what's the financial value of a koala?

You're right, there's no trade in koalas, but the Director of the San Francisco Zoo told me he valued them at about $50,000 each. All the zoos overseas that received koalas have spent a deal of money preparing for them, providing feed, suitable housing – and they've all got their money back very quickly. In Japan, for example, three zoos got koalas in October 1984 and within six weeks of them going on display they'd all recouped their investment!

Because the Japanese are bananas over koalas?

Absolutely, they really are! It's quite incredible, the Japanese reaction. We get one flight a week directly from Tokyo into Brisbane and the normal passage of the tourists is to come *straight* from the airport and spend an hour and a half here. The first thing they want to do is be photographed with a koala – and then they go on to the Gold Coast.

Only six zoos outside Australia have koalas: three in Japan and three in the United States: none in England, or in Europe.

There's an opening for you, back in Ealing!

We might have trouble growing eucalyptus in Middlesex ...

THE CHAMP: JOE BUGNER

I'm one of the greatest British heavyweights, ever ...

Joe Bugner made his third comeback while I was sitting at the ringside with Marlene, his equally statuesque Australian wife. She was watchful and cool as he won – just. He was fighting the American James Tillis, who described the points verdict as 'a home-town decision'; his trainer called it 'bullshit'.

The home-town crowd in the Sydney Entertainment Centre was certainly with Joe through every one of those twelve rounds, chanting *Bug*-ner *Bug*-ner – a new and wonderful experience for the former British and Commonwealth Heavyweight Champion. Afterwards he described the effect: 'Like an injection in the backside ...'

Bugner had not fought for two years and as usual his comeback was greeted with derision. One newspaper report began: 'Don't laugh, but ...' Bugner, an eager and pleasant man, has *always* had a bad press; he believes we never forgave him for out-pointing Henry Cooper in 1971 and thus ending Our 'Enry's career. So he has always been the bad guy and the crowds booed – even when he won. He went on to outpoint two more black American heavyweights – the third on July 24th 1987, the day he'd been made an Australian citizen. 'I wasn't going to let my new country down,' said Aussie Joe proudly, from the ring. That made his score: Fought sixty-one, lost eleven, KOs forty-three.

Arriving in Bedfordshire with his mother from Szeged after the Hungarian uprising in 1956, he had his first professional fight in 1967. He became the golden boy of British boxing and twice went the distance with Mohammed Ali. He believes he won £750,000 during those ten years.

He retired for the first time in 1976 – but later that year won his titles back. He had one more fight, then retired again and abandoned Britain for the United States, amid recriminations and bitterness. He made another comeback in 1982, which didn't take.

The Bugners came on from California to live in Marlene's home town, in the elegant suburb of Darling Point, where he was on the social and eventually the boxing treadmill again. Marlene, once a reporter on a Sydney tabloid, is not just his second wife but his agent, manager and mentor. He calls her 'Boss' – and who would argue?

Still the golden-haired Adonis, he now likes to be called 'Aussie Joe', and though he may suffer from ring rust he talks a more confident fight than once he did: 'My marbles are intact. I can hold a conversation without slurring the words, and my face isn't smashed to pieces. How many boxers can say that?'

At six foot four and 225 pounds he is indeed still a magnificent physical specimen – as is Marlene. I was with them at Sydney's Opera Ball a few weeks afterwards, when both were dressed to kill; an *awesome* sight – even if Joe, with world heavyweight ambitions, has gone a few extra rounds with Father Time . . .

I came out here with Mohammed Ali to do an exhibition tour in 1979. We were here for almost six weeks and I just fell in love with the place – and what's more, the people sort of took to *me*! That's the main reason – and of course the country's so beaut and the weather's outstanding.

I think the Australians like me ... Some of them don't, but most of them've accepted the fact that I'm going to stay, now. It takes a hell of a big Australian to move me around, so I *think* they like me.

And you always thought the British rejected you?

What happened in England is the fact that their old idol, their Henry Cooper, got beaten by me – and they just never accepted it. That goes back to 1971, and unfortunately the whole thing just snowballed down, and even now the cynics and the critics are still knocking me in any way they can. It's really been a very sad situation as far as I'm concerned, with England.

I can't relate to the attitudes of these people – they automatically assume at thirty-six you should have one foot in the grave. What they don't realize is that there are some athletes out there, Alan, who at thirty-six – even forty – are still great achievers. Let's face it, that old Henry Cooper was thirty-seven when I beat him. The fact of the matter is, I still believe in myself at thirty-six – and as far as what they think, who cares a damn?

There was even one critic who said that I looked like Adonis – but it might as well have *been* a statue because I moved so slowly in the ring. Being that slow, if I beat guys how slow must *those* blokes have been? The guy who was rated No. 13 in the world, I hit him with one punch and he went out. They said, 'At last the unexploded bomb explodes.' Shit – I had forty-three knockouts in my career. At *last*! Their thinking is not sensible; when I was younger I sometimes gave them credit for being schooled and educated, but I take it all back now. I think they're all dills – *that's* a good old Aussie term!

I may get a lot of knocking for this, but I don't rate Tyson. I think he's another Frank Bruno. He's been fed a lot of guys who he could form over, and I think when he meets somebody that can box and punch, they'll knock him out. I think Frank had his chance against Tim Witherspoon. Sadly, I sent him a telegram: I said, 'Look Frank, you can do it' – but he had to do it in the first five rounds. I honestly don't believe he was prepared properly for that fight.

So you decided you wanted to make a comeback – or did Marlene manipulate you into it?

Marlene was dead against it, right up to three months ago, absolutely against it. 'Joe,' she said, 'why are you trying to mess up your reputation?' I said, 'Honey, you can't mess up something that has already been established.'

I've given myself a seven-month plan. I'd like to fight for the world heavyweight title before I'm thirty-seven, so I'd like to fight this guy called James Tillis, get rid of him, fight possibly mid-November another one, and then with a bit of luck, swing the world heavyweight title for the America's Cup, and that would just about do me, I reckon.

Sounds a pretty good scenario – but what happens if you lose?

Nothing – I shall just go back to living. I mean, I'm not a man who's stupid, I'm a man who has quite a bit of brains left. I can still go look for ABC, who've asked me to do some commentaries for them. No, no, I'm still *in* there, and you can't take away something that I've learned over a period of twenty years, Alan. You should know that.

Win or lose, you're not going to leave Australia?

Never, no, never at all. In fact, I've already applied for citizenship, and it should be coming through any time. If it does I shall be fighting under the Australian colours – and that's not because I've got anything against England. It's just that I believe if you live in a country and you want to be like one of the countrymen, *be* one of them. I'm going to go all the way.

Do you have any happy memories at all of England, of Bedfordshire, of your old school . . .?

My childhood was fantastic. I was raised in a pretty rough area, if you can call it that, but the people were nice. They were all Italians, Indians, blacks, you name it; they were all very cosmopolitan, so I didn't know too much of the English way of life. Occasionally we were invited over to tea into an English family, it was quite a culture shock!

I have some fond memories. I'm resentful of one simple thing: that I was never appreciated for what I've achieved, and I am – irrespective of what the cynics say – one of the greatest heavyweight boxers *ever* to have come out of Britain. Yet they refused to accept the fact. That I resent. But I think England, at times, can be beautiful country.

What's more, your old Mum is still there . . .

What's more my Mummy's still there, yes, and I think she intends to stay there – she loves the country. She won't come and live with me, she says I'm too odd, have too many opinions, should keep them to myself. I'm a bit outspoken at times. At six foot four and 225 pounds, I suppose I can afford to be!

Nobody's going to argue with you?

Well, Marlene does. Marlene throws a pretty good left hook!

Otherwise you sit just where you want to?

That's right. I'm not a bully, I just don't like fools who write bad things about me . . .

THE STUDIO BOSS: JANE DEKNATEL

If they're well dressed and attractive,
they're not taken seriously ...

Jane Deknatel was a film producer working out of one of those Century City highrises in Beverly Hills. An elegant grey-haired divorcee and a real-life Alexis Carrington, she followed into *Whicker's World* that other Brit who'd made good in the United States, Joan Collins.

Born in Oxford, Jane went to America to become married, divorced and a television executive; she was Senior Vice-President of Home Box Office, dispensing a budget of a million pounds a week and living happily with her two daughters in Santa Monica.

So far, so much achieved; but when I arrived in Sydney for my *Whicker's World Down Under* recce – *there* she was! She had come to Australia while my back was turned to run film operations for Kerry Packer, then controlling his nationwide newspaper and broadcasting empire. She had an interesting house over the Harbour at Point Piper and her daughters were at school in much safer, less stressed Sydney.

After the ferocious hard-driving *Dynasty* life-style of Hollywood she had been unprepared for the more relaxed ways Down Under; nor indeed was the Sydney film scene quite ready for her – only two of the twenty-five

Australian staff she inherited were still in the company. Nevertheless she steamed ahead on various TV series based on Australian themes, but destined for world markets.

Her production plan began to fall apart when Australian Equity refused permission for the use of the major international stars the scripts required. Then the tax structure changed – and Alan Bond suddenly offered Packer £422 million for his communications empire. He accepted.

Next day the removal men arrived in Jane's office, took away the furniture and disconnected the telephones. It was, after all, more *Dynasty* than Sydney ...

The last time we talked like this, you were an English film tycoon doing well in Hollywood – what made you leave Mecca and come Down Under?

I got offered a lot of money, and the opportunity to actually *run* a company, which nobody in America was offering me. I also don't see too many other women running companies in this place ... I thought it would be interesting for my daughters to live somewhere outside of Hollywood; it's very hard to maintain a life-style that's realistic when you live in that kind of environment. When you're in the game of being powerful it's very exciting – but when my children were smaller I didn't really understand how much it affected them. At some point you have to acknowledge that when you go to the supermarket to buy a bag of flour all you see in the parking lot are $50,000 cars ... It has to have some effect, somewhere.

But a powerful woman in Hollywood is an accepted thing, a woman being powerful in Australia is not ...

When I first came here the Australians had a hard time with me. I wasn't quite sure whether it was because I was a woman doing what I do, or whether I was perceived as an American. When they finally discovered I was English, it was even worse!

A powerful Pom – did they take agin you?

There was a great deal of resistance; all I knew was whenever I tried to do anything, nothing happened – which I wasn't used to.

I'd been here several times before, but always as a visitor on business, always representing a major American company – so the red carpet went out. Australians are incredibly hospitable and friendly – except when you come to *live* here! It's very different then because you become one of them, part of the scenery.

You stopped being the flavour of the week?

You don't even *start* being the 'flavour of the week' when you first get here; I literally had – in a very aggressive way – to do it myself: it absolutely stunned me that I never got invited for dinner by anybody. Absolutely incredible. The people I'd done a lot of business with in the States, men who had spent Thanksgiving in my house, dinners or lunches or whatever if they passed through LA or Home Box Office, Australians we did business with – they *never* called. When I called I got answers like, 'Well, you're now with one of our competitors' or 'My wife will think I had an affair with you ...'

The women were frightened you were going to pinch their husbands, the men were frightened you were going to fire them!

(*Laughs*) Yes, maybe you're right! Australians are very straight-forward and generous when you get to know them – more like the English and less like the Americans – but they're very into having equal numbers at dinners! I would get this kind of tentative call saying, 'Do come to dinner and *bring* somebody.' The reality was, who was I going to take? I find that offensive, frankly.

It's couples-country, and they don't have walkers! So what did you do?

I was uncharacteristically aggressive! When I'd spent two or three months without anybody inviting me anywhere, I decided it was ludicrous – so the first dozen people I met every week that I thought were attractive or interesting I said, 'I'm having dinner on Friday, why don't you come, bring your wife or your husband?' I wrote their names down, hoping to God I'd recognize them when they walked into my house.

Didn't you get a lot of taxi drivers?

A couple of attractive taxi drivers! Gradually over the months people began to feel more comfortable, and slowly I made some friends and people started to invite me back.

By yourself?

No. Still to this day, I only have two friends in Sydney who say, 'Come to dinner', and I know I can go alone.

One of the wonderful things about being in Sydney is that one can have all kinds of friends who do different things; that is enormously consoling after spending ten years in Los Angeles, where one had to go to New York or London or Europe to actually talk about something *besides* television or movies.

If you want to meet an architect in LA, you have to hire one!

That's right, absolutely. Here people ask, 'What do you do?' and you say, 'I run a movie company', and they say, 'Oh, that's nice.' Period. Over and out, end of sentence, don't want to know. But that's *great!*

Have you experienced the Australian party minuet: men at one end of the room talking sport, women at the other, talking babies? Does that persist?

What's happening now is that the men are at one end of the room talking about their feelings and being sensitive, and the women at the other end talking about their stock options! Women now actually *like* to talk to each other, and are talking to each other about professional things . . .

This might be absolutely heretical but my feeling is, if a table has to be put out of balance in terms of numbers, I'd much rather have more women than men, because men when they're *en masse* without women get to be very boring. They talk to each other in a *very* boring way.

The thing that's interesting about Australians is that they are very flexible and non-puritanical, and as a result they do lots of interesting things like acupuncture and aquapressure and floating in tanks, go to faith healers and spiritual healers and get into crystals – all those kinds of things.

How did you have to adjust when you arrived here from California?

One has to get used to the fact that there's not the variety of things available that there is in California: movies, restaurants, theatres, records, clothes ... I wanted to buy some additional table napkins for the kitchen one day, and went down to Double Bay; they had two kinds – but only six of each, and I wanted twenty. So I bought twenty tea towels instead. It's hard when you've been living in a consumer society like the United States, not to be able to go and buy *anything* you want.

Sydney now seems to be making a good effort – and then suddenly falls flat on its face! In Woollahara, in Queens Road yesterday, while waiting in the rain, I discovered a very elegant little coffee shop with comfortable bamboo chairs, lots of interesting magazines and every type of coffee: Zambesi and Costa Rican and Jamaican ... Valerie wanted a soft drink so they said, 'A passionfruit?' We thought, 'Wonderful!' A can of synthetic fizz with a straw arrived. So we said, 'Perhaps not, let's settle for orange juice' – thinking in this country, full of fruits, it's going to be fresh, or at least deep-frozen. Not a bit of it – a can of Fanta ... So there's this promising, stylish little place behaving like a caff.

I think it's beginning to happen, though. New restaurants have opened, and it's impossible to get into Chez Oz. If there were more, the demand would be greater.

One of the things that struck me when I first came to Australia, and I'm sure this is a reflection of living in California and in LA in particular: people here *don't* dress-up. The men are still dressing very conservative, and I think culturally Australian women have been taught that if they're well dressed and attractive, they're not taken seriously.

They don't want to be different?

No, and that's a major Australian trait: not to want to stick out of the crowd, because then nobody's going to like you and you're going to lose your friends and the tall poppy syndrome strikes again.

When you arrived to take over the company as hired gun, what happened?

I walked into the office and the man who I was replacing took me around to introduce me to everybody; in the conference room there were six or eight men, the writers and directors working on a mini-series we were about to shoot. The thing that stunned me was that not *one* person got to their feet.

He said, 'This is Jane Deknatel, she's the new Managing Director of PBL.' Two of the young men just laughed and said, 'Yes, right, very funny, tell us the next joke.' They just didn't *believe* it.

So they didn't last long! How many people did you have working for you?

About twenty-five, in the beginning. We are now down to about ten. Of the originals there are only two left.

So you had a night of the long knives?

If they're not willing to accept that you're running something, you have to make them understand that you *are*.

Do you think they were braced for it – or were you a bolt from Santa Monica?

I think they all expected to be fired immediately; they thought some tough-arsed American was going to come in and just blow everybody away.

I did have to fire somebody when I first arrived who'd been with the company for a while and who I thought was behaving inappropriately. Finally the day came when I knew I was going to have to terminate him. I said, I'm sorry to do this, but we have discussed this issue several times, and this is the end. I will give you a very generous settlement, but collect your things and we'll send a cheque to your house. And he leant over and tapped me on the knee and said, 'There, there dear, I'm sure we'll work this out, let's go back to the office . . .'

I guess trying to be taken seriously was not something I've had to deal with before!

How do Australian men look upon a successful woman?

With interest, with amusement. I think they find it a little scary. The reason most of the men who worked for me in the beginning gave for leaving was that they didn't want to work *that* hard.

I was in a meeting one day with men from around the country and they were referring to some woman as a 'sheila'. I said quietly, 'Excuse me, I actually find this quite offensive; would you mind not doing it?' They said 'Oh, sorry – sure', and never did it again. It's not something they do deliberately to be offensive, it's a lack of consciousness.

You don't come here and in six months change the habits of a hundred years.

No, but I can certainly request that those habits get *looked* at when I'm around.

So they don't refer to you as a sheila, anyway?

Not to my face; God knows what they call me behind my back!

I suppose if you've sent a number of people to the guillotine you can't expect to be popular ...

No, of course not, but I don't try to be popular; I mean it's harder for me to fire women because I know how difficult it is for them to survive in the marketplace.

You did tell me, back in Beverly Hills, that the pendulum was about to swing against women ...

If you just look at what's happening in Hollywood you'll see there are very few women left in any positions of corporate power; there's still a backlash in operation. As you hit recessions and conservative times there's always that swing to put women back in the kitchen, or certainly take them out of the workforce. Men are the only people who support families, women are not – therefore women should get out of the way.

The English see Sydney as an Americanized city – has the American work ethic reached here too?

There's not the same effort there is in America, there's not the Puritan work ethic and there's not the same level of intensity – which is wonderful because it's more relaxing, but is terribly *frustrating* because you can't get things done as fast, or with the same kind of precision. When you find Australians who are willing to work hard, they're as good if not better than anybody in the world, because they also keep a balance: they play, they take time off, they sail, they party, they drink the good Australian wines, they like to eat – but they also work hard. On the other hand that's not prevalent, and Australia is going to have to do something about the average work habits. There's a great tendency just to leave it and not to take it the next step, not to push it one stage farther.

Say your contract ran out and they said, 'Thank you, close the door behind you,' is Sydney a place where you might stay?

That's very likely. I have a friend who thinks I'll never leave, which of course absolutely stuns me ... I think we're all getting to an age where we think being somewhere relaxed is more fun than being somewhere like New York. Sydney's easy and comfortable and cheaper, but if I never saw anybody I knew and couldn't get on an aeroplane whenever I felt like it, I'd feel terribly cut off and isolated ...

THE LONER: DENNIS GOWING

*I poured salt water into my right ear
every night ...*

While Englishmen may dream of dancing with Princess Di and Americans yearn to be President, Australians merely long to win the Melbourne Cup – the only race in the world that stops a nation. In 1985 that Cup was won by an orphan from St Pancras who'd been adopted by three fathers and two mothers and could not read or write until he was ten.

A boy-soldier who thought even the Army might be a sort of family for him, Dennis Gowing soon wangled his discharge and escaped to Australia – the only free passage available in 1949. From this discouraging start he went on to create, and sell for millions, the most successful car franchise in Victoria, own the best collection of modern Australian art, have two wives, four children and seven serious relationships – one with a Miss Australia, no less. He also carried off the Cup: What A Nuisance won $625,000 prize money – though it wasn't the cash, it was the glory.

Melbourne Cup Day, despite its power to stop Parliament, taxis and the nation's life, is an innocent carnival, a hectic mixture of Ascot and 'Appy 'Ampstead: elegant marquees dispense hospitality to the *beau monde* in morning dress, who go out to queue at the tote with equally enthusiastic punters in shorts and thongs. It's the outdoor party of the year.

During the Derby, Cup and Oaks Days in November 1986 I was press-ganged into helping judge the fashions – an awesome task. Scores of dramatically dressed women posed on a catwalk in front of the Members' Enclosure, all of them hoping to win a flight to America and $3500 spending money. Were we looking for elegance, or fun? Youthful dash and outlandish style, or wearable comfy mummery? Some of the outfits could have been fancy dress. It was hard to know where to draw the line. A few years ago Jean Shrimpton's knees shocked the nation ... It was all a bit bizarre but we enjoyed ourselves, and one of them went to San Francisco.

Dennis Gowing had a horse running, but she did not show. This Damon Runyon character was out of step in good grey Melbourne, even on its one gaudy day. I enjoyed this little master car salesman who had suddenly decided to deal in art, and could well see him knocking out in the trade an almost-new Sidney Nolan, previously owned by an elderly clergyman who'd only looked at it twice ...

Unusually quiet, small and epileptic, he says he looks like a 'Jewish Cockney'. Certainly he retains a London accent after forty years away, but shares the true Australian passions – horses, sailing, wine, women – while remaining apart, and lonely as an orphan in St Pancras ...

———————————————

I was born in St Pancras Hospital – an orphan, adopted by people with the name of Gowing. All in all I had three fathers and two mothers. I didn't know I was adopted until I was about fourteen, and found out by accident. I'd applied to join a training ship at

Greenwich and they wanted a birth certificate: on the train I opened the envelope and found I had an adoption certificate.

I never went to school until I was about nine, and I couldn't read or write. I sort of bummed around England and joined the Army in June 1946. I was fifteen and a half and put my age up, and eventually ended up in the Duke of Cornwall's Light Infantry, signed up for nine years with the Colours and three years with the Reserves; I was stationed at Bodmin. I remember getting the King's Shilling at King's Cross, where I got recruited.

Why did you enlist? ·

I'd been battling around on my own for a long time, during the War and after. I'd run away from where I was evacuated and bummed around England, and I was fairly screwed up. I could have quite easily gone the wrong way, and somehow felt that at least the Army would give me a home without all the responsibilities of looking after myself. Which it did.

In the first year I spent 113 days in a lot of trouble in the Army: in the Aldershot glasshouse, confined to barracks, in jail, going AWOL and everything else! The second year I spent 365 days trying to get *out* of the Army.

I did get out, I was medically discharged with a very small pension of twenty-eight shillings a week for two years and a £50 gratuity. I'd always had ear trouble, so I aggravated that by pouring salt water in my right ear and ended up being discharged with what I think was called bilateral otitis media.

You poured salt water down your ear?

Oh yes – every night.

Good Lord – has that affected your hearing since?

Yes, I'm still slightly deaf in that ear, always have been.

It's quite a price to pay – was it worth it?

It was bloody *cheap* to pay! In the Army I got four shillings a day – imagine me being in until I was nearly thirty! General Montgomery had come back and he'd arranged you could buy yourself out for about £50 – but when you're earning twenty-eight shillings a week £50 is a bloody lot of money!

It was 1948, and the first thing I did when I got my demobilization suit was to go to Australia House, Canada House, the whole lot, and put in my application to go overseas. The main thing was to get out of England. There was Hong Kong, there was the Gold Coast in those days, there was New Zealand, which cost you £100. America you couldn't go to. The only one you could get to without money and influence was Australia. I landed on 10 May 1949, when I was eighteen and a half.

If you'd stayed, what do you think would have happened to you?

I'd have been very successful. I'm very dedicated in things I do. I had more opportunities in Australia – but looking back I'd have done all right in England too.

If you had nothing but trouble in the Army and were in the glasshouse much of the time – wouldn't you have had trouble outside the Army?

I'm a survivor, and if I have to do something I'll work eighteen hours a day to become successful.

In those days if you'd been in the Army you could come out to Australia for nothing, sharing a cabin with about ten blokes. I think mine were four Scotsmen, three Welshmen, two Irishmen, a couple of other Poms – and the whole lot of them ended up back in England within a year! They all gave it away. They were homesick. They missed the pubs and the people next door, and they wouldn't give the country a go. I'd nothing to go back to, anyhow. They had relations and they had memories. I'd come out much younger, and I could see no reason for going back: I thought it was fantastic.

Do you think any one of them could have finished up winning the Melbourne Cup, if he'd put his mind to it?

No, no.

What have you got that they needed?

Luck – a lot of luck. A hell of a lot. People always say dedication and perspiration; that is true, but not if you don't have that bit of luck going for you. It didn't matter where you came from, you could be a success in this country if you got off your bum and got into it. You weren't held back in those days by red tape.

I ended up working in a general store of the State Electricity

Commission, putting nuts on bolts. I was supposed to get paid £6.13.4d a week, which was not a bad salary, but my first fortnight's pay was half that. They didn't tell me at Australia House that if you're under twenty-one you got half the pay, so I thought: I'd come 12,000 miles, I could have more than this in England, I'd better get out of that situation!

Since '49, since the days of putting nuts on bolts, how many other jobs have you had?

I did between twenty-five and thirty-five jobs in that first four or five years: gold-mining, truck driving, bus driver, nightwatchman, barman, photographer, milkman, rabbit-trapper . . .

But you finished up as the biggest car dealer in Victoria with 550 employees, you're half-owner of last year's Melbourne Cup winner, you possessed what's said to be the best collection of contemporary Australian art – how did an orphan find his way through so many different worlds?

There's a saying that all knowledge is acquired, and I had this tunnel vision. I was the best car operator in Australia, starting from nothing in 1954. The art business I sort of drifted into in 1960/61, spent a lot of time reading, thinking about Australian contemporary art, acquired a knowledge of things, ended up with the best collection. I sold it, along with a big house, because all my cash and my funding was in this one collection and one house. They paid nearly $2 million. The collection's now worth about $25 million.

I was in the stud horse breeding industry and it was very successful, but two people were killed on that stud, so I just got out of it.

I think anyone can apply their mind to any subject and be successful, if they want to. I mean, other people are a lot smarter: I know a lot of businessmen can do all those things at once. I can't. If you point me in one direction and say, 'Do that,' that's what I'll do, and I'll do it very very well, but if you say, 'Do that – and do *that* as well,' then I get confused. Other people can manipulate large loans, but I've never borrowed money – I get confused with all that.

But whenever you're doing well, in business or in your personal life, you break off and throw it all away?

241

I think it goes back to when I was adopted. I think there's some sort of resistance to attachment. I haven't worked it out myself yet, but when I achieve the greatest happiness or success – not necessarily in that order – then I go and stuff it right up, I want to get out. I had the finest restaurant in Melbourne, and when everybody loved it and it was taking a large amount of money, I got out. I had one of the great cruising yachts – I sold it. I had a great car business – I sold it. I developed houses and property. I had the first professional showjumping team in Australia; my horse, Mr Dennis, was the top horse at the Montreal Olympics. This is not an ego trip – there must be a weakness in my character, or something . . .

I'd sold the car business for about $2½ million – twelve years ago that was a fortune – and I went into a few other enterprises, like the entertainment industry and hotels that didn't work, which I lost fortunes at. And I've lost fortunes on the market: I thought I was going to beat the commodity dealers, and I clapped out very badly on that. I'm not rich by today's standards because I've spent a lot of money and I've had a fairly good time. I've sort of been married here and there, and raised children.

How many times, here and there?

Two actual marriages.

And some that didn't take, you mean?

Like a skin graft! I lived with seven other ladies over a number of years, which was all enjoyable.

One of them, I heard, was a Miss Australia?

Yes, yes – marvellous! I was always madly in love with Randy, but funnily enough she was never in love with me, you know how it is. We were together for about three years. It was a time when all of a sudden I discovered a new way of life, and I bought a big yacht. I'd never been on a yacht before and we sailed from Melbourne up to the top of Australia and all around, had a fantastic time; and at the end of three months during the 1984 Sydney Cup, she virtually said, 'Well, goodbye, piss off,' and off she went. And that was about it.

Was it something you'd said?

(*Laughs*) Something I·didn't tell her about? But no, it was good, it was good. Very fond of her, but I don't know if I'd want to settle down again. Hard to say.

Aren't you going to find yourself in ten years' time right back where you began – as a penniless orphan?

No, I can keep making money. I can always make money. I had extreme wealth in those days – today I'm sort of comfortably off; but I'll always have the ability.

You're saying you've lived with all these ladies, on and off; your business has gone up and down ... It seems in Australia people can be bankrupt, can go to jail – and nobody holds it against them, nobody worries ...

As long as you haven't done rotten things – I mean you can't put those people in the same class as child molesters or murderers.

Somebody told me you'd been in jail – that story got about ...

Yeah – somebody told me too.

Was it true?

No, no – it all happened many years ago. It was on a Good Friday and my daughter saw me in the morning, I hadn't had a shave for two days at least and she said, 'Why don't you grow a beard?' So I grew this beard. My advertising agency said I'd been over-saturated on television for so long – we had eight shows running, and 287 minutes of TV commercials.

You're on television more than I am.

Well, I should be, I'm much younger. (*Laughs*)

More beautiful, more clever, richer ...

But I grew the beard and the agency said, 'Keep it.' So I was three to six months off television, and then I came back with this very peculiar campaign and everyone was saying, 'But that's his brother, *he's* in jail.' All of a sudden I've disappeared and this new person's come in – so we stopped the campaign, cut off the beard, and then: 'He's *out* of jail!' This was bloody ridiculous; I've always been reasonably honest. My word has been better than all the partners I've had.

Still, you're better known for winning the Melbourne Cup than for being an ex-convict, I'll say that for you. What was the effect of winning?

I was away with the birds for nine months! I just couldn't believe that somebody in my position was able to win something like that: only a hundred people over 125 years have won the Melbourne Cup. It's a fantasy, and I didn't come down for months ...

I did a very peculiar thing; after I'd got the Cup I stayed for one race – I was with a lady I go with, and my daughter – and I said, 'We're going.' I'd got the Cup and I got hold of a newspaper, wrapped the Cup up and ran through the car park. I got back to my restaurant to get away from all the thoughts, I wanted to be private. The euphoria must have lasted three or four months. I'd get up every morning and I'd look at the Cup and touch it.

It's a special race, a very special horse, a very special thing – a totally Australian thing outsiders wouldn't know. I mean, the whole country stops dead. To get a horse in the race – not to win, just to have a horse in the race even if it runs last – is fantastic. The first prize was $625,000. We gave $130,000 to charities – Save the Children and Variety Club. The trainer got about $100,000, the jockey got about $100,000. What did we get ...?

You finished up owing, right?

(*Laughs*) No, I think we got $100,000 plus; plus bets! But I tell you – you'd *pay* that, not take it!

You can be quite unpopular in certain quarters here, I'm not quite sure why: you're a quiet, amiable chap ...

I suppose in our advertising many years ago as Kevin Dennis Motors we worked on the principle of brainwashing, hitting people. They weren't 'nice' commercials, they were there to hit people over the head. I have a sort of a *look* about me on television that isn't sometimes too nice to too many people – like a Jewish Cockney – and I became unpopular; but I still sold. If I had ten customers, I'd sell five cars. But they never knew me. I never mixed in those days.

I'm not a popular person, I've never *tried* to be popular – it's not my game, you know. I can't pat babies' heads, and if I don't like anyone I tell them to piss off.

You're not tempted to take the bones back, to have them buried in St Pancras?

No, I'm an Australian, I'm very happy here. A lot of people in Melbourne know me. I think you fight to be acknowledged – not to be *popular*, not because you care whether people dislike you, but to be acknowledged as a person. A lot of people I know in Melbourne mightn't like me, but they respect what I've done and what I do. It's very hard to go somewhere else and be a stranger in somebody else's country. I'd be a stranger in England ...

THE SOCIALITE: DIANA FISHER

It's like a circus gone wrong ...

Australians devote much of their lives to the pursuit of pleasure, relishing a dramatic country. Since they also enjoy a fine climate, good meat, excellent wine, they have raised the barbecue to an essential art. It's a poor Sunday brunch that finishes before late evening.

Clothes and manners are as casual as the hospitality – but the pendulum can swing in the cities, where women will get more dressed up and wear more make-up than they do in *Dallas*. The glitzy charity circuit in Sydney, the determination of showbiz and advertising groups to keep awarding themselves Oscars – even the more restrained hospitality of Melbourne ... is a long social mile from all those barbies, when a T-shirt can be dressy.

Such gatherings of expensively groomed women are carefully chronicled in most daily papers by old-fashioned columnists – and though Australian journalists will attack and denigrate any poppy showing the slightest sign of growing tall, these columns carry few barbs about impending divorces or family drug problems. Instead, glowing descriptions of clothes and food and those seen – a gentler pace than we have grown to expect from our diarists: 1950 in freeze-frame.

Amid all this, Diana Fisher (known for good reason as 'Bubbles'), doyenne of Sydney social columnists, radio and television personality, generous hostess and all-round good egg. Once a BOAC stewardess from Southgate, N.14, she arrived in Australia in 1964 when Humphrey – son of the then Archbishop of Canterbury, Lord Fisher – was made BBC representative. They returned to London in '69 but after eighteen months could stand the place no longer, and emigrated – this time, for good.

Since then she has been inescapable on the Australian social scene, imparting a sixth-form Angela Brazil jollity to every charity ball and boutique opening. We went to the Opera's wardrobe department to select her costume for the Opera Ball. I steered her away from a very tight Christmas tree fairy towards a sterner but looser Brunhilde, with the horns, pigtails and breastplate of an invincible social Valkyrie.

Noisy but nice, Bubbles may dress up and clown around, but shows due respect for good form. In a small and charming house in Woollahra she's den mother to English friends' back-packing children on the free-holiday route; but having embraced the quick warmth of Australian hospitality and sunshine, Bubbles has become a mite piqued by the buttoned-up welcome she sometimes receives back in England ...

We came out in 1964 for the BBC and fell in love with it, begged the BBC to leave us behind – but they didn't. We went back and had a year and a half in London; the skies were grey and the pavements were grubby and we missed the vitality and the sunshine and the people – so we emigrated back!

We were ten-pounders who emigrated twenty-two years down the track, and still love it: the open-heartedness, tall blue skies, wonderful vast country. Sad to say it looks like it's being ruined by the government but, if we dismiss that, it still has golden beaches for miles and miles, sea that's crystal clear, and it gets you.

At first it was freer and easier; there was a Liberal Government and everybody was very welcoming. There was an ebullient feeling, which, sad to say, changed. I feel it's sad at the moment, I feel it's like England was when the unions got at it: sort of down in its boots, a bit down at heel. We've no need to be – we have all the resources, we have everything. We just need to do an honest day's work. But the restaurants have become much better, the food is better, we've got all the ethnic people coming in.

You write a gossip column with the sort of social chit-chat we haven't read in England since the Fifties . . .

When I first came and saw all these funny names in the papers I thought, 'Who on earth *are* these people? Who do they think they are?' The *Tatler* in England was full of dukes and the Honourable this and Lord that and Princess Anne's gone here and Diana and Charles are doing something else . . . I suppose because we don't have *them*, we make up our own society which attends all the great charity occasions – like me making a fool of myself tonight! There are people who star at these charity events, and they form the nucleus of the society we write about.

So there's still a market for the goings-on of the almost rich and the nearly well-known?

Different stratas, different rungs of the ladder; whether you're in sport or theatre or films, if there's a grand occasion everybody wants to know about it. They want to get their pictures in the paper.

Len Evans, our friend, tells me there's no interest in Britain here any more?

Bring a royal personage out, bring a star out, bring Sir Laurence Olivier out – there'd be a queue a mile long to see them! They love things that are British, that have made the grade. They love stars – and if you've got a title my dear, they'll be *swanning* around you . . .

I have a host of wonderful friends here, I feel totally at home. I couldn't live in England again unless I married a millionaire, and I don't think *that's* likely . . .

People in England have changed so much – they're *so* Cockney.

I'd say they were ocker, in an English way. They don't talk proper on the radio any more, which annoys me. I had eight years at the BBC and it was almost white gloves and red carpets and you were properly dressed and you did everything properly.

Yes, your original strength here was your Englishness, was it not?

They loved me for that, but I'm not *too* lah-di-dah. Some people come out and they're frightfully frightfully – and nobody takes any notice of them at all. They love dukes and earls and duchesses and things; if you've got a title, they love it. I don't put The Hon. Mrs Humphrey Fisher on everything. I might when I have to answer something that's very proper, and Humphrey would use it only when he's *cross*. I'm Bubbles ...

At the Melbourne Cup, you'll have hysterics! It's like a circus gone wrong: all those who want to be seen to be outrageous and ludicrous are in the paddock with ridiculous hats, like Mrs Shilling. The kids dress up and wear a bow-tie and nothing else, or shorts and boots and a top-hat – and think that's great!

Then the real racing crowd in the Members' Enclosure come exquisitely dressed, and – forgive me for saying – the Melbourne racing scene is *so* bloody stuffy: having been asked down to judge the fashions in the field, I was evicted from the Members' Dining Room ...

THE DISILLUSIONED:
JOHN AND SIOBHAN CHAPMAN

Any sort of change upsets people . . .

John Chapman was a clerk, his wife Siobhan a school-teacher; they left Essex in August 1973 to find a better life. Newly married, they were *so* average that BBC television filmed their departure as a typical pair of young migrants setting out cheerfully for a new world. In Australia John went to work for Fords. With two attractive children and a suitable dog, the Chapmans seemed a traditionally contented family, and their future wellbeing in that sunny land happily predictable. It was not to be. Their dream life turned into a melodrama, acted out in loneliness 12,000 miles from home . . .

John fell for Nancy, who worked with him, and sent Siobhan and their children home to England. He had three more with Nancy, who turned out to be unwell. His daughter Corinna, who was beautiful and only three, drowned in an irrigation canal in front of their home. His other daughter Angelina was found to be stone deaf. Their mother left him, and went to Law.

Siobhan finally returned from England with their children; they are now living in Brunswick Junction, a small township in Western Australia.

So migration has certainly changed their lives – though

not altogether for the better. I asked Siobhan whether she believed the marriage would have broken up, had they stayed at home ...

Siobhan: Possibly we might have managed to stay together in Waltham Abbey, because you have so much more support – you've got family around you and things like that. I mean, here I didn't really have anybody to talk to ...

John: I don't know if it was really Australia's fault – any sort of change upsets people, whether it's changing the job or changing the country. Maybe it wouldn't have gone the same way – but then again maybe it would.

In the first eighteen months we bought two brand-new cars! I worked for Ford Motor Company as an analyst, and it was quite good for a while. Then the bottom fell out of the motor industry in Australia, and the work became very tedious. I had the opportunity to go back into construction, building two very high tower blocks in Melbourne, and I spent a couple of years on that job. It was very absorbing, and I think that was half the problem we had ... I was spending most of the time dealing with the unions, and doing the accounts in the evening, and I became very ragged.

But you can't just blame the work – you found another lady, didn't you?

No, you can't blame the work at all – but that was part of the problem Siobhan had; that I was never *there*. Two days after I started that job she gave birth to Rebecca, a month premature.

You now have two gorgeous kids – I would have thought they might have cemented your marriage, especially as you were earning well?

But we'd gone from two salaries and living very well, to one salary. To earn that salary I was working harder than I should have, and playing harder than I should have. That was really the problem – I was *playing* too hard.

But I suppose if that's your character, it would have been the same back in Waltham Abbey?

It's different here, it's a little bit of 'she'll be right'. It's more chauvinistic, as far as men are concerned. If you want to go out – you *go* out!

And you've got to stay here, Siobhan, looking at formula food and doing the cooking! How did you take to his new-found chauvinism?

Siobhan: He was always a bit like that anyway. (*Laughs*) He always liked to get his own way, so I didn't notice a great dramatic change . . .

So he's blaming his rotten character on Australia! In coming to Australia, you became a more liberated male?

John: Ah, I probably have changed views over the years. In the Sixties I suppose I would have been someone who'd go marching up and down saying, 'Equal Rights for Women', and all the rest of it. Now I would say, fair enough, equal rights for women – but equal *responsibilities* as well.

I could see when I came here the way we were going: it would be exactly the same as in England. I would have ended up as the accountant of a construction company and I would have done that job for the next twenty or thirty years . . . When I saw that happening, I didn't like it.

Siobhan: It was a bad time, and Rebecca wasn't the best of all possible babies; she was absolutely awful until she was two years old, never slept longer than two hours at a stretch, very, very hard work. John would come home and I'd be absolutely exhausted and he'd be exhausted, and it just led to friction or non-communication.

John: I come from a large family and I know what large families and children can do to people. It's hard. As soon as you have children, it changes the relationship dramatically. It's not just a simple change, it's a *dramatic* change. Siobhan wanted children and I tried to tell her it's not quite what it is on television, having children.

I think she was a bit surprised how hard it was, being stuck indoors with someone as difficult as Rebecca. Then I was working until nine o'clock at night quite regularly, and Siobhan didn't trust me. Actually, I *wasn't* playing around or anything, but she didn't really trust me.

Anyway, I met a girl – who worked for me, actually – and she was quite an entrancing person and an incredible liar. She was supposed to be dying of cancer, and all sorts of things. I saw her doctor who wouldn't say what was wrong with her, but said that whenever she felt really bad she knew what to do. But she was an extremely interesting person and probably at the time I thought, 'This is good.' I was very emotionally messed up – and I just sent you home, didn't I?

Siobhan: Just after Nathan was born – he was three weeks old.

John: That's right. I just said, You go – because all the time I was getting, 'I'm dying.' So when Siobhan left I said, OK when this is all over – it'll be about a year – I'll come back and see you. Then about three months after you'd left I found out it was all a fantasy.

But despite this you still started a second family with this other lady?

Yes, I did. She wanted a family, so we had a very, very beautiful child, Corinna, born just before I arrived back in Australia from working in Nigeria. We actually lost her – she was drowned. She was a beautiful little girl.

She was drowned?

Yes, in the irrigation channel over there. It was quite horrific. I was at work and got a phone call with this really hysterical yelling. I came back here, and the ambulance was just going off. You think each day you'll wake up and find it was a terrible dream. She was three.

We'd had a second child by that time, and when Corinna died we had the third child about ten months later; she was deaf, totally deaf. That's Angelina.

So this other lady, Nancy, she took off. What happened was after ten months I knew there was something wrong with Angelina because, although she was such a beautiful baby, she was very quiet. She wasn't coming on like I would expect a child to, so in the end I took her to a specialist who said, 'It looks very much as if she's retarded.' He arranged for us to see another specialist in Perth, and then three days before that Nancy took off. Since then we've had rather a bitter time, I don't know why. It's turned out very bitter, very expensive and not very nice at all ...

It sounds from everything you say that you were the one who rocked the boat, it wasn't Siobhan.

That's probably true. There was a stage about six months after Rebecca was born where I said, 'I'll go up north and earn some money quick-quick and then we'll have that basis and we can do the sort of things we want to do.' She wasn't very happy about that at all, and it was a silly idea.

Siobhan: Well, it was about two o'clock in the morning and you could hardly stand up and you were going there and then – only I had the car keys ...

Sounds like one of those Saturday nights!

John: It was, but at the same time it was a genuine thought ... There are times when I've been really, *really* depressed during the last eight years and I've drunk extremely destructively through very short periods of time, but excessively. Very, very destructive drinking.

Siobhan: You see, you can get very cheap wine here, and it's very easy. Every hour of the day and night, virtually any time you want it, you can go and buy yourself a cask of wine or a crate of stubbies or whatever. You don't think anything of it.

John: Drinking is a frame of mind, a lot of the time. Drinking is so socially acceptable it's way above what it should be for everybody's health. In the business I'm in, which is basically construction, you meet so many people who have a serious problem. Most people function throughout the day heaven knows how, because you know very well when they arrive in the morning they're drunk!

The worrying thing is that they're driving the car that's heading towards you!

It's pretty obvious with most accidents there's alcohol involved somewhere.

Siobhan: There's an awful lot of road smashes which they feature on the news, all the blood and guts.

Looking back over these last thirteen years, would you say your life here has been a success?

Well, ours is a strange case, we're in a peculiar situation. If we'd been together the whole time, then we could probably say yes.

'Apart from that, Mrs Lincoln ...'

John: (*Laughs*) I've had opportunities to move around and earn lots of money. I've done a lot of things which if I hadn't done, I would always have been sorry I hadn't done – so in that respect, yes it has been a success. We've all had a really hard time, but you can make a comeback here.

When you left, John, you said that England was careering downhill from one economic crisis to another, but since then the same thing's happened to Australia?

Australia is basically sound because it's just a mass of raw resources, and that's its strength. Australians are used to a very good life – the 'lucky country' – and an awful lot of them don't realize where that lucky life comes from: they think it's because they're hardworking and good grafters. In actual fact it all comes from primary projects. It comes from agriculture and minerals – all they're doing is digging up big lumps of Australia and selling it. But it's given them a good chance to have a look at themselves and their manufacturing industry, which virtually is non-existent – and what there is is just totally bolstered up by protectionism.

Australians like to think of themselves as a certain type of person, a Crocodile Dundee – they *love* to see themselves as that, which is a total fallacy. There are some people like that and they're the most marvellous people you'll ever meet in the world, but the rest of Australians are like everybody else: they're greedy, very self-centred. Their sense of humour isn't too good, doesn't exist as such; it's really having a dig at someone else – as long as they don't have a dig back! That seems very funny from the giving end, but if they get it back they're not quite so keen ...

If you're from the east, the people from the west don't like you. In Melbourne they don't like you if you're from Sydney – and everyone thinks Queensland is a joke. So they're not selective in who they like to criticize – they like to drop the bucket on anybody, and of course if you drop it back on them they're not too receptive to that.

But you do find this other Australian with a very dry laconic sort of humour, and he can turn his hand to everything and nothing seems to faze him; you couldn't wish for a better sort of man. It's the best side of mateship and the Australian character – but that side is by no means as widespread as Australians like to think it is . . .

THE GARBO: JIM JAGGS

I tried to make the kids talk proper,
but they won't ...

Jim Jaggs came from a family of dockers in the East End;
he moved from Forest Gate to East Ham, but migrated
when he decided there were too many Asians around. He
is now a garbo — a Sydney dustman.

We talked behind his dustcart as he went on his dawn
rounds; then at his home, which many English bankers
would covet: a pole house, cantilevered from a wooded
hillside outside Mona Vale, amid a dazzle of exotic birds.
His neighbours are architects, lawyers, government
officials. A television actor has moved in up the road:
'I told him, "You're going to bring our bloody prices
down!"'

Jim's children ride their horses, his wife is tennis-mad
and he's into boating. In Australia a dustman's life can
be *quite* a happy one ...

This is nice clean rubbish, upper-class rubbish – or so they say
around this area! The smelly stuff's not out yet because it's not
summer. One of our perks is just coming along the other side of the
road here: lady joggers. Hi darling! (*Whistles*)

Is this a job you'd recommend?

Suits me, suits the lads. A lot of time's your own. If you want to get stuck in and really work hard you can get it done in a couple of hours. We're doing fifteen kilometres a night, and loading about ten tons.

You can't even go to the toilet on this game. People will come out, get half way through their round – and go home! They don't want any more of it, half a round's enough. It's too hard for them. Take an office worker, there for eight hours – but by the time they've made their social phone calls and talked about the football at the weekend and made cups of coffee, they're not doing *that* much.

How do people of Sydney look upon you?

We're second worst to prostitutes; there was a thing in the *Daily Mirror* the other day, a prestige rating on jobs, and they rated us just above prostitutes. We work the same hours: sleep all day and work all night. We don't get the dough they do, though!

But do you get the job satisfaction! What made you exchange the reassuring warmth and friendliness of the East End of London for the Pacific?

When we was just married East Ham was OK, when there was the two of us; we got out and we had a good time. When our first child came along we realized there was something wrong in London: you know, a lot of Pakistanis started to move around our way, and things got a little bit bad. There was bomb scares in the shopping centres, when the IRA was here. This was in 1973, there was quite a bit of disillusion really. We worked hard on the house that we had in East Ham, we borrowed the money, put a new roof on, done the house up, but I didn't seem to be getting anywhere.

A lot of people might say that travelling half way around the world to become a dustman is an odd sort of ambition – you're not the Asians of Sydney?

I've never regarded myself as an Asian, actually! I hope not. I really do enjoy the job. You get your bad days and off-days, but it keeps you fit. It's a much better type of dust here!

Could you see yourself as a dustman in East Ham?

No, it never even crossed me mind, being a dustman. The nearest I come to the dustman in London was put my bin out on a Sunday night and hope they don't wake us up – and maybe give them two cigars at Christmas.

Do they go in for Christmas boxes here?

It's a really known thing, but it's gone down a little bit in the last couple of years. About three years ago they used to leave beer out, bottles of wine, bottles of champagne, give you five bucks, ten bucks. There was a television actor that lived at Kirri Billi, he used to give us twenty bucks every year.

Television people are very generous.

He must have got the sack, because he didn't give us one last year.

It's up and down in showbiz ... If people see the house you're living in you'll never get another tip for the rest of your life! Are there any perks apart from the occasional Christmas box – do you find people chuck away furniture and things you can use?

Wednesdays, they call it a clean-up day here. Not so much now, people are getting more aware of what they throw out, but up until about a year or so ago we used to find loads of stuff. We've got some really nice mirrors in the house, chairs, a telephone table, few bits and pieces ...

One of the disadvantages must be the hours – what time did you get up this morning?

Half past two, or a little bit before that. We usually finish about half past eight. By the time you tip and get home, usually about half nine; then you have a shower and ten o'clock you're ready to do whatever you want to do. A lot of guys in the summer will go down the beach, a lot of other guys do a second job. In this game there's quite a lot of sports people; footballers use it as training, while they get paid as well.

I wouldn't recommend it to anybody who doesn't want to run around for four or five hours a night, because it really is demanding work, plus the fact you've got two off-siders with you and you've got to be fair to them as well. They don't really want to be up at four o'clock in the morning with some guy that's not ready to have a go.

There's a mateyness in the East End; this is a mateship country, but it's not like the London style . . .

I don't mind them calling me a Pom – they say it in good humour anyway – but there is mateship here. I've found some really good guys on the garbage, and outside that. You do tend to lean towards English people a bit more as friends – people that's come into the country from outside, you're all in that same boat, you're trying to do better things than you did . . . Over here I find if you really want to work hard you can get in front and get a few extra figures, if you try.

I miss the sense of humour of the guys in the pub at home; most Londoners have got a fair sense of humour – here it's a little bit slower. I find you *do* slow down a bit. I used to hear a lot of jokes, tell a lot of jokes. Here they're few and far between, so you've got to really work at it.

What do you do with the rest of your day when you're not building your house?

I like to go down the beach for a couple of hours to swim; I had a catamaran I used to sail, but I had to sell that to pay for the house.

Now you're living in the stockbroker belt you don't go down the pub, you drift round to the hotel for a cocktail, I suppose?

We don't go out that much because we can't afford it, but it's a big thing in Australia for people to come round your house. The children really like it here, and my wife definitely wouldn't go back – she'd lose her tennis partner for a start, so that'd be out! But it was good fun seeing the missus knock up the cement for the house; that was really good.

She's a pioneer girl from East Ham?

Oh no, she comes from Birmingham. My mum and dad thought it would never last, you know, they never *spoke* to me for a couple of weeks when I said I was going to marry a girl from Birmingham! Well, you know, anybody out of London . . .

Now she really loves it here. The kids even talk with Australian accents; I tried to make them talk proper, but they won't. They've got horses up at Bay View there, they've got two paddocks and they go up and feed them, and go to school after that.

Do they ride to hounds?

I hope not! They do some gymkhanas and they've got a pony club; it's quite cheap, the horses, it's not that much to feed them because they do OK on the grass. We usually get a couple of bales of hay a week and a little bit of feed, and they do really well.

So you've got your splendid house, your daughters have their horses, your wife's got the tennis and you're into boating; this is the life the Australians should advertise when they want migrants: 'Come to Australia, be a dustman, live like a millionaire!'

Paul Hogan does that really well, so we'll leave it to him . . .

THE PROSPECTOR: EDDIE FARRELL

*You couldn't go looking for gold
in Manchester . . .*

Ravenswood, an old gold-mining town up in Dalrymple Shire, Queensland, has rested undisturbed since the years of glory that followed hard upon the day somebody struck pay dirt in 1868. The rush came, the hillsides sprouted tents, the canvas village grew into a weatherboard town, and modest prosperity lasted almost fifty years.

The population reached five thousand before the First World War, but by 1917 the last company had ceased operations. Today about one hundred people remain. One of them is Eddie Farrell from Manchester, who got into the famous Australian meat pie business but has now retired to live in a caravan among the derelict buildings, and do a little fossicking.

An Army cook, he had worked in fairgrounds before emigrating in 1952 to become a hostel chef in Woolangong, New South Wales. After five years making meat pies, he spent another twenty in the tallow department of the Townsville meat works – which, let's face it, must make retirement to a dusty caravan site in a ghost town seem like paradise . . .

There are only a few isolated buildings in Ravenswood today, though one of the two pubs has been tarted up to offer ornate goldfield architecture and, if pushed, a meal. The mining machinery has gone, so most visitors settle for a stroll round the cemetery.

In this distinctive and evocative setting Eddie goes out every morning in the scorching heat, in his regular uniform of vest and shorts, looking for gold. He once found a little, and is confident more will emerge from the old diggings where he and his companion Madge occupy themselves usefully, if not fruitfully.

It is not a serious enterprise, I suspect, but more of a hobby that occupies the day and helps keep him fit, for this sprightly seventy-two-year-old jack-the-lad is as chirpy and contented as any man I've met, although his living conditions are basic and what's worse, he says, the price of a stubby has gone up ten cents!

This is not a ghost town – there's plenty of amenities. We've got two shops.

It'll do until the next ghost town comes along . . .

There's plenty of houses here now. All these things will eventuate, with this dam being built; you'll get a lot more people living up this way.

Perhaps you ought to buy some property quickly, if the dam is going to bring a rush of people?

Seventy-two years of age and I should buy *property*? No, I don't think so.

Most people come to Australia looking for a better life – do you think you've achieved that?

Yes, conditions are different – there's room to move. There's no way in the world could I be as fit as I am now in Manchester at seventy-two years of age. You can go out here with a pick and shovel – you couldn't go looking for gold in Manchester.

There was no prosperity when I first came out. I started work in a hostel, I had twelve months there as a cook, then I bought my own pie business. Had that for four or five years, came up north to Queensland to the sun – beautiful weather, beautiful place. Worked in the meat works here for twenty years.

A lot of people can put up with caravan life for two weeks' holiday, but wouldn't want to spend their entire lives in one ...

In Queensland, you can. You've got the weather, you've got sunshine ten months of the year. You get about one week of winter here. One week. What more do you need?

Some observers might think you're living like a down-and-out ...

They may think that but they've got the wrong impression altogether. We have everything we want here. You couldn't wish for a better life. I don't know what all the Poms are doing – they should be out here! The only thing that's wrong here is the price of beer; too dear. But I don't think I'm roughing it at all, by any means. I've got a hell of a lot more than a lot of people.

You're the caretaker of this caravan park?

I look after this place. I get twenty bucks a week for that. You couldn't get more because of the pension, so twenty bucks is enough. I done it for years for nothing.

You could be living with your four children, your twelve grandchildren in Brisbane, in a cosy house – you prefer a more rudimentary life?

I'm sure my family prefers to live away from me – and I prefer to live away from them. They come up here now and again, stay overnight – and back again they go. I'll go down and stay a couple of weeks, because the beer's cheaper down there, which keeps you healthy; doesn't keep you wealthy!

Something keeps you contented ... I've been travelling around the world all my life and you're one of the first truly contented men I've met.

My word, my *word*! Only I'd be more content if the price of beer went down. I can get up in the morning at five o'clock or before that and I'll be singing and dancing around, cooking breakfast. Madge is the afternoon cook, I'm the morning cook. Contentment, it grows on you. The longer you stay here, the more contented you'd be, it's such a beautiful place. I regard it as such.

At Eddie's goldmine:

Is that fool's gold?

No, this is the McCoy.

But no serious gold's been discovered here for sixty years.

With this mineral here, you've got gold, you have copper, silver, lead – you've got all these conglomerates in that one stone. All has to be treated differently, but *here* it's just gold and silver, through the lead.

So what have you discovered, Eddie, since you've been digging?

Beautiful country. Lovely climate.

But no gold?

There's gold. I found gold this morning. That's three ounces of gold, over there.

You're not going to live on it, let's face it.

At seventy-two years – live on it! Yes, you could live on this if you put machinery in here, with just a jackhammer and a compressor. You have to go down one hundred feet. This is assayed at four ounces to the ton, this stone; well, four ounces of gold for a ton is very well, just now.

But Eddie, to be honest, you really haven't found enough gold to fill a tooth, have you?

I'm finding gold – *health* is gold! What can you do in a city at seventy-two years of age, as far as exercise is concerned? Running's no good, there's no future in that. There is a future here – you might find something or you might not, but you're losing nothing. It's only time you're putting in ...

THE BOY RACER: PETER BRIGGS

*I built up to paper millionaire
by the time I was seventeen ...*

Peter Briggs left Britain at the age of eight, arrived in Perth and set about collecting bottles and old newspapers to sell for useful small change: 'I had an overriding ambition to make money.' He succeeded. And failed. And succeeded, sort of.

He belongs to the junior branch of the Perth financial buccaneers. Starting as a carpenter, he bought blocks of land at a few dollars a month, and sold them for much profit. By the time he went bankrupt, he was a millionaire.

He became a stock market promoter, borrowed $3.8 million, went into various enterprises from boutique breweries to goldmines – and is now clambering back into the money again, relentlessly pursued by the tax men.

Bankruptcy taught this driving workaholic – who met his wife when she was fifteen, he seventeen – that he should enjoy life more, so he took up yachting, but in the competitive way of Perth achievers: his *Hitchhiker I* sailed in the '83 America's Cup trials. He loves cars – so keeps one hundred and fifty of them in two motor museums, and races the runners.

One of the museums is in York, an attractive town

between Perth and Kalgoorlie, where he is the power behind the Flying Fifty, an annual race 'round the houses' by vintage sports cars.

I was persuaded to take part in this unexpectedly hairy event, driving a 1937 Jaguar SS-100 – a classic cream machine just removed from the museum, whose looks were better than her behaviour. Nevertheless for an elderly lady who should have been indoors, she motored impressively – considering the lack of recent racing experience being disguised by *both* of us.

The public turned up in their thousands to line the route around town; according to the organizers it was not so much a road race, more a parade – so why were fifty vintage cars roaring down the straight around me, and behind every steering wheel a boy racer, flat-out and slit-eyed? From my breathless position, struggling to control the deep-throated fifty-year-old Jag, it was a race all right.

Peter Briggs drove the finest machine, as you would expect: a supercharged 1930 bullnosed Bentley – two tons of British craftsmanship which could touch 130 m.p.h. but was then rather hard to stop. This kept him occupied.

I covered several circuits with his great bellowing beast weaving across my mirror, frantic to pass, while Peter's goggled head peered over the steering wheel. He looked *exactly* like Mr Toad.

The race was almost over – and I was flagged in and disqualified for not being 'garbed to the wrist'! Like any self-respecting television man in the Australian bush I was of course wearing a safari suit, but all the boy racers were tarted-up in full Brooklands rig: go-fast shoes, flameproof track suits, significant badges, gloves with holes ...

After all the heats and most of the race, the judges had suddenly noticed my elbows were exposed in an inexcusably amateurish way, so I drove away past the black flag, into the pits and out of the race. You *see* how Australians behave when the competition gets tough ...

I went to about ten schools by the time I was fifteen, and my results were abysmal. My father thought I didn't have any brains, so it was a waste of time learning Latin or anything like that. He was not very interested in wasting good money on me. My sisters went to university and got all sorts of degrees.

My family left England principally, I think, to chase the climate, to get away from the war – the potential war that was going to happen with the Berlin blockade in '48. My parents were reasonably well-to-do and made their own way over here.

Father felt the country needed builders and the way to be a builder was by being a bricklayer or carpenter. Seeing he had assessed my intelligence as fairly low, he figured I should work my way up from the bottom, handed me a nail pocket, a claw hammer and a saw and said, 'You're now a first-year carpenter's apprentice.' Mother thought that was *terrific* because Jesus Christ was a carpenter and if it was good enough for him, it was good enough for me.

So off I trotted; I was rather chuffed at the fact that someone was going to pay me £3.10s a week. I qualified and became a builder – just in time for the early Sixties recession we had. Competition was very hard, so I got a job with the Public Works Department, became a civil servant and studied quantity surveying.

What was your ambition at that time?

To make money. At that particular time I'd had enough of working in the field with tools. I had a few friends in offices, and it seemed rather nice to wear a suit and a tie, to take a different perspective on life.

Meet a different sort of girl?

I'd already met my girl, but the girls were certainly different in business. So carpentry led into building and building led into the quantity surveying, which led into property development. It gave me a view of parleying some money together; I started buying blocks of land in my spare time and selling them at a profit.

The buying and selling part of me was *always* there – from age seven or eight I collected bottles and sold them to the shop, collected newspapers and sold them to the butchers ... so a sort of accumulation of wealth – albeit very small – was going on all the time.

A seven-year-old wheeler-dealer!

I started selling push-bikes and little old cars, and then moved into blocks of land. The idea of buying and selling was always attractive: it didn't require a great deal of work, it just required a native cunning to barter.

This was during the Poseidon boom, so it wasn't a bad time to start climbing?

It was a good time because, although the Poseidon boom was a stock market boom, it also lifted the entire Australian economy – the property market was booming and commodities were booming, everything was. Poseidon was a little tiny company that started at ten cents, discovered a nickel mine – and went to $350! Many, many millionaires and multimillionaires were made during the course of that time, and every man in the street was share trading. I got into the latter part of that boom.

So some of your dreams came true and you made a lot of money?

I did well in the property business and built up to be a paper millionaire by the time I was seventeen! Of course, I always had to sell these things – but on paper it looked terrific.

You were a property millionaire; then the market crashed. What happened to you?

I crashed too.

How deeply?

Well, to despair, really. To an extent that we had a *fifth* mortgage on our house ... The building society at the time didn't normally go in for fifth mortgages – in fact they'd never *heard* of anybody that ever had a fifth mortgage! They thought it was rather amusing.

I had various other mortgages and guarantees on all sorts of properties, and although I never left a lot of small shareholders or small creditors lamenting, I had a lot of what they call professional creditors: banks and finance companies on guarantees and so forth, which I just couldn't meet.

So you went bankrupt; did they come and take your wife's jewellery and your house and your car and everything?

The car they couldn't get because that was owned by somebody else – it had no value anyway. The house went, of course, and most other things. It wasn't one of my better times.

It took a while to go bankrupt. I had an enormous ego at the time, and I only knew success – but when the downturn came and things started going bad, it shook me around a lot. I went up to eighteen stone in weight. I stopped doing anything physical and spent most of my time on the phone talking to creditors and fighting off the evil day. Still eventually, of course, it happened – and we were out for the count.

So you went back to carpentry?

No, but my *wife* wanted me to go back to carpentry; get a steady job! But I just sort of readjusted my thinking a little. I thought, here was an opportunity to start again, do something new, get away from all the things I'd been involved with before.

I was offered a public listed company; one of the minnows of the Poseidon boom that had run out of money and really had no value. That boom created dozens and dozens of little public companies and they all had mineral claims, and the geological reports said they were 'interesting'. That's the most important word of the Poseidon boom: on the basis of some 'interesting' find, people would pay millions of dollars and buy all these shares – and the stock would rocket through the roof. You could have nickel in almost any geological environment, any bit of ground ...

During that, this friend of mine who had the public company had raised $20 million, but before the first Annual General Meeting of the company he'd *lost* all the money and the shares had gone from $1 to three cents! He was petrified, being the promoter, of going to the AGM and saying to the shareholders: 'All the money's gone, the shares are worthless, I didn't do it, I'm a good guy, nothing to do with me, let me *out* of here . . .'

He said, 'Would you buy the company?' I said, 'No, I've just got out of the property business.' He said, 'I'll *give* you the company, pay me later, you be Chairman, you tell the shareholders there's no money . . .' So there I was, Chairman of Siberia Nickel Mining Exploration NL. NL means No Liability – but in this case it meant Nothing Left.

I went and chaired the meeting – and of course the apathy of shareholders in Australia is strange. They're not interested in politics, they really want to be left alone: don't bother me, I've sold them, I've put them in the bottom drawer . . . So out of 2600 shareholders in this company, one old lady turns up! I was getting this little old lady to second all the motions; it was marvellous.

I ended up with six or seven public companies. I remember one we had, the shares were selling at two cents and I thought, 'It's impossible to raise money, you'd have to issue a hundred million shares – and nobody's going to take them anyway.' So we invented this little thing called a CIP, which was Capital Issue Page. We gave them two fully-paid shares, two contributing shares and two options – six pieces of listed paper, all for eight cents a share. We pushed like hell – it was like California in the Fifties. Various little flutters came along.

Then in the uranium boom we were able to raise some quite good money, but stock promoting became a dirty word . . . It's that sort of underlying thing in Australia: unless you get into a really *big* league, people don't understand you.

A stock promoter is the kind of person my grandaddy warned me against?

Just depends whether you made or lost money. We made a lot of money at the time; lost some, of course, but I think we made more than we lost.

So how did you become a bad name in the marketplace?

The problem with anybody that has public company exposure, you do get identified with company shares that go up and go down. My mistake was that I had too many involvements with too many companies, and they couldn't really see which company was doing what. There were a lot of cross-shareholdings and so forth, and the whole thing got a little out of kilter with the market.

When did the tax authorities decide to make an example of you?

The Tax Department took a keen interest in me in the early Eighties. Well, I had a fairly high profile: cars, sailing, big house, and I guess my tax returns didn't appear to reflect an extravagant life-style – as they call it. I think there was a change of attitude in Australia towards tall poppies: they wanted to make an example of a few so the rest would pull their heads in, so to speak. We had a tremendous resurgence of political pressure to make examples of tall poppies.

You were a tall poppy?

I certainly was. I want to be a short poppy, now. The Tax Department would like to see me a *very* low poppy.

They're trying to chop you down, but you don't seem very worried – yet it's a criminal charge and you could finish up in the slammer?

Well, that *is* a possibility, but I believe we will win and I think that justice will be done.

How do we sleep nights?

Well, very, very well. We've just had a success – we've sued the Tax Department themselves, the very people in the Department, for fraud and abuse of power. That's the first time it's ever happened in Australia. They've been trying to sling it out of the courts, and they're losing. I believe we will win substantial damages against them.

What's the reaction of the public – do they see you as you must see yourself, as a sort of white knight taking on an unreasonable Government department, or as a tax dodger?

I think probably as a combination of all that, although I seem to have a lot of silent followers. I get all sorts of letters from people telling me what wonderful things I'm doing – and even sending me money! But I don't want to be a martyr, I just want to be able to satisfy the authorities and the Tax Department, one way or the other.

You've diversified your interests – you've got all these cars, various homes, businesses, you're still in goldmining ...

And we're in boutique breweries: handmade beers and lagers – five or ten different types. I think that's one of the great things about Western Australia: we're able to diversify and be in almost *any* type of business.

In Australia what I say three times is true: if you say you're a brewer often enough, you're an expert brewer!

Everybody's a pretty deft hand at *anything*. That's a disadvantage, too, because everybody gets involved. I remember when I was in property development we were building duplexes and after a while my garage man proudly announced he was going off to build a duplex! Everybody was getting in. That's one of the problems – you've got to be first in, as we are with boutique breweries.

And first out?

Yes. Well, not necessarily – but sometimes.

Can you estimate what you've made and lost during your Australia years?

You don't really sit down to add things up, and take them away. It's obviously *millions* of dollars.

What possessions have you accumulated?

Well, personally of course I haven't accumulated anything.

Everything's in your wife's name?

Everything's controlled by family trusts, shall we say, but certainly we have a very fine car collection – some one hundred and fifty-odd cars and motorbikes, and two Hitchhiker yachts: we sailed for Australia in the Admiral's Cup team in '81 and '83, and we're hoping to do so again next year. Also all the usual houses and bits and pieces that go with them.

If you believe the bullnosed Bentley you're sitting in is worth £200,000 and you've got another one hundred and fifty cars, that's a few quid, I suppose? Is this a rich man's hobby or a serious business venture?

No, they're not a serious business venture.

Are you making money out of your two motor museums?

No, but they contribute to the overheads. At one stage we were restoring a lot of cars, but that's a very expensive business and we're trying to cut that back.

And what's the object of the Flying Fifty road race tomorrow?

It's a re-enactment of the classic 'round the houses' races they've had over the years in all these little country towns in Western Australia.

This fifty-year-old Jaguar SS-100 that you want me to risk my life in tomorrow, she's a goer?

She'll go like a *rocket* – you'll have to hang on like grim death!

Have you lost many of your drivers yet?

Not many – not many spectators either.

Yes, I noticed there aren't too many safety precautions – it's not quite Monte Carlo, is it?

Not really, no; but it's only a reliability run and we're not *supposed* to let our hair down and go mad.

But I'm told you all get very macho and vroom-vroom on the day?

Yes, well one always has a go.

So here you are sitting in a supercharged 1930 Bentley, two tons of British craftsmanship; when you go back to its homeland, to England, do you feel like a Streatham boy made good, or a colonial lad?

I feel most like a colonial lad. I have a tinge of Streatham when I go down there – I discovered we'd lived in a dolls' house! Of course when I left it I was only three foot high, and thought it was *huge*.

Perth has the friendliest and gentlest atmosphere of all Australian cities, yet it's also spawned the country's most flamboyant and successful business high-flyers ...

I understand that *per capita* we have a higher percentage of entrepreneurs. I suppose we're all in one town of a million people and we can't get out, so we can all be observed. We're fiercely competitive here in the west, the opportunities are obviously here, the Government is in favour of free enterprise.

Alan Bond is one of your peers, and in fact at one time you were running neck and neck – but he got away, didn't he?

Yes, substantially! Alan's done very, very well. Most of these entrepreneurs come from overseas. Alan was born in England, I was, Holmes à'Court was born in Africa ... So a lot of us were determined to make good in a new country.

I once heard you say about someone: 'Oh, he's worth $5 or $10 million but he's never really made it.' What have you got to be worth before you have made it here?

I think $5 or $10 million is not real bad, but there's plenty of people here worth in excess of $20 million. I'm somewhere along that path.

Alan Bond and I have this lovely attitude: I said, 'Alan, I'm in trouble, I owe about $4 or $5 million on this deal and I can't repay it.' He said, 'Did you borrow the money?' Yes. 'Did you have fun borrowing the money?' I had fun. 'Did you have fun spending the money?' I said, 'I had *enormous* fun spending the money.' 'So why are you worried – the *bank* should be worried, they've got to get it back.'

His whole attitude is: if you borrow $10,000 the bank owns you, and if you borrow $100 million, you own the bank – and that's always been very true. He was the first billion-dollar borrower in Australia: he borrowed a billion dollars!

Everyone here does seem to sail fairly close to the wind?

If you don't go close to the wind, you're never going to make the bigger dollar. If you don't take the risks you aren't going to get the rewards.

There's a constantly changing background to wealth creation: thirty years ago it was land, then it was minerals, nickel, uranium, gold. What's it all coming from now?

From the stock market; a lot of the wealth has been made out of the stock market in the last ten years.

So it's less substantial, in that case: it could all go again – could be another West Australian bubble?

There's always that possibility. A lot of the things some of us are involved with are highly speculative – high technology things ...

But if you go bankrupt in England there's a stigma – let alone having people chase you on a tax charge! So many Perth millionaires have got a bankruptcy behind them that it just seems part of the growing up process?

Just part of business experience. A lot of people have gone broke that really haven't been broke officially. Technically I've never been broke, but that's only the legalities of it. In fact, I was.

In America you really aren't a businessman unless you've been bankrupt three times. That's not the case here, of course, and I certainly never want to go broke again – but I think people in business take that sort of thing in their stride: hassles with the Tax Department or going broke is all part of the educational programme of the life of the businessman, it's not a problem.

You can shrug off bankruptcy – but jail would be a bit of a problem, wouldn't it?

Definitely, yes. Different sort of hurdle.

It doesn't seem to worry you – does it keep your wife awake at night?

I don't worry Robyn with the problems of my business – but she does like to hear what's happening before she reads about it in the paper!

You've been together for twenty-five years, so she's ridden the roller-coaster for quite a while?

Yes, she's had a lot of fun.

This generation likes to display its wealth: in the old days the rich Australians, the graziers, lived quiet retiring English country-type lives. Now it seems if you've got it, you flaunt it.

A lot of the motivation to *make* the money is not to put it away, but to enjoy it during the course of your lifetime. One of my main motivations in making money is being able to enjoy it. Ever since I went broke I've changed my whole attitude to life: I decided that if I was going to make it again – and I *was* – that I was going to enjoy it, and if when I died my children didn't get much, that's just too bad. I'm not here to create a dynasty.

By nature the average Australian is an outgoing individual. He's a bit brash – a bit *too* brash for the more conservative English – but he does like to flash his money, he likes to flash his toys. He's developing style – maybe not necessarily *good* style, but he's got some style ...

THE WELSH FALSTAFF: LEN EVANS

I am an arrogant little shit –
but I've done a lot for Australia ...

Len Evans, former assistant golf professional at Potters
Bar, was Australia's first Mr Wine. In the Sixties he
contrived to wean much of the nation from its beer,
those inevitable 'tinnies', and redirect them towards their
splendid wines.

A Welsh Falstaff who can stand anything except being
bored and not being the centre of attention, he received
an alarming warning from a heart artery, so retreated
from the excitements of Sydney to live among his vineyards in the Hunter Valley, in a house built with the
help of his family and any visitor who dropped by for a
companionable bottle.

The place was constructed erratically around a collection of bric-a-brac: unusual windows and doors, beams
from derelict stations, railway sleepers, old tiles, leg-
irons ... Our bedroom had a Victorian four-poster – but
instead of wardrobe and cupboards, a couple of hooks; a
wine cask for a bath, an ecclesiastical loo that required
courage and contortion. It was Cessnock Cathedral meets
Clint Eastwood, and if not the most comfortable house in
New South Wales, must be the most amusing.

Outside sheep grazed across a tranquil vineyard

The Welsh Falstaff: Len Evans

landscape, but any guest arriving for a quiet weekend receives a stern shock: *that* sort of behaviour will not be tolerated by his restless and driven host, still the ebullient perfectionist in a land where mediocrity is usually admitted with modest pride. Compulsively firing sparks and making the world turn, this catalytic agent is generous and – to my certain knowledge after twenty years' friendship – his impulsive financial operations have always been *just* about to come good.

He still runs his growing wine empire – now producing sparkling in South Australia – writes an occasionally insensitive column for a Sunday newspaper, loves his four children and long-suffering wife Trish while driving them bananas, and is a splendid host – one of his wines is called Evans Family. How could you knock it? A great mate who constantly exercises his superb palate. Len Evans is an enormously entertaining life-enhancer.

One day at the beginning of 1953 at Potters Bar Golf Club – a Jewish golf club – I was teaching a very wealthy lady who'd been looked after all her life and had no wrists, so she could never hit a golf ball. I wasn't allowed to tell her, but I felt like saying, 'Madam, you'll *never* play golf – why don't you take up tiddlywinks?' I was twenty-two years old and full of pith and vinegar and I thought, 'What the hell's the point of doing this? I'll try to emigrate tomorrow!'

I went to New Zealand House, Canada House and Australia House. Canada said they wanted nuclear physicists. At Australia House the chap said, 'You got £10 and a sponsor, mate?' I had £10 but *no* sponsor, so he walked away from the counter and I never saw him again. But New Zealand House said, 'Certainly sir, *love* to have you, what are you – a professional golfer? We don't have any jobs for golfers at the moment, but we *do* have splendid opportunities for bus conductors, quarry workers and forestry labourers.' So I became a forestry labourer for a couple of years.

I arrived in New Zealand with £2.10s and worked for two years

279

chopping down trees. When I got to Australia I had quadrupled my fortune: I had £10 in my pocket.

Then I mucked around for a while and did all sorts of jobs – welding and everything at General Motors–Holden, and I now have intense sympathy with anyone doing eight hours a day, eight car bodies an hour, the line coming remorselessly towards you ...

Then I went to Queensland and became a ringbarker and sucker-basher. I had a fight with the camp overseer because he hit an abo with a shovel, and they ran me out of town: 'If you don't leave town tonight you'll be dead tomorrow.' I got out of town quick.

I finished up helping build this enormous dingo fence, which remains one of the greatest experiences of my life. I did five or six months on the dingo fence during winter in unbelievable conditions, eating nothing more than corned beef or steak, and damper – unleavened bread. The other dingo fencers were the flotsam and jetsam of the world. They came and went, and there were some terrible bastards and some delightful people among them. I was fit and strong, so I didn't worry much about things, and actually made a lot of money at the fence. I put time-and-motion into it and was earning twice as much as fencers who'd been there for twenty years.

It was very expensive to live there because we had to freight everything in – even petrol, in those days. It was so remote that one fellow said, 'Outback, son – you go through three fuckin' outbacks to *get* there.' And it was true. It was on the edge of the Simpson Stony Desert, right over on the far west of northwest Queensland. It was an immensely hard but a wonderfully exciting life, because we'd been where no white man had been before. No roads. We blasted holes with dynamite in rocky outcrops to set posts in to make this fence. Remorseless work, and a great experience. Afterwards it took me a week of baths to get the red dust out of my pores – there'd be this huge red rim around the top of the bath!

On the way back to New Zealand to become a professional golfer, I went to Mount Isa to earn some money, a very tough mining town. I was lucky to be able to do well at whatever I did: I rose from pick and shovel labourer to office manager of a building company. Met Tricia, my wife to be: she was working as a secretary in the community store. Then we decided to come down to Sydney in 1958 to see if we wanted to get married.

I'd been writing all the time, the endless rejection slip thing, but I was being published by *Man* and *Pocket Book* magazines – short stories. I was going through that terrible phase of loving toughdom: I'd call myself Singapore Evans, that sort of thing! I've still got some of those stories. Then I was writing revue skits for Philip Street Theatre. So I worked as a glass washer at the Ship Inn on Circular Quay from six until ten every morning, which enabled me to be at rehearsals and write during the day.

It was a very hard time: they paid two guineas a script in those days. One glorious day I had work at Channel Seven in Adelaide on a national programme called *Café Continental*, I had a major script going in Melbourne – and my return for that effort was £19.7s. It didn't go far, because the wage at that time was about £25 to £30 a week.

And then the hotel career took off – the things which my nature allows me to be good at: my gregariousness, if you like; my enthusiasm, if you like. I'm not very bright but I'm a fairly hard worker. I became a stocktaker, which is the man who analyses the results of hotels. That led to being grabbed for the new Chevron Hilton. The last job I actually applied for was that of glass washer at the Ship Inn in 1958 – I've never applied for a job since.

I went to the Chevron in '60, the great new glamorous hotel. We had 80 cooks working there, 360 food and beverage staff – over 500 staff altogether to look after 220 rooms. There was this huge service block and only 220 rooms because they were building 700 rooms – but it finished up a hole in the ground forever.

Unbelievably, in the first day I was Assistant Beverage Manager, within three months I was Beverage Manager, within one and a half years I was Food and Beverage Manager, and within two years I was Assistant General Manager.

It was a great, great joy. We worked so hard – eight o'clock in the morning until two o'clock the following morning ... but there was this marvellous hotel thing of Eartha Kitt, Nat King Cole, Patti Page, Ethel Merman in the Silver Spade, the Prime Minister making a speech in the ballroom to tycoons – and then going down to a whole crowd of poofters in the Quarter Deck Bar cutting each other with broken glass – a marvellous sort of life. Wonderful training.

This great feeling for wine really became manifest when I went to Chevron to learn about it and I found that *no one* knew anything about it! I was the leader, the enthusiast. I was the first person in Australia to bring out open bins and decanters, to build bins so that people could handle wine and pick it up.

I actually wrote articles about how to market wine – which was terrific presumption on my part, except that nobody else in the country was doing anything. Typical of this is the Wine Column. In 1962, desperately anxious to learn more, I was having lunch with Peter Hastings who was the editor of the *Bulletin* and said, 'Why don't you have a wine column?' He said, 'A good idea – why don't you write it?'

Did you know anything about wine, apart from drinking it?

No, but I'd been a keen drinker from sixteen when I was a prefect at school and had a study around the quadrangle. I was the one that always had the bottle of Madeira, illegally, the bottle of old sherry. God knows how I did it!

You were successful in Sydney because at the time no one knew about wine, either?

That's right. I used to buy wine and people would say, 'Have a beer, mate.' Even at Mount Isa when I first went to the bottle department of Boyds Hotel, which was a rough fighting hotel, and said to the owner, 'May I buy a bottle of white?', he said, 'A bottle of sweet sherry, mate?' 'No, a bottle of *dry* white wine.' 'What are you, some kind of pansy?'

In those days the average consumption of wine was one glass of table wine per head of population in Australia. Today it's twenty-four *bottles*.

When this column appeared it outraged Melbourne. Who the hell was Cellar Master, this fellow writing about wine? This was 1962, and that's how it started. It's a bit like the British Empire: people have always thought that I've been ruthlessly ambitious and almost predatory, but really it's just happened, I've bumbled along ...

Then the wine industry said, 'We want you to run the promotional body,' so off I went and became Director of the Wine Bureau. In two years we doubled the consumption of table wine in Australia. This was 1965, '66, '67. I only left out of irritation – I could have been there still. In '67 I got an £8-a-week increase of salary from my interstate manager's bureau, and I had to fight all day to get *that*. At the end they said, 'Well, that's *you* Evans, you won't get any more money for a long time.' I realized that the wine industry farmer-mentality was basically very mean, very introverted, very tight. So I resigned, went overseas with Graham Kerr, and had no job. We wrote a book called *Galloping Gourmets* when we returned.

I was $2000 overdrawn at the bank, three children, a totally mortgaged home in Greenwich. I walked into the first place – Miller's Hotels – and said to Harry Alce, the boss at that time, 'You once mentioned that you needed a wine consultant.' He said, 'Start tomorrow, $3000 a year.' In that first year '67/'68, compared to my Wine Bureau salary of $7000 a year, I made $19,000 as a consultant.

Then I bumbled into Bulletin Place, a wine merchant's cellar. Someone told me it was up for grabs and I went and started with $5000 worth of borrowed funds and 5000 bucks-worth of wine.

We actually opened the restaurant on the first day. It happened because I needed lavatories and a tasting room; I built a kitchen for entertaining and thought, 'I might as well open a bloody restaurant.' So *again* we bumbled into it. I had no knowledge at all of finance.

But it took off – I can remember when I visited you at the end of '69 people were waiting weeks to get a table . . .

There was a waiting list for the first three years! It was a great success but I was *so* financially incompetent, though it happened to coincide with the boom period of '69–'71, the mining boom. The money around was unbelievable.

These were the Poseidon days and I should have made a fortune if I'd had any sense. It was just very lucky I was at the right place at the right time, with people spending money. They'd come in and ask, 'What's the most expensive wine?' I'd say, 'Château Latour so-and-so at $24 a bottle' – an *unbelievable* price in those days. They'd say, 'Give me a case of it. I've got to say thank you to a chap who's done me a good turn.' They'd buy five cases – a thousand-dollar order was a common thing.

Just to show you how busy it was in those days, I was turning over $28,000 a month in the cellar in 1970, and by the time I'd grown tired of it in 1984 the turnover was down to $8000 a month.

Then the Rothbury vineyards started in '68 from a casual comment by Murray Tyrrell – we got some chums together and formed a syndicate and got that going. To show you again the bumbling nature of things, we put in $25,000 each, which I didn't have – I had to put in over the years. It finished up costing seven *million* – it grew so quickly, the winery, the four vineyards and everything.

So always, Alan, there's been a strong element of financial crisis in my life, all the time. Always I've been short of cash, always I've been terribly *un*liquid. Peter Fox became involved with me when I had my heart scare – a blocked artery, which I still have – in '76. I was in hospital and we had one of our usual liquidity crises: a shipment of wine – I'd bought too much, you know – was coming and he funded it on the basis that I wasn't to be told; there was no security and no interest. He became my strong friend because of that marvellous gesture, when I found out about it.

So then Bulletin Place ran alongside Rothbury, and I developed both. My writing career was getting bigger all the time. I did five years of television: I had my wine programme, ten minutes in front of the news, for about two years in the Seventies. I did three thousand radio broadcasts on wine. My major book was the *Complete Book of Australian Wine* in 1973, which has gone into four total rewrites and eight or ten impressions. Sold 150,000. There are twelve books now, and they all went well.

So you carved your niche in the wine industry – or indeed created much of it – yet you don't often treat it with traditional respect.

A young man had lunch with me in Sydney recently: very good old Australian wines, lovely French wine, and I really expected him to bow with profuse thanks and genuflect, but he said, 'I'm rather disappointed with your attitude – you seem very flippant about wine.' I thought this was a cruel thrust indeed, but explained: 'I'm immensely serious about wine when we select the vineyard sites, what we put in, the way we grow it, the way we pick it, the way we make it and how we mature it, but once it's in the bottle – you're quite right – I become flippant, because then you can't do much about it!'

I did have a friend who owns fourteen chateaux in Bordeaux sitting at this table and I said, 'Isn't it marvellous to think that we're drinking my wine grown only 400 yards away?' He said, 'Yes – what a *pity* it didn't travel . . .' (*Laughs*)

I lecture in London quite often, and you'll always have the Pommy redneck in the front row who'll say, 'Your wines don't travel, do they?' God, the old colonial lip, it really does aggravate thinking Australians, I can tell you. But Poms who really do understand fine wine would put Australia among the top seven wine nations, although we're only nineteenth in production.

We are more important in quality terms than any other country in the world. We're making wines like Dylan Thomas who said, 'I am a first-class poet of the second rank.' If you reserve the front rank for Shakespeare and Milton and Goethe, then I think the analogy is fairly apt: we don't make Montrachets, we don't make Chateau Lafite Rothschilds, but we *do* make wines which are a damned sight better than most commune Burgundies, most generic Bordeaux, most generic Sauternes and Graves, most Pouilly Fuissé. If only people understood that we make some extremely good wine at that level.

I do a lot of charity work round Australia – I'm honorary member of all sorts of blind societies, deaf and dumbs and things. I'll go and do auctions and tell stories and make speeches and shake hands and all that stuff. I actually got my OBE for services to the industry and to the community. I was very pleased someone knew because I've never actually shouted about it.

But you'd have preferred a knighthood?

Oh, yes, I'd *love* to have a knighthood! A knighthood's lovely. People in the old days of Liberal governments used to say, 'A knighthood would be *very* embarrassing.' Embarrassing, hell! I've never seen a man yet who wouldn't love one – it would be lovely to be Sir Leonard. I've just come back from Hong Kong and I was treated like some sort of sun god there. If I'd had the tag, it would have been even better.

Trevor Lloyd Hughes told me when he got his knighthood he

couldn't believe the change in people's attitude to him. I'm quite honestly commercial about it. I know if I went to the States as Sir Len Evans, my impact as a salesman for Australian wine would be immensely greater.

So that's that side; then there's the wit side, which is the performing, the weekend 'Indulgence' column, the *Woman's Weekly* column I did for four and a half years, the paid speeches, the product launches and all that stuff. It's amazing how much work comes your way in that fashion. On the phone last week I was being offered $20,000 per year to be the chairman of a panel of wine tasters for a wine club. I've been offered $5000 if I'll design a weekend for some top business executives and host and teach them about wine. Speeches now are $2000. People say, 'Will you write an article for such-and-such a magazine.' I say, 'I'm too expensive, I'm a thousand a thousand.' It takes me an hour to write a thousand words about wine; it's $1 a word, and they say 'Fine', so you sit down ... One day here I wrote $7000 worth of stuff. It tends to mount up. Because I'm always so financially bereft, I build all the time.

Yet because you're generous and expansive you always seem to be spending more than you earn – does this concern you?

It gives a certain edge of discomfort, which makes life rather fun. For example, I've always travelled first class – even when I was quite poor – on the basis that I'd rather not travel if I couldn't travel first class. I was living like a bum, working like a bum, but when I took a holiday it had to be done properly. I would hate to have to worry about opening a bottle of champagne, for example: if I ever had to worry when I put my hand in the fridge for a good bottle of French champagne, something would be awfully wrong and I would then start to think I was living poorly.

So you don't worry about your overspending, but do other people worry about it?

I once rang my bank manager at three o'clock in the morning when we were suffering a particularly trickety crisis – he was a friend of mine – and said, 'I can't sleep, what if we did so-and-so?' He said, 'For Christ's sake, see me tomorrow morning, get some sleep.' I said, 'I don't know if I can.' He said, 'Don't worry – *I'll* stay awake now.' (*Laughs*)

Welsh Falstaff: Len Evans

But you do need that old eff-off money ...

That's right: you told me that years ago, and you were quite right. That's *exactly* what you need: to be able to say, 'No, I don't want to do that, thank you very much' – and not do it.

The weekend before last, Anzac weekend, we got through thirty-four bottles of wine here, including a nineteenth-century Madeira, two or three '55 Bordeaux and a '61 Bordeaux. I started to look at the empty bottles and Tricia said, 'How much is all that worth?' I knew it was well over a thousand dollars for wine for one weekend. I said, 'Don't ask darling – because the moment you know it, you won't enjoy it any more!' And really, that is part of the income thing: I have to earn that money to live in that style. I've just developed six acres of Pinot this year, that's $20,000. That dam down there cost $10,000. The Chardonnay would have cost over $60,000 to put down.

The future, the thing that it's really all for and the thing I enjoy most doing, is production. I'm Chairman of Rothbury, which is a $6–$7 million company. It's just got over a disastrous drought, just got over the mistake we made of planting too much red grape – and too much Shiraz particularly. The market has stopped for that, so we had to do terrible things – we had to haul out virtually 400 acres of Shiraz, which hurt me *terribly*.

Australians now drink six bottles of white for every bottle of red and you – the eminence grise *of Australian wine – called it wrong!*

Quite right: I actually created the boom which I couldn't read myself. We didn't predict the swing, we didn't predict the Chardonnay boom – so that cost a fortune. Then we had a drought which cost $1½ million.

For ten years to my knowledge Rothbury's always been about to come good, but it never quite has ...

Absolutely, you're dead right. This time, pray to God, this time we're right. All the signs are there. Next year we'll have 65,000 cases, of which 20,000 will be automatically sold before we start the year. Export is going very well: we've come from nothing two years ago to about 10,000 cases next year. Wholesale's doing very well. We bring in 50,000 cases which we sell as Other Area wine –

Barossa Valley Riesling, or whatever. There's a wine club for our members; we have 40,000 members now to service.

I think really it's a matter of always biting off a bit more than you can chew – and then *somehow* getting it down! Obviously one has assets of a few million dollars – but who's a millionaire in Australia? Anyone who has a decent house is a millionaire.

Rothbury hasn't produced a profit in seventeen years. I'm sure Lafite Rothschild didn't produce a profit for the first seventeen years – that's the category I like to be in! When we start producing a profit this year it'll be a profit for centuries to come, it's something which is there in bricks and mortar and vineyards which I will be proud of in two centuries' time, and I hope my benign ashes – which are going to be cast on the vineyards – will sort of grin from time to time at what's being done down there.

One of the great tragedies of Australia for me is when I see wealth being abused. It's abused in two ways: I shan't mention names, it would be rude, but I see people making millions upon millions of dollars, and they're so unbelievably ostentatious about it. The huge motor-yacht syndrome, the multi-helicopter syndrome. One tycoon built a hotel so he could have a suite in the snow, and if someone's staying there at a cost of $2000 a night and he wants to come down for a weekend, he kicks them out! That's appalling. What he should do is to keep it for himself so he can drop in any time, or not have the bad manners to kick them out.

We see the ostentation . . . There was a recent wedding in which they took over the church they wanted but it didn't suit the bride's dress – so they repainted it for the wedding! Then the day after, repainted it *back* to what it was. I find that ludicrous.

Equally I find ludicrous a vast home on the harbour in Sydney with a magnificent garden, with the hostess bejewelled – overdressed, if you like – serving Great Western champagne to her guests! It's simply incomprehensible to me. I love people being simple, drinking simple and having simple pleasure, but I can't stand ostentation.

I don't think there's enough grace in life in Australia. One of the tragedies is that the people who're making a great deal of money aren't necessarily the people who live gracious lives.

The have-and-have-not thing very much exists in Cessnock: deep,

deep, deep in the psyche of these towns is the socialist idiom; they are the number one voting area for the Labour Party. For example, the daughters of miners who work at the winery, sharp on the dot of five o'clock, mid-sentence, mid-invoice – out of the door like a shot! They would never work a *minute* overtime.

Does this antipathy show itself in other ways?

I believe if I drove around Cessnock in a Rolls, it is quite likely I would get it vandalized, but that would happen in Sydney as well – that's the situation around the world today. They're pretty honest people, sturdy people. The mateship thing is very important. Jack *is* as good as his master. You must never ever put on any side at all, even though it's quite obvious you're the boss and you want what you want, but it has to be done in a semi-jocular way.

In the hotel business, full of Europeans under a great deal of pressure nearly every day, it was very much: 'Do this, Do that, Fix that, Quickly, Hurry up!' But now it's sort of, 'Come on, chums ...' Even so, I know some people feel I'm a little too abrupt.

Many Australians still seem slightly resentful of England, do you detect that?

Yes, there's a great love of England here amongst certain people, and a great disdain. England really hasn't been particularly helpful, once it got the country going. In the last thirty years I'd say England's record is *not* very good – and I'm talking now as an Australian. Having sent large contingents of our sons over there both in the First World War and the Second World War, we're immediately thanked for it by being dumped agriculturally by you and the Commonwealth.

On the other hand there's an enormous admiration for the Queen. Charles is very much liked; he schooled out here, he's a terrific bloke and he's handled Australia very well indeed. I don't see the republic happening for a fair while yet, but inevitably as the ethnic minorities become more and more forceful – and they basically don't have a background of royalty – there'll be a very strong movement towards a republic, it's inevitable.

Australia was an unbelievably isolated insular country, very much tied to Mother Britain. Don't forget, if you'd a referendum in 1955 about republic versus monarchy, you'd have had a 99 per cent vote for monarchy. Today, maybe 60 per cent, 55 per cent. In twenty years time almost certainly 45 per cent, 35 per cent.

You'd be amazed how totally *uninterested* in England the majority of Australians are; it's an indifference. The businessman, the upper-class Australian, the professional Australian, old Australian money … are all devoted to England, but you must understand that the ethnic influence in Australia is enormous. Your Greeks and Italians and Lebanese and Poles and Czechs and Hungarians couldn't give a *damn* about England.

Whitlam encouraged Australian nationalism more than any other Prime Minister: the yellow kangaroo on the green flag, which I find appalling, 'Advance Australia fair'-type thing, the most puerile kind of words for our National Anthem which has replaced 'God Save The Queen'. But don't make an issue of it, Australians aren't making an issue of it.

Don't think that England doesn't have strong colonial attitudes to Australia still, because I experience them every time I go to England and talk about wine. There's very much the patronizing attitude to Australia – oh God yes – which Australians resent enormously, and I resent. Total ignorance of what Australian wine's about. They express the attitudes of thirty and forty years ago. I feel like Rip Van Winkle, sometimes.

You find the Poms are condescending, even here?

Many of them, yes, unbelievably. There's an unknown English club which exists in Sydney, in Paddington – a lot of young Brits from good families, and they stick together. They mix as little as the Greeks or Italians mix. They stay rigidly in their colony, give dinner parties to each other – and they happen to be *using* Australia. Parasites, if you like, on the body of Australia. They intend to go back, don't worry about that, they're living very well, they're all in merchant banking or that sort of thing, an amazing number of them in insurance.

I detect that in New York, where many British say rather apologetically 'When I think about it, most of my friends are *Brits …'*

My reaction is, I believe, an international one, just as yours is. I can't think of anyone who's more international than you. I know almost without you saying what you like and dislike – I can see it in your mannerisms. I've twigged what you're about and what you're not about, but you're very urbane, very sophisticated about it, or you handle it brilliantly. You're very relaxed with people, because you're so secure within yourself. Well, I'm very secure within *myself*.

I cringe sometimes when I see my rich Australian friends overseas behaving the way they behave. Equally I cringe when I see rich Englishmen behaving beyond the normal. I don't know if you've thought much about it but the assumptions of, not the *nouveaux riches* but the *nouveaux* meritocracy? I think television has a lot to do with it, but by God, some of the people I've met who've some small talent ...

Look at bloody Clive James as an Australian example of someone who went to England and became a celeb! I find him appalling, and yet stripped of all the gunk he carries around with him today he's probably quite a nice fellow. But I certainly haven't seen it, because he behaves appallingly most of the time: centre of attention, I am. Everyone in this room revolves around me. When he comes out here now he's very much: 'I am the sun'.

I don't mind egocentricity, nor do I mind people who genuinely do what they want to do: if a man eats his peas off a knife, that's totally OK with me as long as I don't have to sit and watch him. But I do mind when the little finger curls, intellectually, and there's a lot of that. There's a lot of intellectual pretension when people make money ...

Bond is a very good example of a man who really is a very direct, hard-going, hard-working, rather crass, vulgar man – and yet he's getting a veneer of almost-respectability.

But is he pretending to be something he isn't?

Oh, yes, he's starting to, my word! He's starting to try and control the farting, yes. Again, I speak intellectually. I don't like any form of pretence, and we're talking about the pretence of people who've made it. I can't stand people who don't allow themselves to be themselves.

Is there an aristocracy of wealth here, as there is in America?

If you make money, you're regarded as being one of the aristocracy: 'She was a member of Sydney society' – if that's not a contradiction in terms! That's pretty valid; you get an awful lot of people who thrust themselves forward when they've got a bit of money, and when you consider that half of Sydney society are people who fled Hungary in 1956 and came out and did very well, it really does make for fairly egalitarian living at the top!

I presume you have your critics?

Oh Christ, yes. I've got my critics because I can't bear fools lightly. If I was nice to fools I wouldn't have a critic in Australia because people would say, 'He's made it, good old Len, he's lovely.' Some people say that, a lot of other people say, 'That arrogant little shit', because I *am* an arrogant little shit. I quite recognize I've done a lot for Australia, as far as wine and food is concerned. I'm not modest about it; I have.

When you've been in the news so much and knocked around so much, you become a tired old palate ... people no longer see you as a threat. I'm on the verge of becoming an institution – an interesting old fogey!

In my own little world I'm Chairman of Judges here, Chairman of Judges there – a lot of people *call* me Chairman because they don't like saying Sir, they don't like saying Mr Evans when they've known me for a long time, and they don't want to call me Len because it's a bit too familiar; so they call me Chair.

I can remember once when I was a senior judge in Adelaide and Mick Tanapsin, a very great wine man in Australia, was one of my judges. We were discussing the sparkling wine style and this young associate judge said, 'Excuse me sir, but do you know anything about champagne?' Tanapsin looked at him in absolute horror and said, 'Son, he's *spilt* more than you'll ever drink!'

Well, you do become a legend in your own lunchtime ...

It seems you're about to become the Australian Falstaff ...

I rather fancy dying slowly in a great four-poster bed in the Cask Hall. I want to gather all my cellars together – I've got four scattered around the world – and arrange for my friends to come from everywhere. I want a bacchanalian party: oxen being roasted, people drinking and carrying-on behind the casks, pretty girls being raced-off, all that sort of thing.

Then eventually the butler will come up and murmur, 'Terribly sorry sir, but we've run out of wine.' I shall say, 'Thank you Jeeves,' put my head back on the pillow – and die very peacefully . . .

THE SEIGNEUR: TONY MOTION

I don't think I was a spy . . .

Western Australia is strong on nickel, black swans, new millionaires, wine, yachts, gold . . . but distinctly weak on stately homes. It has not, after all, been in the business long enough. The first settlers' ship, the *Parmelia*, did not arrive in Fremantle until 1829; and afterwards, because of its poverty, Western Australia became known as the Cinderella State. It had a good climate – though not for the creation of dynasties.

Today a handsome two-storey colonial homestead built in 1874 at Irishtown, some seventy miles outside Perth, is as close as you get to a stately home: Buckland was the home of James Dempster, an ex-seaman who with his wife Ann founded that successful Avon Valley dynasty. Used to naval discipline, Dempster would ensure his sons were working hard enough on the family's grant of 8000 acres by sitting on his balcony and observing them through his old sea telescope. Unfortunately, one night in 1890 he fell over that balcony – nightscopes had not yet been invented – and thus provided a ghost, without which no stately home is suitably furnished.

Buckland was dilapidated and crumbling when bought in 1982 by Captain Tony and the Hon. Mrs Penny Motion, granddaughter of Lord Ebury. After restoration, they opened to the public. It is not large or splendid, but it is interesting enough for at least twelve thousand people to take the three-dollar tour around its various rooms each year, listening to Tony's cheerful commentary and buying Penny's souvenir teaspoons.

Tony had been a soldier who went to work in Whitehall, and was posted to Melbourne and Moscow. At one time he shared an office with Peter Wright – who also came to live in Australia and caused a flutter in MI5's dovecotes, and for whom he has little sympathy ...

He was metal-trading when the Poseidon bubble burst, so took over an outback residential pub for a while, setting out his supper table in the middle of the street – the only place where there was electric light. As Western Australia flourished he built this unpromising pub into a small group of hotels and restaurants – 'for the gifted amateur there *are* more opportunities here' – and sold out handsomely to Brunei interests.

Penny says he's a people person, while she's a gadget person; indeed she swoops triumphantly around their 1250 acres on a fearsome three-wheeled motorbike with fat tyres – her fiftieth birthday present – mustering the sheep. More sedately, he greets paying customers arriving in minibuses to view their mini stately home ...

I started off as a career soldier: I was in the Ninth Lancers for ten years, decided that playing polo and showjumping were terrific fun but that perhaps I ought to do something better – not better, but *something*.

In 1961 I was working as a civilian for the Ministry of Defence, attached to the British High Commission as First Secretary in liaison with the Australian authorities. We stayed in Melbourne for three years, my first overseas posting. I think if I *had* to live in any city in the world, Melbourne would be my choice.

Before Paris, Rome, London, New York?

Oh yes, yes. Partly because I'm a bit insular, I'm very bad at languages; but it was extraordinary at our age – we were in our mid-thirties – to suddenly make so many new real friends, who remain friends to this day. There's something about the people, they're so completely genuine, with so little side. I always describe Melbourne as whisky-and-soda country and Sydney as dry-Martini country – one seems more solid than the other.

Then I was posted to Moscow after two years; it was a marvellous experience and I thoroughly enjoyed it but I wouldn't want to go back and I *wouldn't* want to live there!

You were the spy who went in to the cold?

I don't think I was a spy, but I certainly went into the cold. I enjoyed Moscow and two years there was a fascinating experience, but our love relationship with Australia had started, so, after Moscow and a couple of years in London, Penny and I wondered whether really Australia wasn't *it*, particularly as we left breeding children until very late – not on purpose, it just happened that way.

Then one day a company in the City of London called Metal Traders was silly enough to say, 'We need somebody in Australia; you get on well with Australians ...' This of course was when the nickel boom was starting and the share market was going berserk – just before Poseidon. So I came out as State Manager of the company in 1969.

You were in at the start of the boom, and on the inside – so you should have made a fortune?

I took the view that the people who were going to make good legitimate money were in the service industry to the mining boom, rather than in the mining boom or the share market boom itself. Then one day I was rung up by my Chairman from Sydney saying had I seen Reuters tape that morning, because Metal Traders London had gone bankrupt! It was a little bit of a jerk.

We were left here without a bean, so I thought, 'For the first time in my life I'm going to make some money!' I'd left it a bit late, but didn't do too badly: this is the result, actually. Penny and I hadn't got any money: we were earning a very good salary but we never saved any. Anyway, after a visit back to England we put a few friends together and bought the West Australian arm of Metal Traders off the liquidator, and one of its assets happened to be a pub. I don't suppose you've ever heard of Nullagine?

Certainly not.

Well, it's about a thousand miles up there, in the Pilbara.

So it's a place where they need a pub.

Yes, they do, because it's very hot and there are an awful lot of people milling about – geologists and stockbrokers with blunt pencils, needing somewhere to stay at night. It's right off the map, Lang Hancock territory ... One day when I was drunk I bought this old pub: it was a corrugated iron shack which could take about fifteen people if it was crowded. Penny and I restored that and made it into a very successful little outback hotel with comfortable accommodation. We turned the mat which said Keep Out over to Welcome, and went on from there.

We bought another pub, then we bought a motel about 300 miles over there which we got at a ridiculously cheap price, and the thing built up and I suddenly found myself with these outlying situations, all of which were doing extremely well.

You'd been a professional soldier, you were a diplomat/spy ...

Diplomat.

Diplomat, you were a metal trader/commodity dealer ... what was your experience in running outback pubs?

Experience was nil, but my mother was always a very good hostess.

(Laughs) It was in the blood?

It was a bit, I mean even in Moscow, where I wasn't really a very good diplomat, I suddenly found I was the chap who ran the British Commonwealth pub for the Canadian Embassy, the Australian Embassy, our own Embassy – and turned it into a fun place to be. At school I was the chappie who was responsible for the school dance ...

But having lived at the High Commission in Melbourne, your favourite city, was running a pub in the outback the right kind of advance?

I was probably drunk when I bought it. We paid $30,000 for it, and I had $5000 in the bank at the time, so five other friends put in the other twenty-five. Then we developed the company – and sold it in 1981 to some people from Brunei for $1.8 million!

Not a bad capital appreciation.

Wasn't all mine; I wish it had been. In the meantime, of course, we'd added a restaurant to it, which went well, with the first sort of – I hate the word up-market, but, yes, let's use posh – restaurant in Fremantle. Admittedly we were a bit ahead of our time, and while it was tremendously popular it didn't give us a very big capital gain, but I was building up a little chain.

When I first came to Perth in 1962 on a visit there was only one restaurant where you could get a reasonably good meal, and that was Luis. The rest were just steak and chips. Emotionally I wanted a restaurant, so we created one. As a child I was always taken to the old Berkeley Hotel in London, and the maitre d' there was a wonderful Italian called Gino Galbiati. I'd heard that Gino had just retired, having set up the restaurant in the new Berkeley, aged seventy-two. I rang him up in Como and said, 'Mr Galbiati, sir, it's Master Tony, would you ever consider coming out for six months and setting up the best restaurant in Western Australia?' And like a flash I remember him saying, 'Mr Tony, it'll be no problem. One condition, I must go down to Rome to have a new dinner jacket made, my little tummy has increased.' Sweet.

The Perth culinary media couldn't get over it, because his stories and his personality and his natural talent were just unreal; the staff adored him, and it worked beautifully. So that put me up front a bit in the hospitality trade, because one had done something really quite eccentric. It wasn't an Italian restaurant, it was up-market international, the first restaurant in Fremantle in its day – going back to '71 – with a super hors d'oeuvres trolley, silver service, everybody in black tie. It got me fired up to say: 'Look, I can *do* this!'

From there we moved on and eventually we'd created enough to borrow money, and so we bought what was the West Australian Club and converted it into an hotel called the New Esplanade and ran what I like to think was the best restaurant in Perth, The Room With A View, which I named after the great Noel Coward song.

The whole of the Australian hospitality industry had one really basic problem, which was distinguishing the word 'service' from 'servile'. The Australian is very anti being servile, it's not his form at all. The training I tried to instil in my staff was: 'Look, I'm not asking you to lick the guests' shoes, I'm asking you to *clean* them.'

The majority of our staff realized that if you happened to spill tomato soup down the lady's dress you didn't use a four-letter word, you immediately jumped in and said, 'Terribly sorry madam, could we have it cleaned for you?' It was just a change of attitude. The result, the restaurant was packed, people enjoyed themselves, the staff made more money, they got good tips, realized their jobs were secure – and the atmosphere and therefore the morale of the regiment built up.

So now that's behind you and you're a rich gentleman of leisure?

I wasn't very rich, I'm not sure how much of a gentleman I am, but I certainly became at leisure for six months.

So with all this in the blood and business going well, why aren't you back in Perth looking after the crowd?

I suppose one's career has changed about every ten years; I was ten years a soldier, ten years a diplomat ...

Spy. You didn't decide to pack up and head for Sussex?

No, certainly not. Western Australia is our home. Penny and I took the view that it would be quite fun to be ancestors, and not descendants. Each generation really must think of the next generation.

One fundamental difference between Australian countrymen and English countrymen is that we in England work in the city to enable us one day to retire to the country. The Australian basically retires to the city, to suburbia. He doesn't want to stay *here* when he's seventy. When *I'm* seventy I want that little cottage out there which I built for my mother-in-law, and my children can have this.

So how did you come to own Western Australia's stately home?

I think I've got enough Irish in me to say it was meant. I've got a feeling if my Irish grandmother was still alive she'd be saying, 'Well done boy, that was what your career in Australia was really *for*.' I have no ambition left now, other than that my ashes be scattered over these 1250 acres ...

I'm planting a thousand trees a year here. Do you know that horrific piece of trivia on trees? The first jumbo that takes off from Orly airport every morning consumes the entire oxygen supply put out by Fontainebleau forest the night before – and there's still another three hundred aircraft to go!

In England this place would still be handsome, but not quite as exceptional as it is here ...

It *is* exceptional in Western Australia, which was very poor and always called the Cinderella State. There wasn't any great inherited wealth, unlike Melbourne, and there were very few country houses built. It would have been a tragedy if this had fallen over – and there was a very good chance it *might* have done.

It actually looked a great deal worse than it was: structurally the stone and the woodwork were sound. It was just things like the ceilings falling in and the plaster off the walls, the front verandah had to be renewed, there was no garden – everything was a mess. We said to ourselves, 'We're going to have to make it commercially viable.' The farm is not capable of supporting the cost of operating this set-up.

Is it financially viable now?

It's more profitable than the farm, which must be a lesson to farmers around ... They've got to learn to diversify, whether it's into tourism, whether it's into long-stemmed roses ... but their syndrome wheat-sheep-wheat-sheep-wheat ... have a bloody drink!

The reason in my opinion why farmers in this part of the world are in trouble is because they're grossly overborrowed. You and I, whether we're running a restaurant, a TV programme, we would not capitalize ourselves say eighty to ninety per cent borrowing. And that's what they're doing, with interest rates at 22 per cent and 23 per cent. So they're going bust because they're overborrowed. They're encouraged by the banks and the pastoral companies ...

So what do these Australians who didn't understand the idea of service make of a stately home?

A lot of the people who come to Buckland have come from, shall we say, retirement villages. They aren't living in poverty but they're living in dullish and fairly small surroundings and it's rather lovely for them to come and move around a house that's big and open and quite glamorous inside. There's some lovely furniture, some lovely paintings and they talk to Penny and I and they find it slight • escapism – slightly romantic, if you like. It's perhaps like reading a Barbara Cartland novel . . .

But you go and mingle with them – it's part of the entrance fee?

Well, I don't like to put it like that, but you're quite right; I mean, people are paying three dollars to come and spend an hour, two hours, at Buckland, therefore they've got to be properly looked after, not just have a look, they've got to be *shown* things. Some people know very little and love it to be explained; I've got a beautiful desk in there that was my grandmother's and her grandmother's before that; it's a lovely piece and to be able to talk to them about it, does bring the place alive.

But can you occupy them, because it's not Blenheim, is it – it doesn't take all that much time to walk round?

It's not Blenheim, no! Well, we seem to be successfully occupying them. Some people only stay three-quarters of an hour, but others picnic on this lawn and spend all day here.

You have some pretty things lying around. There are no chains, nothing's roped off; do you ever miss anything?

I take the view that most people who pinch things souveniring, are *thick*. They're a bit ill. They like the challenge. If you put a rope up you're giving them an extra challenge, because they have to get to the other side of it. If you have a notice saying 'Don't Touch', they want to touch, and so on. So we said, 'This is our home, please treat it as such. Sit down, have a cigarette, smoke, play the music box' – and the result is that people behave far better. In other words, if you treat people like gentlemen, they behave like gentlemen, if you treat them like pigs, they behave like pigs.

So you've had no light-fingered visitors?

Had *one*. We've been open three and a half years and we've had one – and it was a Pom! I suppose it takes one Pom to smell another, but I could sort of sense this woman. She was wandering around, she kept nudging me and saying, 'How do you like living here then – it's not like 'ome, is it?' She lives here, she wasn't a visiting Pom, she was a migrant Pom – but there's that sort of Pom who thinks that we Poms will all get together and be better than the Australians. And I could smell this woman, you know.

Later on during the day I went into the drawing room – I've got a sort of eye check, I can flash my eye across the mantlepiece – and one beautiful little Sèvres powder box, patch box, was missing. I thought, I bet it's that woman! I waited until she'd gone out into the garden at the back and about fifty people were out there. I shut the door and said, 'I'm terribly sorry ladies and gentlemen, we've just had something stolen and I am going to ask to look in your handbags.' I went up to her and opened up her shopping bag and the first thing I picked out was a rotten little china ashtray out of the loo. I said, 'That's not yours, dear, is it? But I tell you what, you can keep that as a present, provided I don't find anything else.' I went down to the bottom, and out came this little box. And do you know, she didn't turn a hair! Nor did her husband, nor did her mother, nor did her daughter. Not a hair. I very nearly said to her, 'Could I have your address, madam, because I'd love to have a look at your collection some day.' I should think she'd gone to all the National Trust houses and got a beautiful little bundle everywhere.

Why do you believe that some Poms – perhaps like yourself – get to the top in Australia more quickly than others? Are there more opportunities here, more openings?

For the gifted amateur – and I suppose that's what I am to a certain extent. As you pointed out earlier: what experience have I got? How could I ever have become the manager of the Savoy Hotel in London? I'd have had to go through Lausanne and speak three languages. So for the gifted amateur who's got a bit of guts and go, yes, I think there undoubtedly are more opportunities.

It's a funny thing we *do* seem, we ex-Poms, to be able to have some influence, whether for the bad or for the good. I was Chairman of the Tourist Advisory Council, Western Australia, I was President of the Restaurant Association – one seems to be able to get to a good position of influence, whether it's because we've got a better command of the language, or are more persuasive ... I don't know what it is, but we can do it for good and bad, and there's an awful lot of them doing it for *bad*: the Pommy stirrers – those lunatics – and the whingeing Poms.

Also, Australia's not quite so – shall we say – stuck by tradition. I mean, can you imagine Penny and I doing this in her family village in Oxfordshire, in my family village in Sussex? Taking over the local pub – I mean, that would be going into *commerce*!

Not the done thing?

A little bit way out!

Australia'll always be lucky, in my view. Nobody will ever die of cold: we don't know what the word hypothermia *is*. When I'm ninety-five – my father's ninety-one so there's a good chance – and I'm wandering about here, I'm not going to pay enormous bills to keep myself warm. My hot water comes from the sun. I can grow tomatoes out there, have a couple of goats to milk, I can survive. I don't see myself doing that in Manchester.

I would prefer to spend the rest of my life here because I love it and my children love it too. They're growing up very well, very healthy, and they're not on pot, they're normal heterosexual decent kids and they really haven't got the awful temptations and pressures to be anything else. So, we love it as a family.

I have absolutely no wish to live in England. I didn't leave England – I *came* to Australia. There's a difference, I think: I wasn't running away from anything ...

THE CASINO BOSS: PETER BARNARD

*That whole scene of
quasi-respectable orgies has gone . . .*

For years the ex-Servicemen's RSL Clubs of New South Wales, with their shining acres of fruit machines, have been doing tremendously well for themselves and their members – so it seemed to the Australian Government that nationwide gambling, carefully controlled, might be one answer to the country's economic problems. There followed a scramble in every state to provide 'pokies' and all other games which satisfy the determination of locals and tourists to have a punt.

Monstrous casinos – Aztec temples, Persian playgrounds, brutal monoliths – grew up across the land: on the Gold Coast, up at tropical Darwin, over in Perth, at Adelaide, Townsville, even in the heartland of Alice Springs . . . The world's biggest casino, planned for Sydney Harbour, will cost $500 million and accommodate 15,000 players.

Australia's very first casino was built many years ago, paradoxically, in the gentle green island of Tasmania, where life is sane and subdued. At Wrest Point on the Derwent River just outside Hobart, they created a great circular concrete gasometer twenty-two storeys high –

and sent to England for gambling men to run it. In the early Seventies Peter Barnard arrived with a planeload of other ex-Playboy types from Park Lane to set up the scene. He is now Gambling Director and his casino is Tasmania's best-known landmark.

Dark, compact and watchful, he looks like CID to me but was in fact a £14-a-week croupier in Torquay back in 1962 and worked his way up the casino ladder. In Tasmania his wife and four children became Born-again Christians, so he married one of his croupiers and had a couple of babies. Peter now loves his home, his $50,000 yacht and his life – and in fifteen years has never bothered to return to London.

Inside his hotel complex – which has spawned a convention centre – acres of crimson carpet and gilt furnishings; but not even the draped four-poster beds upstairs can create a wicked atmosphere. The casino remains a cosy place where croupiers with cropped hair and their brothers' dinner jackets are young and polite; even the pit bosses look as though they should be serving Big Macs. They're all a long happy way from the hard-eyed hoods of Las Vegas, the usual steely casino mafiosi we know and dread.

In Tasmania even the punters seem more like pensioners on a bingo outing than gamblers, though Wrest Point and its associated casino at Launceston on the north coast turn over $100 million a year – so there must be *some* high-rollers around.

Since Peter's gamblers are so honest, his croupiers untainted by avarice, I wondered about the inevitable peripheral hookers – which casinos around the world employ heavies to keep out of their players' hair, so they may concentrate upon losing. 'Can't get *enough* of them,' he said. 'There're only two escort agencies in town, and

if we have a big conference the delegates want some
action ...'

I joined the Merchant Navy because I didn't want to do National
Service and two days after I joined National Service for my age
group was *out* – so I blew that. But I went round the world twice,
which was tremendous. Then afterwards I thought, 'Well, I'm
normal and I *do* like women and I don't like staying at sea for forty
days, as they would want me to do', so I gave that away and became
an executive trainee with Unilever, all round England. I worked for
Walls Ice Cream as a management trainee and that was ghastly,
terrible. You had to call people 'sir', and bow and scrape.

My father had a hotel in Torquay at this time and he decided that
he was going to run a casino in it. This was in 1962, and he
was the second casino in England which was allowed to open
subjudiciously, before the Act came in. The police said, 'We're not
going to do anything about it, so go for your life – as long as there's
no complaints!'

It was called the Academy Club. I went down with my brother
and learned how to run a roulette table with a plastic wheel and a
sort of ball-bearing going in the middle. The whole thing was on
chipboard laid over a dining table, so after people had finished their
evening meal it all changed: put the velvet drapes back and the eye
shades on and away we go! It really was George Raft ...

We had chemmy, roulette and poker. We ran the roulette until
we earned enough, then all on to chemmy; we'd play for quite
substantial amounts: all locals – bookies, horse trainers ...

When you first start up a casino there's always an available
amount of biscuit-tin money; the place is full of hoteliers who've
got ten rooms for the income tax and two rooms for the holiday –
that's biscuit-tin money: 'Oh let's have a flutter, never done this
before!'

We ran that for about eighteen months, and then Newton Abbott
races opened and we had visits from bookies and jockeys and horse
owners; they'd given us a good go and we'd come out on top. They
came round this particular year and played chemmy. We were very
naïve. There was four of them sitting that side and four of them
sitting this side, and the four of them *that* side lost about £23,000 –

one loses to the other in chemmy – and they demanded cash. The other paid us with a cheque, and it bounced all the way to the bank. We weren't making big money, we were making a comfortable living – there were families living out of it. So we sold our houses and we sold our cars. We all went to the wall, and that was *it*.

So I became a rep, to keep body and soul together. Just after that, the Royal Bath in Bournemouth opened up as a French casino and I thought, 'I'm a croupier, I'll go along here.' I walked in and this French fellow said 'We only take Frenchmen.' I said, 'But I'm a fully-qualified croupier.' He said, 'Let's see what you can do: come in every night at six o'clock.' So from six o'clock until two o'clock in the morning after work, six days a week, I went in and trained and studied, learned to speak French, the whole bit ... Nine months that took, nine months' solid study.

As a rep I was earning £14 a week, which was enough; I was surviving on that. He said, 'We can only afford to pay you £22.10s' – which was a fortune, just for being a croupier! It's an easy job, really is, once you've learnt the basics. I could speak French and it's only a question of manual dexterity and a bit of flash – and it's fun. Money for old rope, and you're amongst the nightlife and birds are available ... Lovely – I adored it.

So I stayed there for about eight months, and then somebody said that they were looking for croupiers at the Victoria Sporting Club. I applied, had a table test, and that once again was all Frenchmen. I got the job. This was in '65, and the money was frightening. Weinberg, who ran it, was a front man for the Corsican bandits, the Mafia ... Jewish. Then he disappeared, because I think he had sticky fingers. That was a great place; we used to have £60 a week – which was a fortune – and on top of that every Friday a little brown envelope was distributed which was your share of the tips – and there was another £100. So £160, in 1965!

I used to buy clothes all the time, bought a house ... Anyway it was just too much: it didn't last long because it suddenly became too apparent, and wages were then sort of pegged. The Gaming Board came and said, 'No tipping any more, clean it up generally, make people accountable, no credit, no cheque cashing ...'

Playboy was just about to open and they wanted pit bosses. I went along there as a pit boss – and that was a mind-blowing

experience, incredible. I'll never forget that because of the birds ...
frightening! There were all these vestal virgins who were deprived.

*They had to keep it in-house because they weren't allowed to go out with
the clients?*

Absolutely – quite right. Once again you get so naïve because
there's a bird you're talking to, she's dealing away and you're
saying, 'You went out with Abdul Razziz last night?' And she says
'Yes, he gave me this Cartier watch and all I did was have dinner
with him!' And I'd believe them! I'd think, 'Aren't you lucky, wish
I was a bird ...' Some of the Bunnies made fortunes, literally
hundreds of thousands of pounds!

Did they hang on to it?

Oh yes: birds seem far more squirrely, in that regard.

So that was a fascinating experience. It was the most professional
casino in the whole of London, run very much as a business, a
superb grounding for any manager. I made it up to Shift Manager
there, and the money! It was in the days when Poseidon went mad
and we used to have stockbrokers coming in during the day after
they bought in, bought out and sold and bought in again on their
daily take of Poseidon. They used to have these people from the City
coming with a quarter of a million! It was the most incredible thing
I've ever seen, because it suddenly meant there was all this money
available that they'd turned round – and there it was, coming in to
us.

*This was when the Park Lane Playboy Club was supporting the entire
Playboy empire?*

Yes, very much, and you're constantly having to justify or excuse
the excesses of people ... I think that whole type of scene where
you can put on quasi-respectable orgies has really gone.

It's all a long way from Hobart ...

Yes it *is* a long way from Hobart. Hobart is the most respectable
place I've ever been in my life.

*So you came from the Playboy Club, with all those Bunnies, to Tasmania,
with all these sheep. How did it come on to your horizon?*

The Boy Racer: Peter Briggs

The Welsh Falstaff: Len Evans

The Seigneur: Tony Motion with his wife Penny

The Casino Boss: Peter Barnard

The Producer: Phillip Emanuel

The Optimists: Geoff and Edie Taylor

The Pilot: Malcolm Hatton-Ward

The Medical Missionaries: Drs Clare Jukka and Neil Beaton

The Artist: Patrick Kilvington

The Inventor: Tom Law

The Curator: Edmund Capon

The Cricketer: Tony Greig with Ian Botham

The Intrepid Colonial: Diana Bowden

The Country Gent: Major James 'Slip' de Courcey Mitchell

The Bush Brother: Noel Allen

The Valley Girl: Annette Wilde

I'd been asked to open a casino, a right battered joint slap bang in the middle of Manchester in a basement with a disco next door. That lasted about eighteen months and the fellow who'd been appointed to manage this place said, would I be interested in going out to Tasmania. I jumped at it.

You were married then?

Yes, married, four kids; she thought it was a great idea.

Anything to get out of Manchester?

Manchester is the pits. Oh godfathers, it was terrible – but I lived in the village of England, Prestbury, just before you get to Macclesfield. All the local hunt Masters live there. I'd got this lovely brand-new house, and my children had taken up horse-riding.

You joined the squirearchy?

Very much so.

Then why did Tasmania look good?

Change, I think. Not better money, not necessarily. The possibility of being able to do more *with* it. We were in horses then and I thought, I'll be able to get some land over there and raise some horses. I have never, from the day I set foot in this place, ever thought I've made the wrong decision. *Ever!*

What age were the children?

Twelve, eleven, eight and six – and it's worked out for them. They're all Australian. They have no desire to be called British, English or anything else. My eldest daughter's a hospital sister; she's married, has a child and is expecting another one. The son makes surfboards. The other daughter's doing an Honours degree at the university here and the young fellow is running a Christian bookshop, so we're all sorted out. They're all in Hobart, it's smashing; just across the water, and I can see the lot of them.

How about your first wife?

She's a student nurse in the local hospital. She's got the distinction of being the oldest trainee of her intake. Everybody had said, you'll know after two years whether you can handle Tasmania, whether it's part and parcel of you. The two-year mark was a slightly magical time because up to then she'd had problems coping with it, with the alcohol excesses. You go to parties and alcohol is *it*, it really is. You take casks and flagons, you don't take good wine to a party – people knock it over.

She found great difficulty coming to terms with that, working out her spare time because she'd had babies in England, here they were schoolchildren. At two years she made a statement which sort of summed it up: 'I really *like* gum trees!' And that was it: she loved it.

She also started a business which made fortunes: she became an antique expert. She read books, she bought five brass firescreens for $4.50 each, real rubbish, took them home, cleaned them up – and sold them for $12 each. She said, 'This has got to be it!'

Is she happy now, despite the fact that you've separated?

I still see her, and my present wife and her discuss me – what I'm like in bed ...

Will she not get married again?

No, she's a committed Christian, they all are, all my children.

Even Christians get married ...

Not when they consider there's no such thing as divorce.

Born-again, is she?

Yes. They're Baptist sort of people.

No one would accuse your punters downstairs of being very stylish, would they? Even in Manchester there must've been a bit more flash than there is here ...

Yes, there was. There was a little more class, a little more on the side. There was also a lot more dishonesty – a lot more, both in persons and in actions. For instance, here we cash cheques for people to gamble with and the amount of cheques returned as a general percentage is less than 0.01 per cent since we opened. In America they work on 4 per cent of all cheques given are returned.

People are basically quite honest here – in variance to when I was in England, where all the teams of shoplifters were Australian, all the teams of people trying pull swifties in the casinos were Australians. We came out here expecting real trouble ...

If you're getting some high-rollers here from the States they must be a bit surprised? Some of your pit bosses are nice healthy youngsters with spiky hair ...

We go for youth, we certainly do ... We've been very fortunate – we've recently had to staff 90 per cent of all the casinos going up in Australia. They all come and pinch our older employees, which has given us a great fillip because it's left us with great blanks which we filled with youngsters.

A lot of them are very naïve – naïve in the nicest way. We're also naïve in the management of the casino, in that for fourteen years we haven't been exposed to hoods, we haven't been exposed to the Vegas-type jungle. So we accept a lot of people on face value: we get very few bouncing cheques, we get no cases of dishonesty amongst staff that we know of, we get minimal amounts of dishonesty amongst players.

If we get the Sydney casino, it'll be a whole new ball game, we'll have to be like steel traps. It'll be a relearning process for a lot of us – back to what we were at Playboy – keeping an eye open, never trusting anybody, making sure what was ours *stays* ours. But, in the meantime, this is very pleasant.

You'll notice, though, that we have one inspector to two blackjack tables, or one inspector per roulette table, which is very high. We've also got a huge number of local permanents, customers, *real* permanents, 'Hello Fred, hello Wally ...' who are in day after day. If anybody tried to rip us off, they'd tell. They're like our watchdogs.

Is there a reservoir of high-rollers around?

Victoria is our main drawing area – geographically it's the closest place. They're traditionally mostly Jewish schmutter-merchants, cloth manufacturers, dyers, printers ...

So how do these people differ from the punters in London or Manchester? You said they're more honest ...

Streetwise, is the top and bottom of it. You can see it in employees as well. You get a London dealer, a London inspector – they're crafty. It's just streetwise, that's all. They're after the main chance –

and the punters are the same in London. For instance, if you overpaid a punter £10 in a London club the chances of getting that back are zilch. Here you stand a fifty-fifty chance of the person giving it back, which is really nice.

And the other side of it, it breeds ... In London if you're in a club and there's an opportunity to give a punter the benefit of the doubt, he looks a bit iffy, he's got this scar – forget it! Out here you welcome the opportunity to be seen to be a contributing person, like, 'Sure, we believe you ... if you *say* you had a piece there and we've moved it off, it's quite likely we did – we'll pay.' Because we know that that reciprocal situation only enhances the thing. He's either going to say, 'They're good lads down there' or 'I've put one over them.' It doesn't matter whichever way – he's going to come back, because he thinks he's going to do it again, or he's a nice lad who's going to give us some more custom.

We've just had a party of sixteen Americans who we've treated as we treat all our high-rollers, and they've been absolutely flabbergasted at the attention they received. We're never absolutely certain whether it's going to work. The breakeven point is sometimes too close for comfort: it's always on the knife edge.

It's going to get better now, though. The more bombs that go off in Beirut, the better it is for us – which is a terrible way of looking at it. I read one of the principal actors in *Dynasty* or *Dallas* changed his holiday arrangements and came to Australia instead.

Rambo was frightened to go to Cannes ... So that's all on the asset side; is there anything on the debit side that you feel you've lost?

I'll tell you what I *have* lost: my sense of proportion, in certain instances. Like, I'm still in touch with my relatives in England and it's difficult to relate because I've got a house, I've got a couple of cars, I've got a $50,000 yacht, I've got the ability to go out and buy a new set of golf clubs tomorrow if I want them. I can fly to wherever I want to and they can't. This isn't because they earn less than me, necessarily, but their ability to expand their use of money is limited. It's not limited only by restraints of finance, it's limited by their imagination as well.

Their horizons are smaller ...?

They are, they've shrunk. Maybe ours have expanded. We say, 'We'll go to Fiji', they're still thinking – which isn't wrong – they're still thinking about going to the Boy Scouts' camp, going to the Lake District walking ...

Almost every Briton I talked to in America wanted to go home – not to live, but to visit. You're unique in not even wanting to visit!

I look at it this way: I'd like to go home and say 'how do you do?' to my brothers and sisters, and I imagine that after I'd said, 'Do you remember?' for about three hours we'd then find out whether we've got any similarities left. Then it would be a question of taking Kathy around to show her the various places: 'That's where I went to school ...'

Take her to Bond Street and Harrods – she'd like that!

That's a straight tourist thing: to get there and to have that much enjoyment's going to cost fifteen grand: the fare for myself and Kathy and a couple of little babies – we're talking three grand each, nine grand for fares ... The things I could do *here* with fifteen grand are quite extraordinary.

So what would you do with it?

Buy a bigger yacht ...

You're not concerned about the recession?

Hotels suffer from recession because companies say, 'We can't afford to do that ...' Casinos die in depressions, but *thrive* in recessions. The reasoning is that any person who has $100 – there's always someone with $100 – knows that in a recession it's worth nothing. What are you going to do with it? It's not worth putting in a bank, so they say, 'It's only $100, I'll have a go with it.' So they gamble.

In a depression they haven't *got* $100, so they can't do anything with it. In a normal time we have normal runs, in a recession, up she goes. Casinos *thrive* on recession ...

THE PRODUCER: PHILLIP EMANUEL

As a film producer, one is accused
of being a bullshit merchant ...

In the Seventies a few Australian films became internationally noticed. Having regarded the antipodes only as a cultural desert and home of the technicolour yawn, critics fell over themselves to recognize this new-found sensitivity.

The industry was also going well financially, thanks to unusually generous tax breaks for investors who were allowed 150 per cent deductions, with the first 20 per cent of any income tax-free; so high earners and the star-struck jostled to become angels. The industry went on to produce a few good and a lot of awful films, working up to the triumphant *Crocodile Dundee* which unexpectedly broke box-office records around the world.

A sensitive Bradford boy climbed eagerly upon the back of this boom: Phillip Emanuel's father Julius was a Manchester oculist and part-time gag writer who knew his son was stage-struck but also knew that any nice Jewish boy should be a doctor or a lawyer, at *least*, just in case. He sent Phillip to Bradford University to graduate in Pharmacy.

With a chemist's shop to fall back on, Phillip founded a theatre club in Edinburgh, married an Australian

choreographer and in 1978 took one of his productions –
East, by Stephen Berkoff – on an Australian tour. There
he met Wilton Morley, son of Robert, and after a few
stage ventures they struck it rich with *The Rocky Horror
Show*.

When he observed the tax-incentive thrust behind the
industry, Phillip decided to stay in Australia and produce
films. His first feature was Ibsen's *The Wild Duck*, with
Jeremy Irons and Liv Ullman; then *Rebel*, with Matt Dillon
and Debbie Byrne. When we met on his set in an old
Federation house he'd hired for $2000, he was producing
a black comedy called *Those Dear Departed*, with Pamela
Stephenson and Garry McDonald. The budget was just
over $1 million, which he called 'highly minuscule'.

Phillip, small, warm and smiling, has an attractive
house at Mosman, a pretty wife and two picture-book
daughters, so his home life seems perfect; his low-budget
films are also doing well. Yet with all these happy scenes
he still does not feel *quite* at home in Australia ...

Feel at home? Not entirely, no. I don't feel I belong here, my roots
being somewhere else: I feel wedded to the UK. I'm enjoying myself,
have a good lifestyle, I've done well – but if I'm being perfectly
honest, I don't feel at *one* with Australia or Australians because for
some reason I'm not relating to them as well as I'd hoped I might.
I felt that way when I first arrived in '78 and I *still* feel that way. I
can't put my finger on it, but I'm not relating in an intellectual
sense or a cultural sense.

I knew nothing about Australia, although I married an Australian. I honestly believed it was going to be like England, but *hot* –
and of course it isn't. Australians are a different race and you have
to get used to a different country, a different way of life. It doesn't
altogether appeal to me. Being perfectly honest, I think I'd be more
at home emotionally in the UK. I miss the general way of life, I miss
the accessibility to world-class theatre, I prefer the drama there,

the television there, I prefer the informed opinion, I prefer the newspapers – I don't particularly enjoy Australian newspapers.

I don't miss the climate and I don't miss the fact that you can't do what I'm doing, which is to make films. I'm very happy to be here for that reason, I'm very grateful Australia's given me the opportunity – so when I say I'm not feeling totally at home it would be churlish of me not to admit I'm enjoying what I'm doing.

We have a close circle of friends, Australians and non-Australians, whom we *can* relate to, but it's difficult to explain: it's the people I *don't* know that concern me more than the people I do know. It's the man in the street, if you like, who I don't feel at one with. But that doesn't mean to say I'm going to hightail it back there!

You were a pharmacist who dreamed about being a film producer?

I *am* a pharmacist – it doesn't go away. I was brought up with a theatrical background, although I did take some time off to get a degree in something as an insurance, at the behest of my father.

In England you've got to be established to find film finance; here you've just got to be plausible ...

In England you've got to be established, you've got to have money; producers often have a private income, or come from a moneyed family. I didn't have either. But you see, there isn't any money in the UK for films, it's a very high risk venture business and people are simply not investing in it – it's very, very tight.

What's helped me here is the fact that several years ago the government, unbelievably, introduced an amazing tax incentive scheme to encourage people to invest in feature films. I came to Australia at a time when that was just beginning to happen, so what I've got going for me is a fantastic incentive for investors who used to get 150 per cent deduction on their money. Now it's 120 per cent – and people are *complaining*. A 120 per cent write-off! The first 20 per cent of income is tax-free.

Also, it's quite a fun thing to do ... They're angels, these people?

They're angels, but in London, in the West End, angels are looking for a profit, here they're looking for a tax profit. Once they've achieved that, anything else is a big bonus. So that's what we've got going for us here: it's not even a question of being plausible, it's a question of being able to put together a package that can find its way into the marketplace.

Anyhow, Australians seem very proud of their productions – yet in the main they're art house films?

Yes, I believe they are. You've got to crack the American market, that's the big problem. Not even the English have cracked it consistently in the last few decades, and they're making some marvellous films. Here the Australians talk in a different way and the language is hard to understand, so we've got that going against us for a start. But they *are* regarded as art house films, almost foreign language films; very few have broken out into mainstream.

Australians have a perception of their films that I don't feel is strictly accurate because the Press here are blowing them out of all proportion. They're not as well received overseas as the Press would have us believe – I *know*, because I'm going overseas and getting reactions first-hand. Only a handful have done anything at all outside these shores.

They like to export the Paul Hogan image – and then get rather affronted they're not seen as thoughtful intellectuals ...

Yes, but to be fair to them there have been a number of films made by directors such as Bruce Beresford and Fred Schepisi and Gillian Armstrong which have been remarkable: I'm talking about *Gallipoli* and *Breaker Morant*. *My Brilliant Career* and *Picnic at Hanging Rock* have a considerable amount of intellectual content.

Is this a place, Phillip, where it's easy to bullshit your way through?

Bullshit your way through? Well, um, I don't know whether I've operated on that level ... As a film producer one is accused of being a bullshit merchant anywhere in the world, because one has to build things up to attract investment in a very high risk area.

Australians are fairly canny people, and it's tough here; I think you've got to have some depth in business, you've got to know what you're doing. I don't think bullshit works, no. I can't put my finger on it, I can't actually articulate what it is that makes you successful and why you can make money here ... I guess it's the same anywhere in the world, if you bring together the right elements and the chemistry's right and you're plausible and feasible and what you're doing works, then you'll make money – but not bullshit, no.

Is it true that if you've got a bit of spark, you can't help but make it here?

I'd go along with that, to a degree. There's a lot of xenophobia around in Australia, generally. That's a real paradox, I find – there's xenophobia, but they'll give you a go! If you keep banging your head against that door, eventually it will open for you.

The Australian is a very complex and complicated individual, and if you think you're coming to 'England with sun' you're in for a big surprise – they're a race apart. There's unquestionably still a chip on the shoulder, there's unquestionably still an inferiority complex. On the other hand, they're very open people. Despite the xenophobia, if you keep pushing they will accept you – so there's a contradiction. There is not, in my view, an incredible standard of excellence across the board here, in *any* field.

Yet it's a place where a film-maker like you can achieve some of his dreams – but once achieved you want to scuttle back to Wardour Street?

I don't necessarily want to scuttle back to Wardour Street. People say to me, 'While you're in Australia, you're a big fish in a small pond', and I say, 'As far as filming is concerned, I'm a very small fish in a huge pond, which is the world's film industry.' I'm hitting Wardour Street from *here*!

Your film Rebel *is going to open in London, but only in four cinemas; so that's not going to make you rich.*

In London, and then right across the UK and then in twelve cinemas in Paris and right across France, in New York, LA and right across the USA ... If it breaks out in any *one* of those territories, we'll do very well, thank you very much. Now I'm not sure that I could have raised the equivalent of six million Australian dollars to make a major drama musical in London; but I did it here.

You bring your investors to your home, ply them with champagne – and sweetheart the money out of them?

Or we do it in my office or in various brokers' offices or I just do it on the phone. I mean, there's any which way; as long as they put the cheque on the table, I'm happy. You have to have a certain background in law, in accountancy and business acumen to get money out of people on that level. It isn't easy, but it has to be easier than it would be in the UK, where all my friends that are still working in the theatre would love to make films but simply cannot make the break. I'd like to think I can go and live in the UK again, but I know if I want to continue making films, I'm much better off here.

You can't afford to go back to Manchester?

Manchester – you've *got* to be joking! Manchester's a long way away. No, I wouldn't go there, but I would consider one day going back to London. I suspect I'd be emotionally and intellectually happier back where I belong, which *is* in the United Kingdom ...

THE OPTIMISTS:
GEOFF AND EDIE TAYLOR

It was a bit isolated – a thousand miles to Darwin ...

Charters Towers is an old goldrush town in Queensland, eighty-five miles inland from Townsville along a dead straight road which takes about an hour to cover, illegally. On the way you pass one garage, and an occasional kangaroo lacking road sense. The Flinders Highway then carries on for another five hundred miles or so to Mount Isa; this is *wide* country.

The gold, discovered in 1871, vanished around 1916 after almost seven million ounces had been mined; one nugget alone weighed 143 ounces. Then Charters Towers dozed for a while, but now Australia has begun to value its history some of the town has been restored. With iron lace, curved awnings and elegant facades on Gill and Mosman, the Towers is today a gentle town Disney would love; on its wide streets only the Deadwood Stage is missing.

The old Stock Exchange has been transformed into a shopping arcade, the ornate buildings that were busy banks have become libraries or offices; the corner pubs with swinging Wild West doors merely adjusted to quieter days, as the population fell to 9000.

Old Stan Pollard, who started the town drapery more

than seventy years ago, is still there keeping an eye on things – though considering selling ... His store's slingshot money exchange system – overhead wires that whizz invoices and cash to the central desk and send back the change – must surely be worth saving. They're not making those any more ...

A couple of miles out of town along dusty tracks that take over when the tarmac ends ... and there's the Bark-a-Bit Kennels, baking on red earth under Queensland's stunning sun. Only the occasional bark, as advertised, shows this tumbledown collection of ancient caravans and corrugated-iron sheds on five acres of barren earth represents thirty kennels, a cattery – *and* the hopes of Geoff Taylor, a colliery electrician from Coalville, Leicestershire, and his wife Edie. They emigrated as £10 Poms in 1969 and now live with children aged twenty-five, fifteen and three, and a mother-in-law, in and out of these caravans, and are perhaps less well housed than the dogs.

They also have a new business making concrete garden ornaments; Geoff uses imported American casts, Edie spray-paints. Then the animals, urns, cherubs are left on parade in gaudy lines, awaiting purchasers.

Unfortunately, in the Queensland scrub amid derelict mines there are few passers-by, few impulse buyers for these florid frogs and gnomes – not even for the precast concrete lavatory seats sprayed purple and black and inscribed: 'If you sprinkle when you tinkle, be a sweetie wipe the seatie'...

Geoff: We were sick of the life in England – seems as if you're *born* to a job over there: you're a Coal Board employee, you work at the Coal Board for so many years, you die at the Coal Board, you're buried by the Coal Board – and that's your life! There's no outside life at all. It's too narrow, too bloody cold over there, innit mate?

Edie got a bit of wanderlust, being Irish. We wanted a change of life, wanted to look at how other people live.

Coming out was the best holiday we've ever had, or ever likely to have – a whole four weeks on a boat! We landed in a totally strange country, entirely different ideas. We didn't like what we saw when we first arrived – but we wouldn't go back now.

One thing you cop over here: you land in the hostels, as they call them – a quarter of a Nissen hut. When you leave England they're supposed to be these nice flash places over in Australia for you to live in until you find work and a house and a job – but it's not quite so glorious when you *get* here!

So you were a whingeing Pom?

I was a *dissatisfied* Pom. How can you put it – we didn't get what we were led to understand we would get: a better life, nice housing, all sorts of things. You finish up in a quarter of a Nissen hut with a job smack in the middle of the city from eleven in the morning to God-knows-what at night.

Made Leicestershire look pretty good to start with, did it? Was there ever a chance, Edie, that you might have packed up and gone home?

Edie: Yes, there was: about twelve months after we arrived we got to that point where we felt homesick. We were living in Melbourne, which is a funny place – it's got a climate where you can have all four seasons in one day.

Like England?

Yes, which we found a bit hard to take. The funny thing was, we asked our son Jim – who was nine at that time – we asked him what he felt, and he *cried* at the idea of going back to England! He was so happy already in Australia, so we thought we'd better give it a fair go. If that's how he feels, it *must* have something ...

Geoff: We got a little bit fed up, we thought we were settling back into the same old rut we had in England: you've got a job in town with Mr A or Mr B, you go to and from your job every day, you've got a house upon the hill and you've got a mortgage around your neck, you go to and from town to do your shopping just the same as we did in England – but twenty degrees warmer.

Well, Edie virtually persuaded me that we should be gypsies, because that's what she wanted when we arrived. I said no, and went for a house instead – and then came home one day with a Land Rover! She didn't believe it. We came across a twenty-five-foot caravan, and we sat there patiently waiting for the house to be sold. When it was sold, we started the Land Rover up and headed north, headed towards the sunshine, eh!

After about three years, we finished up in Alice Springs for four or five years. It was a bit isolated – that was a nuisance. It's a long way to go anywhere – a thousand miles to Darwin. Down to Adelaide, at that time, there was six hundred miles of dirt road. They were the two nearest cities for local booze-ups, for a party.

But you're not exactly in the centre of things here, outside Charters Towers – and it's a bit basic, isn't it?

Very. It's more than basic, mate, it's a bit rough, innit?

But you find it's better than Leicestershire?

You can't sit out in the middle of the day in winter in England. I know it cooks you here in the summer; all you do is you just sit and sweat – and then you go and have four showers a day instead of one a month!

Occasionally it'll get to forty-four, but not very often. That is the extreme, and it's unbearable. But the big advantage of Charters Towers from our point of view is that it's very rarely humid. Forty degrees here is bearable, forty degrees in Townsville or Darwin and you just go *phut* . . . That's a big difference.

And you're still living in a caravan? You don't ever feel, Edie, you'd like a little home with a new kitchen and all mod cons?

Edie: Ah yes – I'd be wrong if I said no. But I think you've got to be practical; we started off here just on the dole, and you've got to do things in the right order.

Geoff: I'll be honest with you: Edie would love a modern house with all the frills and a bedroom and everything else.

So you're lucky it was her idea to get a caravan!

Yes, and I'm also lucky in another respect too, Alan. I don't know any other feller's wife who would be prepared to put up with things like that – and she's been doing it now for quite some time.

We made a decision after we got here: we got two choices, either the home or a business. If we can get a business going, we can provide a home from the business. If we buy a house – it's a house and dole money! That's no good, so we opted for this. We make a lot of sacrifices, but we've got the bare necessities. We'll find out in the next couple of years. We've got two businesses, nearly, which should give us a living and provide us a house.

It's baffling to me why you should have chosen this spot; I get the impression your car must have run out of petrol here!

It could well fit in like that. Where're we going when we leave Alice? How about Charters Towers? Where the *hell's* Charters Towers?

Edie: Every little town in Australia, they've all got a similarity, they all look much the same, but Charters Towers didn't. It had something different, because they've preserved the old buildings. It's got a very romantic feel about it, because it was the old gold-mining town.

If you were going out for an evening at home, you'd go down to the pub – what do you do here?

Geoff: Social life we don't have time for at the moment. We're spending all our days trying to develop these two projects, both of which cost far more than we thought. We're only looking for a comfortable life out of it anyway, I don't want a fortune. But social life we don't have too much of.

I'm led to understand a normal routine here is, knock-off work, go down the boozer, grog-on for a while – and then go home. But I'm different, because I'm not a grog merchant. We might go out now and again to tea, but it's not so very often at the moment because of financial necessity. I don't think we would anyway, if we were worth a quid.

The Australian government – when they used to allow you to come over here – said you have to stay for two years, or pay your return air fare. That two years was very clever because it takes you two years to get immune to it, believe you me! You may listen to the Aussies and they may laugh, but it takes a long while before you stop getting your back up. After a while you get used to it. You can pick the genuine nasties from the rubbishing, and a lot of people were rubbishing.

We've been here since '69; that's a long time, but we're still Poms and we still get rubbished, and we respond. Some people are nasty with you, some people are not. You get the occasional vindictive one that really likes to get the boot in.

They'll run down the Poms from now 'til the day blooming Australia blows up. That's the national pastime, innit, Pommybaiting, but you live with it. When you arrive here you find the Aussies have three pastimes: rubbishing the Dagos, rubbishing the Greeks – and rubbishing the Poms.

I'm an Aussie now, see, but I'm still a Pom as well. I'll be a Pom 'til the day I die, but we're living in Australia, working in Australia, we hope our customers are Australians, if I break the law I go to jail in Australia, we pay tax in Australia, we get Social Security from Australia, we get work in Australia, so why not?

They did a television programme with a family of Poms who came from England and expected Australia to be England, but it didn't work out. They seem to pick out the middle-class snobbery. If you come to Australia, you've got to learn to adapt to the Australian ways of life. Fortunately they're not typical; but if you stick a white sheet in front of you and put a black dot on it – what do you see? You just see the black dot. Well, that's the black dot we're talking about. That kind of Pom blames Australia, not themselves; they blame the people in Australia and the country itself. It's unfair, to my mind.

But you're not a middle-class snob, Geoff.

Well, I can't *afford* to be, can I – yet! I'd like to be a little bit better off than I am at the moment, but I'd hate to be a snob. If I was in a similar position in England, I suppose it would be possible. When you get a few bob in the bank you start thinking you're clever, you get careless, you make mistakes, and it soon brings you down to earth again. But there's no *need* to be snobbish over here, you get people even in Charters Towers, they're worth bloomin' millions, eh, and they run around with scruffy old hats and teeshirts.

If you've got a lot of money, people will sort of look up to you a little bit more, I guess, but in England you can be as poor as a church mouse but if you've got the right name, everyone looks up to you ...

It's not very often their rubbishing is serious, is it?

Very rarely. The Aussies seem to have had the idea that the Poms are coming to Australia to take over – ironically, when you look at the multiracial system in Australia, that's a fact! We often say, 'The only true-blues are the black fellers' – which is true. The rest have only got two hundred years of history, anyway; *all* the white Australians are immigrants, even if it may be three generations back ...

THE PILOT:
CAPTAIN MALCOLM HATTON-WARD

Lovely days for the rest of our lives...

Captain Malcolm Hatton-Ward has lived in Australia since 1963, but remains as English as can be: thin, tweedy, church-going, serious, patently honest and undevious, exactly as he must have been when he left his Hertfordshire village a quarter of a century ago. He jokes that in the world's most casual country, other pilots say he wears a stiff white collar to clean his car...

He had left the RAF to join Qantas, and is now a Senior Captain flying their 747s around the world, and instructing on the simulator.

His wife arrived in Sydney with him, pregnant and resentful, and gave birth to their second son while he was heading for San Francisco on his first flight as a Second Officer – yet today 'she's a much better Australian than me'. Though Australians tend to move home as often as Americans, the Hatton-Wards still live in the house they bought twenty-two years ago.

Qantas is one of the best – if not *the* best – of the international long-haul airlines, and Captain Hatton-Ward the kind of pilot you always hope will be up front: concerned, assured, believing in good manners and discipline, quietly competent. His decision to join Qantas and not BEA all those years ago showed financial judgement, at least: British Airways pilots now get one-third the wage of Qantas pilots – who in 1984 earned US$88,650, while an Air India 747 pilots got US$11,800.

Unlike almost every other airline in the world, the twenty-five Qantas 747s carry a crew of four – not three – on the flight deck, and their flying time is limited to one hundred hours a month. Certainly they fly high among Australia's working aristocracy...

We came to Australia twenty-two years ago, very largely because I was in a desperate plight: I'd left the Air Force and been on the dole for some period, and needed a job. Up came Qantas *and* an offer to join BEA at the same time, so there was a decision to be made...

The BEA attitude, with typical British undersell, was: 'Of course we can't promise you a command and your prospects aren't terribly good and you'll be starting in the Outer Hebrides...' Qantas on the other hand – and in those days I thought it *very* American – said, 'You'll be in the top two per cent salary earners, you'll definitely have a command in seven years, it never rains out there' – all that sort of thing! They were looking for what they called 'instant captains'; they felt they'd exhausted the supply of Australians. So I came in as a Second Officer, and worked through from there.

Certainly if you were with British Airways today you'd be getting one-third the salary you're earning with Qantas?

Quite possibly, yes. It was a consideration, but it's not one that came into the decision making.

I got into Sydney late on a Sunday night, and had to start work on the Monday morning – so the first impressions were that it was a rotten place: it was raining, the hotel wasn't friendly, poor quality accommodation ... disaster. We've come 12,000 miles, please can we get on a plane and go straight back?

When we moved into a house on the water we began to feel at ease. This was the height of summer '64, and we were made very much at home because our next-door neighbour, while we were still waiting for the key to be delivered, ran over and introduced herself and her husband. I can vividly see her trotting down the path in a way that wouldn't have happened for *years* in England.

For example, when I was based up at Church Fenton – just outside York – although I went to the pub and the local church and all those sorts of things, people didn't really accept us at all. We were led to believe we'd been well treated if some of the villagers *spoke* to us!

So when you looked around, was this instantly God's own country?

It was a mixture: you had the natural beauties of the area we lived in, but commuting between that suburb and the airport, the place seemed very *crowded*. Many of the houses were what I would call old-fashioned terrace style, and those that were not terraced seemed to have very, very small gardens.

Yet Australia has endless space . . . ?

This is one of the anomalies! We had to smile when people said, 'You must be pleased to come to this great big country and have *so* much room – a house of your own with a garden.' I found it jolly hard not to say, 'I come from a place which has much *bigger* gardens and the houses are much further spread apart!' And to start with, we didn't like the taste of the water! We thought, 'We'll never be able to live in this country – the water's *awful*.' Actually it's the cleanest in the world. The water in Hertfordshire is quite salty, very hard.

Once you'd got over the shock of having to live so close together, what did your wife think about Australia?

She found certain day-to-day things very easy: the house cleaning, the upbringing of the children – no welly boots or wet weather gear – made for an easy life. We'd wake up in the morning, open the windows, look out and see yet another lovely day. We'd remark about this for a long time, not realizing that this was Australia and we were going to have lovely days for the rest of our lives!

I think she's a much better Australian and settler than I am – she seems to have fitted in psychologically far more readily. She's a first-rate local citizen now.

What does it take to be a good Australian?

An acceptance of your surroundings, coming to terms with the reality of where you are and what you're doing. I've been very slow in the transition, largely because I still move around the world and seem to have held on to UK ties far more than she has. I think it's been more difficult for me than for her.

Have you ever been made to feel a Pom?

Extraordinarily so – but *deservedly* so because of the way I behave. I don't slop around in thongs, and it's a company joke that I cut the lawn with my tie on! Initially I took a lot of ribbing for this, but I determined that I was what I was: an Englishman – there was little point in me changing. I determined that I would stay the way that I felt comfortable.

Quite a lot of others came out: ex-military, Air Force and Navy, and I found it interesting because I felt very much at *one* with them, and watched their approach to this new country. One or two made an overt move to become Australian: their dress, their speech, their mannerisms ... I thought this was not for me, but I could see it might do them some good.

I think they've fitted in, but I now see them as in no-man's-land; they can't genuinely call themselves Australians, they can't really see themselves as Englishmen – they've passed half way over the river. I'm led to believe some Australians now see them as turncoats trying to please. I didn't bend over backwards to please people.

Their speech changed a bit, but other than that how did they alter their behaviour?

Their outlook was reflected in the way they did things, their mannerisms, their dress at barbecues or for shopping or any off-duty thing where uniform wasn't involved. They seemed to assimilate more readily than I did.

There are one or two individuals who still have a smile at me – they put an extra couple of surnames into my already hyphenated surname, just to accentuate the point that they still see me as pretty damn British. You've got to laugh, there's nothing you can do, no point in being upset about it. In view of the fact that I'm not in any way ashamed – or to put it another way, I'm *proud* to be an Englishman – it doesn't bother me. Yes, the finger is pointed and I think I straighten my back a little bit more and play the part.

My wife's really come to terms with the fact that she is living in Australia – I tend to have half a foot in England. She's happy to live here for the rest of her days, I still hanker for some of the aspects of English life. I love the countryside, the villages, the country area where I come from around Bishop's Stortford in Hertfordshire. I miss the antiquity, she doesn't seem to mind that all the buildings are new. I find this is a very integrated society of many races; to some degree I've found that a little bit hard to accept.

We were on the far side of Hertfordshire from London, just south of Cambridge. My wife was a little bit closer to London, coming from the Pinner area – I don't know if that had any bearing, but I just feel she's made an easier transition.

Is it possible that the England you dream about today is just a dream, that the place has changed in these twenty-two years?

I'm quite sure there have been really significant changes. I still see things as they were, not as they are now; I tend to put on blinkers, you know, to the change I don't like to see.

So after twenty-two years your heart's still there?

Partly in England, but as the years pass I come to terms with reality; my sons are growing up and there's no way *they're* ever going to be Englishmen. It's very good, of course, that they've adopted the attitude that they're one hundred per cent Australian, because this is largely their country – it's a young person's country, and good luck to them.

Have you made many friends here?

I don't think I'm an overtly friendly sort of person; I don't have masses of people I call friends, but I've got all that I can cope with, quite enough.

I'm still a little bit on edge in certain places where I'm not familiar with the groupings of the people; I do feel a bit of an outsider, but it doesn't really bother me. It depends what the cause is: a school function, I'm happy enough there, and the people in the church scene, I can fit in there. It's if I get with a group of people who haven't had much contact with Englishmen . . . I just feel uncomfortable, a little bit out of it. I become aware I'm dressed with a tie and other people have no ties, or that the way I express myself, verbally, is a little bit out of keeping with their way.

They're only small things, because I know that within their heart of hearts they *are* good mates. I wouldn't call them mate – and though they call me mate I tend to feel that I'm *not*, you know, a mate of theirs . . .

THE MEDICAL MISSIONARIES:
CLARE JUKKA AND NEIL BEATON

'I'm the receptionist – but I fill in when they're busy.'

Clare Jukka and Neil Beaton arrived in Katherine on a motorbike, wearing their leathers and carrying a guitar. Clare, a pretty young blonde with an ankle bracelet and a distinct cleavage; Neil, dark and green-eyed. Another couple of hippies passing through? They were in fact two young doctors come to give the conservative little outback town a fresh medical experience. They had been practising there for a year when we met.

Dr Clare, one of nine children of a Liverpool wages clerk, is twenty-three and very modish. If her Northern Territory patients expected their first woman doctor to be a motherly *Woman's Weekly* figure with grey hair, sensible shoes and useful recipes, they received a considerable shock as this blonde child with cropped hair and a Scouse accent swayed into the clinic in a miniskirt ... They then discovered she wasn't cosy, but she was bright.

She sees white patients in town every afternoon, but goes into the bush to work with aborigines in the mornings, whereas Dr Neil has his surgery at the Kalano Community Association and devotes all his time to them.

Dr Neil Beaton comes from a medical family in Scarborough. He is twenty-seven. He spends his working life caring for aborigines in camps around Katherine, accompanied by his paramedics – quiet and watchful middle-aged aboriginal women. In the evening he plays his guitar and sings most appealingly in a restaurant – which has perhaps enhanced his reputation with patients even more than his medical skills...

I went with them to the Rockhole Camp, home to a hundred aboriginals: 'The best camp, the most sophisticated.' Once, perhaps, it had been a showplace of community care, but now it was a scene of desolation: squalid shacks, scattered refuse, wrecked cars. A third of their aboriginals are severe alcoholics, one in seven has syphilis, ten have leprosy.

The young doctors in white moved around, checking sick and grumpy old women and sad monosyllabic alcoholics recovering from the drunken fits that follow their dole days. Although they would be loath to see themselves as such, Dr Clare and Dr Neil are modern street-smart versions of those good nineteenth-century missionaries who carried their care and concern out to the colonies...

Dr Clare: We started out down in Victoria; we'd heard all about the Aussie males, and that when we met them they might not offer me their hand to shake, so I'd have to nod acknowledgement. We arrived at this practice where they'd been short of doctors for a while, and I remember one of the major doctors coming in and he says, 'Oh well, I suppose one and a half doctors are better than one,' assuming that I was only half a doctor! I just turned round and said, 'Neil's not *that* small, is he?'

That was a town in which they'd never had a female doctor, and that's the situation here as well. So I find that all of a sudden I'm different – an enigma, you could say – and people come to stare at me. The women are fascinated that there's this person they can tell *all* the problems they've read about in the magazines.

You're a young blonde, you wear miniskirts; this is not at all the mother-figure they expect?

I feel very dubious about the elderly woman who comes in and asks me advice about the fact that her husband goes out bush, and she has relationship problems with him. She's asking *me* – a young girl who's only had relationships for a couple of years of her life – for advice. I find that really difficult to cope with, but these women up here in frontier country – where there's still the image of the macho male and the oppressed wife – they do have a lot of problems. The isolation, the loneliness is a major thing.

But women are lonely in Croydon and Camberwell and Liverpool – the lonely housewife's not an Australian monopoly?

Those women, if they walked out their doors into the street, they could say hello to a million people. If you walk out your door here, all you can see is trees and landscape. You really *are* alone. If there's a relationship barrier with your husband, you've got no one to talk to. There's lots of difference.

You're at the aboriginal clinic in the morning, but in the afternoon you're here in town dealing with the local ladies. How do you adjust – do you find you're confusing your prescriptions?

Yes, I do: my language is different. You tend to skip words when you talk to the aborigines, because they understand better – especially when you've got a Liverpool accent like mine! So many times I say to the white mother, 'This kid got fever – he eat no tucker?' They *look* at me!

Your friend Dr Beaton tells me many aborigines here have syphilis and leprosy and drink problems – what are the white problems?

The main one probably is drink, as well. White people drink *just* as much as the aborigines but it's not as explicit, it's a bit more closeted. Of course, in the heat there's always the tropical diseases, and I see a lot of female problems and children's ailments.

I get male patients who are sort of tricked into seeing me, and then horrified that it's a female! It's obvious what his trouble is as soon as he walks in the door, because his face sort of drops. I usually see if I can break the barrier down by saying, 'You don't think you've got the clap, do you?'

That *puts him at his ease! This outback life's still fairly tough – have you got time for the psychological problems, the neuroses that modern medicine supports ... or is there a tendency to adopt the Army cure and say: 'Take an aspirin and pull yourself together?'*

There's never been a psychiatric service up here, so if somebody really does go off the rails, it is a difficult thing. Sedation's most important until you can decide whether you're going to refer them to Adelaide – and referring people to Adelaide is like sending them from London to Egypt! Would you do *that* every day of the week?

So you've got to decide whether somebody really needs psychiatric help and that's why GPs in these sort of frontier towns have to be priest, confidante, social worker... You're all these things, apart from just being their doctor.

A lot of these men really *are* bushmen. They're out for a couple of months at a time, and you can understand that when they haven't seen a lot of people they find the town quite overpowering. All they want to do is get themselves cleaned up and race round for a couple of days. They find relationship problems difficult, usually ending in fights. Then females, of course: because of this relationship problem, the mix with females does become difficult.

I noticed to my surprise that this tiny town on the fringe of the never-never has an escort agency!

It's a stream of ladies who've been shipped up from down south, who've settled in business here, because it's a thing in Australia that's well recognized. It's not the same in England – you have to go down Soho. These women obviously are quite concerned about their health and come in to have swabs and things to keep them clear of the sexually transmitted diseases that we have a major problem with, so we do see them regularly.

I'd say there's more than seven girls working. The first time one girl came in she was obviously suffering from some sort of infection, and could I check her over? I was interested that this lady was an escort, because I didn't know then if they were just dancing partners or whatever – and we didn't seem to have many dances around here! I'm chatting away to her, saying 'How's business, then?' And she says, 'Actually I'm just the receptionist – but I fill in when they're busy...' I was stunned – this woman just helps out when the traffic is brisk!

At Rockhole Camp

The aborigines are doing now what they've been doing for centuries – sitting around and letting the world go by. You're racing about frantically. So, who's right?

That's what I think to myself – who's right? We're trying to sort out their poverty and malnutrition and alcohol problems, and if you tell them, 'You keep drinking, you die', some of them turn round and say, 'That's what happens to *all* of us, I know it's going to happen to me.' It doesn't seem to bother them: it's going to happen *anyway.*

They get drunk, then they get violent – but as a young girl operating among them, you've never felt threatened?

No, I still feel they're frightened of the white man. The image. When the Europeans first came they knocked out the people who said, 'We don't want you here.' So you're left with a race of people who are frightened if they do anything, they'll be shot. These people just worked basically for the European, became scouts, worked on the out-stations.

They're speaking four or five different languages, none of which you understand – so how do you diagnose their illnesses?

One language they use is called Creole, and it's like a combination of all of them. Basically it's just like phonetic speaking, I don't think many people have written it down, people just talk it; it's passed by word of mouth.

I remember asking this fellow with a chest infection, 'What colour's your spit?' He looked at me really quizzically: 'What's she talking about?' So I got one of these aboriginal girls and she goes, 'Hey man, what colour spit you got?' Exactly the same thing I said, but he *understood.* I couldn't believe it.

It's your Scouse accent – he'd have understood if you'd come from

Camberley! What are the differences of malady between the aborigines and the whites?

The malady of the aborigines is anything related to filth and dirt, like sores, infections, malnutrition – the aborigines have got the lot. When it comes to the white fellow, you get tropical diseases, and every single mosquito bite gets a bit puffy. Then on top of that you get the neuroses, of course. There's a lot of the clap around and there's a very high incidence of syphilis in the aboriginal people. As we get more and more advanced there's intermarriage, so they pass it on to the Europeans.

The nice thing about this place is you never see much theft. You can leave your car and your door open, you can leave keys in your ignition. The only time you get stealing is maybe if they want alcohol, or if you get drug addicts in town. We tend to get a very transient population drifting in from Sydney and down south. The black fellows are not druggy – they get a bit of amphetamine from the truck drivers. Those guys take a *lot* of amphetamines to stay awake. They drive for forty-eight hours non-stop, and that's why we always say, 'Get off the road if you're passing one – because he probably can't *see* you, he's too stoned out of his brain.'

Go to one of these truck stops and watch them: they don't seem to look, they just stare. They drink about ten cans of beer – and then get back in the truck. Incredible – you've just got to get off the road...

Masses of money have been poured in, through guilt...

Dr Neil: My father's a consultant physician at Scarborough Hospital in England, my mother used to be a nurse years ago and my eldest sister is a nursing Sister married to a GP in Scarborough; my older brother is a gynaecologist... The next sister is a lawyer, my younger brother is a teacher.

They fixed up a quick visa for us because they were desperate for doctors in Victoria, and we flew straight out. We travelled round Australia on a motorbike which we borrowed from two mates in Melbourne, with a sleeping bag, a water bottle and a guitar.

Is it easier to make money playing a guitar than it is doctoring?

It's about the same money, per hour – but you do more hours doctoring!

You said you didn't like the social class system in England, yet it doesn't seem to have done your family much damage?

I do feel that money is unequally divided in England. There's too much massive land ownership under one or two names, and an awful lot of very poor people. I don't like that system. What I do like about England is the sense of belonging to an area; there's also incorporated in that the feudal system which is still there.

I feel that it's unfair that people are very immobile; in Australia, you move around. In England it's very difficult to move from, say, Newcastle to Birmingham for job and cultural reasons. You'd stand out like a sore thumb if you're in Birmingham and you're a Geordie. It's difficult to move your roots.

Are you serious? What about London – it's full of people from every known place...

London's no longer English, that's my impression. Too cosmopolitan. It's the same as Sydney and Hong Kong and New York.

It's a very mobile population in Australia: they can go anywhere, and they don't feel out of place, their language isn't any different. That's the major difference between the cultures; we speak the same language, but it's two totally different worlds apart. They're very well balanced, most Australians – a chip on *both* shoulders! The well-balanced aborigine has a wine-cask in each hand...

This is probably the best camp in Katherine. They've got electric light, a water tap, but no drainage – and there's no potential. The problem I see with community development is that there's no long-term plan teaching aborigines to use inside showers, inside toilets, and gradually progressing from this camp situation with the humpy made out of corrugated iron, to the kind of house you're living in.

You specialized in anaesthetics, in intensive care; what will you carry back to Scarborough, what will you have learned here?

I'll have learned a lot about the problems you come across when a modern culture clashes with a very old culture. I'll understand Ethiopia, India and places like that far more, because the problems are blatantly obvious. It's basically one of communication.

But these people seem further away than the Third World . . .

Somebody described it as the Fourth World, because they've got all the diseases you'd expect to see in Ethiopia or a real Third World country, plus *our* diseases from their diet – such as high blood pressure and diabetes.

The problem with the alcoholic here is that he usually started drinking about age twelve or thirteen. They leave school and get into the ritual of drinking in a circle, with their peers. It's very hard to break out of it.

An aborigine drinks to get drunk as quickly as possible, preferably to become unconscious. I can only guess that they want to escape – some people have thought that they're wanting to commit suicide when they're having fits and are unconscious. They don't really *want* to wake up. In actual fact if you take light beer to a community and hand it over free, they'll throw it in the rubbish bin because it doesn't get them drunk quick enough. I've seen that happen. One of the problems with alcohol in aboriginal people is they *will* drink for two or three days solid after pay day, and eat no food at all – so they get short of sugar and occasionally have fits, if they go too far. Quite commonly they'll go into peculiar rhythms of the heart, and feel very ill indeed. After a long time, because of the vitamin deficiency, their heart gets large, a thing called cardiomyopathy – a large heart that isn't pumping very well.

But it's not an experience that's bad enough to stop them drinking?

It doesn't appear to be. Some thirty per cent have a drinking problem, fifty per cent actually drink – but remember, we're talking about a town population.

This is a community of alcoholics who've been picked up by our counsellors: one's called Barry Robinson, the other's called Electric Motor – a really good name! Or they're referred from me or from the courts. One of the problems of course is having *something* as an alternative to drinking when they've finished their counselling. It's not like treating a white person, where you try to get them back into a work force. These people have never been *in* a work force, so when they leave here it's very easy for them to go to the camp and get straight back into the peer-group drinking circle.

We did a survey of this area earlier in the year, and out of 350 people, 52 had syphilis. We have trachoma, which is a disease picked up from the dust which makes people blind. We have leprosy; because of their particular immunological make-up it seems they're fairly prone to leprosy. If you have crowded conditions and poor living areas, leprosy will thrive. If you keep yourself clean and live in a clean environment, you won't get leprosy. It's not a very infectious disease.

Preventative ideas are very difficult for an aborigine who doesn't understand that if I stop eating chips today – I won't get heart disease in twenty-five years' time! It's very difficult to put that concept across when you live for today, when over the centuries you've just collected what you've needed, day by day.

The history of the aborigines is that European white settlers came and committed mass genocide, not only in Tasmania but in Queensland and up here as well. Then gradually in the Forties the aborigines came into the work place. The Fifties, more integration – and then in the late Sixties there was a referendum that they get the vote, and they became citizens. Then they got the dole cheque! From then on, masses and masses and masses of money has been poured into the situation, through guilt. Largely it's been wasted because there's no coordinated effort in social support. It's coming in from forty-seven different agencies!

You can't eradicate the Third World diseases unless you improve public health, basic hygiene education, good sewage, good drainage, proper education. The problem is that health should have an input into how the houses are built, because these are built by a Canberra architect who's probably never *met* an aborigine.

Perhaps they've gone too far towards being Europeanized and used to Toyotas, used to videos, used to *things* too much to be able to go back to the nomadic life. There are people out in the bush at the moment who're living more or less a traditional lifestyle; they have the trappings that we have, but they still go out fishing, still go out hunting and still believe in all the dream time and the rest of the traditional cultures.

It seems that, like the Eskimos, the Red Indians, the Maoris, they've absorbed all the worst aspects of Western civilization?

They've certainly absorbed a lot of the worst things that we have, things which are *easy*. They've taken to fast food and cigarettes – and booze, of course. If you're under stress and you want to relieve the stress, alcohol's an easy option.

It might seem the least stressful life in the world, sitting under a tree all day!

The stress is that their culture is under threat, and they can recognize that. They're not communicating very well, but their culture is definitely under severe stress. In fact, the Northern Territory is a fairly racist place. Most people in southern Australia, in Sydney and Melbourne, very rarely see aborigines; they know as much about them as English people do. There's hostility and aggression, and the feeling that aborigines are second-class citizens. The cultural difference between these people and us is enormous, it's like a clash of two civilizations which are diametrically opposite. You can't think of two cultures which are *more* different.

It's not a normal culture jump, it's being pushed from the Stone Age into the Space Age.

Absolutely – remember these people were living out bush in a nomadic life-style, and now we're expecting them to cope with work, with an eight-hour day, with achievement... Australians expect them very quickly to adapt from a life which is essentially no different to what it was two hundred years ago. He doesn't need to hunt, because he gets dole money, so he buys tucker with that – or occasionally buys alcohol. Yet the white Australians in town despise these people because they aren't achieving. My question is, *what* are they supposed to achieve?

Down in the southern cities they're viewed with scorn and sometimes with fear, I think – taxis won't pick them up, that kind of thing?

When the aborigine's had a few drinks, his inhibitions disappear and his anger appears at the surface.

Not all that different from us!

Very, very angry person. He's bitter, but it's unusual here for an aborigine to attack a white man. Very rarely happens, but the anger is there and they look very fierce indeed. Incredibly good fighters – that's what they're trained for.

If they're put into modern housing, they pull up the floorboards and use them for fuel...

That's true. Those people have come from out bush living under trees, and they're expected to live in the environment we live in, and behave accordingly.

If they can't find a station on a radio, they'll smash it?

Or just leave it behind – yes, everything's discardable. Fixing it isn't the answer, get a new one.

Petrol sniffing is the latest craze?

That's very poorly looked on by the aboriginal people. We don't have any petrol sniffing in the town, luckily, or any major drugs – marijuana of course, but no other drugs that we know of.

Out in the bush communities there's petrol sniffing, but it's severely dealt with. For example a community further north found two boys petrol sniffing, reported by the police. They were taken to an island off Bathurst with no water on it and told, 'You're going to be here for a week, boys; you can have a forty-gallon drum of water – or a forty-gallon drum of petrol; take your choice.' That was it. That cured them. Other people have had violent methods of traditional punishment inflicted on them.

Why should they object to sniffing and not to grog?

They seem to recognize the danger of petrol sniffing as being abnormal, while grog is a thing Europeans do – so therefore it's all right.

You're dealing with a group of irresponsible children, is that your approach?

In many ways we are, yes. Many projects are paternalistic for that reason, because you need to lead people by the hand.

Is there an argument for not trying to push them into the twentieth century?

There is. There are no long-term programmes for gradual social development – they're all very *quick*. Every programme I come across seems to be a very makeshift Band Aid in many ways, not thought out over fifty years. After a forty-thousand-year history people are saying, 'Come on, you've got to learn to be a technician.' They can't *do* it. You can't expect a chap who's lived out bush all his life to suddenly turn up at work every day at eight o'clock in the morning, but the local people expect that and despise them for not doing it. That's what irritates me.

The local Australians are fairly racist in their views, particularly in the town. I can see their point of view; a lot of them are pastoralists, the growth and development of the Territory is important, but they're very intolerant of aborigines. I work as a musician in a restaurant and I frequently listen in on conversations. I've encountered lots of examples of severe racism.

It happens whenever races are in proximity like this – whether it's Brixton or New York, you're going to get all sorts of antipathies.

It wasn't long ago that the Ku Klux Klan was running in this town, you must remember that; there was a squad of people who used to wander around in the usual gear. A few years ago there was an aborigine beaten to death with a spanner from the boot of his car by young white youths. They were given a short suspended sentence, and it didn't even reach the local newspaper.

That's not one of those pub stories, like the Flying Doctor refusing to turn out for whites, is it?

No, that's a real story.

So is there any light at the end of their tunnel?

The only light I can see is with the children. I don't think there's any point in spending a lot of money educating adults who're already trapped in the suspicious circle – although the resources should be there, if they need them. I don't think vast amounts should be spent in trying to change these people. They've made up their minds they're going to live this lifestyle, and that's it ...

THE ARTIST: PATRICK KILVINGTON

I crusaded myself into a £250,000 writ ...

Patrick Kilvington is a *cool* man, self-deprecating and laconic. He was cool about the tuberculosis which invalided him out of the Army after nine years, in 1948, and even cooler about his recent lung cancer – though irritated that this major operation should destroy his taste for alcohol. He is also a very considerable artist.

Educated at Eltham College, he sailed for Australia in 1951. For health reasons? No, for *sex* reasons ... He married the Queensland girl he had followed to her home, but the only job he could find was cleaning cars – at which he was little more successful than in the various jobs attempted in England.

He did not begin painting seriously until he was forty-nine, when a recurrence of TB gave him time; it seemed preferable to playing with Plasticine. He instantly showed remarkable ability to capture outback life and action, and his pictures sold well; since he was again out of work, this was stimulation enough. Today, in convalescence from cancer, he has stopped painting.

Divorced, with four sons, he now lives in a small jumbled cottage at Southport, on Queensland's Gold Coast, where he lay in the road in an attempt to stop the building of a neighbouring McDonald's – but suffered one more defeat.

His bush paintings show all the verve and humour of this unusual man; I wish he would start painting again ...

I was invalided out of the King's Shropshire Light Infantry. I tried to sell encyclopaedias for two or three weeks, then landed a job as wine consultant with a firm in Park Lane selling to the Diplomatic Corps. This was about 1949. I was *worse* at selling wines than I was at selling encyclopaedias. I worked out that I wasn't really fit to do anything – and as I was living on an Army pension of £5 per month, things were getting a bit strained.

I eventually got a job in an advertising agency by using someone else's photo layout which was a bit too good for me. I was exposed the first day, but the studio director was kind enough to keep me on. I was there for about a year, probably the longest I've ever had a job.

You came out to Australia in 1951 for health reasons?

No, I came out for *sex* reasons! I got engaged to a girl from Brisbane and followed her out four or five months after she'd returned. I didn't come as a migrant because of the tuberculosis, so I had to pay my own passage. I think I was one of six people on board this bloody great ship who'd paid their passage: the rest were £10 Scouse gits and Glaswegians, about five thousand Greeks. That was a bloody terrible trip, that one – six weeks stuck in a ghetto.

It's a helluva thing to go thirteen thousand miles – and find you can't get a job when you *get* there ... The girl I was engaged to was well-connected and introduced me to the Managing Director of a car company in Brisbane. After an interview he handed me down to his General Manager who handed me down to the Sales Manager who handed me down to some other manager ... and by the end of the day I was being interviewed by the factory foreman just to see if I could get a job as a car *cleaner*, which I did. I just scraped in!

After four months of car cleaning I decided *anything* was better than that, and got married. I went farming then, and worked like a coolie. I had 5000 hens that I kept – they were supposed to keep *me*, but it didn't work out that way. They wouldn't lay any bloody eggs and they irritated me, and I wasn't a very good farmer either.

Ex-officers are supposed to run chicken farms – that tradition that started about 1919 . . .

A bloody awful rotten tradition, believe me.

Were the Australians pleased to find a Pom arriving in 1951 to help them renovate their country?

The Australians did not like English then. I don't think they like them any more now, but in those days it was the only group of people Australians could dislike in *one* hit! We were almost keyed up to fight our way down the gangplank when we got to Australia.

That's thirty-five years ago, when Australians were a different race of people; they were very Anglo-Saxon anti-English Australians. Now the Australians are composed of Swedes and Bulgarians and Germans and Turks and Greeks and Italians and Albanians and you name it, we've got it. It's very rare that you find a genuine dinky-di Chips Rafferty-type Australian around.

The anti-Pom thing is still being kept alive by the media, to an extent, but there are *so* many people to be anti these days that the Poms have to take their turn in the queue.

I mean, you've got the Armenians fighting the Turks, the Turks fighting the Greeks, the Vietnamese fighting other Vietnamese, Lebanese fighting Lebanese . . . Occasionally if you're lucky you'll get an Australian involved, but they don't really know *who* to dislike these days. You're not allowed to call an Italian a wop or a dago or whatever, but the term Pom is still used.

But we're always assured it's a term of affection . . . ?

They assure you of that, but I'm not so certain. It's like the term bastard: there are about twenty forms of bastard, which they tell you again is a term of endearment . . .

Anyway, in 1954 I went back home, and struck the worst smog that London's ever experienced. I think about five hundred people died of yellow fever, or something. I found I was wandering around wearing a surgical mask. I thought, 'This isn't worth it' – so I came back to Australia again.

The Brisbane set my fiancée and I became involved with went in for a lot of these box-wine parties, all-male functions where they try and get the guests rolling helpless drunk. At one of these some drunken Australian rushed up, called me an effing Pommy bastard, and took a swing at me. He was so drunk he fell over, cracked his head on the rockery – and knocked himself out! Other people heard this crash and looked around and said, 'My Christ, he's dropped him!' My reputation after that was: 'You don't want to tangle with that bloke, he's *savage*!' I sort of got through on that incident, I think. If I'd been an Australian I would have dropped *me* many a time – but it's the only way to handle the natives. They quite like it – they're used to being denigrated.

I was involved in a company making office furniture, and when I came back I brought the rights with me and negotiated with a firm in Sydney to see if they'd manufacture an office cabinet under licence, and pay the parent company royalties. A day before I was due to negotiate this deal I got a call from England saying they wanted £500, on top of this royalty arrangement – which frightened the hell out of me. I thought, 'There's no way in the world I'm going to get £500 out of this company.'

I went down to Sydney all of a cringe, was ushered into the boardroom – one of these twenty-metre-long tables with six people in grey flannel suits at one end and me the other. The Chairman said they'd decided to take it on. While I was thinking, 'Christ how am I going to ask them for £500?' he said, 'We can offer you £5000.' I was still worrying about this £500 and so I didn't take much notice, and there was a silence. Then he said, 'Well, we can increase the offer to £7500.' I thought: 'And I came in asking for £500!' Then he said, 'Look, we'll make it £9000, and that'll be our last offer.'

I sort of came to and realized the stupid berk was offering me £9000 for something I was trying to sell for £500 – so I graciously accepted. That taught me a lesson: if you're going to negotiate, say bugger-all and let the other people do the talking.

What is this Sir *Patrick Kilvington I see on your letter-heading?*

I've been a Knight of the Hutt River Principality for ten years. Never been there – I got my knighthood through the mail.

Prince Leonard also made me a Knight, and a Roving Ambassador, when

I was doing a Whicker's World *there in 1975. He made Frank Pash – a brother artist of yours – an Earl . . . but, unlike you, we don't use these titles . . .*

Well, I admire anyone who can thrust two fingers up the nostrils of bureaucracy – and get away with it. I find it tremendously useful for getting seats in booked-out restaurants. People don't really know whether to genuflect or not.

When Frank Pash was stopped by the police while driving home one night, he'd had several and his speech was slurred; but one copper said to the other, 'It's all right – earls always *talk like that' – and they let him off! Prince Leonard gave me a diplomatic passport which I've always thought I'll try to use going into some country where I don't mind being thrown into jail . . . Anyhow, you were a hard-up Knight?*

I had two or three years of baked beans on toast as a regular menu. I took on any occupation I could, to get in some money. I worked as part-time journalist for a couple of years; worked as a Press secretary to a fellow who was standing for Parliament, who's now the Minister for Mines and Energy in the State Parliament. He slipped me $100 a week underneath the counter. I worked for him for three months – and that was the only election he ever lost.

At one time you were a crusading editor here – you ran a Gold Coast newspaper?

I had about six years of crusading, and I crusaded myself into a £250,000 writ – and decided that the crusading should be left to those who could afford it! I also decided to leave that field of occupation – likc my encyclopaedia selling and my wine selling and all these other failures I've had in life . . .

I was a great promoter of tourism at a time when tourism was a dirty word in Queensland, but my target was corruption. I've always had a hatred of corruption, an instinctive dislike of anyone making money from his fellow men illegally. The whole of Australia is, I think, probably one of the most corrupt countries in the world.

Corruption here is an accepted way of life: it starts at the city council level, goes to state government level and ends up at federal government level, but it's accepted. The average Australian is totally indifferent to corruption.

Yet this was originally an Anglo-Saxon country, it's not Central America; is it still convicts and warders?

I think that came into it. Australians are now very proud of their ancestry – in fact they're queuing up to find a sheep-stealer they can somehow claim as an ancestor: 'He stole a potato and got sent over here for life!' In actual fact he probably ripped off half a village, raped half the girls and stole half the Crown jewels . . .

But my painting came good; I discovered after a while I'd become what they call a name, where people don't buy the painting, they buy the signature that goes underneath it.

Come tomorrow, which is my Happy Birthday, I'll be a thirty-five-year-old Australian *and* a twenty-nine-year-old Englishman. I don't really belong to Australia – I pretend I do, but after thirty-five years I still refuse to become an Australian citizen and I don't feel Australian, I feel British. When I go back to England I don't belong there either because I've been far too long off the place. And apart from that, London is so bloody filthy I wouldn't *want* to go back until they do something about it.

I went back a couple of years ago and was disgusted with London, it's matching Bombay – or Calcutta even. You've got more black people over there than we have over here. I don't necessarily like nor dislike the blacks, but I had a whole hassle getting into England because I was accosted by a Pakistani customs official. The hotel I'd booked into was a sort of Fawlty Towers in Gloucester Road, run by Pakistanis again, and everything went wrong.

Once you get out of London there's not a great deal of change. After the harshness of Australian scenery I found the southern counties – Kent and Sussex – were a little too neat, a little too lush, a little too green for my liking. I still prefer Yorkshire and the Lake District, that more rugged beauty of England.

I recall in England waking up, pulling the curtains aside to find out what sort of a day it was . . . Here you don't do that because you *know* what sort of a day it's going to be: it's going to be superb. Every day is better than the last day . . .

THE INVENTOR: TOM LAW

Haven't seen my sons for forty years...

You'd think the hard life in the Northern Territory outback might wear a man down. Tom Law, from Stoke Newington, and his German second wife once ran a fifteen-room guesthouse in genteel Cromwell Road. Now his home is in Humpty Doo, forty miles south of Darwin, in that fierce tropical climate: the Dry is scorching, the Wet just that. An unforgiving place, even for a loner.

He lives without air conditioning or any visible amenities in the concrete bungalow he built. The ground outside is spread with rusty tools and engineering debris – like a rundown garage after the burglars have turned it over. That is his workshop; he's an inventor.

Inside the rooms are festooned with grime, cobwebs and dead flies; a mop growing into the floor sprouts fungus. In the Cromwell Road the place would have been condemned. He has a characteristic reason for leaving the squalor untouched...

Tom takes care of himself, after a fashion, and the life must suit him, for he looks about fifty-five. He was born in 1907 – but behaves as though it was 1957. He chain-smokes, plays golf – and is learning to fly an ultralight so he can tour Australia with the girlfriend for whom he plans to advertise, just as soon as his latest invention comes good.

I went to watch this Royal Flying Corps pilot (year of 1929) take off in his fragile canvas and fibreglass contraption with its tiny phut-phut engine, into which I would not have entrusted my life. Tom was full of confidence despite being heavier than air, once again.

He had left London to escape taxes, gone prospecting, worked on the Arnhem Highway for eighteen years, and only retired from a Government electrical workshop following an accident when he was seventy-three.

He claims to have invented the bubble car and in 1946 sold the rights to a German firm. Now he is working on some indoor-golf games, a golf buggy made from bits of a motorized lawnmower, and a broad-based plastic tee that holds a ball – since peg tees cannot be driven into the baked soil.

At the parched Humpty Doo Rural Area Golf Club, goats munch their way through the dust as he plays his daily round. His handicap, apart from the goats, is twenty-four. The course has browns, not greens . . .

An accumulation of things made us come out to the Territory: couldn't cope with the tax situation, couldn't cope with the work situation . . . We had a job all right because we had an hotel, but things just didn't go *right* – and of course my wife wanted more money and more money and more money . . .

She's a good kid, mark you, a bloody good kid, but she wanted money and we just couldn't cope with it, so the present wife and myself said, 'Right, let's get out, mate.' Out we came, and never regretted it.

This is about as far from a guesthouse in the Cromwell Road as you can get: but what about the squalor – why the cobwebs, why all the dirt?

There's a reason behind that. You see my wife – I've got the most *perfect* marriage – my wife lives up in Darwin, and I live down here. She doesn't like spiders and cobwebs, so I let them grow – and she doesn't come anywhere near me! Beautiful.

We're good mates – don't get me wrong, we're damned good mates – but she prefers to live in Darwin and I prefer to live in the bush.

Two things I hate: housework and cooking, so I don't do any cooking except an egg or bacon or something like that, and I certainly don't do any house cleaning.

You look about fifty-five to me, but I'm told you're in your eighties ...?

Yeah, I was born twenty-eighth of the third, 1907.

So you're doing something right – instead of inventing tees and golf carts you ought to be bottling whatever it is you're taking! What's the secret?

Damned if I know. You see up to about five years ago I was drinking a bottle of Scotch a day. I was never sober. The doctors just got hold of me and said, 'Right, give the grog away or it'll give you away.'

The only thing that annoys me now is, when I was on the grog and I woke up crook, I knew what was wrong with me. Now if I wake up crook I don't know what the *hell's* wrong with me!

At eighty the juices may be running a little less strongly?

Not according to what the doctor says – he reckons I'm good for another twenty years or so ...

The Territory is a place, it seems to me, where people come to do their own things; they appreciate the offbeat here, and I suppose they regard you as an eccentric?

Oh, yes, I am, and the beauty of it is, I can get *away* with things now. On my second time round I'm doing all the things I ever wanted to do as a youngster: fly, play golf and sports and tell people what I think of them! A younger man would get a smack on the nose, but they just look at me and say, 'Poor old bastard, let him go.' So I get away with murder, and I enjoy it.

Are you concerned about living alone? If you ever became ill, what would happen?

Well, I just don't *get* ill, that's about it. If I feel crook, I get out somehow and get help.

You've got no telephone, you're miles from anywhere; shout and nobody's going to hear you...

I can always stagger into the car and drive down the road somewhere.

Touch wood, you've never had to do that; but what about security – are you liable to be invaded by a bunch of bikies?

If they come down I've got a perfectly good gun to stop them – me and my mate here! I've had this .357 Magnum for about eighteen years; got a special grip.

Have you had to shoot many people?

Er, no – I've been very close a couple of times, though. A carload of larrikins came in one morning and I asked them what they wanted, and they turned round and said, 'What's it got to do with you?' I said, 'This is private property, get off.' They said, 'Who's going to turn us off?' I said, 'Me and my mate.' 'Oh yeah?' With that one of them advanced towards me, so I just put the gun up in the air and – *bang!* They were gone ... Apart from that I've never had to use it in self-defence or against anybody. Used it plenty of times on snakes, but that's about all.

At one time you were prospecting around here, did you have any luck?

Yes, took out about $6000 worth of gold, but it was $123 an ounce then. We took out about forty-four ounces. But it's too much like hard yakker.

You don't think you might make more money prospecting than inventing?

In the short term yes, but not in the long term. I won't reap the benefit, it'll be my grandchildren if ever I get round to seeing them, of course. They're somewhere in England. I haven't seen my sons for nearly forty years, *never* seen my daughters-in-law, and never seen my grandchildren. I'll get round to it one day.

That's rather sad, isn't it?

Just part of our way of life . . .

You wouldn't be happier living back in the Fulham Road in a nice little pad with a telephone, near Harrods?

No bloody way. There's nowhere else, excepting going up to Arnhem Land, where I can get *farther* away from civilization. I love it on my own . . .

At the bush landing strip

You got your pilot's licence in 1929, Tom, but when did you last fly?

In 1944, the end of the war. I took up flying with the RFC, which then became the Royal Air Force. I was invalided out in 1933, after a crash. When the war broke out I went back to it again but they wouldn't accept me into the RAF, so I went into the Auxiliary with Amy Johnson, Jimmy Mollison and all the rest of that gang, and we used to ferry the machines.

I told you I'm on the second time around so I've decided to do what I always wanted to do, and now I've got the time I've started to fly again.

When most people are putting on their slippers and relaxing, you're starting to take on the world again! But don't you notice a certain feeling of impermanence about these microlights?

No way, they're beautiful. It's like everything else: you drive a car, it's dangerous if the person that's driving is dangerous. You fly one of these – it's dangerous if the person that's flying it is dangerous, but normally they're quite good.

How long before you get your microlight licence?

About another eight to ten months, twelve months . . . Then I'll buy my own plane and fly round where I want to play golf. I can land, pull to one side, play a game of golf, take off and fly on to the next course . . .

On a back-yard golf course

So this plastic golf tee is going to make your fortune, Tom?

I hope so; it's quite revolutionary. In the Northern Territory the ground is so hard you can't get an ordinary peg tee into the earth, so I just devised that idea: you put it down, balance the ball on top, and then hit it. It's going to be marketed – there's two or three enquiries after it already.

What do you expect you might make out of this?

After about three years into production, I reckon $40,000 a year royalties – be able to afford an extra can of beer!

Has any other invention ever done you any good?

Yes, the Messerschmitt bubble car; I sold that outright when I left Germany to a German engineering firm and they gave me twenty thousand marks, so that was that.

How are you going to spend your expected $40,000 a year?

Find meself a girlfriend – you soon get through it...

THE CURATOR: EDMUND CAPON

Sydney's suffering from
premature decadence . . .

Like all right-thinking megamillionaires, Australia's young tycoons are moving into old art, hesitantly approaching the Impressionists by way of early Colonial. Pleasing but ordinary Australian landscapes, executed in the romantic European style of the nineteenth century, now change hands for enormous sums.

Inspiring these new collectors is a dapper forty-six-year-old guru from Orpington: Edmund Capon qualified as a chartered surveyor but became Assistant Keeper at the Victoria and Albert's Far Eastern section. Since 1978 he has been the Director of the Art Gallery of New South Wales, moulding taste and appreciation. He was one of the final three candidates for the position of Director of the V & A, but was pipped at the post by an insider.

Gregarious, amusing, fluent, he became a friend of the Murdochs, the Bonds, the à'Courts, the Packers . . . also, and most usefully, of the then Premier of New South Wales, Neville Wran; Mrs Wran is his agent. However, he is not obsequious; he refers to another potentially useful politician as having had 'a charisma bypass'.

Edmund Capon says for three-quarters of his time he is an impresario for the Gallery, publicizing and raising

money. His innovations include a free bus service to The
Domain, occasional parties for Sydney's taxi drivers so
these new Australians will know how to find the place –
and personal appearances everywhere. This urbane
publicity-seeking has increased the Gallery's visitors from
400,000 to a million a year – most of them prized from
Sydney's beaches and encouraged into a new artistic
world...

I came to Australia by accident and opportunism. I'd been asked to
write a book about Chinese archaeology, which I happily did; came
out in '77 to launch it, and went back to the V & A, to my ivory
tower in London, and forgot all about Australia.

I was approached about this job over a year later, and I thought
they were absolutely cuckoo. Running a museum, *not* my business
at all – so I said, 'No thank you, I don't understand that.' Then it
came up again, and I said to myself, 'Think about this', because
English art museums are as stuffy as hell, there's nothing more
boring than a British museum – the dullest place on earth populated
by the *dullest* people. The V & A's the same. The real problem with
all of them, they're not interested in the public – they couldn't give
a *stuff* about the public.

And life in that sort of semi-fringe academia is like living in an
inverted cone, where you go round in ever-decreasing circles. I'm
actually interested in everything; I like looking at modern pictures
and old pictures, everything – and yet people couldn't understand
why I, in the Far Eastern department, a serious student of Chinese
and Buddhist art ... what was I doing in the Tate Gallery on a
Sunday afternoon? A bit odd.

I came out for a few days and it was fantastic: firstly physically
it is the most attractive place, a seductive city, you can't ignore that.
Living here is very enjoyable, very comfortable. Secondly my deeper
interests are in the Far East, and we are actually a bit nearer China
and Japan than London.

This is a bit of a yellow profession in Australia; it's an odd thing,
this gallery has actually existed for well over a hundred years but

it's sort of immature business, an immature profession . . . I came to *save* them from immaturity. I don't think the interest that exists now existed ten years ago. I mean, we had well over a million visitors last year – that's an awful lot of people.

The institutions in London are rather stable, fixed, and don't flex their attitudes, their philosophies or their approaches to the public very much. This place is much more gregarious, hedonistic . . . As I said, it may have been here for a hundred years and it's sort of young, sort of immature – but it's going through a wonderful adolescence! You can do things with it.

Did you have to alter your sights when you came here – socially, intellectually, artistically?

I suppose there are two or three things you miss most of all: one thing in my game are the resources that are available in London in terms of works of art, libraries, colleagues, scholars – all that sort of nonsense. You miss the great works of art, which we don't have here.

I have a theory about Australian art: some of the great names did their best paintings when they went to Europe for that first experience in the late nineteenth and early twentieth centuries – these are essentially European paintings done by Australians.

Socially, of course, Sydney is one of the most active and gregarious places imaginable. You can go out for three quid a night here, you'd never have to buy any food or drink if you didn't want to, you can live. The other day we discovered we hadn't had a night at home for twenty-nine successive days!

With the credentials of the museum behind you, you were instantly a social arbiter?

There has been a tremendous rush of interest in the arts in the last twenty years in Australia, and this institution's in the vanguard of that – so you're pulled along in the wake of it all.

Sydney is a physical place, not an intellectual city?

That is a charge that's levelled against us. We're called the 'flavour of the month' city, and that kind of thing. There's a certain amount of truth in it, but a city of this size, this activity, doesn't survive without a certain amount of thought. The art community's very lively and it's the home of the opera – music's always been very strong.

But you've got a lot of competition from the beaches and the footie?

Of course you have, but we can get a whole lot more visitors into this Gallery than the National Gallery of Victoria – and Melbourne has *far* better paintings than we do. I hate to say it, but they do.

The problem here has been this pseudo-egalitarianism – it's always a problem – and the concern about money. If in America you ask people about somebody who's made a lot of money, they applaud it and say, 'I wish I could do that!' Here, the instinctive reaction tends to be, I wonder what rule *he* bent to do that? It's extraordinary, but that is an attitude.

I think it's changing a bit, maybe, because the economy and the use of money is no longer in the hands of that Anglo-Saxon mob. It's changed: you go down to Double Bay and you'll see it.

I have quite an interesting reaction: I started something years ago called Celebrity Choice, when I get a famous person to come in and go through the entire Gallery, stores, everything – and pick out their favourite twenty-five pictures. Patrick White first did it, then Joan Sutherland, then I got Mel Gibson, and it was very popular. And last year I was looking around Australia, and in the normal way you'd expect an entertainment star or sports star, but the two names that came up were Alan Bond and Holmes à'Court – the maverick money-makers!

Do Australians enjoy art – or are you making them feel guilty for not enjoying it?

I don't want to make anybody feel guilty about anything, unless they owe me money! I think they do enjoy art, they also enjoy what art means and the place art has in society – they're tremendous collectors. There's not a house, I guarantee, that you will go to in Sydney that hasn't got paintings all over it. They'll be Australian paintings, most of them, so what we've got to do now is broaden their horizons, their collecting instincts. I'm just dying to get some Chinese things in there, Japanese things – a couple of Renoirs and a few Van Goghs and Cézannes.

Some time ago I was asked to give a talk on the Gallery at a shopping centre in the southern suburbs. They had four or five hundred people there, so I talked for an hour and told them what we do and how we did it, what sort of monkey-business went on, that sometimes we were serious and sometimes we weren't. The next day they phoned up and said, 'We've got eight busloads coming today, and eight busloads next week.' And they'd never been to the Gallery before!

I get the impression that art here is like wine: they didn't discover it until about twenty years ago – and now they can't get enough of it...

I think it is. The art market in Australia really is booming. We've had our first million-dollar Australian painting, and living artists are getting well over $100,000 for their pictures. The trouble is, it has absolutely no market outside Australia, it's a very closed national market.

Do you now identify with Australians?

When I get off the aeroplane at Sydney after I've been away somewhere, I don't feel I'm coming back to foreign soil – I suppose that's quite a telling moment? It's a very compatible city. Things in Australia are never grey. There's a wonderful sense of unreality, things are either underneath the earth – or up in the stratosphere.

That's an American quality...?

It is – it's actually quite a vibrant quality, but it means that the real sensible objective view is not very tenable.

One of the joys of working here: you can get things done, you actually can. There was no bus service at all to the Gallery, which is silly. I thought, I'll write firmly to the Minister of Transport. A year later nothing had happened, and the Premier, Neville Wran, was having lunch with me in the boardroom. I said, 'Look Neville, for Christ's sake can you do something about getting a bus service to the Gallery?'

He picked up the phone and said, 'Put me through to Peter Cox' – who was the Minister of Transport. 'Peter, put the fucking Gallery on a bus service, will you?' *Bang* – puts the phone down. Next day there was a bus practising its turns outside. Now we have two. I didn't ask for a *free* bus service, but we got one.

Charity is a vital part of the social scene, so the organizing matrons must rely upon you?

Oh absolutely! We've inherited this sort of English system where art is seen to be a government responsibility, and that's something else I'm trying to change, because I wanted people's attitude about us as an institution to be much more flexible.

With all this new money, I would have thought your nouveaux riches megamillionaires – like their American counterparts at the beginning of the century – would be very anxious to help you?

The first thing they've got to do is buy their pictures – they're in that *first* stage. We're sort of early J. P. Morgan at the moment. There are plenty of them – I mean Alan Bond has got paintings coming out of his ears, and Holmes à'Court. The other thing that's happening is that big corporations are collecting – that again is much more American.

So that's why it's a bull market and they're paying millions for paintings that would be worth much less elsewhere?

Yes indeed. That picture, if you sold it here, you'd get your six-figure sum, no problem at all. Put it into Christie's or Sotheby's in London and you'd probably get a fiver for it if you're lucky. So there's a moral there: buy your Australian paintings in London, then sell them here!

One thing they have done in Australia is that donations, support for the arts, is tax deductible. That's terrific – well over half the things we acquire every year are gifts, one way or another. Our acquisitions budget is tiny and it's sort of quadrupled by funds, by gifts from other people and private sources.

Also, there's no doubt that once art becomes a very expensive commodity, the whole idea takes on a certain glamour because it *means* money. That's a fact. When we have a big exhibition like the Monet, or make a big acquisition and we have the media in, the first thing they all ask is not 'Where is it' or 'What's it like, is it beautiful?' ... it's 'How *much* is it?' That's all they want to know. Once they've got that, they've got a yardstick.

I have this theory about Sydney, that it's suffering from premature decadence. Decadence can really only be achieved after you've gone up right to the top of the great cultural ladder and popped off the end, like Greece and Rome – and the French of course.

Sydney put up the cultural ladder, went up two or three steps and said, 'Oh, sod this, hedonism looks good', and popped off rather early. That's my theory of our premature decadence...

THE CRICKETER: TONY GREIG

All English captains are given a hard time ...

Tony Greig stands out in our happy catalogue of Poms, Welsh, Scots and Irish – for he is of course South African; but how can a man who captained England and had twelve years in Sussex be anything but the best of Britons, at heart?

So here he is, tall and assured. He was swept out to Australia after the 1977 World Series cricket to play in Kerry Packer's cricket circus, and now runs one of his many companies – an insurance brokers. He stopped playing cricket a couple of years ago but keeps closely in touch by doing commentaries for Packer's Nine Network, now taken over by Alan Bond. Totally Australianized, he loves the place although 'It's a *long* way away ...'

I was part of World Series cricket when Packer arrived on the scene and turned cricket into turmoil for a while. My deal was to come to Australia, play cricket – and then to settle here thereafter and work for his organization, which is exactly what happened. I run a company called Lion Insurance Brokers, a subsidiary of the Consolidated Press Group.

Some people say that your departure signalled the end of cricket as we knew it?

I don't think that was the case at all, I think in England things started to change quite dramatically once the Cambridge and Oxford elements began to have less influence on the county game, and the amateurs started to disappear. It's a great tragedy really because you lost that mixture of the general population playing cricket ... It then became very much of a muchness – by that I mean the people were all much the same.

You lost the Gentlemen but kept the Players?

Yes, and that was a great tragedy. I was probably a beneficiary because the Englishman has always had an acceptance that the educated should lead, and all of a sudden there was a shortage of captains – so I got the captaincy.

A lot of the old-stagers tend to say that Test Match cricket is being destroyed by one-day cricket. To a degree that's true, but it's something that's going to have to be accepted, because people don't *want* to go and watch the Geoff Boycotts of this world any more; a tragedy, in a lot of ways.

But you were one of those who first transformed cricket into a carnival?

No, I didn't, it started long before; talk to Ted Dexter and Bagenal Harvey and those guys about that, because they actually started the one-day game. The reason it's kicked on is because people love it.

When you were captain of England and playing in Australia, were you given a hard time by the crowds?

Incredibly so! All captains, all English captains are given a hard time out here. The Centenary Test is a lasting memory – I'll never forget putting my head out of the door at the Melbourne cricket ground: I think I'm right in saying that the booing didn't stop until Dennis Lillee ran in to bowl – when I couldn't hear it any more because they were cheering him! That's very common out here.

After all that booing, how are you accepted here today?

I think I played my cricket rather the way Australians play their cricket, and they perceived me as being perhaps more of an Australian than they'd have *liked* me to have been, when I was playing for England. The aggressive English cricketer they tend to want to adopt here, because they believe that's really not very English – so I have a great time. It's not hard to get on with Aussies, as you would have found out; they're a pretty hospitable lot, especially if you've played some sport against them, and done reasonably well.

In a lot of ways I do miss the Sussex scene; I found the twelve years I spent in England were marvellous years. I loved Brighton, loved that county ground, loved the beach down there – although it doesn't compare with these! Going right back to South Africa, I miss my school friends, and you can't replace those when you emigrate. Then the camaraderie that went with playing for England ...

My wife, like myself, found she missed her friends a lot, especially her English friends – because she made some great friends there. It's a little easier for the men, because we get into the work scene straight away. She had the kids to look after, so her association with the school helped a bit, but it's taken her a little longer to settle. She's back in the work force now, working for a bank.

So she doesn't spend her days on your family estate?

There's a little place of about eighty acres down on the south coast, but it hasn't got a house on it yet, so it's not much use to us. I'll be working on it ...

This is a great country for kids. I'm not a great one for the Australian Government school education system, which is not very good – I think that's one of the few weaknesses in this place. The standards are low – and that's a serious problem, because the majority of kids are coming through those schools. That's a bit of a sadness, but I'm lucky enough to be able to afford to send my kids to private school, and they love it.

If you play cricket or any sport nowadays – especially if it's a profession, which I think is bad news – you've got to start thinking about what's going to happen for the *next* half of your life ... So I'm very grateful to be in Australia, where opportunity abounds.

You know people tend to think sometimes that emigrating's easy! It's *not* ...

THE INTREPID COLONIAL:
DIANA BOWDEN

I don't fit in England any more –
I'm just a bloody colonial ...

Port Douglas is an attractive harbour and fast-growing township in Northern Queensland; the only place of consequence further north is Cooktown. I visited these way-out communities in the early Sixties and filmed a local character, Diana Bowden from Sussex, a wartime cryptographer. She was designing shell jewellery and selling it not only to George's department store in Melbourne, but also to Saks Fifth Avenue in New York. At the time this was a remarkable breakthrough into chic, from Conrad country.

When I went back a quarter of a century later she was still in the same white bungalow on a forest hillside, still chain-smoking indignantly, still selling the same home-made jewellery ...

It was not hard to see why the adventurous old lady had come to rest on this glorious and almost empty coastline. The two-hour drive from Cairns to Port Douglas, up the Marlin Coast, is one of the world's scenic experiences: lush rainforest swoops down to the Captain Cook Highway as it runs round deserted palm-fringed bays. The smooth Coral Sea inside the Great Barrier Reef laps mile upon mile of fine white sand – with never a footprint. It's like some magical South Sea island – where you can drink the water!

But civilization – if that's the word – is approaching. Vast development companies are building resort villages – one, on 345 acres at Four Mile Beach on the road into Port Douglas, is costing $163 million.

Qantas sees this area as the world's next major tourist resort, a touchdown for the millions of Japanese tourists who're beginning to discover Australia, a vast improvement for Americans bored or offended by Hawaii. So Port Douglas is about to be given the kiss of life – or the kiss of death; it depends upon which side of the rainforest you live ...

Diana Bowden, alarmed by the approaching footsteps, remains one of those indomitable well-bred English-women the world seems to be running out of these days. She was a code-breaker during the War, then an interpreter in Berlin – where she fell in love with her CO, a major in the Gunners. To stay with him she stowed away on one of the first peacetime ships to sail to Australia. They landed at Christmas 1945, cleared virgin land at Innisfail and struggled to create a banana plantation.

Cane grubs ate their first year's crop, drought ruined the second and flood the third. She worked as a waitress and a cook, while the Major turned his hand to labouring. Then in 1948 they reached Port Douglas, where they live like some remnant of the British Raj in a crumbling bungalow full of elegant mementos.

With the prospect of descending tourist hordes awakening the sleepy port, her property increases in value every day. Diana is not quite sure whether she's *happy* about that ...

I went into this code-cracking thing during the War. I cracked one of the German naval codes when I was about seventeen. I got no kudos for it at all – they were livid, absolutely furious! They had all those Girton girls around, all brainy with huge spectacles and what have you, but none of them spoke languages. I was left one night with this code coming through, and I thought: some bored little man the other end . . . It all went round his girlfriend's name! It was one of the scoops of the War.

I became so absorbed in codes that I couldn't sleep at night – you get these passions for things. I knew when the *Ark Royal* was going down. You know how in England everything goes in a Morocco case by foot to Admiralty House? I said, 'Look this is *urgent*, somebody's got to know now!' They all said, 'Calm down, dear.' But this was a matter of minutes. And waiting for that little man with his little Morocco case to go round to Admiralty House, the *Ark Royal* sank!

I nearly went round the bend over that, the slowness. Absolutely incredible. And Berlin was the same – I was interpreting there. The English never took anything seriously at all. I went to some very urgent conferences, but they got bored – so they rolled up all the conference papers and played cricket with them up and down the place . . . typical English.

I came out here in 1945, because there was nothing to do in England, nothing to do anywhere else. We were going to South America, but there were no ships – they didn't *have* any. Max had been to Australia previously when he was about seventeen, stoked his way out in the stokehold of a ship. He went opal mining and said, 'God, it's the end of the world.' He said he'd *never* come back to this country. He was a major in the Artillery, and we'd met in Berlin. He wanted to get away from it all – he'd had a hell of a war.

But when it all boiled down, he said, 'There isn't anywhere to go *except* Australia.' We weren't married at the time, as he was going through a divorce. Lord Gowrie got him a job immediately and said, 'You can sail on any of my cattle boats, but Diana can't go.'

I went to see him off, and at the bottom of the gangway this man gave me a shove and said, 'Give some money to the man at the other end – and hide for four days.' It was quite a good idea, otherwise I couldn't have *got* out here. I wasn't going to wait three years.

We landed Christmas 1945 – arrived in Australia with £2.10s! An Australian sold us the idea for this area: it was the banana boom, but by the time we started our banana plantation the whole thing had fallen apart, and we were completely and utterly broke.

Then we did anything we could think of: scullery-maiding, working on boats, anything. They talk about there being no jobs for people now, but if you really *want* to do something, you can. We did anything and everything.

So you were a cryptographer in Intelligence, he'd been an Army major ... but he ended up labouring and you were waitressing and being a domestic – was this a satisfactory progression for you?

No, it wasn't, with long red fingernails and golden earrings – which were lost in the bush! Nobody had any pride in those days – if anybody needed a pair of hands you did it, didn't matter what it was.

Anybody could come here then, there were no restrictions. People who came out from Europe were all saying, 'This Godforsaken country, we're off to America.'

The north was very underdeveloped, it really was wild country. We were so lucky, Alan, that when we came here in '46 it was the last of the pioneering. People were packhorsing, there wasn't any transport, there wasn't any sophistication. I mean, Cairns wasn't destroyed; we just had ten years before it all disappeared.

Then gradually, with both of us working, we bought another tin shack and then moved uphill and bought another tin shack. We were saving like crazy, and everytime somebody died and a plot of land became available we kept on buying 'til we had this whole acre and a half. That's a lot to look after, there's so much work involved. After the rainy season everything grows like mad, and I was given the job of lawn-mowing! *Great* fun....

I did my Capability Brown thing – having vistas and views – because this place had nothing to start with. We planted all the trees down the middle of the main street – which they later yanked out. We planted all the coconuts down the beach, and they pulled them out for the tourist buses!

You know how Australians, much as I love them, talk about soil as 'dirt', and the garden's a 'backyard'? I've never forgotten that, it still sticks in the gullet. It's heartbreaking – there's no love in it.

I've tried to save a lot of buildings here in the past. No way – nobody listens. We had a funny little Anglican church which really was an historic piece. The last time I went there was to the funeral of a local lady – we all fell through the floor, and hung on to the coffin!

But it was so romantic – all the flowers laid out on the ground, and that was it. They had a double island wedding there – and *they* all fell through the floor too! So that was the end of that – it was pulled down. But Alan, there must be a bit of romanticism left, it doesn't have to be *all* commercialism, does it?

We're terribly lucky, we have so few snakes and spiders. We have children's pythons, funny little green things, entirely harmless. You do get the odd black one, but we just leave them be. One came in to hibernate, but I'm afraid I destroyed that.

We built the restaurant thirty-two years ago, and opened it the day my first daughter was born. We weren't open for dinner because the roads were so bad nobody could come up here – but lunchtime! It nearly killed me – a 4.00 a.m. start! Then I had this brilliant idea of having the most sumptuous afternoon teas, sort of Fortnum & Mason kind of thing for elderly people who didn't have a large lunch but liked to woof into the cream …

That became quite a big thing too, but I had no help, I had to do it all myself. These were all holidaymakers from the south; they mostly stayed in Cairns and came up by taxi for a little tour. And they had three coastal boats running and people used to come and stay in the north for three days. The boat itself was a holiday – they could get as drunk as they liked. But then the wharfies killed that – they wouldn't load or unload. Union strikes, and all that, so we haven't had those ships for years.

Then my jewellery thing started: I'd collected shells and bits and pieces and wondered what one could do with them … Lady Blayney, old General Blayney's wife, came up on a private yacht and said, '*Wow*, we can do something with these', and shipped some back to George's in Melbourne – they're like Fortnum & Mason's out here.

From there on it sort of kicked off, but we had to keep this pretence that we were a *huge* concern, with machinery and God knows what.

They got us mixed up with Bowden Pearling Company, a very famous old company. We never said no. If we couldn't complete a thing we'd say, 'The fleet's out for a little while – when it comes in we'll send you your order ...' But the two brothers who ran the business, the George brothers, found out in the end and sent us the most charming letter, saying, 'This mystique's been going on for a long time, but we now know the whole story ...' Still it grew and grew, and other people got to hear about us and it got completely out of hand, a bit top-heavy. We had to show tax returns ...

An American woman did a television show in one of the fountains in New York – she was sitting there covered with my jewellery. The difficulty was the cost of getting it there, the freight, and they wanted everything dirt cheap so they could put their mark-up on. All our stuff was selling in Saks for hundreds and hundreds of dollars, which they bought for £2.10s here. So that failed. But then we had other outlets – they came and they went.

In my little shop now it's the Americans who quibble and haggle, always – in fact one day my husband couldn't stand it and said to this couple, 'You're not in the Middle East!' They wanted two for the price of one, and thought we were half-wits living in the sticks.

Actually, Australians are the best buyers: if they really want something and they've got money, there's no hassle. The French are the worst, they quibble. I never let them know I understand every word they're saying.

The rates are fantastic now, so we sold the restaurant, we sold our other shop, and we condensed ourselves. It's very slack at the moment. Come and look at my little shop ...

How many accommodation units are they going to build along the shore here?

I think they said nine thousand, at one stage – but there's only seven thousand of us in the *whole* of this Shire, so they've got to put in their own water, they've got to do everything. Meanwhile they're destroying all the land there. There's this forest country between the road and the beach which made it all very private, and they said they'd never destroy that – but now there's little openings ... It'll soon be untenable. It's a huge concern, absolutely enormous – and they had to pick on *us*, here!

The cruel thing is that all these years ago you made a decision to get away from the mainstream – and now the mainstream's coming here to get you!

That's the tragic part about it. We've tried to create something sort of low-key in tune with what we lived with, that everybody appreciated, and now suddenly it's being taken from under us.

Everything in Australia they try to do in ten years, when it's taken a hundred years elsewhere. They want to be right up-front with everybody else. People have walked round here and said, 'Gee, you could make some money out of this, you could build that there, and that there . . .' There's no point.

Australia doesn't seem to go in for restrained development – it's the Gold Coast or nothing!

Got to copy the Americans, it's policy – *everything* they do. The hotel people look to America, instead of designing their own rather low-key slightly bush thing with all that good atmosphere. They don't realize how many Americans come here and are so disappointed; they say, 'We've got this at home.'

When were you last at home, in England?

1977 was the last time. I hated it – I didn't belong. I don't fit in any more because I'm just called a bloody colonial. I mean, the whole family's lost touch in that respect; they know we're here, we're doing different things – but there's no desire to come and see what we're doing, our alternative lifestyle. We're known as 'the dropouts'. None of the family terribly wished to see me – they thought I was a bit odd!

I found London so grubby. Going to the theatre there were people in jeans, with old boots and macs. The glamour seemed to have gone. And I lost all my sense of direction. We used to live at Strand-on-the-Green – we had Hogarth's house – so all my orientation was from there. Suddenly I was dumped in a most ghastly bedsit in Chelsea, and I could never get my bearings.

The nicest people in the world were the West Indian bus drivers – they actually used to get off the bus and take me across the road and say, 'Look, lovie, you catch that one there.' Absolutely sweet. But my London as far as I was concerned had absolutely *gone*.

You're always bound up in clothes, you can't look elegant – and after here where you wear so little, it seemed absolutely horrendous.

So I'm a bit lost at the moment, except doing odd funny things. I still keep the mind ticking: a lot of reading. Crossword puzzles, in desperation – like the Queen does ...

THE COUNTRY GENT: MAJOR JAMES 'SLIP' DE COURCEY MITCHELL

*I got out with a staggeringly ridiculous
sum of money ...*

Major James 'Slip' de Courcey Mitchell is the quintessential English gentleman farmer – indeed he once towed the Queen and her car out of a ditch with such charm and discretion that he was rewarded by the gift of a Royal labrador. His family home in Gloucestershire is now owned by the Prince of Wales.

Slip sold his two thousand acres of Norfolk rather well, and replaced them with another two thousand on the other side of the world: Arraman Park at Scone, at the top of the Hunter Valley in New South Wales. He's lived there for nearly twenty years, has three huge sons helping to run his stud, and is wonderfully at home in his new egalitarian land.

They have 180 mares at Arraman; they're in Australia's thoroughbred game, part of a $1000 million industry with a workforce of 200,000. The 16,000 breeders have another $750 million invested in bloodstock – catering to this gambling nation. The annual prize money for the five hundred race clubs tops $100 million, and every second taxi driver seems to own half a leg of some promising two-year-old running in the 2.30. The first money available to most upwardly mobile Australians goes in joining a syndicate owning a future Melbourne Cup winner ...

Slip is not a betting man – but even he makes exceptions: 'I had a syndicate once – I was in hospital with six nurses, and they had a marvellous time. Luckily our horse won a few races – they thought it was wonderful ...'

I came out eighteen years ago. To start with, the arthritis was getting the better of me, slightly. My wife has always been mad keen on the sunshine, too. I lived just over Newmarket, two thousand acres in Swaffham, Norfolk, had a lot of nice neighbours and three sons – none of them very brilliant it seemed at the time, average lads. And I thought, 'What the hell am I going to do in England?' because the property there wouldn't have divided up. It was the time when land prices boomed, and I got out with what I thought was the most staggeringly *ridiculous* sum of money!

I'd never had any money at all, and suddenly acquired some. The ten per cent deposit, when I sold, was exactly *double* what I'd bought the whole goddam place for in about 1953! I bought it for £12 an acre and when we sold it made over £500 – that's a large profit on two thousand acres. So I suddenly had a bit of capital.

Everybody said, 'You'd better go to Ireland.' Luckily I didn't fall for that: in those days land prices were sky-high and Ireland was having a little boom. Now of course it's gone straight down the plug. I resisted that – but where else do you go? I contemplated Kenya ... I'd been to South Africa and I didn't care for the Boers, I'm afraid. My missus said, 'I don't want to go to a black country, they're all a bit dicey.'

I happened to find a very nice attractive place without a shadow of a doubt, four miles out of Scone at the top of the Hunter Valley: two thousand acres for £40 an acre. It's a stud. We have cattle and crops too. It's not the size, it's what it'll *do* and what it'll carry. So I bought this place in 1968, brought my family – my wife hadn't even seen it.

We've now got twenty mares of our own, but some of them are away visiting stallions. There are three stallions at the place. The overheads are high, even though you need less manpower here than in Europe: the horses don't have to be brought in every night. Brood mares, and mares and foals, live out all the year round – we don't even bring them in to foal. It's more the natural way of doing it, I suppose – it's very artificial in Europe. We have a floodlit paddock and a nightwatchman, and we get very little trouble.

So I'd left Norfolk with a sack of gold; I'd always had a huge mortgage hanging round my neck – but I've never had a mortgage since. I've got another property near Tamworth and a very nice flat in Sydney and I don't owe anybody anything. Not even the bank, very much. I think it's fair to say the *real* farmers who haven't got any back-up capital – which very few farmers have, the money they're supposed to be worth is all in the land – are having a hard time.

You're living more or less the way you lived in England?

Yes, I lived in a village in England, I've never liked the cities – I'm a mountain man. We've got mountains all round us, which suits me. I wouldn't go back to Europe now, I don't think. It's those long winter days when it's not light 'til nine in the morning and dark again at three ... you get out of the habit of it. It's rather nice to see the sun shining in the middle of winter, isn't it? I probably still have more friends in England than here, I suppose, or more acquaintances.

After all this time, you're still very much a Pom?

I can turn the accent on occasionally if I wish to ... I like to call myself 'accentless'.

All right – turn it off, then!

(*Laughs*) Somebody said to me in England the other day, 'You must be an Australian?' I was slightly surprised, but not offended at all. I've got an Australian passport. Got *two* passports: British and Australian.

I don't think I'd have come this far if I was not able to get back when I wanted. Lots of people are much braver than me; I didn't really consider I'd stepped off the deep end into nothing because I knew damn well I could afford to get back when I wanted to. We go back nearly every other year.

So the tyranny of distance means jetlag to you – not financial lag?

For a lot of people who came here, the financial thing was the hardship – those who came on £10 assisted passages. I brought three staff, two of whom are still with me. They've not been back yet – one's contemplating going this year, after eighteen years.

Wages here are the highest in the world. I pay my man a long way over the award rates – but he works ninety hours a week. The trade unions have been down on my neck three or four times and threatened me, saying, 'We'll fix you up! We can't force your men to be unionists but you'll find you won't get your petrol delivered . . .'

I don't know what I'd do if it actually came to the crunch: I can't *make* my men belong to a union. One of them would have a purple fit – he's so anti-unionist it's not true! Unions are a red rag to a bull to him. Probably votes Labour, but he wouldn't belong to a union – he'd be off.

We pay good money because they don't get overtime as such, they don't fill in a worksheet. Occasionally, once a week when we're not very busy, I'll say, 'How about an afternoon off to go to the races?' It's give and take, but with their perks I suppose they're averaging $600 (£320) a week. That includes a house – well paid, aren't they? The same man in England might get £150. It's OK if you've got good fellows. My fellows will turn out on a Sunday if they have to and there's not a murmur of surprise, so it works.

The Australian Workers' Union covers all the agriculture side, plus a lot of others, and we've got a particularly nasty man in our district, too. I'm very careful not to have a run-in with him. I say to my boys, 'For God's sake don't *you* talk to him, you'll get stuck into the so-and-so and you'll muck it up. You send him to see me – play it on a very low key.' I don't want them saying: 'Come outside and I'll give you one!'

A couple of years ago when I was away in England and the boys weren't here, the head union man arrives in a large car – you know, suit of clothes and a collar and tie – and comes in and says, 'Where's the boss?' My man said, 'I'm in charge', and showed him all round, took him into his own house and gave him a nice cold glass of beer – thought he was a potential customer, arriving in the big air-conditioned car and all that.

The first question he fires is, 'How many hours a week do you work?' My man scratched his head and said, 'Well in the season I'm the boss-man here and if the nightwatchman gets me out of bed for a foaling or something, I suppose it runs between ninety and one hundred hours a week, I never count.' The fellow nearly had a purple fit! 'Do you get overtime?' And he didn't; he got all sorts of bloody perks, he didn't *want* any overtime, he'd got free board and three or four horses of his own – it worked beautifully. So the union man came to see me afterwards, said it was outrageous – typical Pom!

I said, 'I look after my fellows or they wouldn't be here, would they? He's got no written contract, he can give me a week's notice, and go. Would he have been here ten years if he didn't find it suited him? He could get a job tomorrow morning: the number of times he's brought me letters from far bigger operations blatantly trying to entice him away ...' In the end he was defeated. He couldn't *force* him to join, so he went away in disgust.

The unions here are getting terribly worried, they've been reading that in England members are going down, in America they're down to less than twenty per cent ... The trade unions are doing the wrong thing here anyway, they're only bothered about the people who've *got* jobs, and getting more lovely lolly out of them – and go hang the fellows who're out of work. That's where I think they're a bit naughty. If you're a competent operator and you know your job you don't need a trade union; and there's no such thing as being out of work if you're a skilled man of any sort.

Do people want to work here ...?

I sometimes really think they don't. The Welfare State's gone berserk – the hungry tiger fights a lot better than the overfed one. The young kids of eighteen, they're all drawing their $80 a week or whatever it is on the dole. Four get together, $320 a week, live on the beach, surf all day, do a bit of gentle thieving on the side ... It's not like England, you know, you *can* sleep on the bloody beach. There's no incentive, really.

I think the younger generation are getting a bit workshy – including my sons, sometimes. Five o'clock comes and they think, I'll play tennis. I remember before I was first married there was no end to the day – it was twelve hours a bloody day! And when your ordinary job was finished you went round to see what had to be done next day, and look at the stock – and then spend two hours in the office doing the paperwork ...

One youngster's father rang up and said his son was mad keen to learn this business, would love to work on the stud. I said, 'OK, we start at six o'clock in the morning because it's cooler, less flies – and the mares don't get upset.'

He arrived the first morning quarter of an hour late, the second morning ten minutes late, so I said, 'Oi, you're needed here.' All he had to do was open and shut one gate. Anyway, he was late the third morning as well so I said, 'If you can't come to work on time you'll have to leave.'

Well, he was late again – so I paid him off. His parting words were, 'It's a fuckin' awful job where the *boss* gets to work on time ...'

THE BUSH BROTHER:
CANON NOEL ALLEN

The wedding reception went on for a week ...

Noel Allen was a Butlin's redcoat before his ordination in 1963. His first parish was St Mary's Abbey, Nuneaton. Three years later he went to Australia to become a Bush Brother in the Northern Territory, to join that far-flung band of young English clergy recruited for three-year tours to bring the church to the remote outback.

The Brothers were not paid but were given food, accommodation, transport, $6 a week pocket money, and expected to be celibate. Brother Noel's parishes around Tennant Creek and later at Alice Springs were about the size of England: 'The biggest pressure on people coming here is the loneliness, the vast space – you can't ever nip round next door. The distances frighten a lot of people ...'

He says he lived quite well on his $6 a week – even managed to save! Such is the hospitality of the outback that in twenty years of travel he only twice had to stay at an hotel.

After seven years as a Bush Brother he became a parish priest in Darwin. Today he is Canon Noel Allen, ministering to the Parish of the Good Shepherd in Humpty Doo, forty miles to the south. His church has not yet been built, so Sunday services are held in the rectory carport. Parishioners arrive by car and tractor, on horseback, to receive communion while babies gurgle from carry-cots and children scamper around in the morning sunshine.

After racing down the Stuart Highway to conduct another service in a local community hut at Berry Springs Reserve before a congregation of six women and one man, Brother Noel returns to his carport to join parishioners at a 'bring your own' barbecue, wandering around in shorts and sandals wearing a trendy wooden cross. His yellow T-shirt reads: 'St Fred's of the Carport'.

He smokes a lot, but gave up beer: 'Australia's a very drink-orientated society and in all honesty I found it was beginning to affect my work, so I decided I didn't really need it.' His dog Emma Lou, inherited from a close friend who died of cancer, keeps him company while he works at his tapestry. He appears a lonely figure, but much loved ...

In the 1890s people would come out and visit the bush, and they'd find there were families that had never been married, children had never been baptized – knew nothing about it. Quite often people had been buried, but no one had said anything over the grave. The Church realized that the work just wasn't being done, so they went back to England and some of them trained as clergy, some as laymen, and then they came out so that these places could have *some* kind of ministry.

They decided to work it on a three- or five-year promise that they would do it for nothing, except food. Originally there was one who did all the far west of New South Wales – by bicycle! He would cycle anything up to one hundred miles to take a service; this was the kind of characters they were.

You were a Bush Brother, but you're now a Canon?

Canon in this diocese is really just a thank you from the Bishop for nineteen years' work – and the Bush Brotherhood in fact has ceased to be.

That's very sad.

It *is* sad; it was a special ministry, but I think with more transport and different ways of financing parishes, the Brotherhood didn't need to be, any longer. It was basically English, and very few Australians would join it.

Because it was a rugged life, you had to be celibate and you didn't get paid?

Well, we got $6 a week pocket money for smokes, and such things. During seven years, all told, I managed to *save* money because all food was provided, and car and house. I think the main thing was it wasn't a religious order, you just signed on for three years, and then went into normal ministry. It was the only way in these very large areas you could ever get a ministry – my first parish was four times the size of England.

You're very foolish in the outback even today if you don't tell people where you're travelling to, because with this kind of heat you could be lost for an hour and you'd be lost for *life*! Whenever you travel you always say where you're going and when you hope to arrive; if you don't arrive, then they'll look for you. You could be hundreds of miles from anywhere.

Quite often I've celebrated the Eucharist on the tail of the Land Rover with nobody around – but it's a good training ground to deepen your own spiritual life!

You were ordained in Coventry, so why did being a Bush Brother in the outback seem more attractive than being a parish priest in Nuneaton?

Wouldn't *you* like to travel? It was a good way.

Not on a bicycle around the outback! But living on $6 a week was no problem?

No.

How about celibacy?

No, um, might sound a bit selfish but at times I like to be on my own, always have done. It's demanding work, and being a celibate I can answer demands with no other ties, so I've always felt personally I can do the ministry better as a single person than a married one. It's not a vow of celibacy and I suppose if the right one came along – you never know your luck! But I suppose I can run pretty fast . . .

So you were going around your vast parish with your begging bowl, like a Buddhist monk? Australians are so hospitable I'm sure you never went short . . .

What astounds most visitors is how Australians love hospitality. You'd go bush, you'd take a service, then my idea as an Englishman would be to move on: 'No, you stay today . . .' I took a wedding once and the reception went on for a *week*! Everybody came in from hundreds of miles around. Fellowship and hospitality are very important in the bush.

Once upon a time you were a Butlin's redcoat – was that good preparation for the life of a Bush Brother?

Marvellous, because I was trained in a monastery, very closed – so where could you meet people and get on with people better than a Butlin holiday camp? To keep eleven thousand English happy for a week on holiday was *very* hard work!

It must sometimes be quite hard for you to achieve a rapport here? One feels Australians are loath to admit sensitivity and weakness to themselves, let alone to anyone else . . .

What you've got to do is to show them that it's not being weak to be a human being. This so-called macho Australian act is more of a city idea, it's not the bush people. The real bush people are quite happy to be honest with themselves, and I think the honesty of the bush is what really hits most people – hence you've got to be honest about yourself. If you put a face on, the bush people just don't believe you *whatever* you say.

A lot of Australians are shy of coming forward to worship, but in many ways they're very basically concerned about each other, and hence there is a foundation that Christ could work very well on. Whether you'll ever get them as a worshipping group doesn't – and

I know this sounds potty, as a clergyman – it doesn't really worry us very much. My attitude is to try and get them to be caring and loving about each other, and I think Christ will judge them accordingly.

They don't seem particularly caring and loving about the aborigines, do they?

There's a lot of bad publicity about what's happened, and unfortunately at the moment the aborigines have a very large political clout. You've only got to mention them and everybody's hackles go up – but a lot *is* being done for the aboriginal peoples. Unfortunately they are stuck between two cultures – they just don't know how to use what we give them.

A lot of them are stuck with that awful problem, drink: they can't hold it, it completely ruins them. Another awful problem, even in the bush, is petrol sniffing. They don't know what they're doing.

Our own young people have been brought up that if they don't work, there's something wrong with them. Well, the aboriginal people, if you didn't hunt and care for yourselves there was something wrong. In our own society we've got a lot of thinking to do if we're virtually getting rid of work; what do we put in its place, and still keep our dignity?

The real aborigines don't look to the future, they never saved, they get food today and eat it today because tomorrow may not come. To give them money is an awful sort of turn-round, completely, in their whole thinking. So our way of life is absolutely foreign to them, and we're expecting them to do in one generation what took us a thousand years.

We've taken away their whole culture and expect them to change in two generations and think like white men. Well, they won't. So there *is* quite a bit of friction. I think it might get nasty as time goes on, mainly because they're being used by some for the wrong ends.

We now have five aboriginal clergy priests – four who were ordained this year – and they are taking Christ and *not* the Church, which is good. Instead of taking our funny ways of doing things – an English attitude to worship – they are very much looking at their own culture and seeing how they can interpret that to Christ, as we did in the mediaeval age and for some unknown reason stopped.

Hence a lot of the aboriginal music and dance and theatre is being brought into their way of worship.

I think a lot of the real aborigines say, 'Just leave us alone and let us have time to work it through.' And they are, they're growing in Arnhem Land – the Church especially has grown ten times in about five years.

There's suddenly been an idea that Christ isn't a white man, he's *ours* and we'll use Him in our way. They're getting their dignity back through Christ, which is lovely. It's wonderful to see, though a lot of the church people don't like it because they don't sing Anglican hymns in Anglican ways – they clap sticks and jump up and down and enjoy it and look at Christ through aboriginal eyes ...

THE VALLEY GIRL: ANNETTE WILDE

They thought I was somebody from Dallas ...

The Diorama was a dream for Don Figgins, a quiet man who owns chains of shoe shops but wanted to build the most beautiful department store in the world – which he may well have done. His temple to fashion as a high art has been furnished from Europe, and offers sedate Melbourne every international designer label. Customers may be collected from their hotels and homes by a choc-olate-brown Phantom Rolls with a tiny curlicued 'F' on its door.

Sited in the middle of good grey Collins Street, the opulent Figgins Diorama is so impossibly up-market many people not captive in the Rolls are frightened to go inside. It provides a European shopping spree without the jetlag for the five per cent of the population who control forty per cent of Australia's wealth. The place would be considered impossibly luxurious in the Rue Faubourg St Honoré, the Via Condotti, Fifth Avenue, Bond Street ... and it seemed questionable whether the people of Melbourne were up to it: they are a somewhat puritanical breed and not deeply into hedonism.

The more intrepid may enter through a high revolving glass door imported from New York and move into a marble passage lined with small boutiques: perfumery on one side, Paisley scarves on the other. Then they stand amid potted palms and wrought iron balustrades looking up at a circular space three storeys high: all is black and white and elegant. Among the crystal and mirrors, each surrounding floor is lined with the showrooms of discreet names: Fendi, Emmanuel Ungaro, Issey Miyake . . .

Within this atmosphere of hushed and hyper-expensive luxury, a smiling Welsh girl, plump and golden. She is selling Chanel cosmetics and perfume but nevertheless exudes an aura of home-made scones. Unlike the pushy polished salesgirls standing around she is a warm and caring Welsh nanny. This gentle and hesitant welcome, it transpires, increases the turnover.

Annette Wilde was secretary to the Mayor of the Lliw Borough Council, outside Swansea. Her husband Nigel – a draughtsman in Llanelly – became redundant, so they emigrated. The small town girl who was frightened by the traffic in Melbourne – let alone London – is now Chanel's top salesgirl, and considering the amount of make-up Australian women wear, has to be in an expanding business. She can hardly believe how much her life has improved . . .

We arrived on the Saturday, and I had a job with Chanel on the Wednesday. It was luck really, because I've never done this sort of work before in my life – I just looked in the paper. I thought I'd meet more people, I'd get more confident. My accent was worrying me – will everybody be able to understand me properly? It still worries me a little bit.

They're very nice – the Australians always say they love the accent and ask me if I can sing, and I get so embarrassed! They're much more friendly – they make me feel warm. I was only in

Australia for one week and I didn't know the money – and my *accent* – but the people just helped me along the way.

You don't seem to meet many Welsh here, they must all go to Patagonia!

Exactly – I haven't met one.

So as a Mayor's ex-secretary, how has your life changed in the three years you've been here?

The social life I have is fantastic – it's very motivating. We had a mortgage in Wales like everybody else, but you seem to get *more* in Australia. You earn more, but you can plan. You can say, I can get a fridge or whatever in six months, you haven't got to have hire purchase or any of that.

My standard of living has improved tremendously, like I wouldn't have a swimming pool of my own if I lived in England. I've got much much more – you can go out on a Saturday and buy a microwave, you haven't got to make *do* with things, that's what I like.

My husband's earning three times, three and a half times as much as what he did in England, and mine's about two and a half. If we lived in England we could never afford to come to Australia to see my sister, but I can afford to go back to Wales for six weeks' holiday, which I could never have done if I was still working at Lliw Valley Council offices.

When you went back to the Valley this summer, how was Wales?

I'd been staying in Hong Kong, which is spotlessly clean; when I first got off the plane at Heathrow I'll never forget walking into the toilet there! It really *disgusted* me, because it was so terrible, it really made me think, 'What on earth have I come home to?' Then I thought, 'Don't be silly Annette, must be one of their off-days.' But people just weren't very helpful.

My picture of England was much brighter than when I went back, and even my husband was shocked. In Australia it's all so nice and clean, with the plants and the trees.

Wales was the same, but *worse*: the place was disgusting, again. Everybody's supposed to be on the dole and I thought, 'Why don't they have a system where anybody can keep it all nice and clean?'

The churches were disgusting, too. It just wasn't a pleasure to be there.

There are people out of work, just living in the pubs all day. They'd all put on weight and didn't care about themselves and had six children all following behind them, couldn't afford things in the shops and yet their husbands were in the pubs all day, or in the betting office – they always seemed to have money for *that*. You know, nothing for the children but they still go up to the pubs – that's what really upset me.

Even my little niece of ten, she's frightened to go in the parks because she tells me these people pick her up and take her in the car, and all these sorts of things. She said, 'Please take me back with you, Annette, I don't like living here any more, I want to come to Australia with you' – and she's only *ten*! She says, 'What am I going to do when I grow up?' There's no jobs – it was heartbreaking, to be honest with you.

All the people that I'd missed in Britain, when I saw them it wasn't what I expected – if you know what I mean? I'd gone on much further – and they'd still stayed the same, that's what I couldn't believe. It was amazing, everybody *looking* at you all the time: they thought I was somebody from *Dallas*!

Because you're better off and better dressed?

They said, 'You always liked dressing and having make-up and things.' I looked much more prosperous, that's what their words were . . . Even my parents kept saying, 'You look much much better, the both of you, healthwise as well.'

So you're not going back to Wales again, ever?

I'd still, like, go for holidays, but the people weren't the same, because you've got that little bit further. My parents thought it was a bit of jealousy involved, which I would have thought would have been the other way: when you come to Australia and have a job with Chanel you would have thought Australians would have been more against you – but they weren't like that at all. I was only out here a couple of months when my parents came to stay and people were offering me all sorts of things, helping me, inviting them for meals – people I'd never been to their homes before!

The only thing I miss is the Saturday shopping and those little pubs ... the cosiness. And teenagers here have got to be very dependent upon their parents: eighteen- and nineteen-year-olds have got to be picked up at night-time, because everything's such a distance ... At home you go to one disco and then to another one, but here you need to be more dependent upon your family.

You're working for perhaps the most expensive cosmetic house; do you find that Australian women are prepared to spend a lot of money on themselves?

One client spent $1700 and another one spent $1200, and they were just ordinary people. One didn't have a handbag or anything, just walked in one morning, very casually dressed. She said she'd terrible trouble with her skin, she was from Canberra and nobody took trouble with her there.

One does notice that women use a lot of make-up here – they tend to plaster it on more than they do in Britain?

Oh much more! Well, they noticed *me* when I went back. You can imagine, me with all my make-up going round the supermarket with my Mum, and people looking at me! Even my Mum, she wears a little bit. She lives in a Residential, a sheltered complex for the elderly, where they have little social evenings, and because she wears a bit of make-up they say, 'Here's a dolly bird coming!'

My Mum is sixty-five, but she wears a little bit of blusher and lipstick. I said, 'Don't take any notice of what they say because they're in their eighties and they don't put anything on.' This is why she was so much happier in Australia, she felt more with-it, younger. She said, 'You're past sixty and you're supposed to forget about clothes.' She likes to look smart, but they just don't like that there.

You've come directly to Melbourne, which is perhaps the most sophisticated city in Australia, from your unpronounceable Welsh town ...

Exactly; it's very, very small isn't it, there's no comparison is there, really? Even London didn't frighten me any more after living in Melbourne, there's just all this hustle and bustle. I love all of it.

When I first came out all the traffic and everybody rushing everywhere, I couldn't believe it and I was frightened to go to any other street. I'll never forget when I had a morning teabreak, they told me where the coffee shop was but I got lost and was about an hour – and only had twenty minutes! They couldn't believe it ...

It seems strange, but I do miss those little pubs. Here it's on a bigger scale, you've got the Regent and all those lovely places to go for cocktails after work. I wouldn't *ever* be doing that if I was home, would I?

Here you can do everything everybody else does. In England it's only the rich that can. You're either a working-class person and you're just surviving, or you've got money; there's no in-between. But in Australia you can have your wages and go out every night if you want to spend it that way, or you can just go out the odd weekend and save your money, and then go home and have nice holidays.

It's more exciting, especially here in the Diorama because you're meeting people like yourself – I'd never have met you if I was in England, would I ... ?

NEW-AUSTRALIAN KALEIDOSCOPE

*Dr Michael Willoughby: I'm grateful the Unions made me
look elsewhere . . .*

Think of people we can *least* afford to lose down Britain's brain-drain, to see carrying their skills and knowledge away to another land . . . Engineers, professors? Pity, but we have others among our 56 million. Pop stars, movie people, television men? Who cares. Bankers and businessmen? Goodbye and good luck. Builders, brick-layers, miners? Hope you do well. What about a cancer consultant – a specialist in children's leukaemia whose wife is a radiotherapist? Let's hope *they* won't leave . . .

But they did, driven out of the country by union militancy when shop-stewards at the Royal Hospital for Sick Children in Glasgow one day refused to let Dr Michael Willoughby operate to save the life of a dying child; when a succession of disputes during three years disrupted the care he was trying to provide children with cancer. 'Mounting militancy culminated in strikes, walkouts and restricted services, when technicians would not work on a Saturday. Operating lists were being monitored by shop-stewards who threatened to close the Hospital if operations of which they did not approve were carried out.'

Dr and Mrs Willoughby left Scotland in despair, amid militant fury – first at their presence, then their departure. They were in their fifties and had never considered changing their orderly and

393

supremely useful lives. With their three sons, they flew to Western Australia.

Dr Willoughby was so deeply wounded by his experiences, by the abuse he and his wife had suffered, that even today he cannot discuss those distressing years.

Since 1983 he has been Director of Haematology at the Princess Margaret Children's Hospital in Perth, which has more than doubled its success rate with leukaemia patients in the past eight years. There are sixteen beds in his wing, and he had just completed his eleventh bone-marrow transplant. His wife Fiona runs another hospital's radiology department.

Direct from dismal Glasgow, they had landed in Perth's perfect climate to be greeted by a basket of flowers from 'Judy' – who turned out to be his new Matron. He soon found most of his staff using his first name. A formal and exceedingly shy man, he was disarmed by the warmth and friendliness of a hospital where he now visits young patients in his oncology wing in shirtsleeves, wearing a colourful name-badge designed by a child with leukaemia.

At the King's Park Club near the modern Hospital the Willoughbys play in the Twilight Tennis Tournaments – and have more friends than they made during twenty years in Glasgow. He remains awkward and self-effacing, but his whole family now delight in the new life into which they were driven:

It's a rare thing, especially in Britain, to have a sort of professional shake-up – more a shake-up, in the event, than I probably realized! A cultural shock – but looking back, I think it's a good thing. We find the patients and families here demand a much more personalized service and explanation, and you have to rise to that. We were always a bit attuned to that approach and it's lucky we were, because you couldn't get away without proper explanations to your patients here. It's a far less hierarchical society here, much more democratic. All members of my team come up with great ideas, a dietician comes along to tell me that she'd thought

of some solution to that transplant ... We're more
of a family here ...

Tony Packard: I've got what every schoolboy dreams about –
a Centrefold ...

Back in his hometown of Reading, Tony Packard would be regarded
as the perfect product of the Thatcher economy: a self-made hard-
working achiever. In Australia – where a workaholic is eccentric –
he has still contrived to make his fortune as the biggest General
Motors–Holden dealer in Sydney, helped by countless hard-sell commercials in which he harangues viewers like some strident Pommy
ocker: 'Let *me* do it right for *yew*!'

Despite such public Strinery his business is not run on Australian
lines: his razzmatazz and salesman's eager sincerity seem American,
his work ethic Japanese. On the celebrity speaker circuit he lectures
about motivation: 'There's nobody in this town who doesn't know
who I am – it's amazing.'

Tony won a scholarship to a Winchester school and worked as a
bank clerk before arriving on a £10-passage in 1967, when he was
twenty-three. He was rejected by a Sydney bank so, unaware that
there was a dole, turned to selling cars. General Motors–Holden
gave him seven years to repay the loan which built his vast Packard
Motors spread in the Baulkham Hills; he had it cleared in twenty-
three months.

He is now as Aussie as any born-again convert and proud of his
beflagged business and second wife Kim – a Penthouse model. His
first marriage to an Australian girl he met at his arrival party had
failed when he spent too much time wheeling and dealing while
she preferred a quieter life in the country – where to Tony's dismay
she showed considerable aptitude for fixing fuses and doing-up the
house. While she did-it-herself and he sold more and more cars,
they had four children, then divorced. She was a 'man-woman', he
says, while his new model – a hardly run-in second wife – is a
'woman-woman'.

In their comfortable home at Glenhaven they exercise in a mir-
rored bedroom amid weights and equipment for keeping bodies

beautiful. He has not yet discovered whether Kim is a closet fuse-fixer:

> We've got enough Government here to run Russia
> and America and England put together! Take our
> 16 million people ... Only 7½ million of them have
> got a job, so that's half the people out of work –
> they're not eligible, they're wives and that sort of
> thing. Then 3½ million of the 7 million that have got
> jobs are in the public service. So there's about 3½ or
> 4 million of us paying for the rest of the country.
> That's why the taxes are so high – there are so
> few people in this country *creating* the wealth that
> everybody else lives on ...

Bob La Castra: Who's an Australian – the Queen?

We know Poms can be given a hard time in Australia, but with the old white-Australia policy and all that talk about dagos and wogs and abos, can you imagine how they'd treat a *black* Pom? That has to be asking for trouble. Bob La Castra had a West Indian father he never knew; a Barnardo boy from Romford, he went to white-Australia in 1981 on a working visa.

He and his English schoolteacher wife Lyndsey *never* had a difficult moment – no problems at all. Everyone, he says, was great!

This might be because he's attractive and cheerful and well-balanced and appears on television: he became a regular on *Wombat*, a children's television programme networked from Brisbane. On the debit side, he still has the sharp East End accent which completely floors Australians expecting some deep voice from the Caribbean:

> They often burst into fits of laughter when I speak!
> My mother wouldn't marry my father because they
> both had families. When she fell pregnant she wasn't
> sure whether it was my father's or her husband's,
> so she kept her fingers crossed and hoped I'd come
> out white – but I didn't, so she had a bit of explaining
> to do! The biggest joke now is that all round

Australia they won't use me for commercials: 'We
can't use you because you're black, we want Australians.' I said, 'Who's an Australian – the Queen? A
European?' It's such a multicultural society – and
yet they won't use a black in commercials, not in
Brisbane they won't . . .

Tony Holt: *I tried celibacy – but I fell back* . . .

Tony Holt left Weston-super-Mare thirty-four years ago when he
was six, and spent two years with his family in a Nissen hut at a
Sydney reception centre. He is now an acupuncturist on the Gold
Coast, the Miami Beach of Australia – where he also treats animals.

When we met he was sticking golden needles into the twitching
brown hide of a four-year-old mare who had become lame and stiff:
'I got some more-solid needles in Korea for treating horses, because
they bend ordinary needles when they flex their skin.'

Well over six feet and well-muscled, with a great blond mane and
large white teeth – and that's just the acupuncturist, not the
patient – he is a telling salesman for the simple life. Tony is concerned
about his spiritual being and invisible life-force, practises healing,
lapses into ashram-speak and lives the careful holistic life as we
know it today – though his girlfriend is a dancer at the Surfers
Paradise Casino:

> I'm not celibate. I *tried* it for a year. You have to
> transcend a lot of senses, being celibate. You have
> to be really devoted, but I fell down, back into the
> sense-of-gratification world again. The physical body
> changes every seven or eight years. I'm just a spirit
> soul on this planet, temporarily in this body, whereas
> I think of my soul as spiritually eternal. I try to live
> a simple life, high-thinking and simple-living, rather
> than the other way around which is what *most*
> people try to live: high-living and simple-
> thinking . . .

Ray Willmott: Kangaroo scent is very much stronger . . .

Riding to hounds is a country pageant well suited to Australia's wide spaces and lack of wire – though it can sometimes be difficult to keep hounds on-line when a fox trail is overpowered by some more exotic scent . . .

Ray Willmott, Master of the most northerly hunt in Australia, the Hunter Valley Hunt, left Somerset in 1961 with the Big Brother movement to work as a jackaroo in Inverell. After six years in Australia with only hard and poorly paid jobs, he returned to Bristol to start The Cavern, a folk-music club. He and his wife Barbara also took part-time jobs at the Bristol zoo – she looked after the souvenirs, he the birds and monkeys. Then after another three years and rather to their surprise, they became homesick for Australia. They returned, opened shops selling videos around Newcastle in New South Wales, and prospered.

He founded the Hunt in 1977 in the wine country a hundred miles north of Sydney, and is Huntsman as well as Master. Twice a week from late April until September they ride across Pokolbin country, with local vignerons and farmers as hosts. A subscription is $120, a day's cap fee $12.

Ray cuts a stern and splendid figure as the Hunt rides out; while MFH may not carry *quite* the clout in Australia that it does in England, members of the field still jump to it when the Master speaks:

> People are beginning to understand that the colours of the Hunt are worn for a purpose, that it's not simply fancy dress. That all helps. Of course every meet is an educational programme for somebody. Initially they're very surprised we can even *show* sport – a lot of people expect it'll be something like a paperchase . . .

Chris Barnes: My friends use my Christian name –
I'm Mr Barnes to you . . .

The Chairman of the Hunter Valley Hunt is also a Pom, from Herefordshire: Chris Barnes now runs Blaxlands, a Valley restaurant, and is President of the Vineyard Association. He left his family property near the Malvern Hills some twenty years ago to go wine-making in the Hunter – where it took him some time to adjust his approach to the workers:

> I'll never forget standing there in front of about sixteen potential employees, telling them what I wanted to do. I must have seemed extremely English. I know I had cavalry twill trousers on and a pair of gumboots and a checked shirt, a Viyella shirt, and I remember one of them saying 'Before we start, we don't even know your name,' and I said, 'Oh I'm terribly sorry, my name's Mr Barnes.' There was a horrified look on their faces, and they said, 'But what's your Christian name?' I said, 'Look – my friends call me by my Christian name, but I'm Mr Barnes to you . . .'

Alister Norwood: *Jeans have been up, and jeans have been down . . .*

In the early Fifties Alister Norwood celebrated his sixth birthday on a migrant ship; with his mother and father, brother and sisters, he was on a £10-passage, and got suitably ducked as they crossed the equator. Landing at Fremantle, they went to live on a cold-water estate of wood-asbestos shacks the State Housing Commission put up for migrants in the working-class suburb of Bentley.

He now lives in one of the grandest houses in Perth – a city that has adjusted to his extraordinary white showplace of glass and huge rooms on the bank of the Swan River in posh Dalkeith. It was Perth's first $6 million property.

The two white Mercedes outside have personalized numberplates: hers belongs to an exotic Anglo-Indian model, his wife Gerri. They have two children: Alister and Ayesha.

Blue denim bought that splendid home, for Alister is Chairman of a public company with a turnover of $40 million and sixty-four shops around Australia – more are planned – selling jeans in vast quantities. He is on the list of Australia's two hundred richest people.

Tall and muscular with blond curly hair, he has enormous drive and is narcissistic enough; one of the best rooms in their riverside mansion is a professionally-equipped gymnasium where the Norwoods pump iron for hours ...

The classic example of rags-to-jeans, he is the emigrant's dream of success: the boy who came from nowhere – via the Kent Street High School and selling ice-cream in his local cinema – to become a business phenomenon, mainly through sales indoctrination and motivation techniques. At his firm's College of Retailing commitment meetings he has taught Australian sales staff to *serve* – which has to be a breakthrough of sorts.

> Australians don't have an awful lot of drive, and they've been brought up with: 'The Government will look after you.' It's, 'What can they do for *me?*' I've got friends, and that's been part of their downfall: 'It's a lucky country, it'll take care of me.' We've now been overtaken by the rest of the industrialized world. Third World countries are actually barking at our heels, and it shouldn't be too long before – you know what our Treasurer said about the banana republic – they'll be saying, Australian white trash ...

Ron Taylor: *The London Underground looked like we were in Bombay ...*

After driving a bus around Bolton and trying his hand at coal-mining, Ron Taylor left Lancashire in 1965 and became a lighthouse keeper at Cape Leeuwin, where the Indian and Southern Oceans meet at the very bottom left-hand corner of Australia. He is so content that when he takes his retirement from the Commonwealth Lighthouse Service soon he'll go to live in a mobile home on a piece of land nearby.

On this bleak and windswept southwest tip of Australia, his nearest pub is ten kilometres away in the hamlet of Augusta – so he brews his own. He does not miss England at all.

His light guards one of the busiest sea traffic routes on the

Australian coast, where all ships turn on their way to and from the eastern States. It was dedicated in 1896 by the Premier of Western Australia, who said that in constructing the lighthouse from its own resources the Colony had done its duty to all the mariners of the earth.

It is still on duty. The white light flashing every seven-and-a-half seconds from its 160-foot tower has an intensity of a million candlepower and a range of twenty-eight miles to the horizon.

I climbed the 185 steps with Ron, a little bantam of a man. With the light on automatic, his main duty – shared with his wife Evelyn – is weather observation. They report every three hours – and certainly there's a *lot* of weather about. The Easterlies are fierce, and each time the South-westerlies blow off the scale, past 75 knots, they can't even stand up outside their little grey home in the south-west:

> We've personally known people who've gone home – and then want to come back here! We've been back twice since 1966, and the changes that's gone on – I could *not* go back again. Don't like it. The changes that we've seen are that great since 1966 it's unbelievable. Everybody seems to be black, not just West Indians, I mean the *lot* – ordinary Indians and the other ones. We were amazed. We went on the London Underground to Tottenham, and it looked like we were in Bombay ...

ACKNOWLEDGEMENTS

I am indebted to everyone concerned with this book – particularly those eighty Poms-and-others who welcomed us so warmly into their homes and lives, and provided such revealing insights.

Valerie and I first travelled Australia for a couple of months on a reconnaissance, when I met again some new-Aussies I'd known for twenty years, and discovered many others who soon became friends. We later returned with our Heavy Mob – the *Whicker's World* television team: two Poms, a Scot, an Aussie and a new-Aussie, led by the amiable pipe-smoking, cricket-loving, cat-worshipping Roger Mills. We then zigzagged happily around Australia for four more frantic months while a mountain of film crashed into the cutting-room of our favourite assertive woman, Liz Thoyts – who this time did not throw a joiner at anyone ...

Tony Luker was there at the start of both book and series with encouragement and advice, and later joined by Ken Boys. Glen Kinging alerted his Channel 7 stations around the land, which were then showing my QE2 series, and some – like Ian Duncan and colleagues in Brisbane – were most helpful.

Then there's Denis Horgan, Bill Gray, Peter Janson, John Haddad, W. Ted Wright IV (an American who became a Mikado before our very eyes), Kevin M. Carton, John Lyneham, Roger de Lima, Rob and Judy Hirst, Sheila Scotter ... where do I stop? I've yet to meet an unfriendly unhelpful Australian, old or new. Must be that weather, again!

Back home John Shearer, Head of Television South and West,

was in at the birth of the series; then BBC Television's Director, Michael Grade, ensured our transmissions were supported from on high.

My eternal gratitude to Valerie, of course, for being there, taking the pictures, offering fresh original thought, tenacious loyalty and over-reaction at all times; and to Laureen Fraser, who faced the mini-mountain of microcassettes and notes with her usual imperturbable competence . . .

No point in listing all my Australian friends, since they've just had their say. I can only warn those who, because of the usual pressure on space, ended on the cutting-room floor or in my files: don't think you've escaped – you're *bound* to be in the next one!

Fontana Paperbacks
Non-fiction

Fontana is a leading paperback publisher of non-fiction. Below are some recent titles.

Armchair Golf *Ronnie Corbett* £3.50
You Are Here *Kevin Woodcock* £3.50
Squash Balls *Barry Waters* £3.50
Men: An Owner's Manual *Stephanie Brush* £2.50
Impressions of My Life *Mike Yarwood* £2.95
Arlott on Wine *John Arlott* £3.95
Bedside Rugby *Bill Beaumont* £3.50
Agoraphobia *Robyn Vines* £3.95
The Serpent and the Rainbow *Wade Davies* £2.95
Alternatives to Drugs *Colin Johnson & Arabella Melville* £4.95
The Learning Organization *Bob Garratt* £3.95
Information and Organizations *Max Boisot* £3.50
Say It One Time For The Broken Hearted *Barney Hoskins*
　£4.95
March or Die *Tony Geraghty* £3.95
Nice Guys Sleep Alone *Bruce Feirstein* £2.95
Royal Hauntings *Joan Forman* £3.50
Going For It *Victor Kiam* £2.95
Sweets *Shona Crawford Poole* £3.95
Waugh on Wine *Auberon Waugh* £3.95

You can buy Fontana paperbacks at your local bookshop or newsagent. Or you can order them from Fontana Paperbacks, Cash Sales Department, Box 29, Douglas, Isle of Man. Please send a cheque, postal or money order (not currency) worth the purchase price plus 22p per book for postage (maximum postage required is £3).

NAME (Block letters) _____

ADDRESS _____

_____

_____